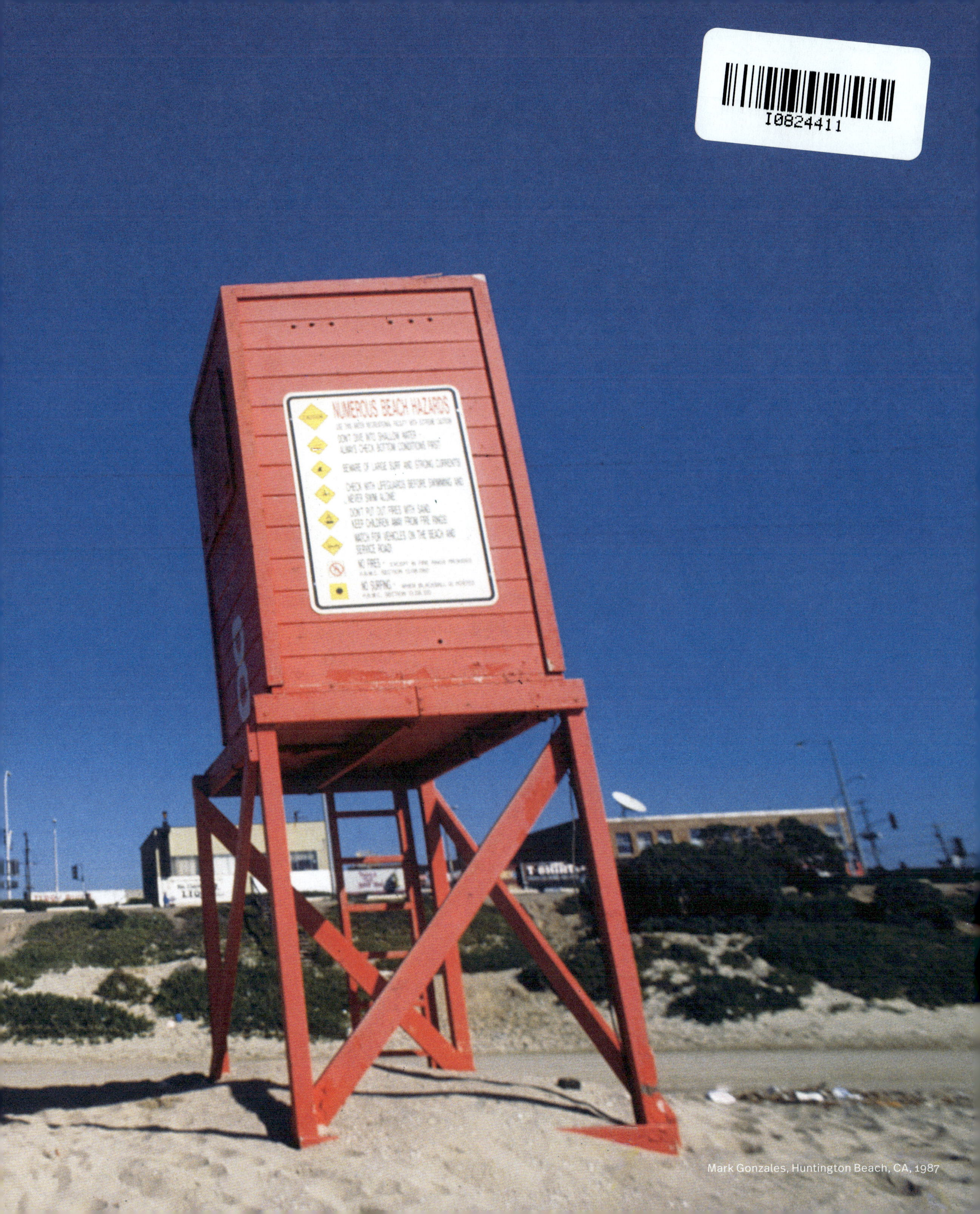

Mark Gonzales, Huntington Beach, CA, 1987

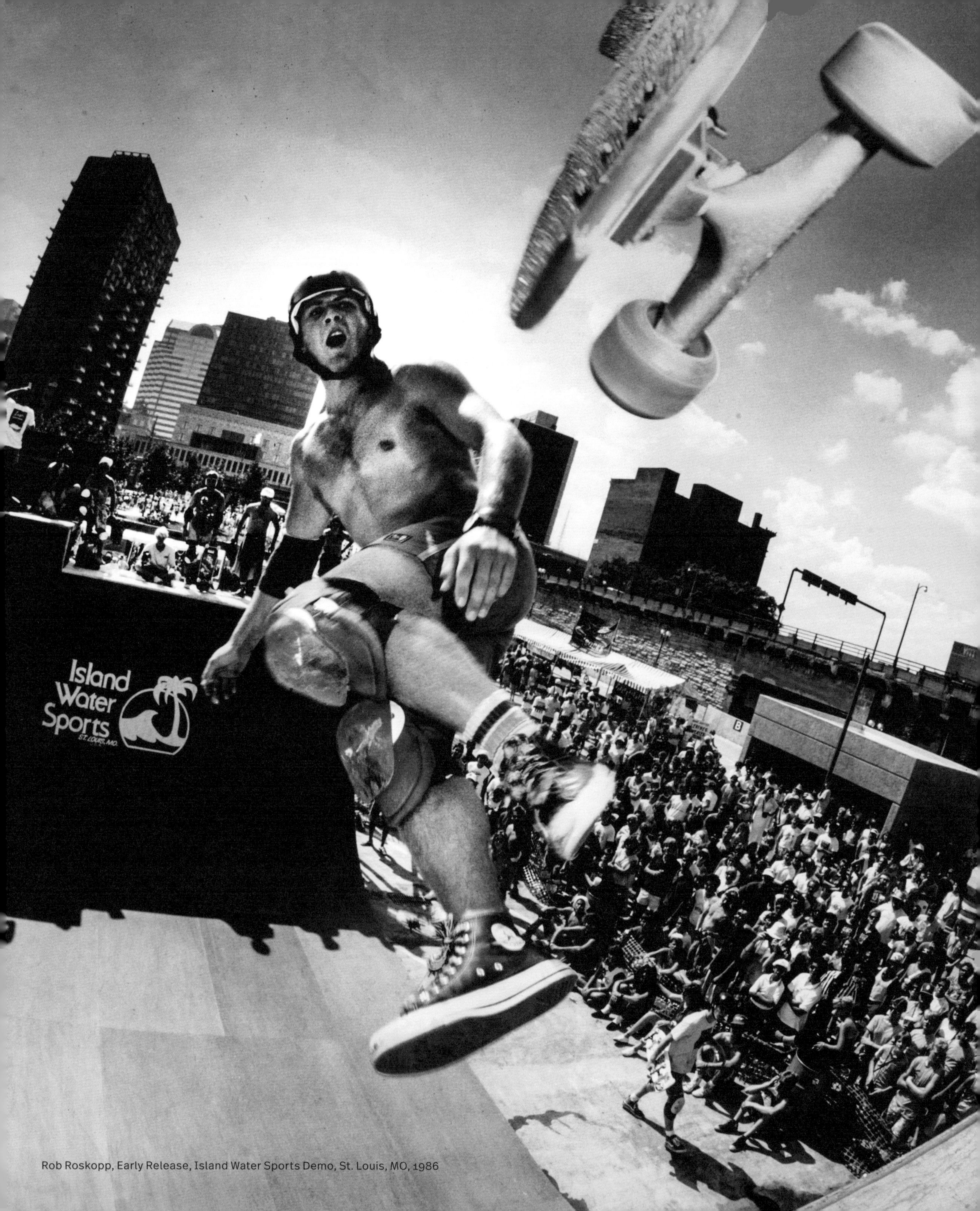

Rob Roskopp, Early Release, Island Water Sports Demo, St. Louis, MO, 1986

PUSH

J. Grant Brittain 80s Skateboarding Photography

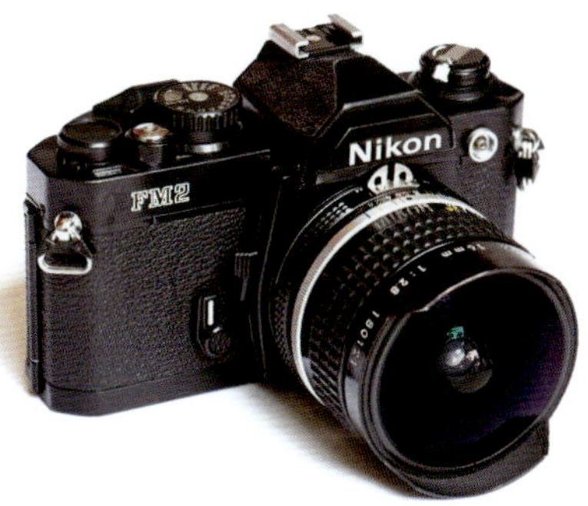

GINGKO PRESS

PUSH J. Grant Brittain 80s Skateboarding Photography
First Published in the United States of America, January, 2022

Third Printing
Gingko Press, Inc.
217 W. Richmond Ave, Ste. B
Richmond, CA 94801
www.gingkopress.com

Foreword: Miki Vuckovich
www.mikivuckovich.com

Introduction: Tony Hawk
www.tonyhawk.com

Design, Art Direction: Gordon Eckler, Plaid Again Creative Co.
www.plaidagain.com

Concept, Layout: Josh Higgins
www.joshhiggins.com

Copyediting: Laura Brittain, Brittain Editing

J. Grant Brittain Timeline: Garry Scott Davis

ISBN: 978-1-58423-765-5
Library of Congress Control Number: 2021942019

Printed in China

Front cover image:
Tod Swank, The Push, Del Mar, CA, 1987

Back cover image:
Tony Hawk, Del Mar Skate Ranch, Del Mar, CA, 1984
This slide was lost in 1984 and found in 2021.

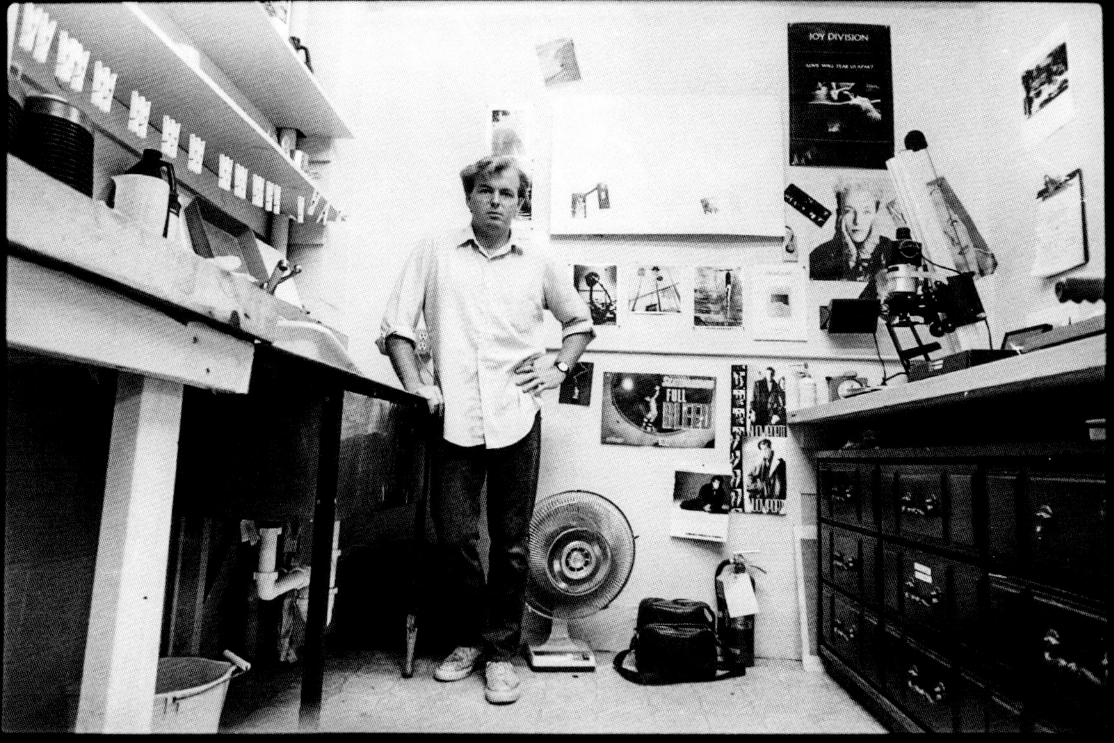

DEDICATED TO

Laura, Zoe, Sage, Joyce, Jerry,
Keith, Clay, and Sherrill.

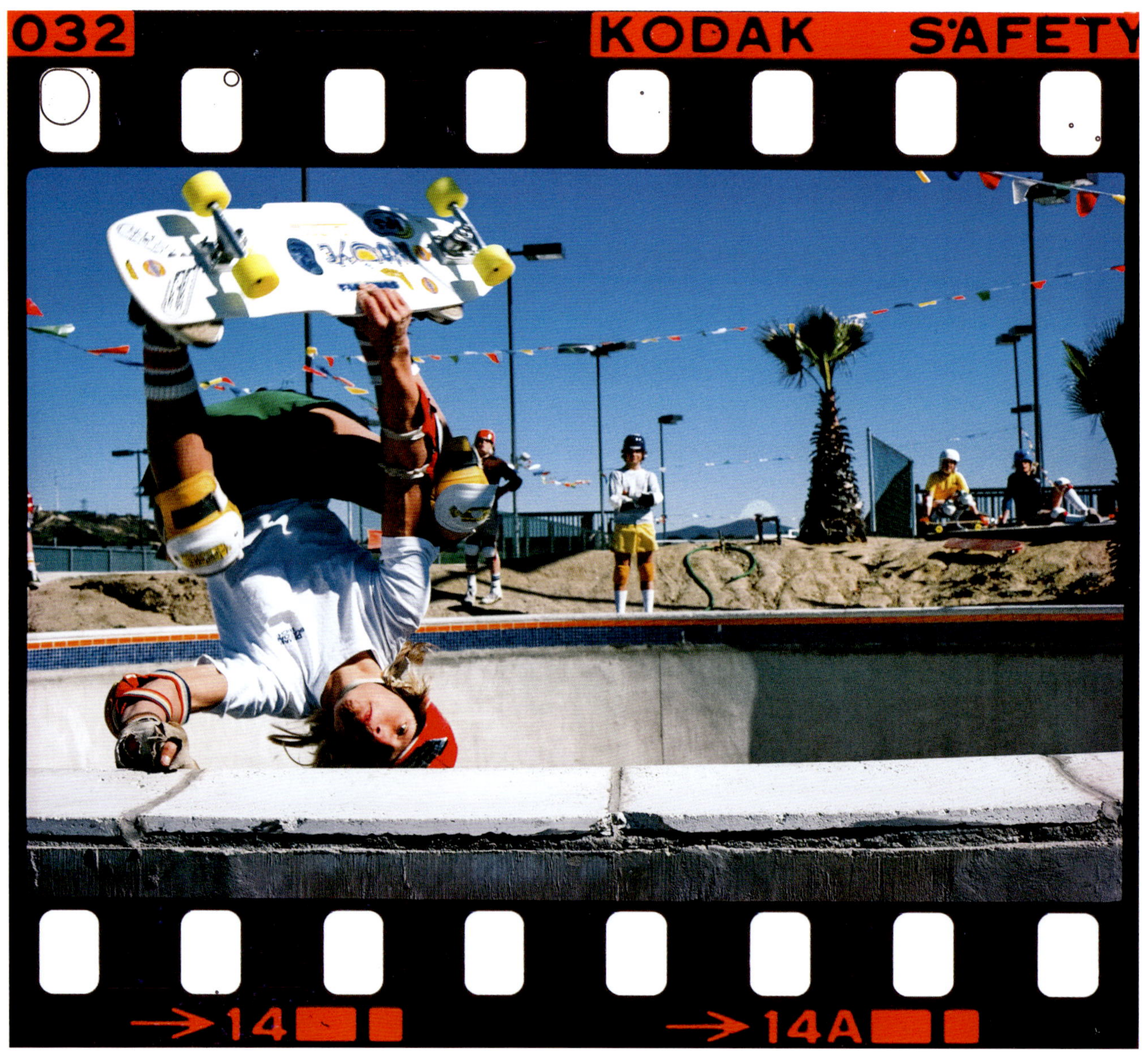

Photo from first roll of film shot, Kyle Jensen, Invert, Del Mar Skate Ranch, Del Mar, CA, 1979

CONTENTS

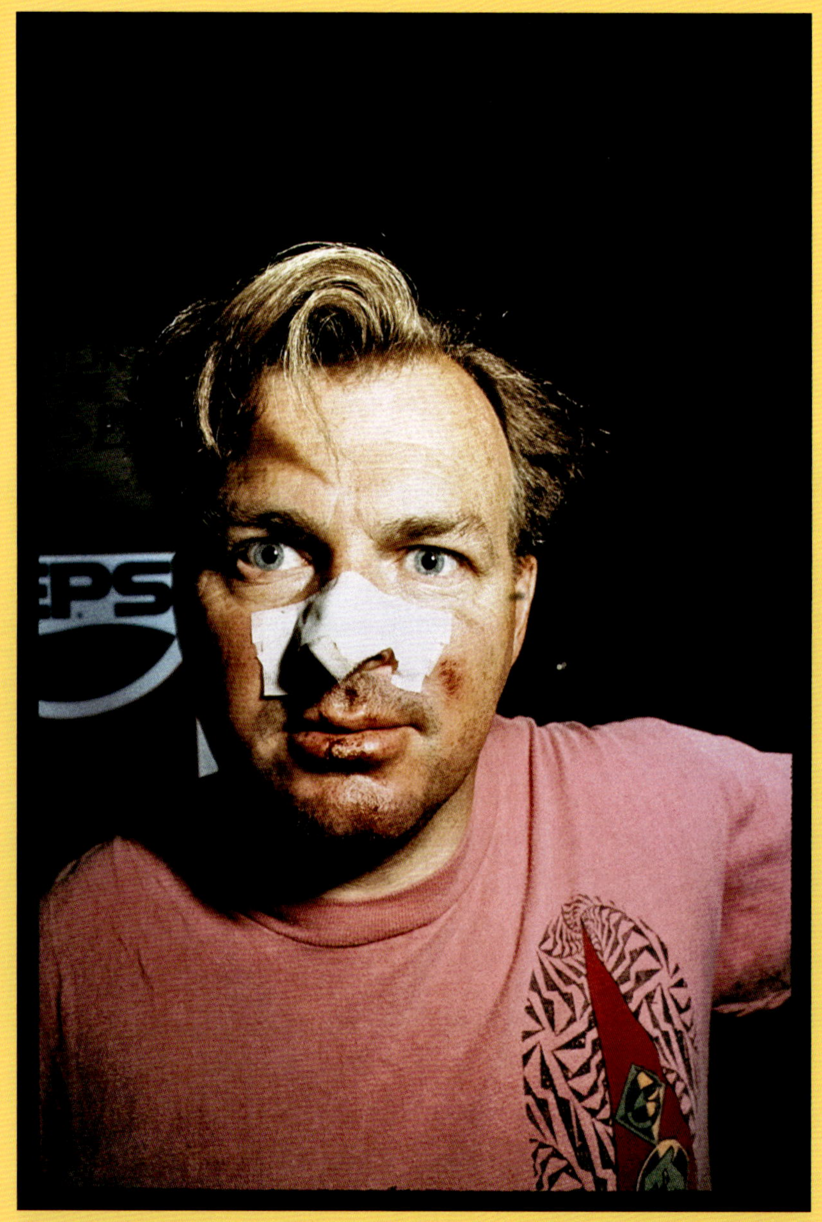

Grant Brittain, Dallas, TX, 1990 – Steve Sherman photo

PREFACE

by J. Grant Brittain

Golden Years was the original working title for this book, as it embodied my feelings about my skate photography of the era. Whenever I think of those times now, I think about how lucky I was to have been in the middle of it all and to have picked up a camera. Neither I nor the young skateboarders I photographed had any idea that people in the 2020s would even give a damn what skaters in the 1980s had done.

Looking back, I am not even sure I knew that I was documenting anything–I was just doing it for the moment and having fun with my friends–in the now. I was lucky my parents bought me a skateboard at ten, lucky I started surfing at fourteen, lucky I moved to Cardiff-by-the-Sea at eighteen, lucky I lived next door to skater Wally Inouye and that he got me a job at the Del Mar Skate Ranch at twenty-two, lucky my roommate Richard B. Apple lent me his Canon camera at twenty-three, lucky surf/skate photographer Sonny Miller introduced me to Palomar College's photo darkroom at twenty-five, and lucky Larry Balma and Peggy Cozens started up something new called *Transworld Skateboarding* Magazine and gave me a job when I was twenty-seven. All of these lucky events put me in the right place at the right time to capture some lucky moments–in a period I think of as the Golden Age of Skateboarding.

I hope you'll enjoy this collection of my personal favorite photos from that decade, and if any of the photos make you smile, I will have succeeded.

J. Grant Brittain

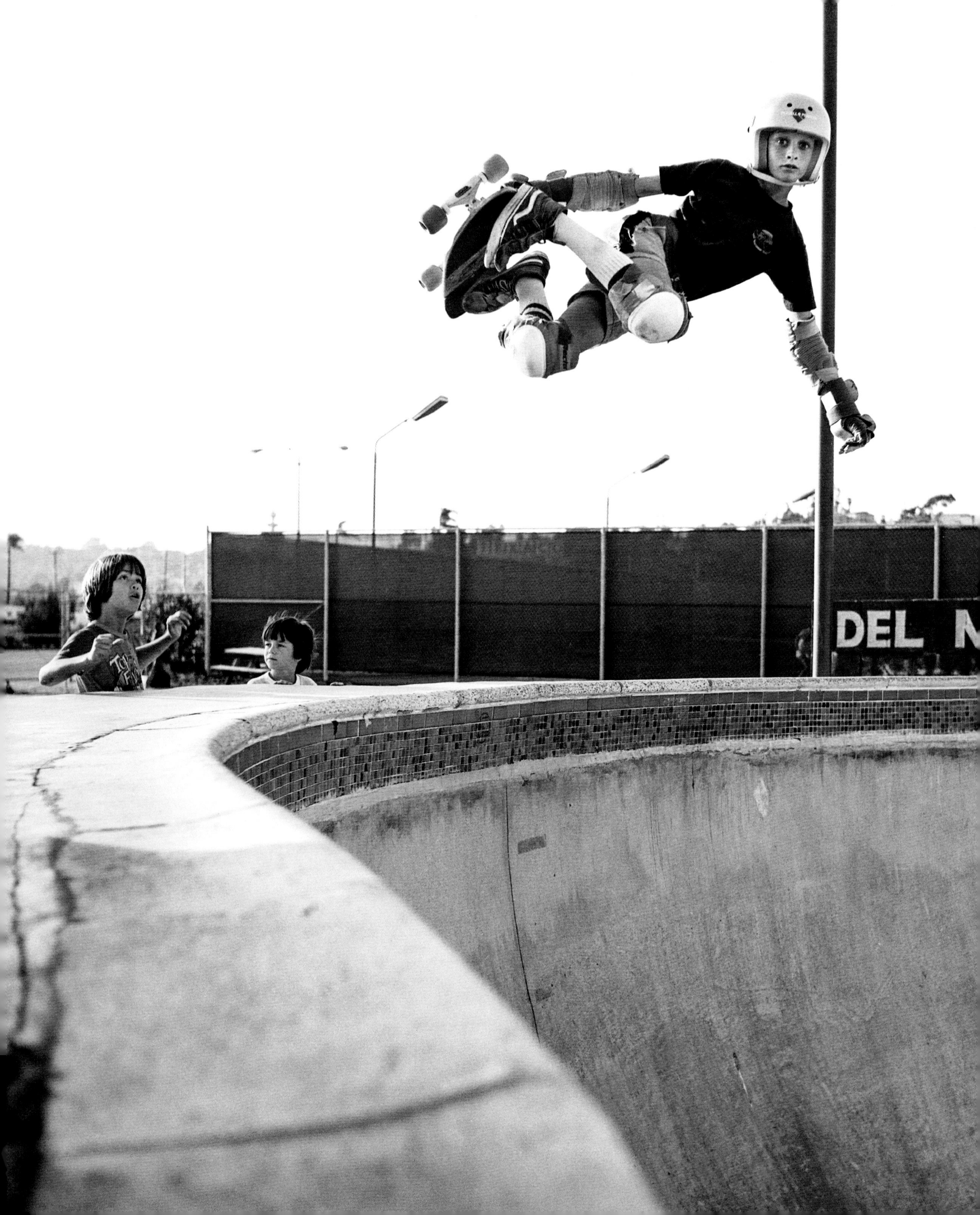
DEL M

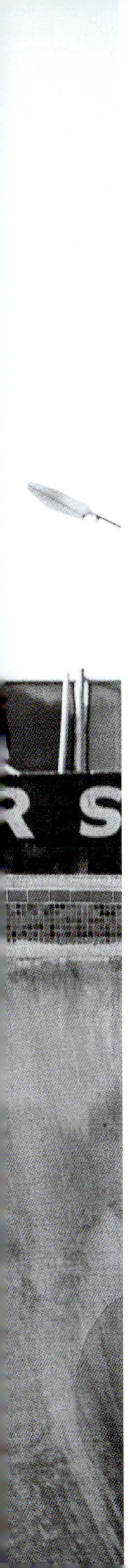

SEEING THE IMPOSSIBLE

by Miki Vuckovich

There are artists whose body of work survives them to inform and influence future generations. We stand in awe of these individuals for what they saw. Their legacy is their visual catalog.

And there are teachers who influence a generation, and we stand in awe of what they allow us to see in ourselves, and in our own work. Their students are their living legacy.

Grant Brittain is both.

The late 70s was arguably the most transformative era in the relatively young history of the skateboarding movement (which dates back to the 1940s). The epicenter of the skateboarding world was Southern California, and at the time most of the action was focused in the couple of skateparks that remained. With such a concentration of talent at these few locations, the skateparks had become hubs of innovation by the early 80s. Inexplicably, this was happening right as the masses were drifting away from skateboarding; just when there was the most to see, nobody was watching.

Skateboarding had gone underground. What used to happen almost exclusively in skateparks was now unseen but thriving in empty swimming pools. And if you couldn't find a backyard pool (or were arrested one too many times for trespassing), you built a plywood ramp in your own yard and limited access to your closest friends.

No kooks allowed.

Skateboarding was exclusive, but it was also dynamic. Its closed system incubated innovation, and innovators like Caballero, Mullen, Hawk, Gonzales, Guerrero, and Kaupas fed off one another like cross-fertilizing organisms in a petri dish.

If you were there, in the lab, you would have seen the most revolutionary thinking being expressed in the actions of–essentially–kids. Kids with a vision and the skills to manifest their thoughts in movement, in flight. They saw where skateboarding could go, then they took it there. Simply

Tony Hawk, Del Mar Skate Ranch, Del Mar, CA, 1982

because no one cared enough to stop them, to tell them it wasn't possible.

In the summer of 1982, I had the great fortune to walk into the Del Mar Skate Ranch as its newest local. It was the most unbelievable scene a teenage skate rat could imagine. Yet, there I was.

All the locals were kids, and the only adult in the room was skatepark manager Grant Brittain, who seemed to have a knack for keeping a lid on all the antics that went down at the park. Which still couldn't have been easy. And he did a lot for the locals. Some got jobs helping run the park. In my case, I got rides home every night when the park closed. And there was no way I could have afforded the regular fee to skate there every day, so Grant let me pick up trash to earn my entry. And that kept us all there, every day–together, skating.

A keen photographer, Grant could often be seen crouching next to the keyhole shooting locals like Owen Nieder, Billy Ruff, or Tony Hawk, or using the curvy skatepark features as settings for avant-garde portraits. None of the nuanced innovations going down in that bowl escaped Grant's lens. And as incredible as it was to see new tricks and styles being invented almost daily, it was even better to see how Grant captured them. I remember once standing in the pro shop at the park, sifting through a pile of his black-and-white prints. They were immaculate–the contrast was perfect, and the images were futuristic because his subjects were ahead of their time, perfectly framed, and often distorted by a fisheye lens. So, when I began taking photo classes in high school, Grant was my go-to for tips, or to borrow a flash or a roll of film. He never said no.

Grant eventually left the skatepark to work on a new magazine called *Transworld Skateboarding*. There wasn't a lot to love in the first few issues of *TWS*, but the photography was pristine. In fact, the new magazine very quickly established itself as the mag you wanted to be in. If you got in front of Grant's lens, you were guaranteed to produce a memorable photo that kids like me would, decades later, still be able to describe in detail: Chris Miller's pole-cam nosebone frontside air over the Upland Combi Pool; The Bones Brigade in mid-handplant symmetry at the Animal Chin Ramp; Steve Rocco pushing past a NO SKATEBOARDING sign toward a strolling police officer; the Godfathers of street skating, Natas Kaupas and Mark Gonzales, leaning into a young Mike Vallely, pointing at him prophetically; Rodney Mullen perched in a mid no-handed 50/50, silhouetted against the banks at Del Mar with his hands extended just so; Tony Hawk's crossbone Lien air over the Del Mar keyhole, viewed from above.

And a thousand others.

I and some very talented photographers contributed to the pages of *TWS* over the decades, but it was Grant's work that established the brand that became a media empire. When skaters were laying the groundwork for the eventual resurgence of skateboarding in the popular realm, Grant was there, documenting the progress and building the culture's visual history. Every issue, his photos showed us what impossibilities had recently been conquered. And for any serious skate photographer, *TWS* was the mag of record. Publishing your work anywhere else was a concession.

The best skate photographers, he'd say, are skaters. Because you can teach a skater photography, but you can't teach a photographer skateboarding. Every photographer he worked with has stories of Grant encouraging them, or downright busting their balls when they got lazy and held their fisheye lens out at arm's length (Grant could tell if you didn't look through the

Grant didn't mentor photographers—he nurtured individuals who happened to shoot photos.

camera). And each became the photographer they did thanks to Grant. And much more—Grant had a way of being supportive, but he challenged you to be at your best.

Grant went on to help found *The Skateboard Mag* in 2004, where he mentored another generation of young photographers. You may not realize it, but you're seeing Grant's influence everywhere you look—at least where skate photography hasn't been replaced by video. Though even in the video age, I would argue, Grant's influence is still visible. Just ask Ty Evans, or Jon Holland, or Greg Hunt, or Spike Jonze.

Everyone has a Grant story. And they're not short. And it's not the same story. But what they have in common is that they're each transformational. Grant didn't mentor photographers—he nurtured individuals who happened to shoot photos.

Grant's work isn't limited to his photography. He helped shape generations of photographers who have told the visual story of skateboarding over the past few decades. And that story has reverberated well beyond the pages of skate mags and has influenced our culture. The world's cultures, in fact. It's skateboarding's universal appeal, and the excitement that skate imagery has generated in recent history, that has opened the door to the Olympic Games, with skateboarding making its debut at Tokyo 2021.

When the world tuned in, they saw a sport that was spawned by a culture—a sport that is redefined by new generations who've taken the lessons of those who came before and added their own layers, influenced and inspired by what they've seen and read from the past to build a foundation for the future.

That's Grant, in a nutshell. He didn't just create images, he made an impact on a culture that has grown far beyond the confines of the Del Mar Skate Ranch. And people are finally paying attention.

What they're seeing is the story of a sport and culture being told by skaters themselves. Participants who are embedded in their culture. Like Grant is. And the dozens of skateboarding's storytellers he mentored have influenced a new generation of photographers and video makers. So his legacy continues.

Every new image of skateboarding you see online, in magazines, or in other books can be traced back to the collection on the following pages. Whether directly or indirectly, the former skatepark manager who took these photos has informed the way we see skateboarding, and what we think about it.

And if you're one of those kids, today, out there skating and inventing, you have a very rich visual history to draw from. It's up to you where it all goes from here, but Grant's made your decision much better informed. Just turn the page and you'll see what I mean.

You'll be inspired to make the impossible—possible.

FULL CIRCLE

by Tony Hawk

Grant Brittain and I have careers that have paralleled, and in many ways, complimented each other. We first met in 1979, when he was a college student managing the Del Mar Skate Ranch pro shop and I was a scrawny, hyper, aspiring skateboarder who spent every waking moment outside of school at Grant's skatepark. Neither one of us thought we were choosing our careers at the time; we just enjoyed the skate/surf culture and the eclectic misfits that surrounded it. He was content to have a job in the "industry," and I was content to have a place to skate. We had no idea that DMSR would become an epicenter of skateboarding for Southern California a few years later, especially since it seemed that skateboarding was one of the least popular activities at the time.

One day I was skating with a couple other locals in DMSR's keyhole pool. It was a typical weekday afternoon at the park: sunny with a scarce crowd, with perhaps a few looky-loos that wandered over from the nearby miniature golf course to see where the punk rock music was emanating from. Grant emerged from the pro shop with a camera in his hand and asked to take a few photos of me skating. I was stoked to get any documentation of my efforts at the time, and Grant found me to be a cooperative subject for his self-education in photography. We became friends quickly, regardless of our age gap, and he introduced me to some early new wave bands that I enjoy to this day, such as Visage, Ultravox, and Killing Joke.

Skateboarding began to slowly increase in popularity in the years 1982–86, just as Grant and I were developing our separate skills in simultaneous leaps. He became photo editor of *Transworld Skateboarding* (*TWS*) in its 1983 debut issue, and he already had a volume's worth of iconic images of the best skaters before it was even printed. At the same time, I was beginning to dominate most pool / vert competitions, so *TWS* was featuring a picture of me in almost every issue ... almost exclusively taken by Grant himself. If any sponsor of mine needed a photo of me, Grant was the obvious choice to shoot it. We rode a wave of success that seemed unreal–both getting to do what we loved for a living even though we never imagined being able to get paid for our passions. Del Mar eventually closed, but our lifelong career paths were already set in motion.

Through the late '80s and early '90s, we continued to work together shooting various editorial, ads, posters, and "lifestyle" pictures. We traveled the world thanks to skateboarding's growing reach, and experimented with new techniques and tricks in our respective fields. It was all very whirlwind, and I never imagined that some of these images we were creating would be considered iconic or timeless. We just loved what we were doing and kept trying to get better at it.

Grant mentored plenty of aspiring skate photographers through these years, and as our paths started to diverge, I worked with a few of them very closely. They would credit Grant for sparking their passion and for invaluable advice he imparted to them. It has been an honor to be the subject of Grant's influence as it has transcended over decades. To this day, if an opportunity comes up to shoot a photo for an ad, social media campaign, or promotion of some kind, I still call Grant to shoot, and he is still usually agreeable to work his magic. Or sometimes Grant will have an idea to revisit an iconic image we've done (or just test out some new gear) and I'll be down for the cause.

As Grant and I get older and our kids near the age of parenting themselves, it's been incredible to see just how far our combined efforts resonated across generations and borders. I realized how much our lives and careers have come full circle when my oldest son Riley recently opened a coffee shop and requested a print from Grant to hang in the middle of the store: a picture of me skating Del Mar keyhole in 1985.

Thank you, Grant, for documenting my life in skateboarding in a comprehensive way, like nobody else could have, and for documenting skateboarding's formative years with grace and in an iconic style.

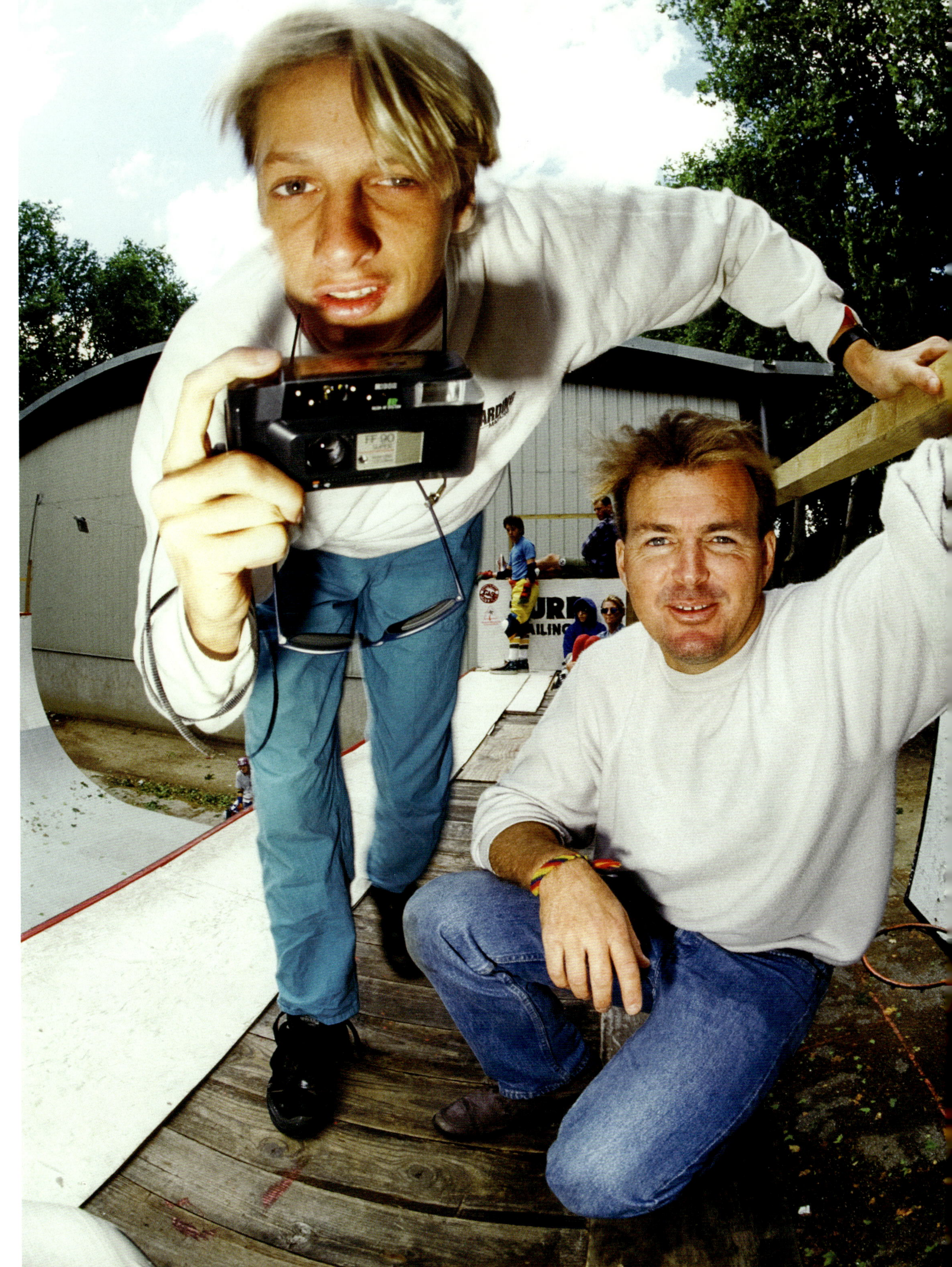

Tony & Grant, Bourges, France, 1987 – Laura Brittain photo

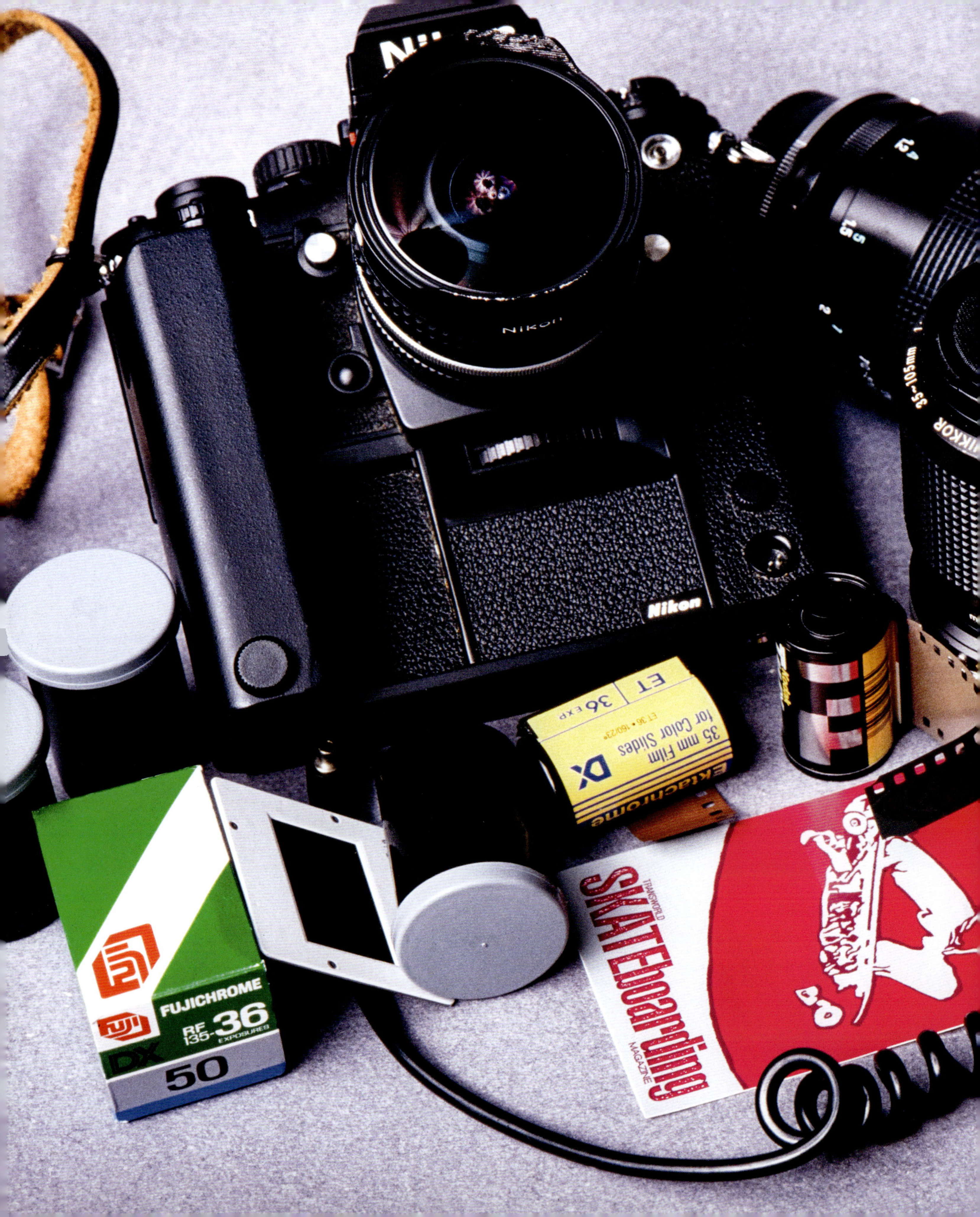
Nikon
Nikon
Nikon
35–105mm
NIKKOR
ET
36 EXP
35 mm Film
for Color Slides
Ektachrome
DX
FUJICHROME
RF 135-36
EXPOSURES
DX
50
TRANSWORLD
SKATEboarding
MAGAZINE

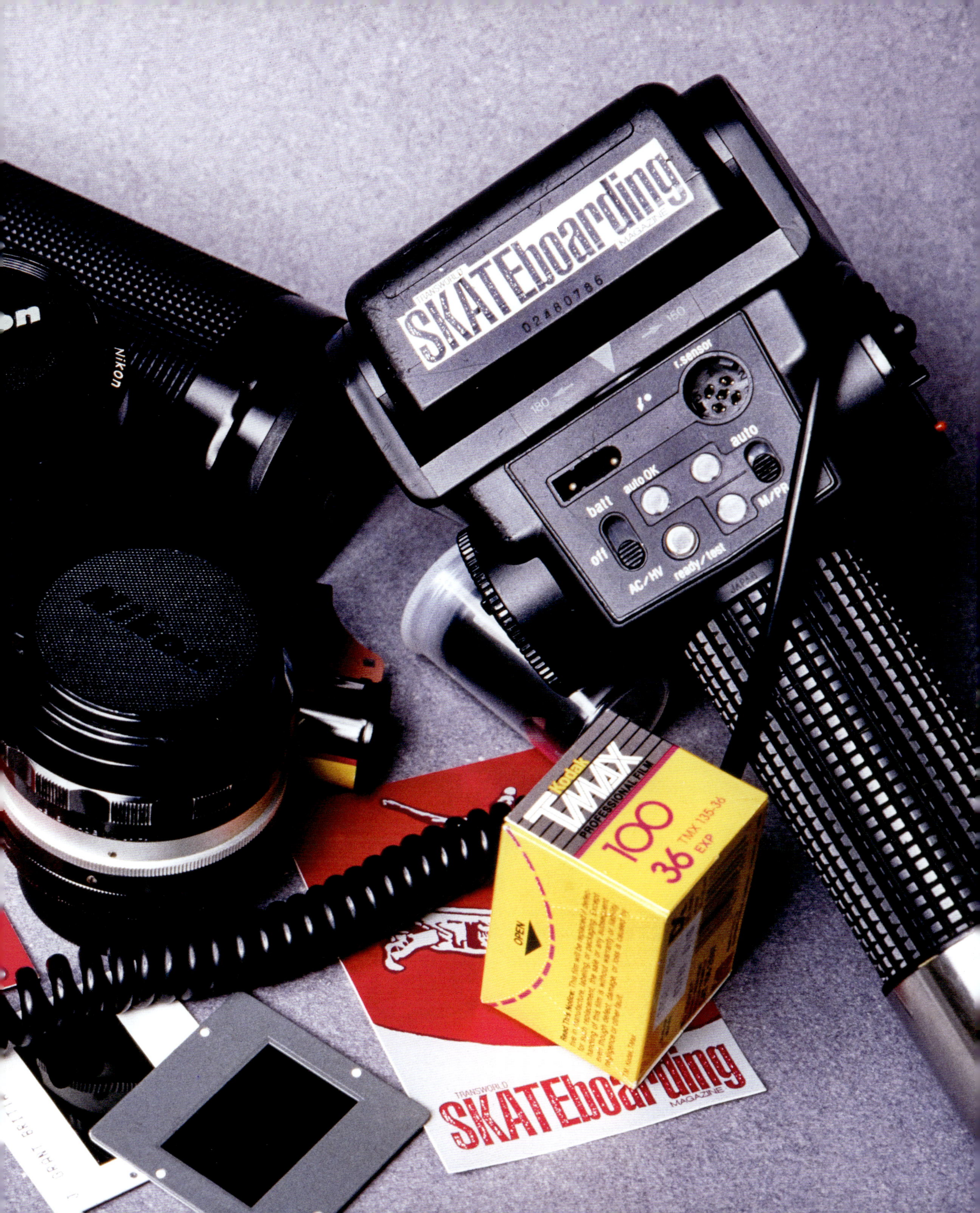

TRANSWORLD
SKATEboarding
MAGAZINE
02480786
Nikon
t.sensor
auto
auto OK
batt
off
AC/HV
ready/test
M/PR
Kodak
TMAX
PROFESSIONAL FILM
100
36
TMX 135-36
EXP
OPEN
TRANSWORLD
SKATEboarding
MAGAZINE

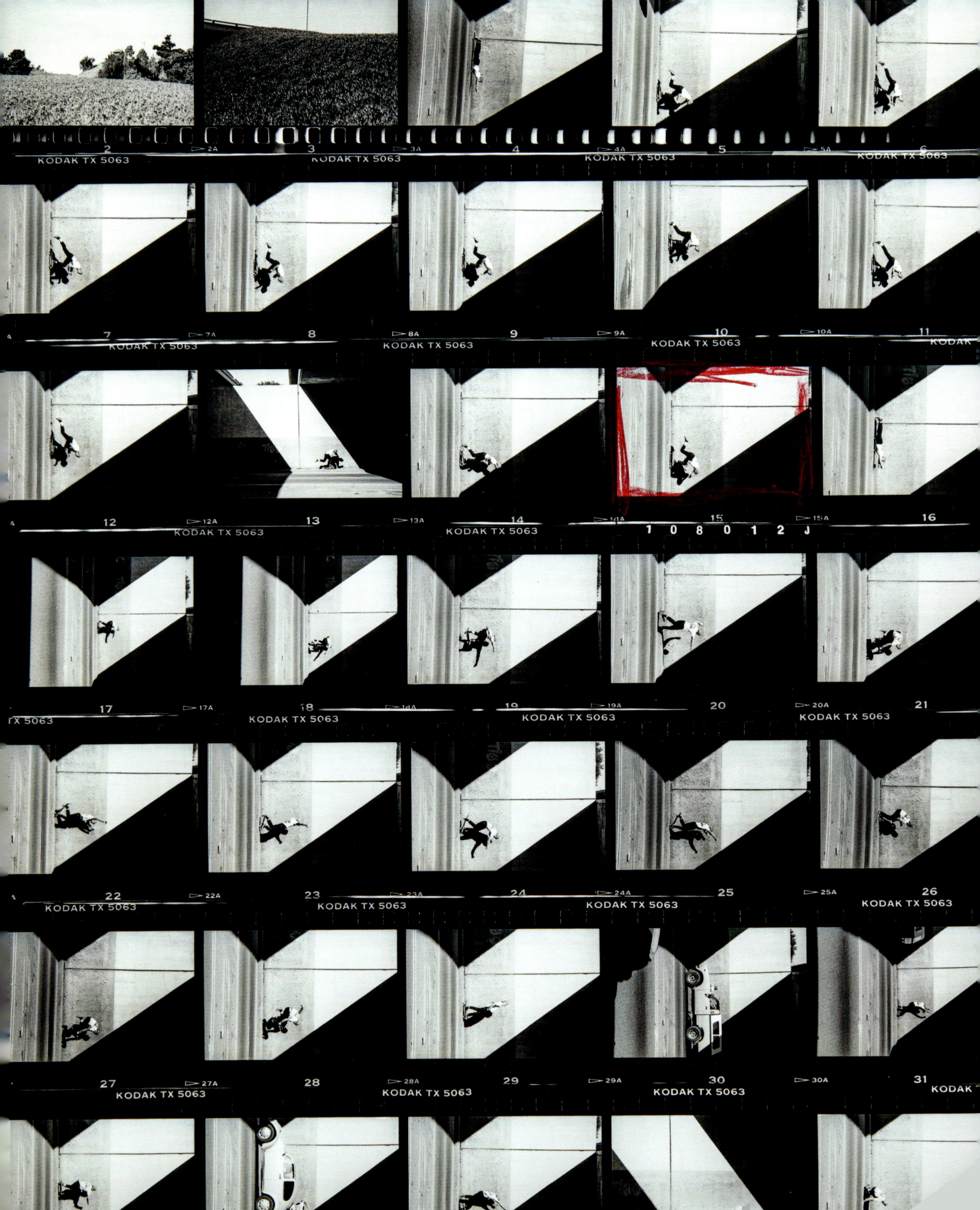
2
KODAK TX 5063
3
KODAK TX 5063
4
KODAK TX 5063
5
KODAK TX 5063
6
7
KODAK TX 5063
8
KODAK TX 5063
9
10
KODAK TX 5063
11
KODAK
12
KODAK TX 5063
13
14
KODAK TX 5063
15
1 0 8 0 1 2 J
16
17
TX 5063
18
KODAK TX 5063
19
KODAK TX 5063
20
KODAK TX 5063
21
22
KODAK TX 5063
23
KODAK TX 5063
24
KODAK TX 5063
25
26
KODAK TX 5063
27
KODAK TX 5063
28
KODAK TX 5063
29
30
KODAK TX 5063
31
KODAK

Previous spread: Nikon F3 and film, Sequence camera, 1987

THE PUSH

by J. Grant Brittain

In late 1986, I would drive east on Via de la Valle in Del Mar, California, and pass beneath the overpass of the I-5 freeway on my way to get coffee at The Pannikin. As a photographer, I was always on the lookout for a good photo or background, and I had long admired the shaft of light which shone through the gap in the bridge above, a gap which was between the north and southbound lanes and bisected the ferroconcrete wall below with contrasting shadow and light.

I am often asked, "Do you see in black and white?" The answer is "Hell yes, a lot." There are certain scenes that scream black and white, and this simple geometric shape cast by the sun onto the massive backdrop was projecting strongly onto my photo brain. I started to previsualize a photograph of a skateboarder passing in front of the textured wall, and I began to calculate what time of day to shoot it. Over the next few days, I would see the angle of light change daily as the earth revolved. I finally figured that early afternoon would be the best time to capture the shadow's diagonal shape in my Nikon's viewfinder.

At this time, I was the photo editor and senior photographer at *Transworld Skateboarding* Magazine (1983–2003), and Tod Swank, who was a great skater and skate photographer, was my darkroom tech. I enlisted Tod as my photo stunt dummy, and we met up at The Pannikin. We walked over to the shoot location and sussed out the light situation–it looked pretty good. Once I took up position on the opposite side of the four-lane road, I directed him by shouting commands and waving my arms wildly. There was quite a bit of traffic, and we had to wait for a break in the cars going by. Tod pushed back and forth on his board, doing a variety of maneuvers, some pretty comical, including one in a Superman stance. I ran two rolls of Kodak Tri-X 36-exposure film through my camera and felt like we had something usable. We'd captured what I'd envisioned.

Let me point out that this was not shot specifically for the cover–that idea came after we developed the film in the darkroom–I just wanted to have a photo for the mag. Tod developed the film and gave it to me with a contact sheet, and I placed it on my light table and squinted through my magnifying loupe. One image stood out–the frame with Tod simply pushing along the sidewalk. It was so basic–it was the foundation of skateboarding, it was the first thing we all learn to do after stepping on a board, it was the essence of this activity we, who do it, love. We all have this in common: we push.

I showed the chosen frame to David Carson, who was the art director (later to go on to become a design guru), and he was stoked on it. He suggested it for the cover of *TWS*, and I thought this was a great idea. David also thought that the cover should be designed without any Day-Glo cover blurbs, which were common on New Wave-style 80s covers, and that would muck up the clean design and crowd the pushing skater out of the frame. This would be the perfect cover to go with Garry Scott Davis's article "Soul Power," which was scheduled for the June 1987 issue. This photo seemed to us as the Everyman/ Everywoman skate photo: everyone could relate to it, and it said soul power big time! That's what we thought, but what you think isn't always what others will think. We presented the design at an editorial production meeting, and the rest of the staff hated it. It broke all of the magazine distribution and skateboarding world rules–it had no Day-Glo cover blurbs, it was shot in black and white, and it showed a non-pro skater. It wasn't a guy-in-the-sky peak action shot of a skater on a logoed-out skate deck. I was a bit surprised by the response of the other staff members, and the meeting was getting more and more heated. After the meeting ended I retreated to Carson's office and tried to calm down. I pretty much thought our Push cover was a dead design idea after that argument, and I was pissed!

I stayed away for a couple of days to cool off. Eventually, I went back to the office, and the June 1987 issue came out miraculously, with the Carson-designed Tod Swank cover, photo by me. The photo caption on the contents page read, "It doesn't matter who, where or what. It's just a skateboarder... skateboarding. Photo: Brittain". That was what it was all about! It didn't matter that it didn't have Swank's name, that was the point, it was any skater! (For the record, Tod didn't mind not having his name on the photo.)

You would think that the commotion would all end there, all hunky-dory, right? Not quite. Just as many of our skate readers hated it as liked it. Friends told me later that they hated or didn't get it and wondered what the hell we were thinking. I tried to explain it to those people, the every-skater photo thing, the feeling of freedom through the simple act of pushing down the street, you know... that thing we all do, but it was a hard sell.

The mag took some heat for a long while, but I started to notice skateboard mag covers changing over time. I think the Push cover opened up some thoughts on what could go on a skate mag cover and made it clearer that you didn't have to stick to newsstand consultants' rules. After all, we're skaters; we don't need no stinkin' rules! People warmed up to that Push cover after twenty or so years. I even heard the old haters say that it was one of their favorite covers and even one of their favorite skate photos. It's that old saying, "Time will tell"–well it did in this case.

Now, in 2021, I regale young skaters with the story of the Push Cover almost not being a cover and the reasons, and they are amazed, because as a cover it would be so tame by today's standards. I am proud of that.

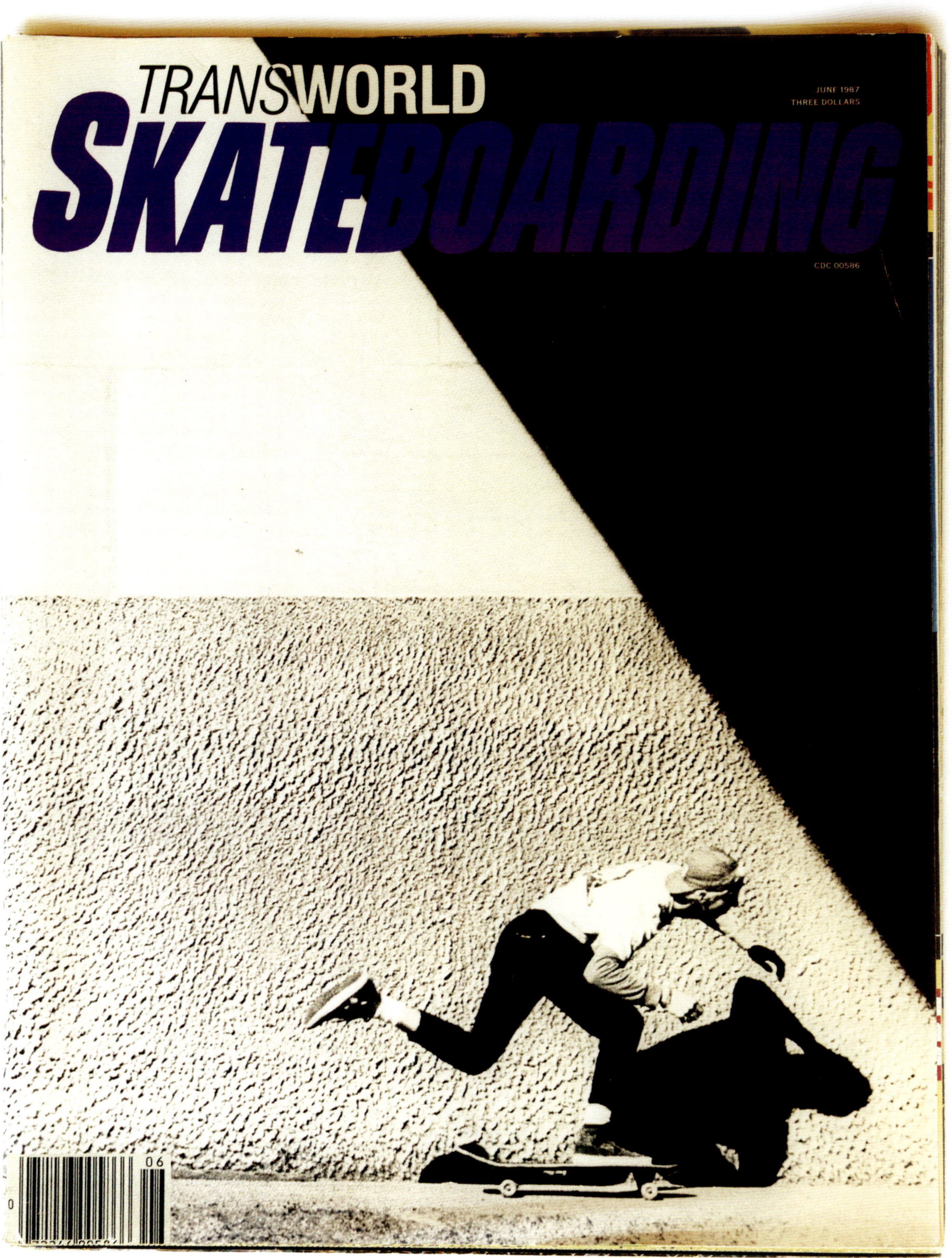
TRANSWORLD
SKATEBOARDING
JUNE 1987
THREE DOLLARS
CDC 00586
06

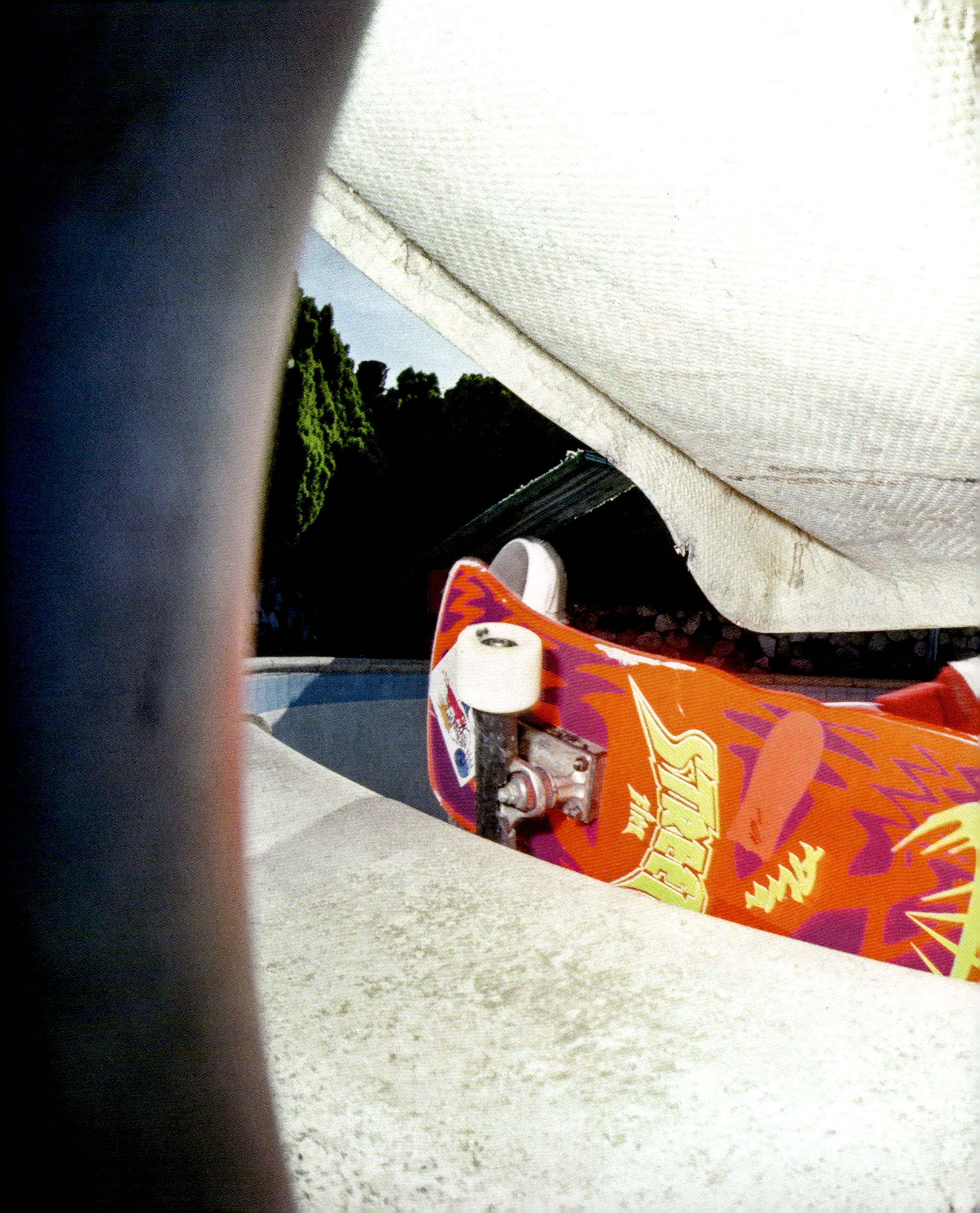

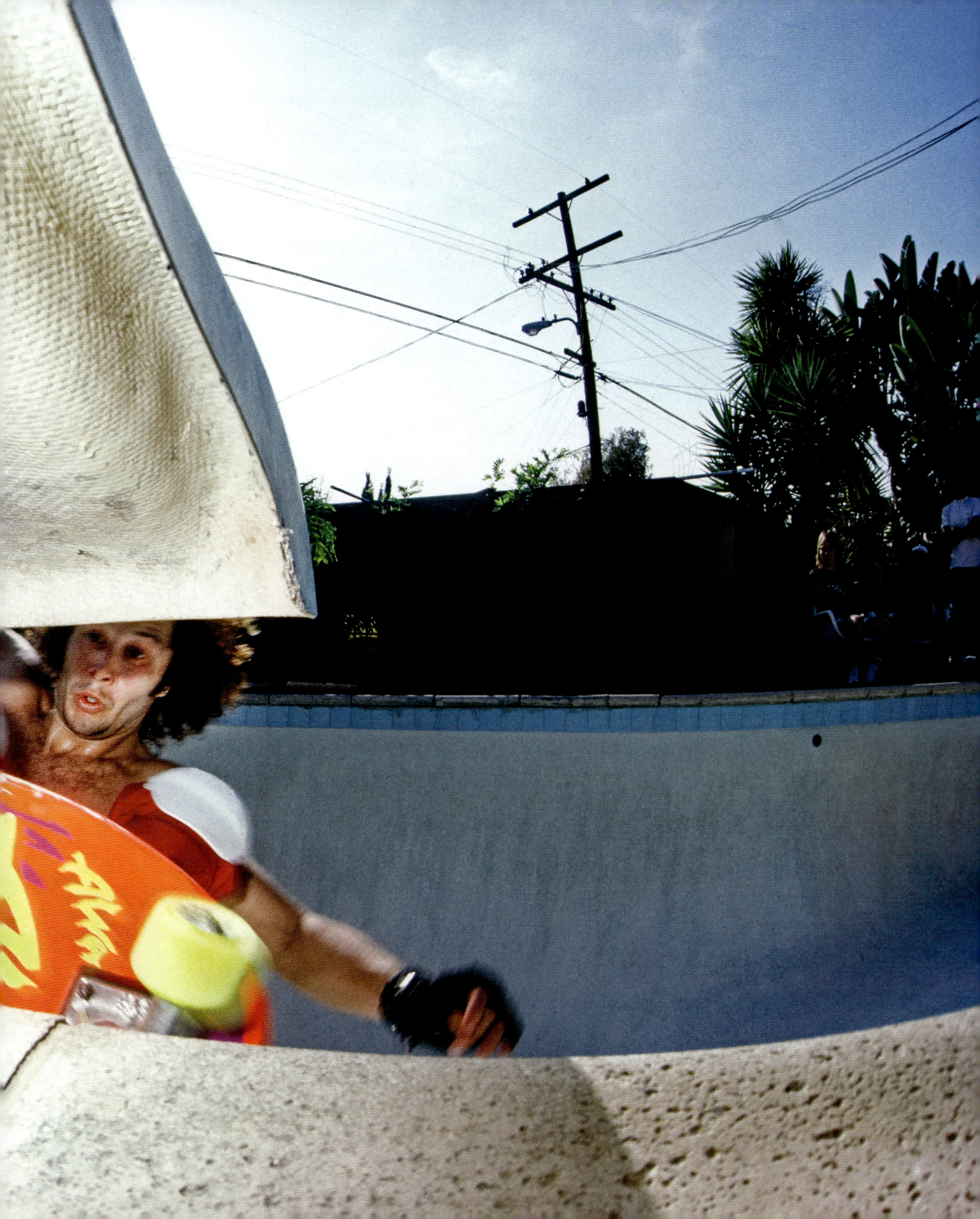

Previous: Tony Alva, Gonzales Pool, Mar Vista, CA, 1986

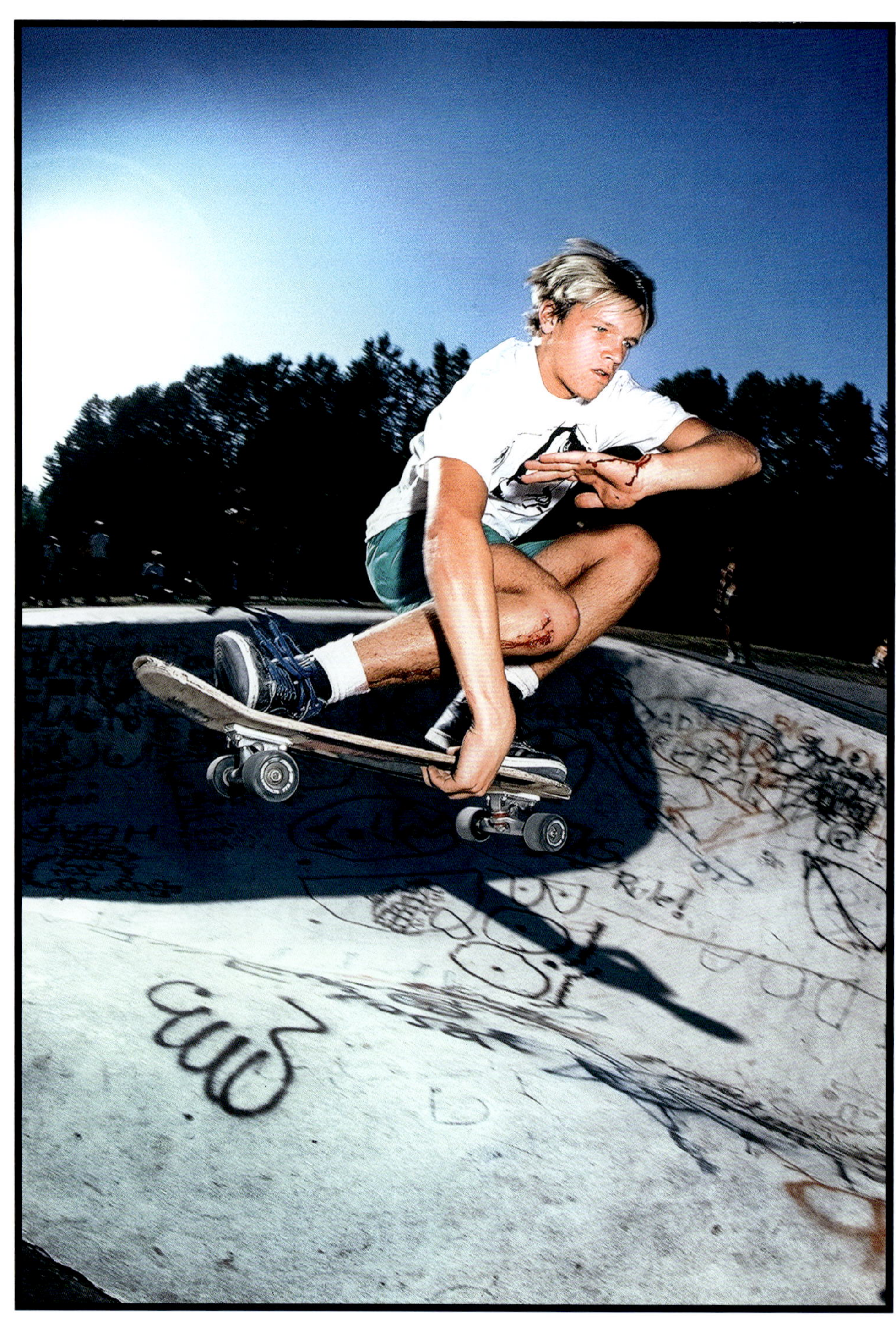

Chris Miller, Seylynn Bowl, North Vancouver, BC, Canada, 1986

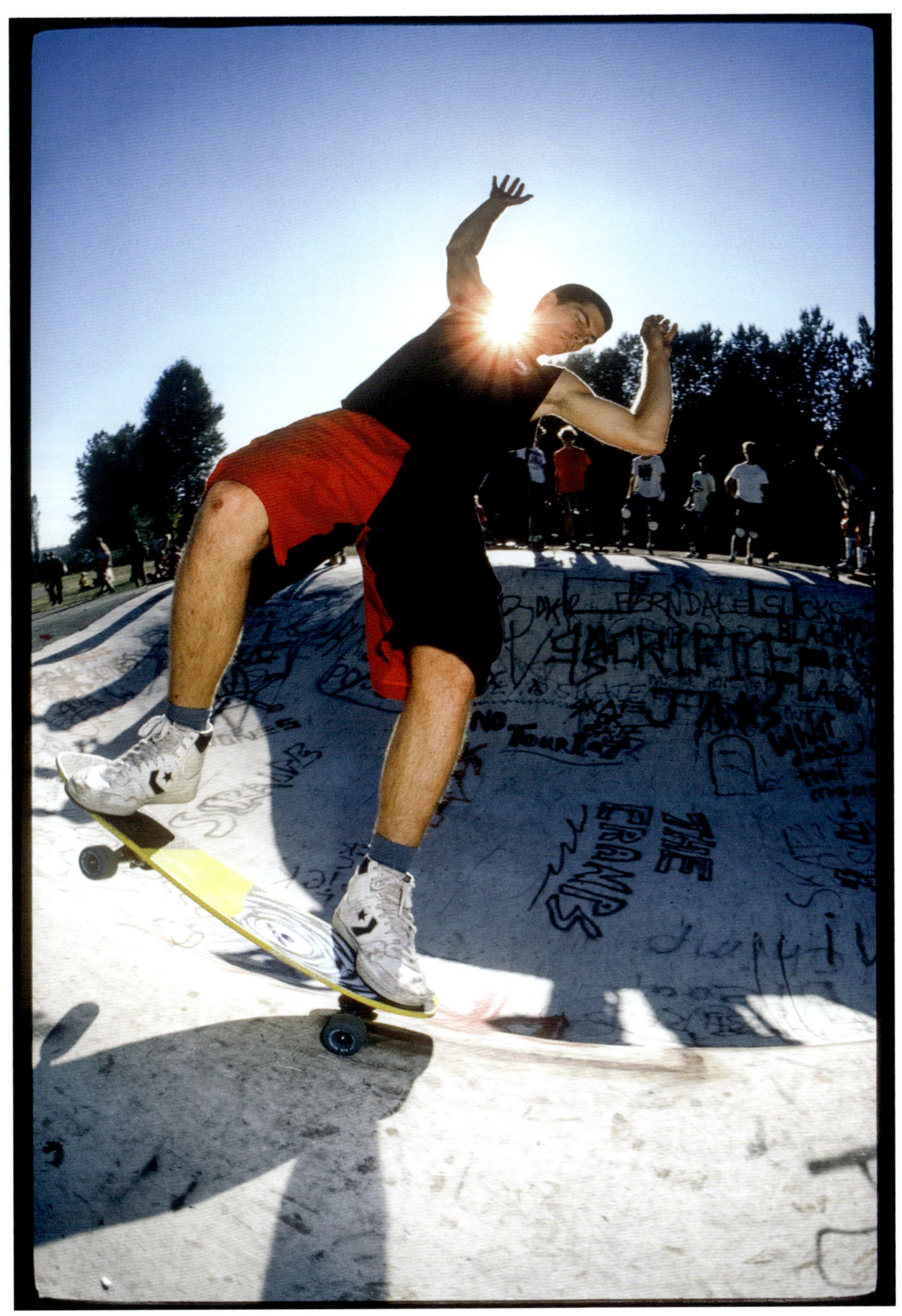

Neil Blender, Seylynn Bowl, North Vancouver, BC, Canada, 1986

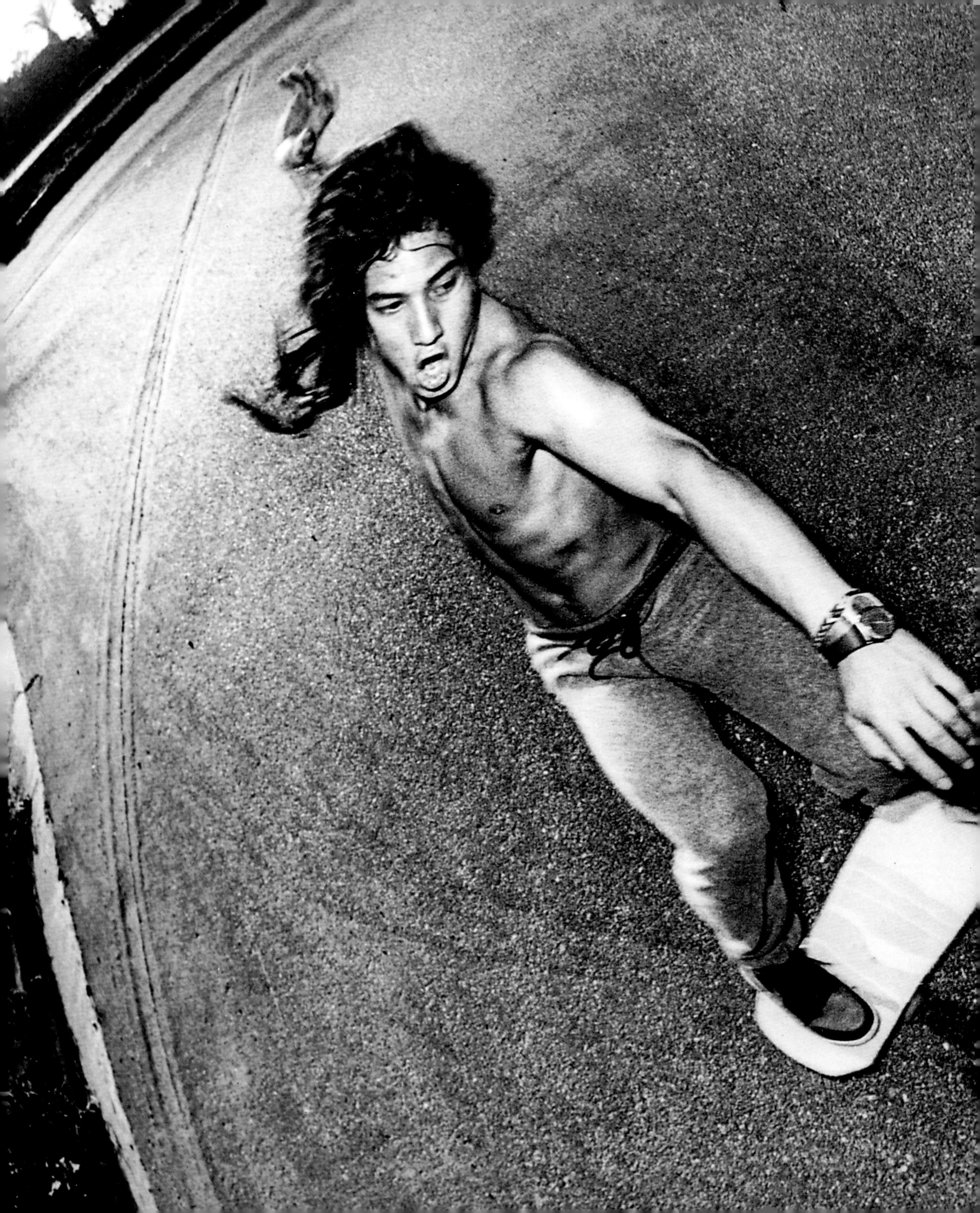

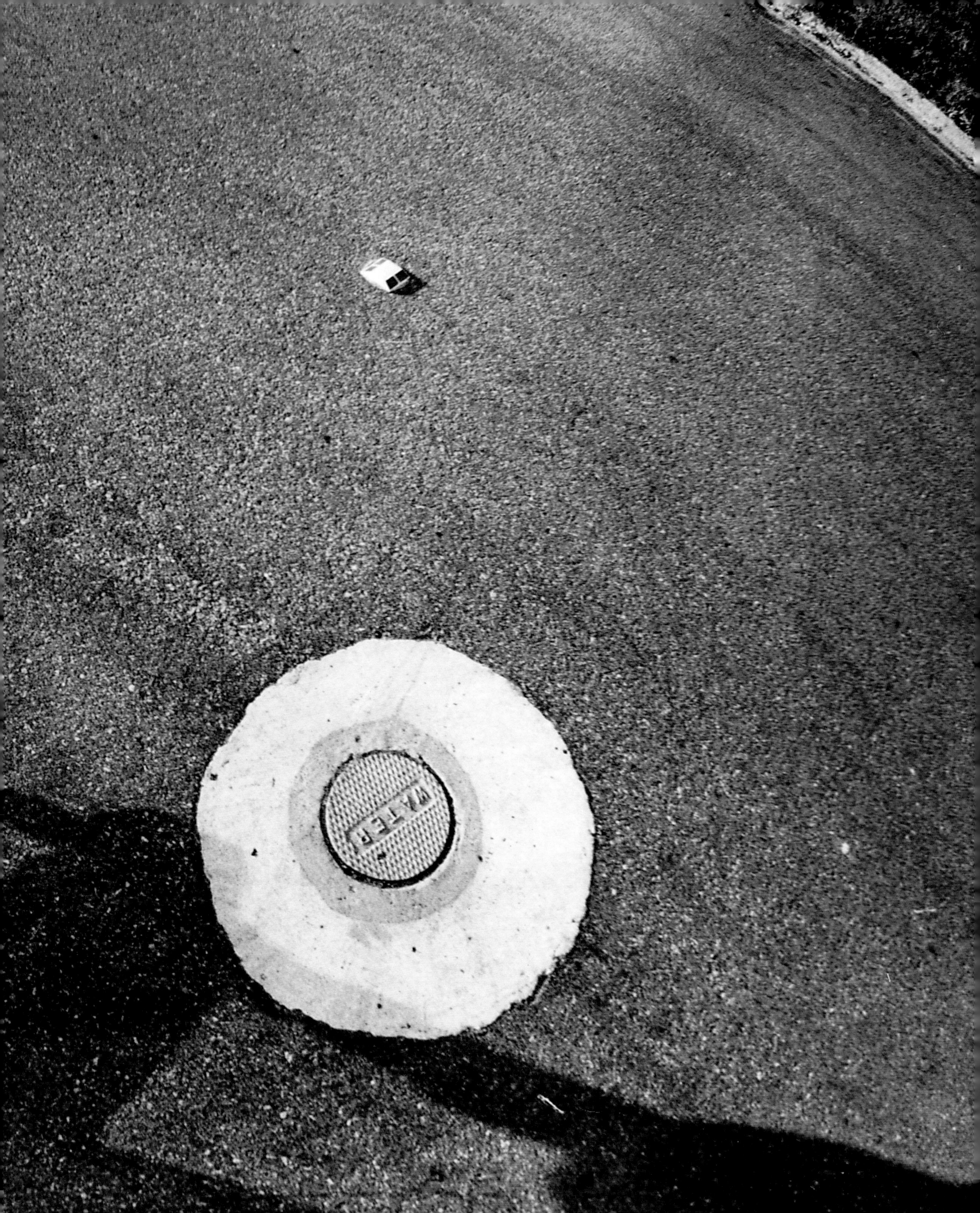
WATER

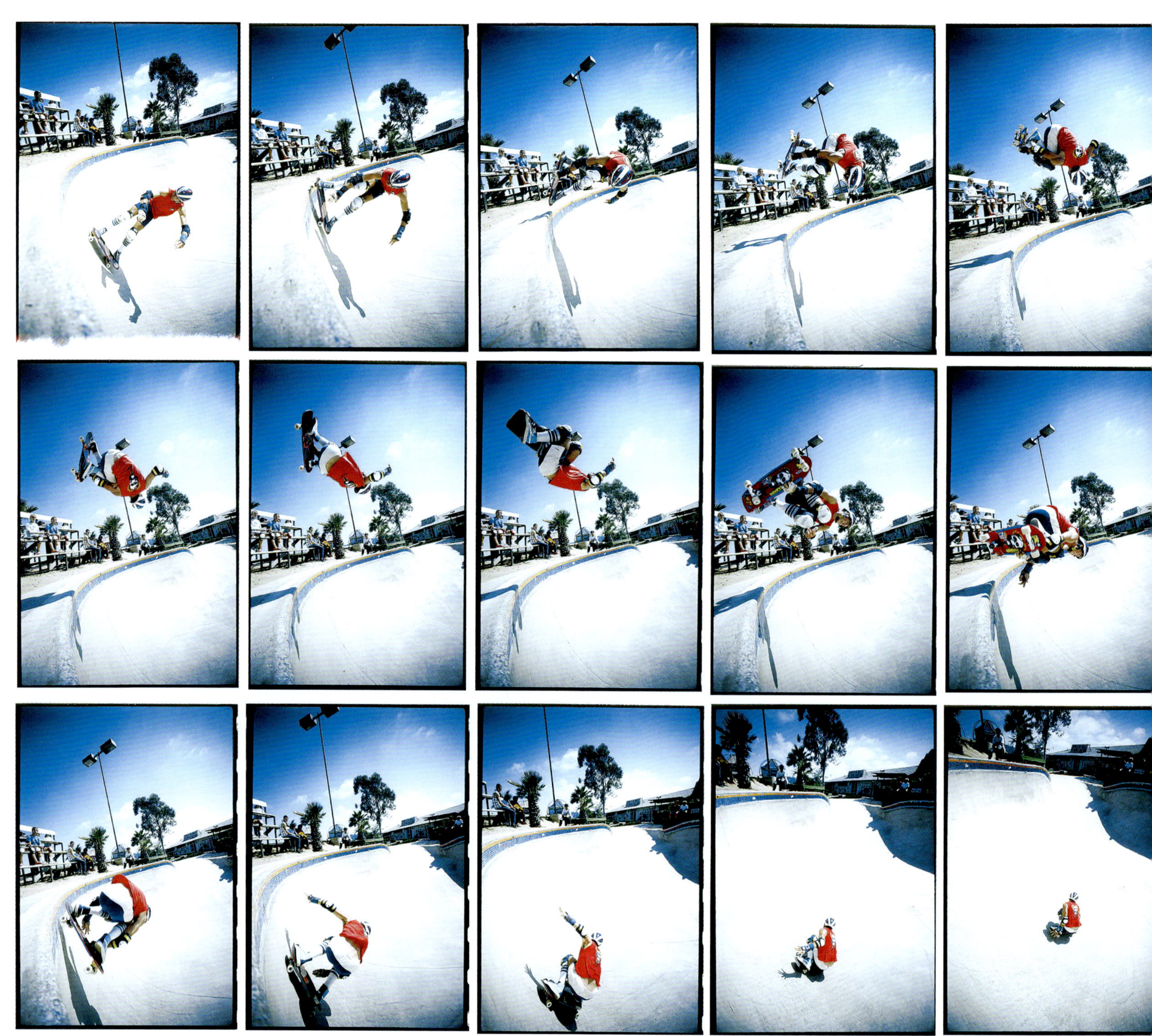

Mike McGill, The McTwist, Del Mar Skate Ranch, Del Mar, CA, 1984

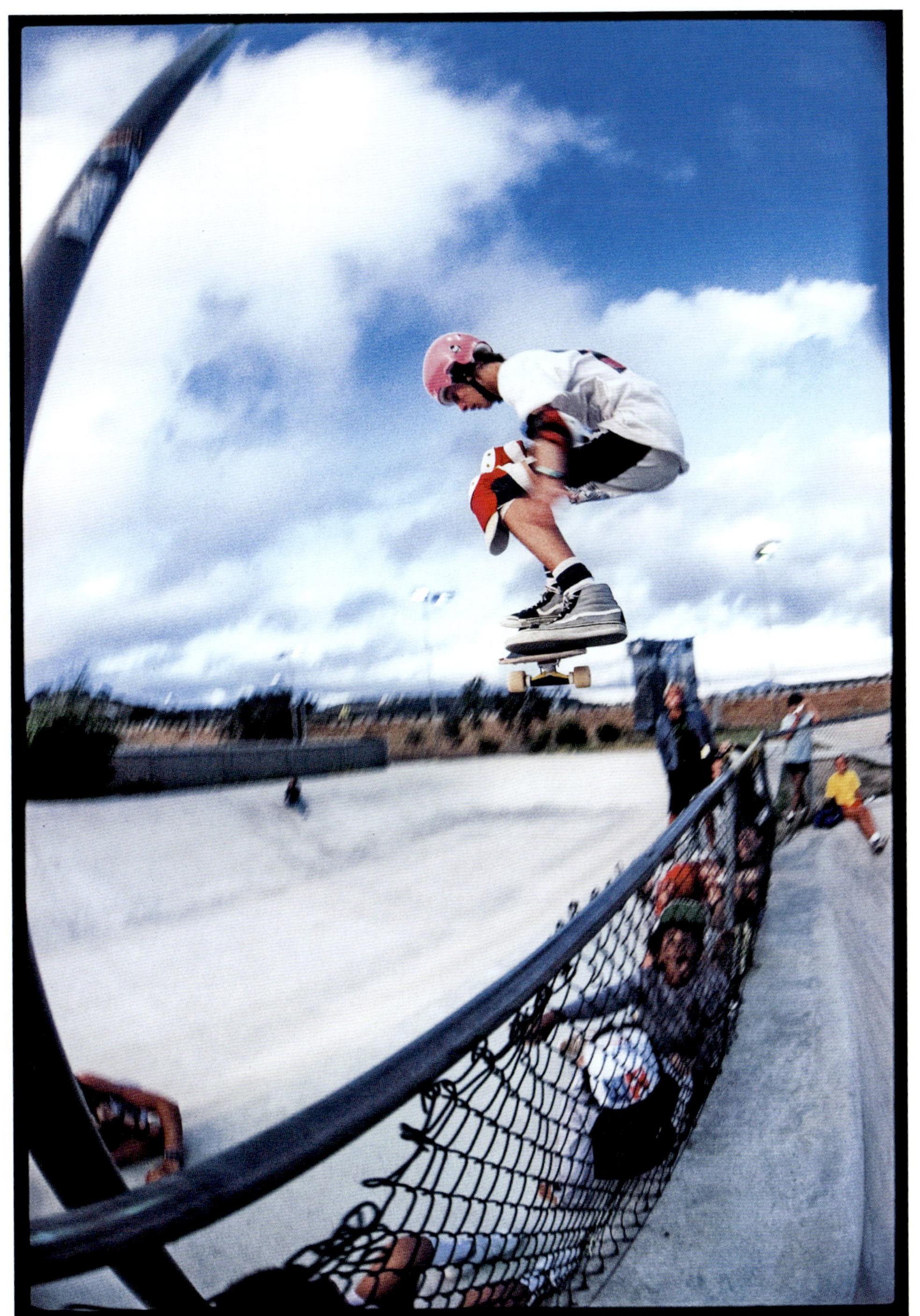

Tony Hawk, Fence Ollie, Del Mar Skate Ranch, Del Mar, CA, 1986

Previous spread: Christian Hosoi, Powerslide, Del Mar, CA, 1987

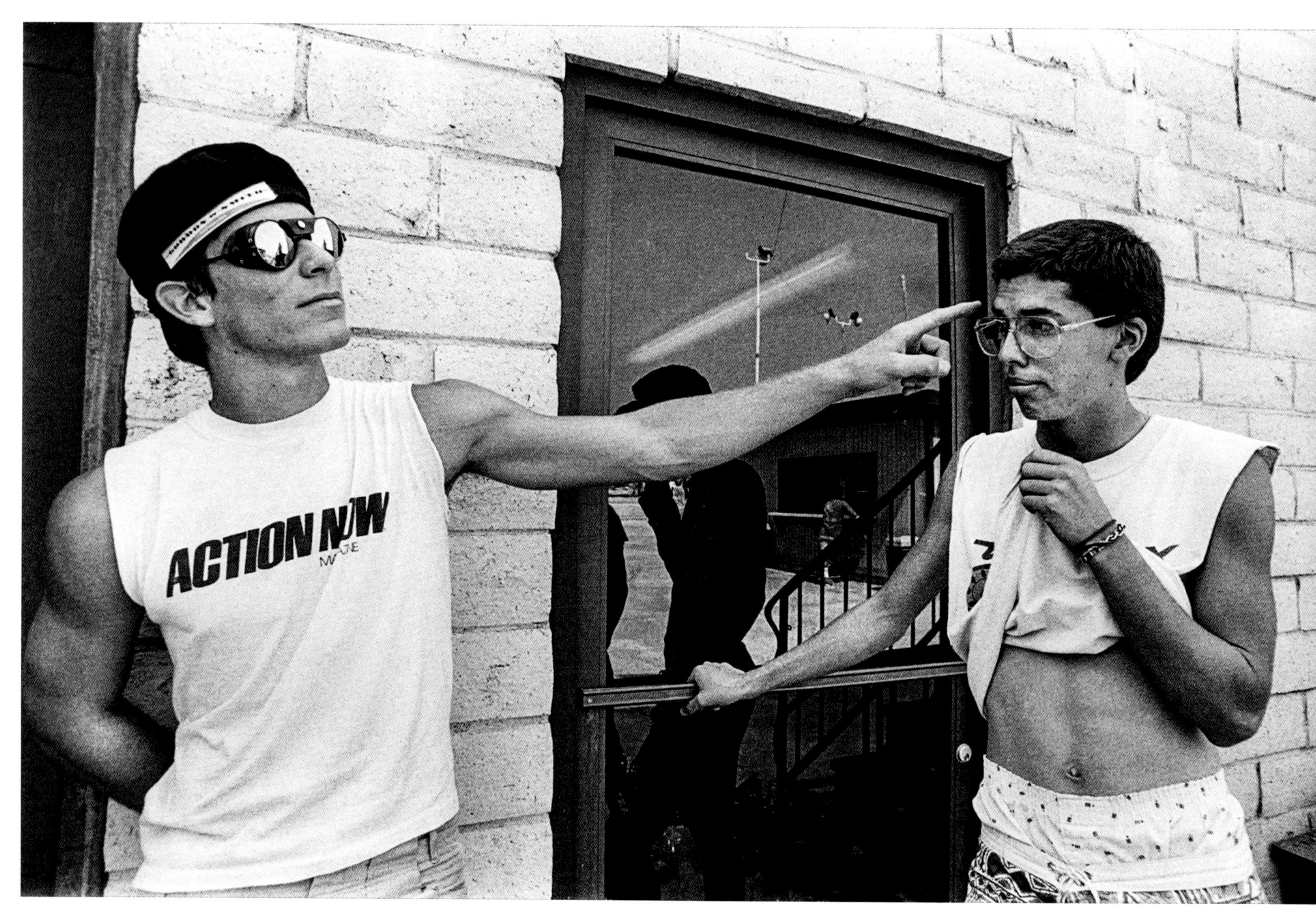

Neil Blender and John Lucero, Pipeline Skatepark, Upland, CA, 1983

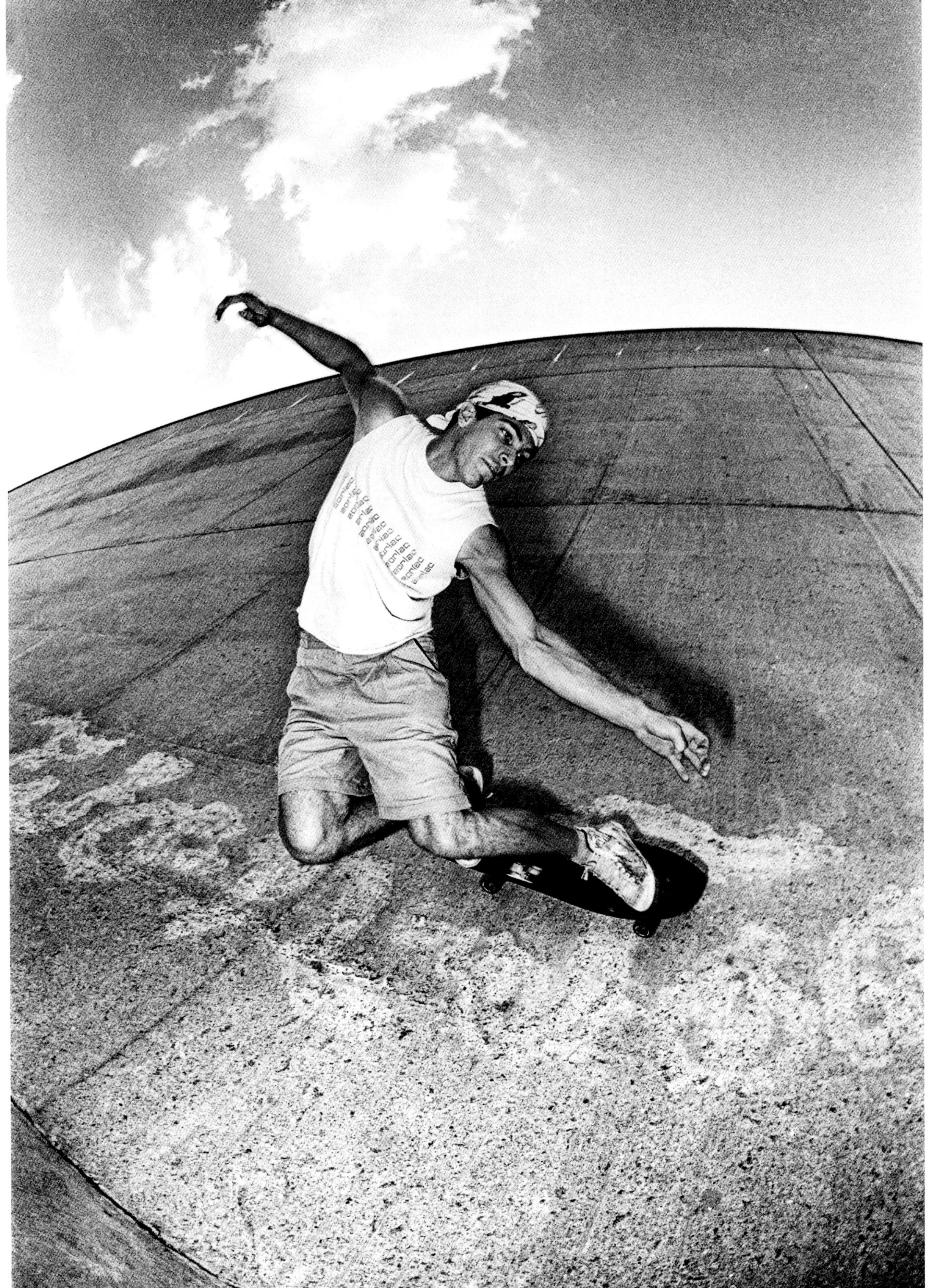

Neil Blender, Wallride carve, St. Louis, MO, 1986

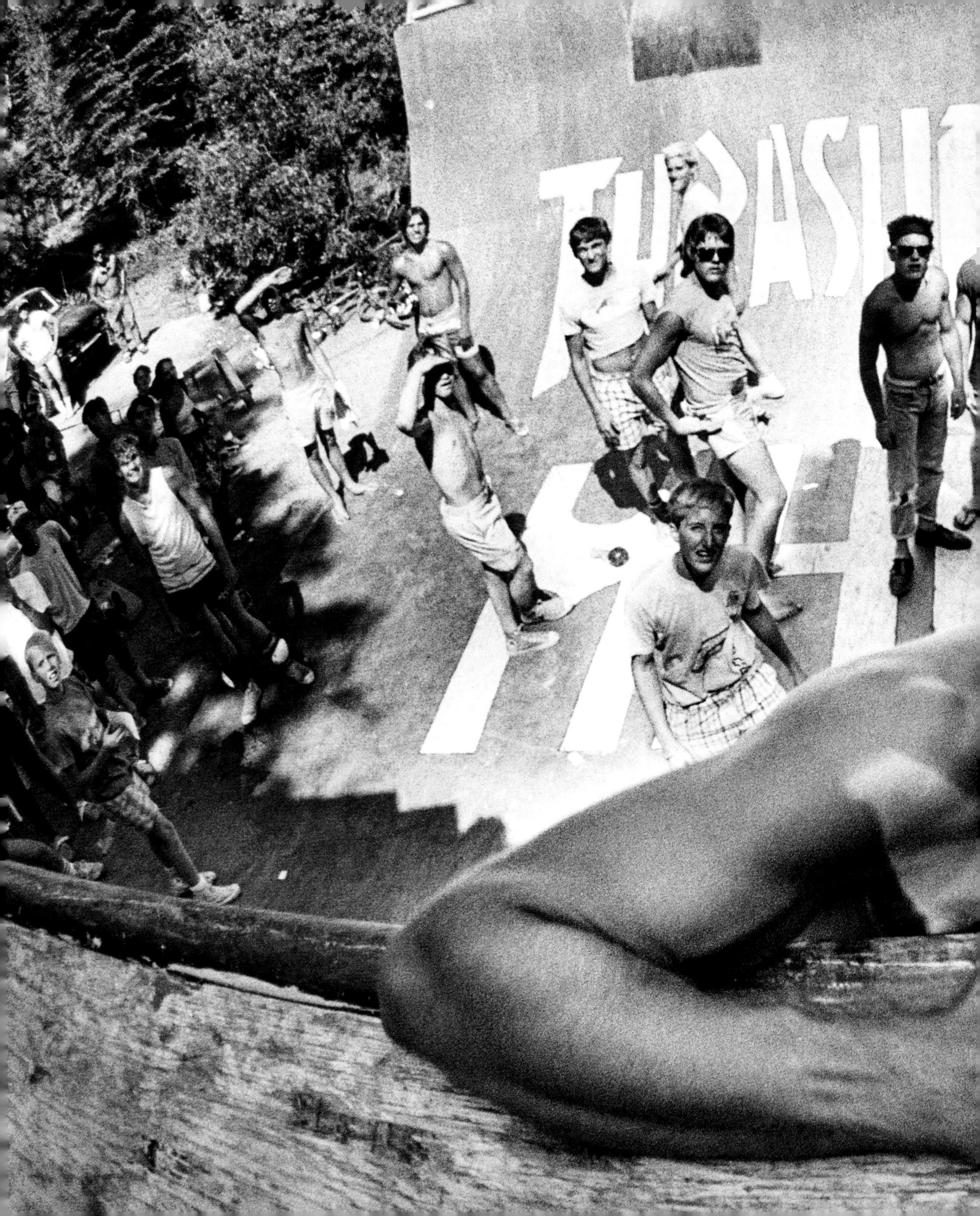

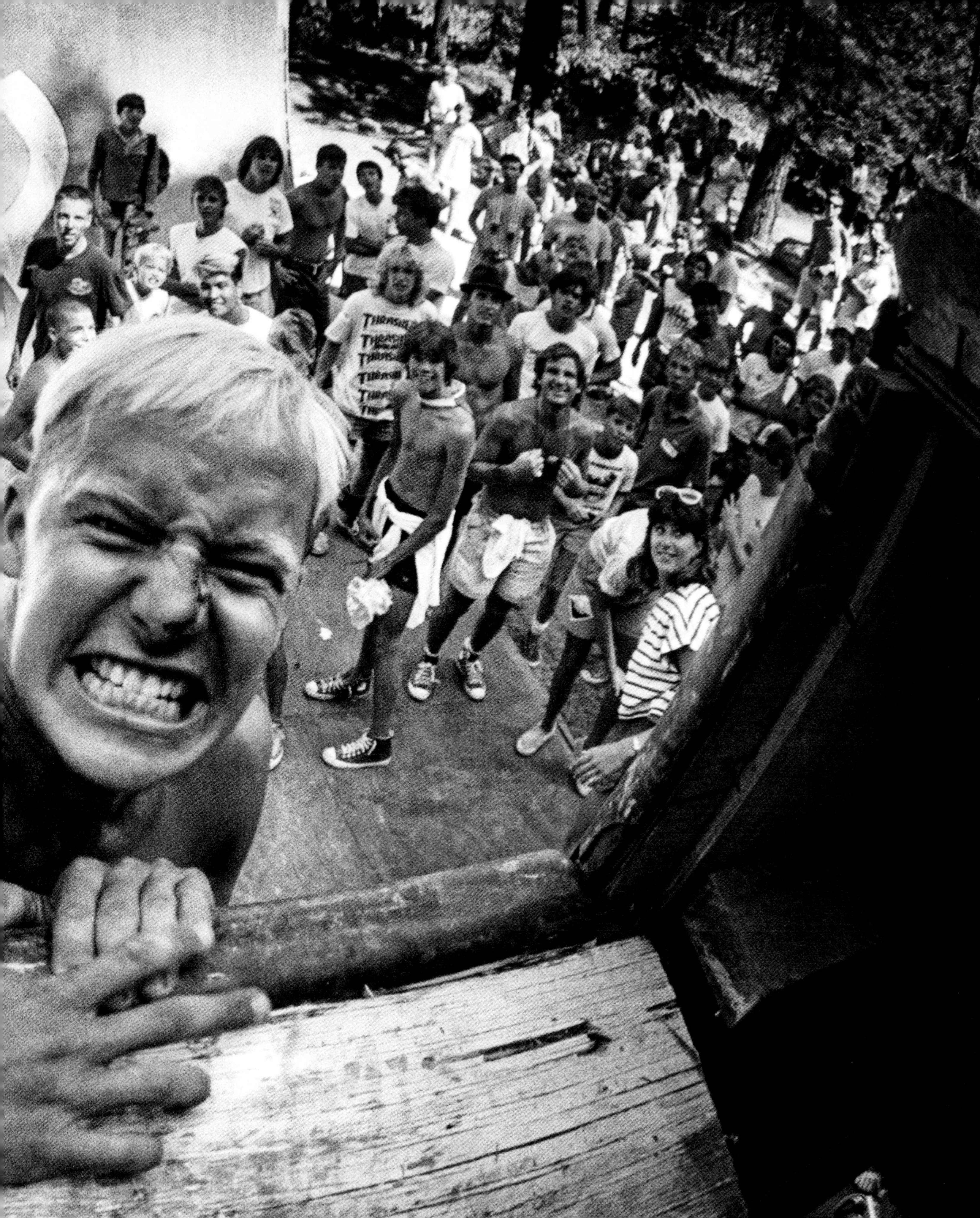

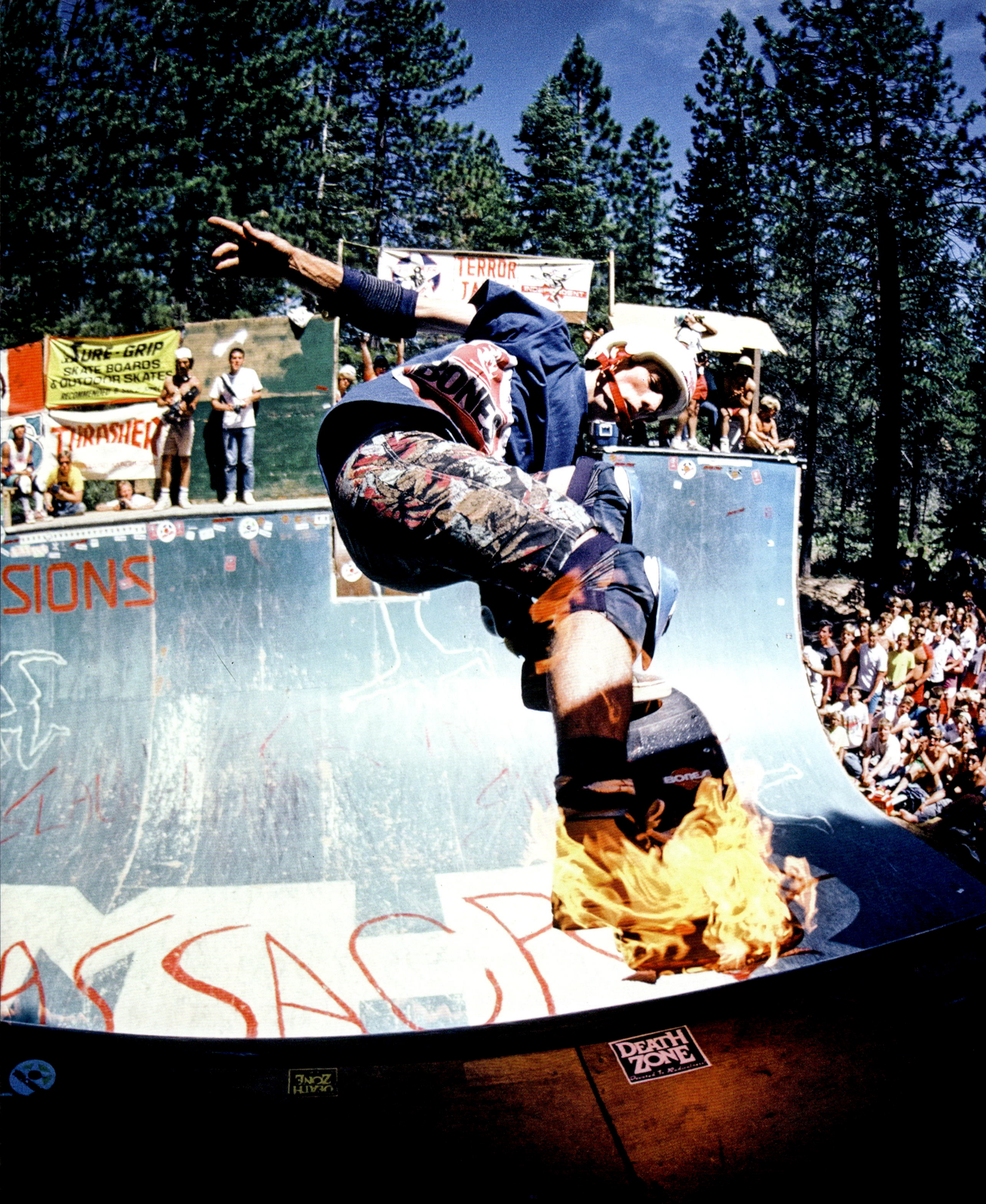
TERROR
SURE-GRIP
SKATE BOARDS
& OUTDOOR SKATES
THRASHER
BONES
SIONS
DEATH ZONE

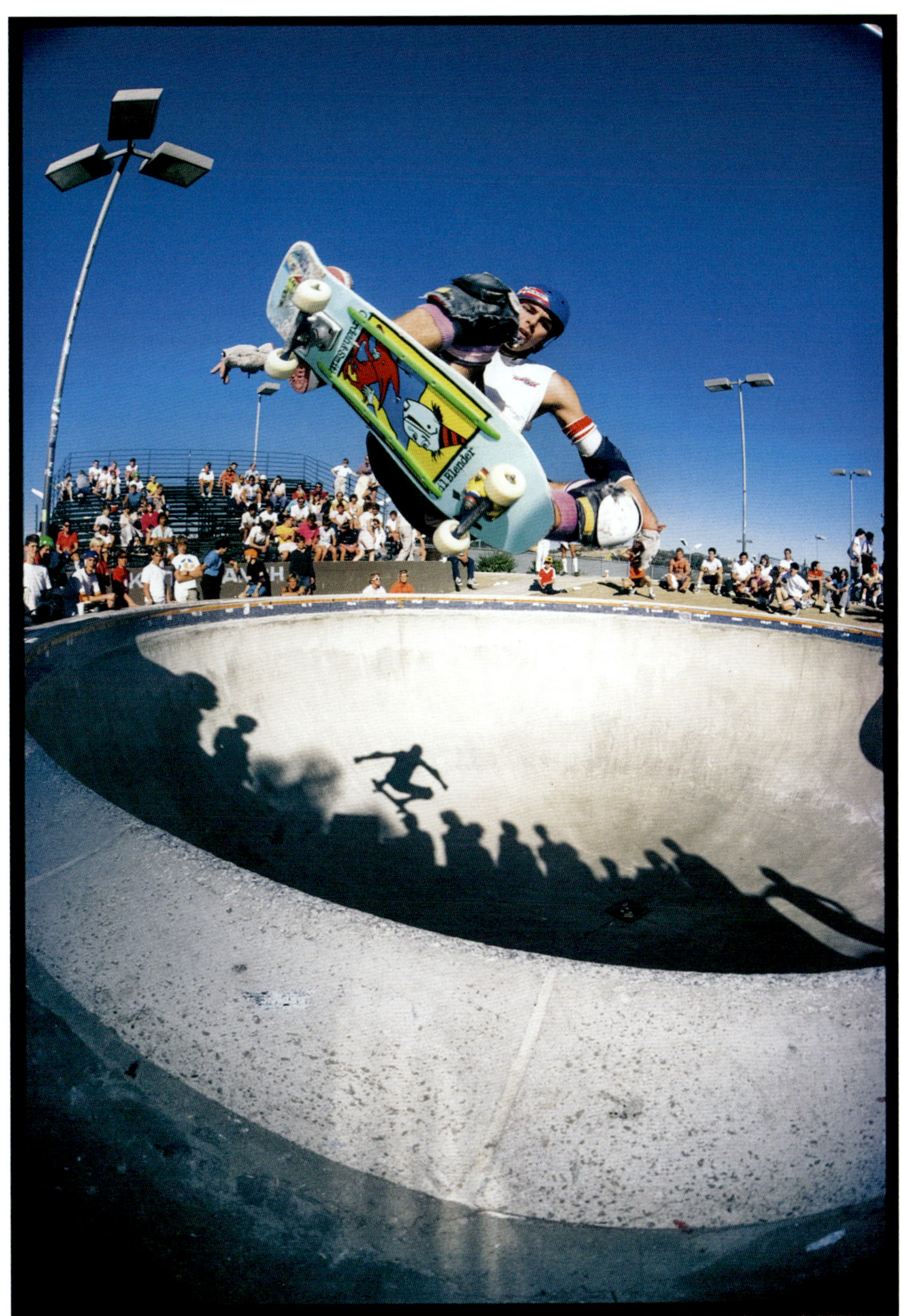

Neil Blender, Ollie, Del Mar Skate Ranch, Del Mar, CA, 1985

Previous spread: Tahoe spectator, North Lake Tahoe, CA, 1984

ance Mountain, On fire, North Lake Tahoe, CA, 1985

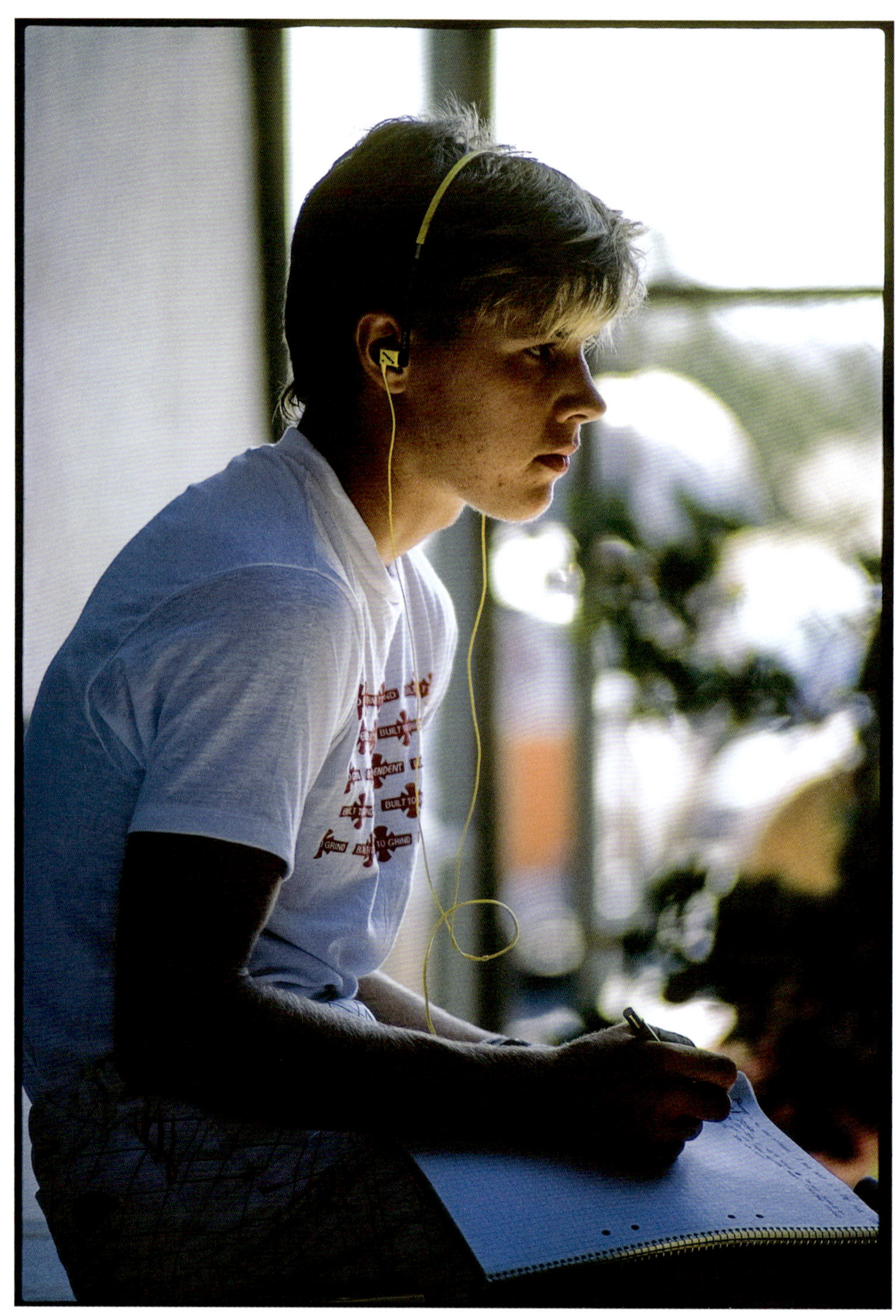

Rodney Mullen, Portrait, Kona Skatepark, Jacksonville, FL, 1984

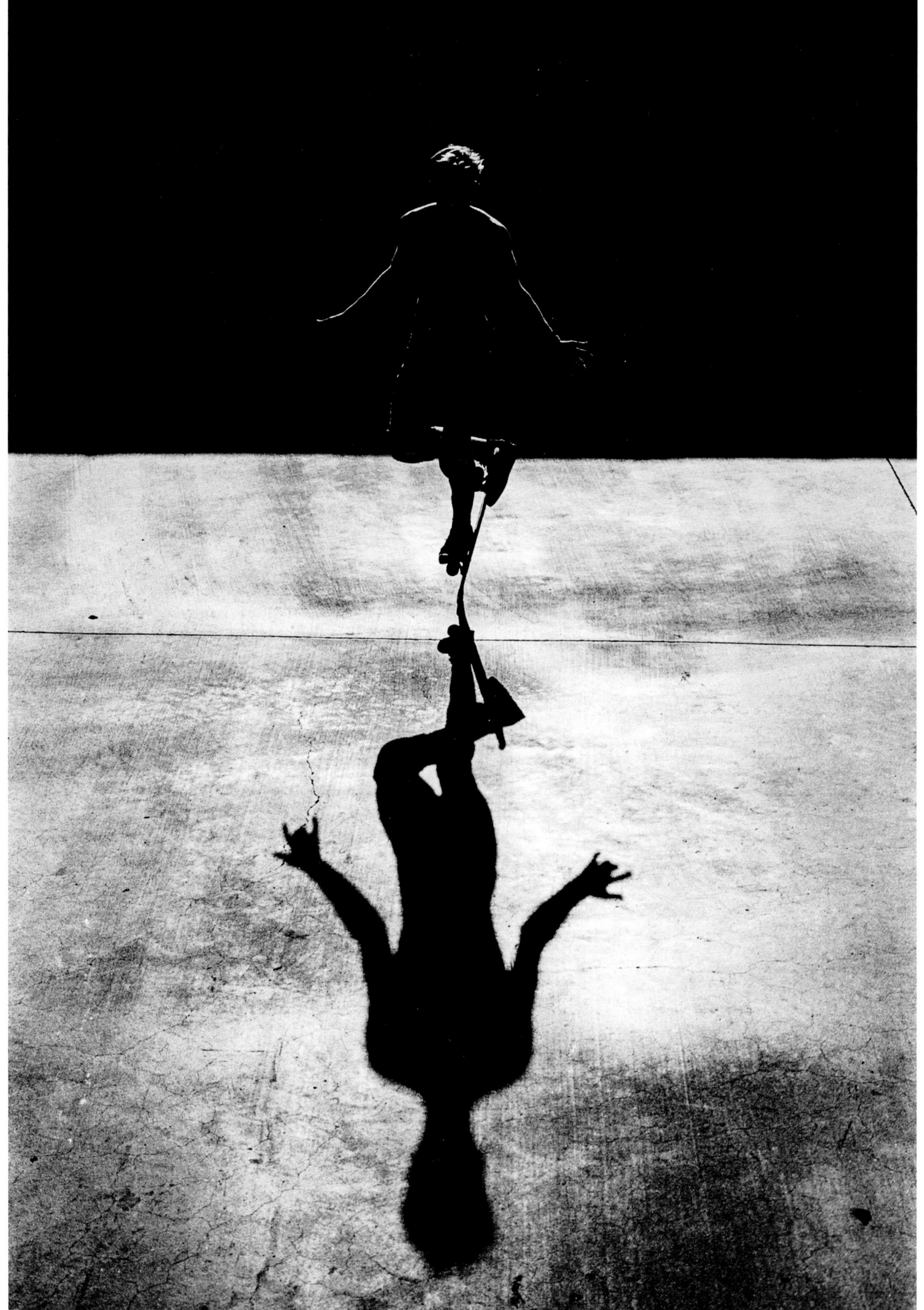

Rodney Mullen, Silhouette, Del Mar Skate Ranch, Del Mar, CA, 1985

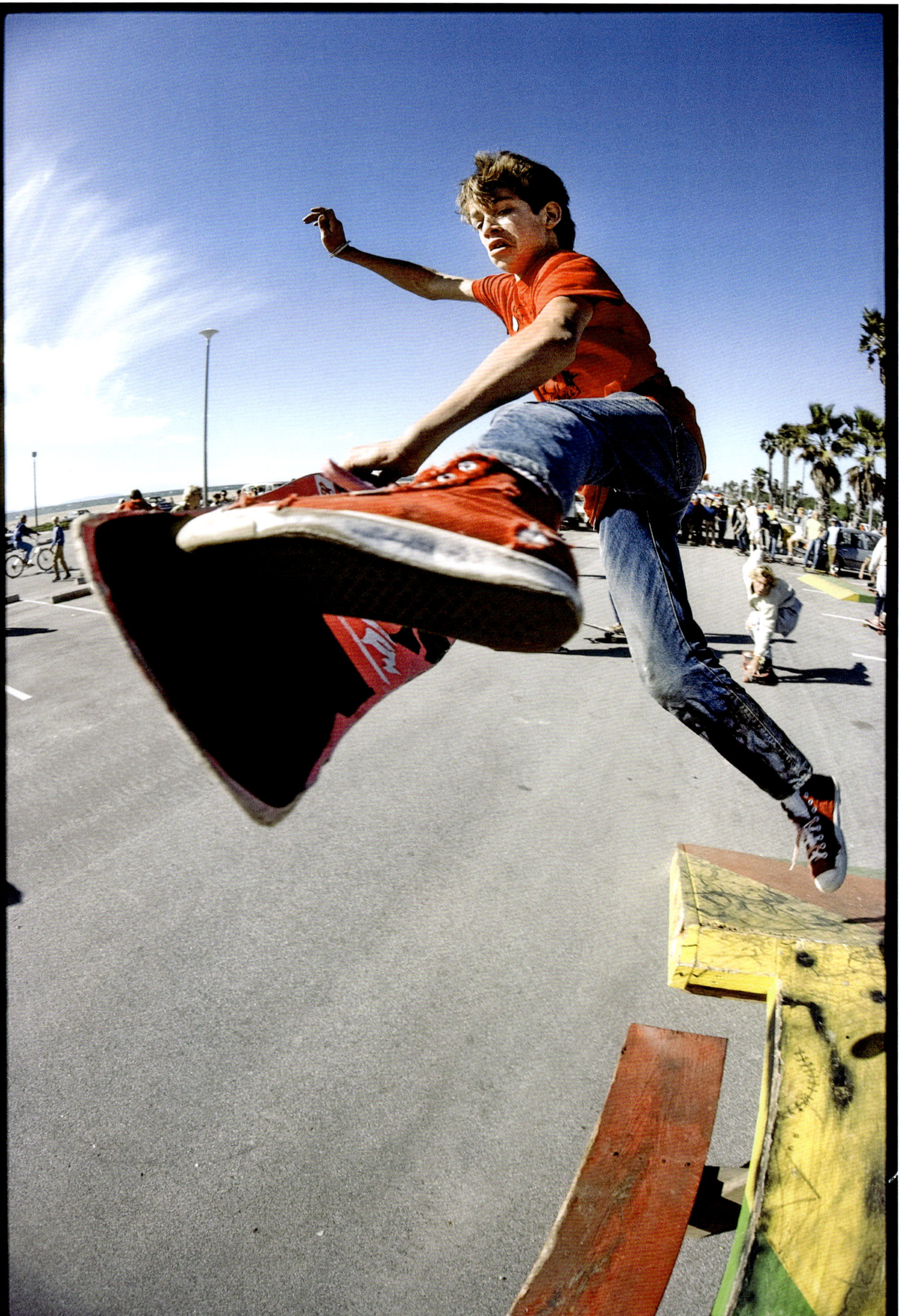

Mark Gonzales, Frontside boneless, Huntington Beach, CA, 1984

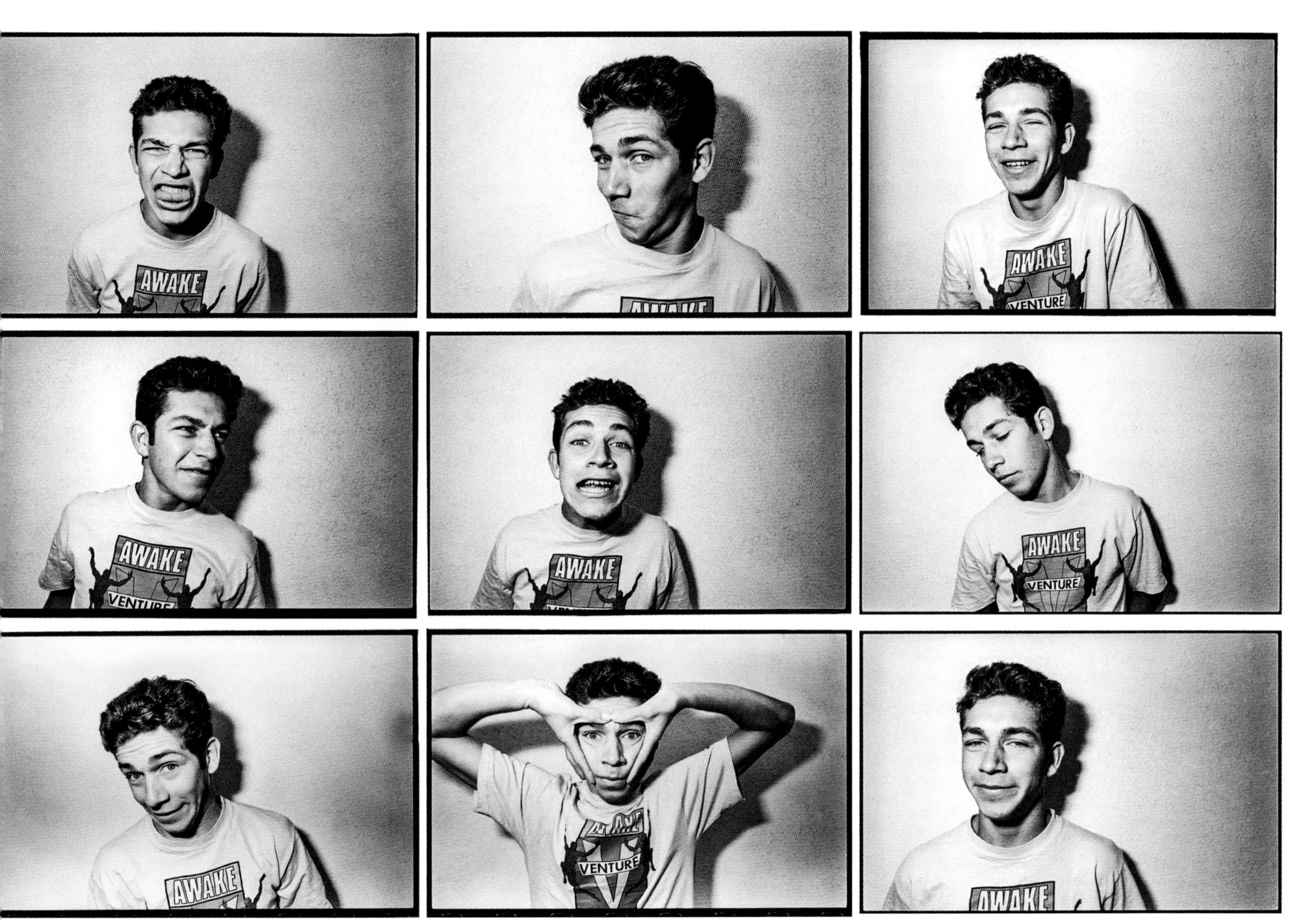

Mark Gonzales, Portrait series, Oceanside, CA, 1986

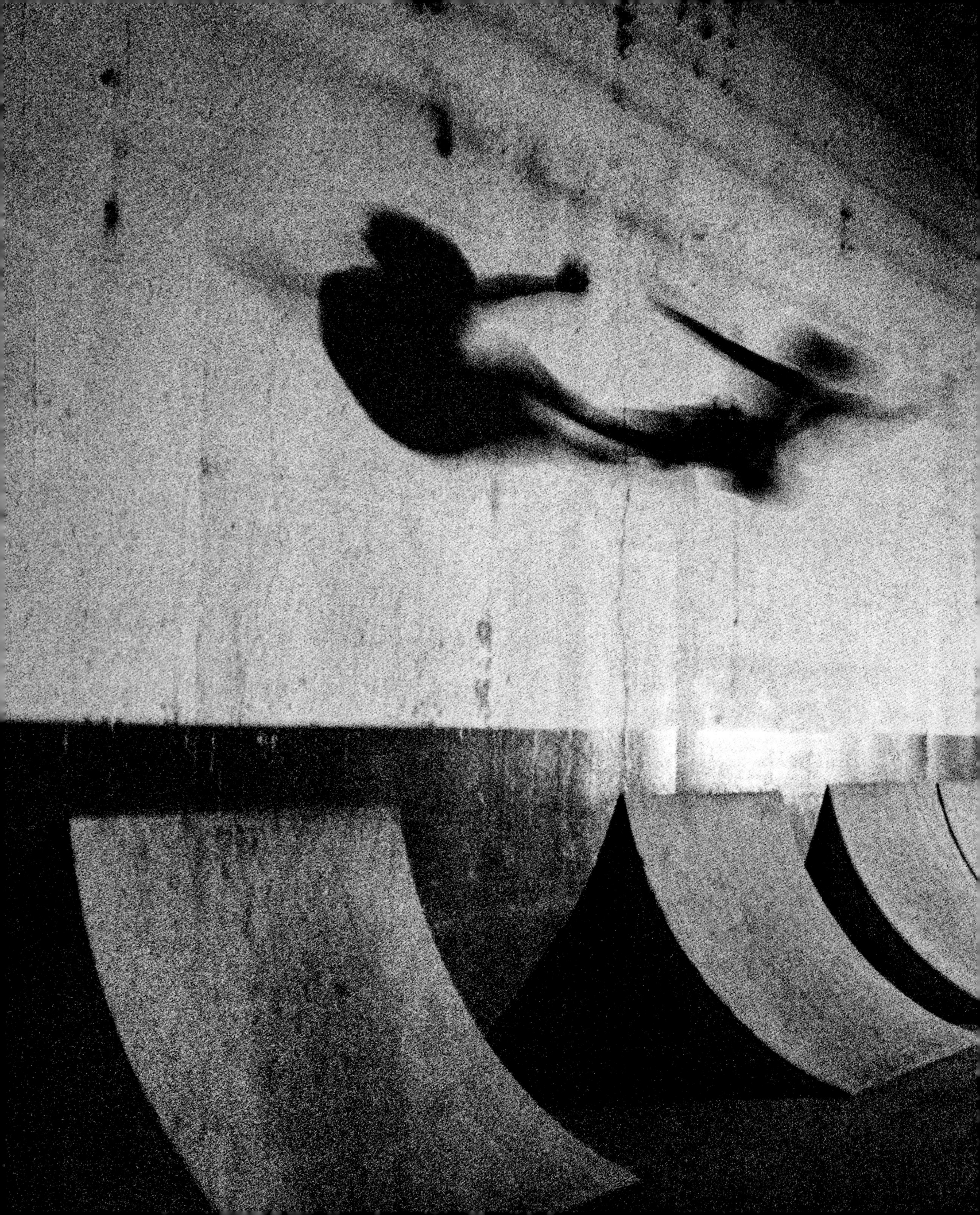

Previous spread: Mark Gonzales, Powell-Peralta building, Goleta, CA, 1988

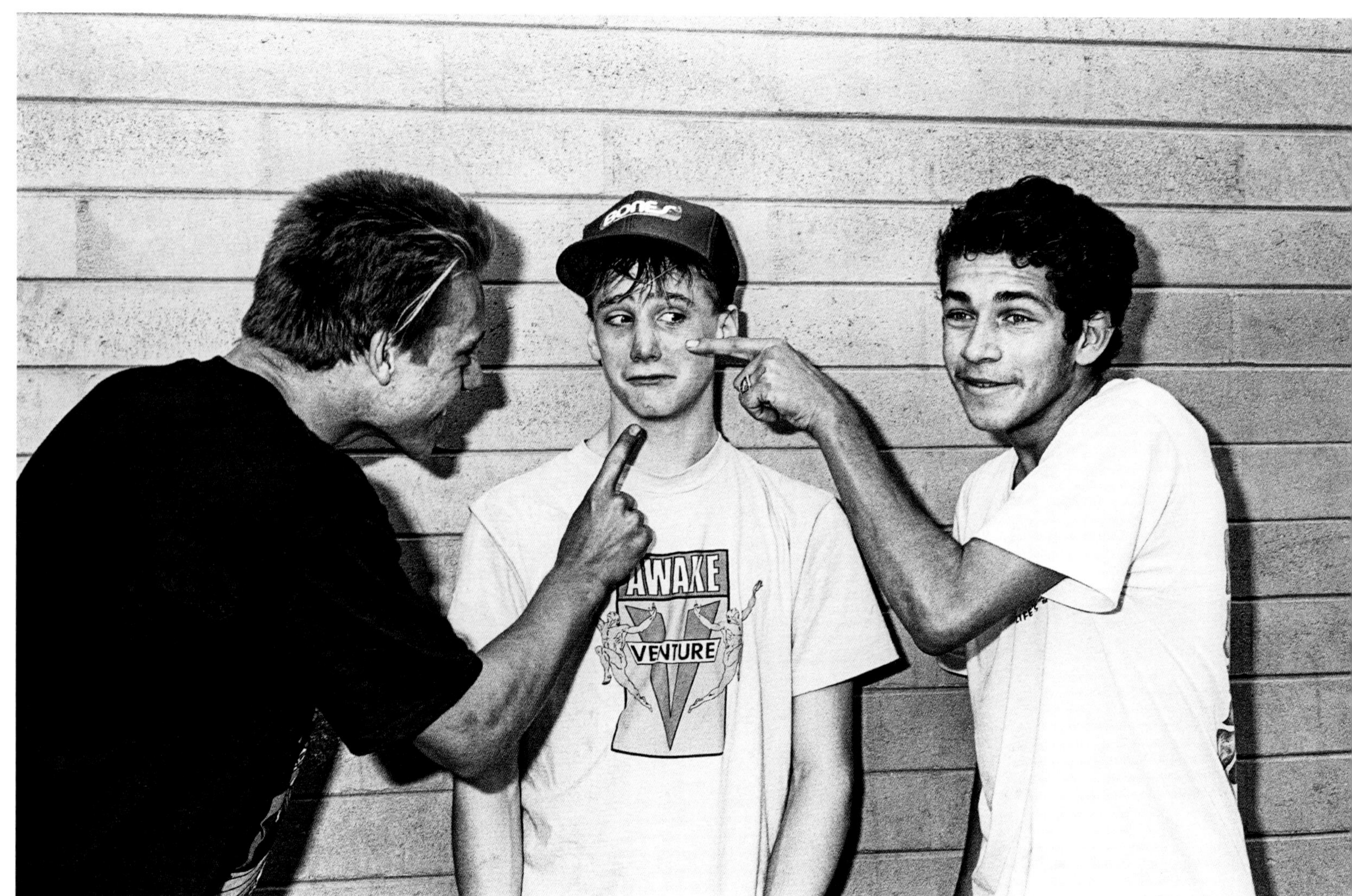

Natas Kaupas, Mike Vallely, and Mark Gonzales, School W, San Diego, CA, 1987

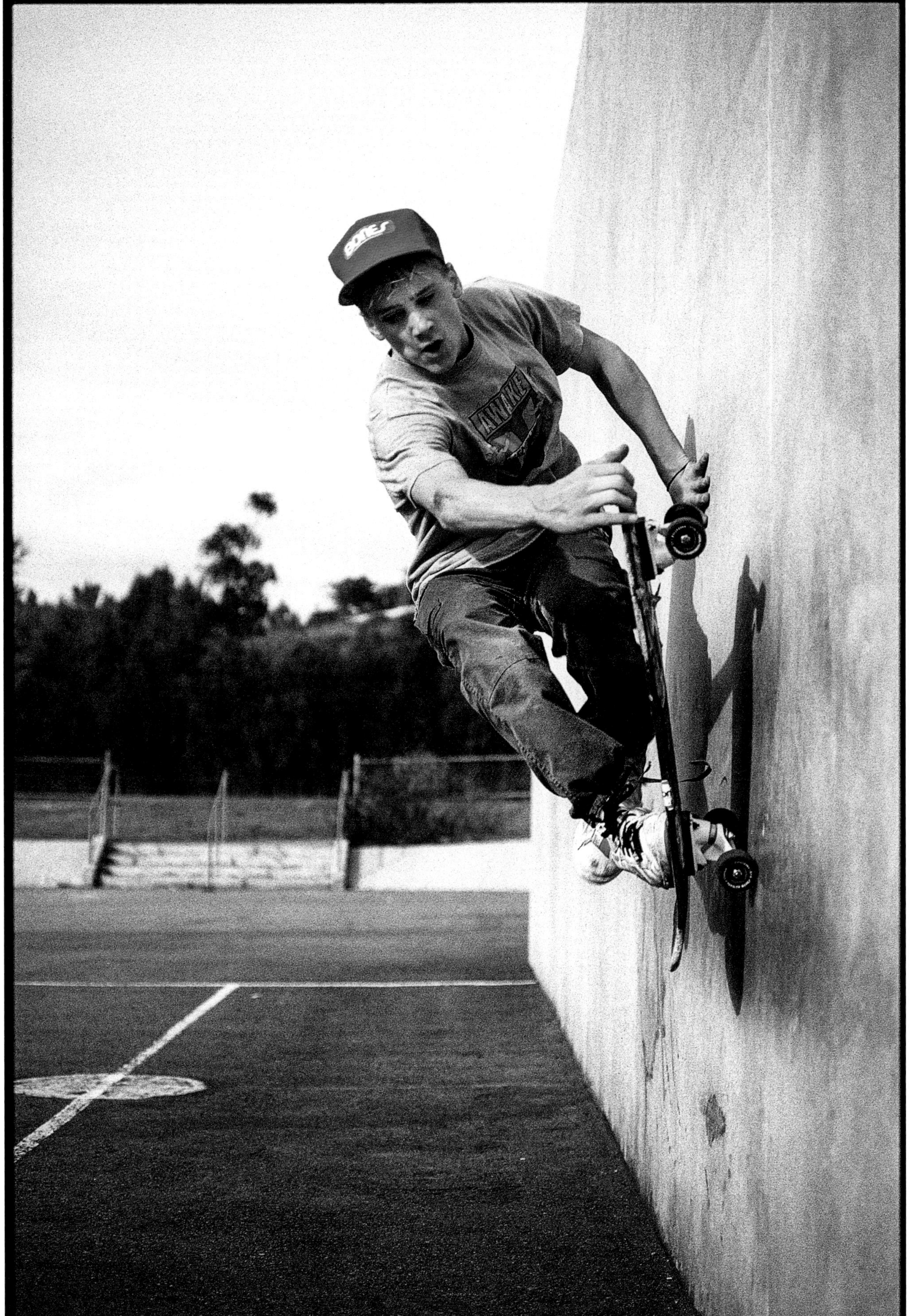

Mike Vallely, Wallride, School W, San Diego, CA, 1987

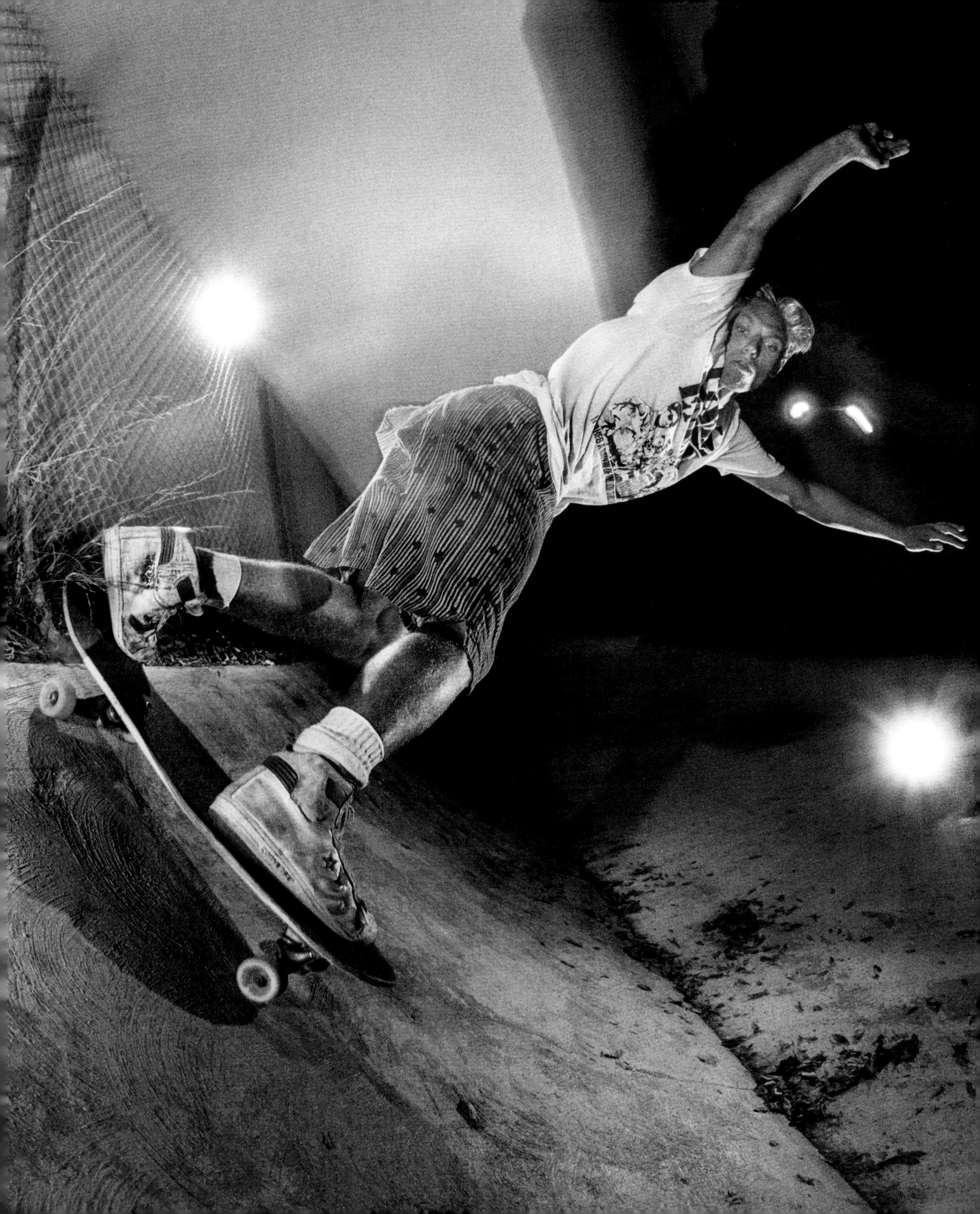

Natas Kaupas, Backside powerslide, Pacifica Banks, Culver City, CA, 1988

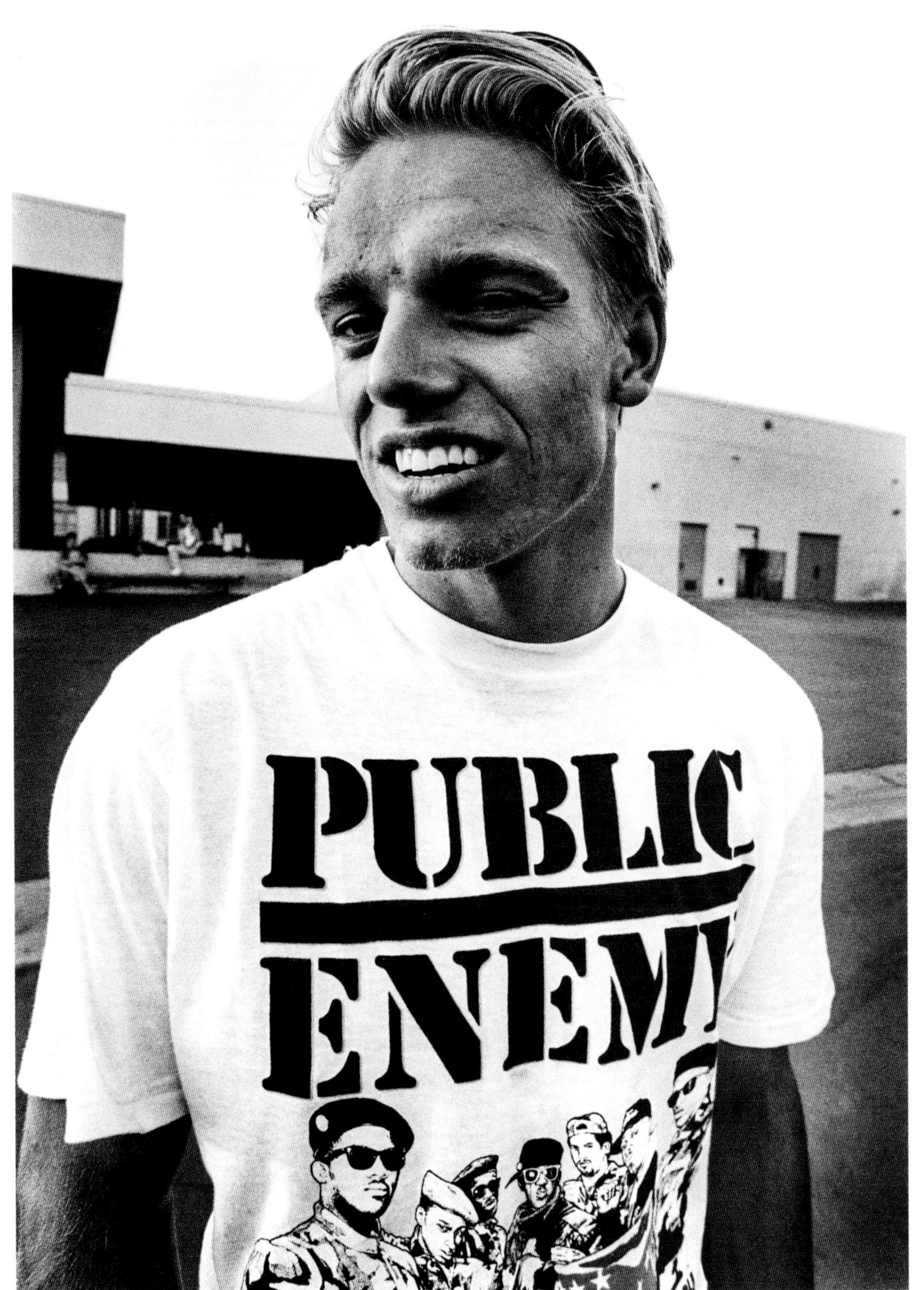

Natas Kaupas, Portrait, Venice High School, Venice Beach, CA, 1988

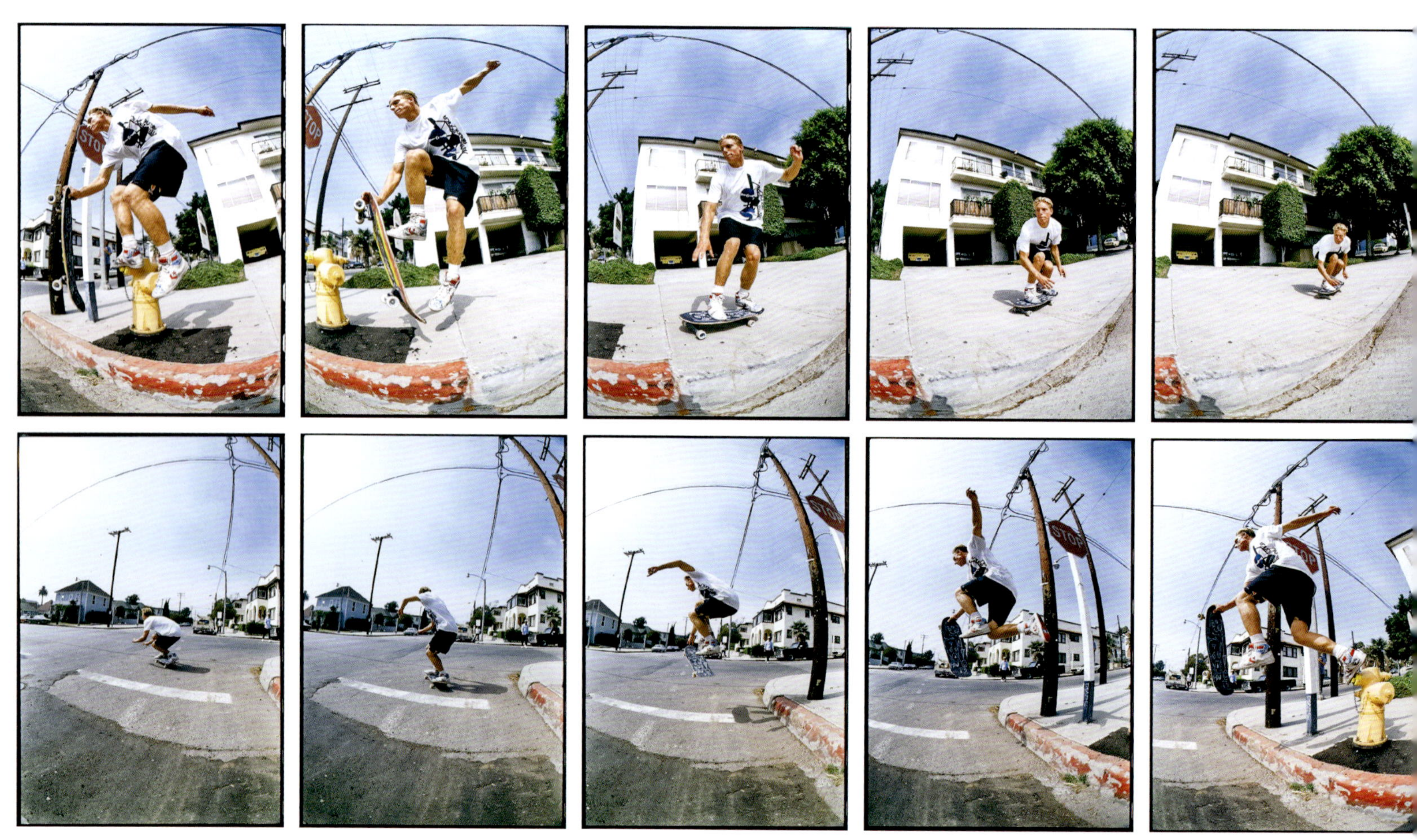

Natas Kaupas, hydrant footplant, Santa Monica, CA, 1988

Natas Kaupas, Melonchollie, Venice Beach High, Venice Beach, CA, 1988

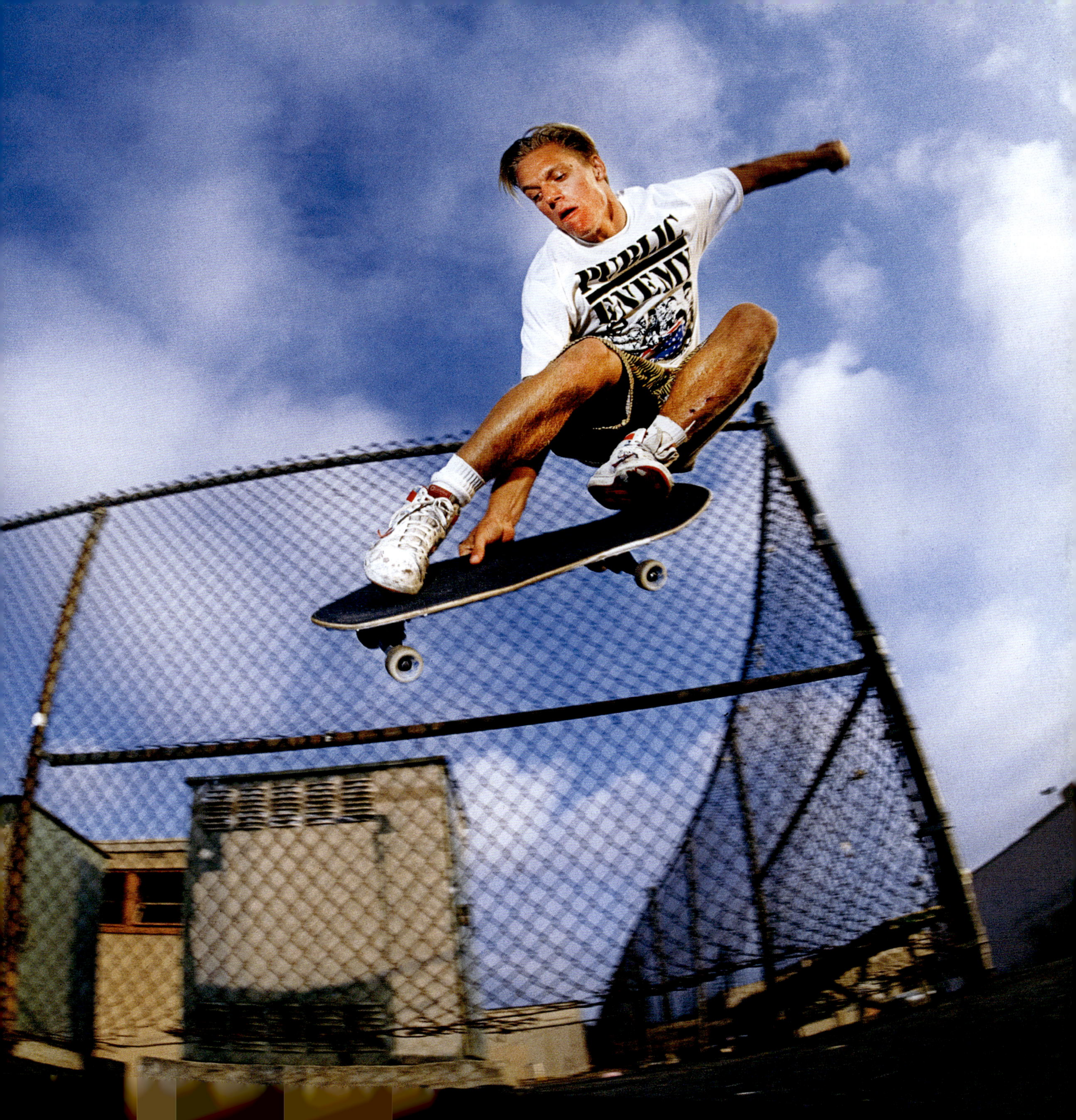
PUBLIC
ENEMY

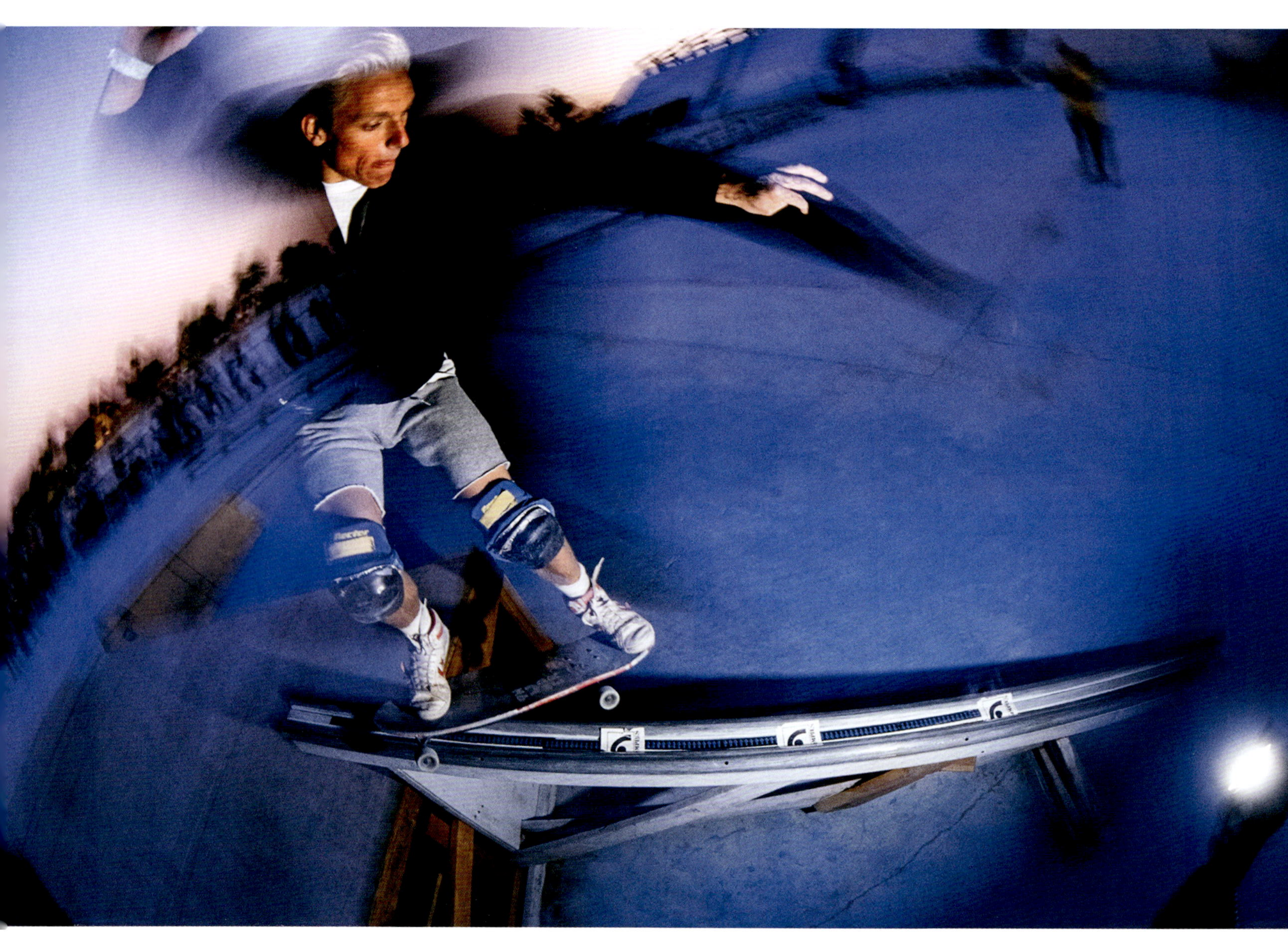

Natas Kaupas, Big Surf, Tempe, AZ, 1987

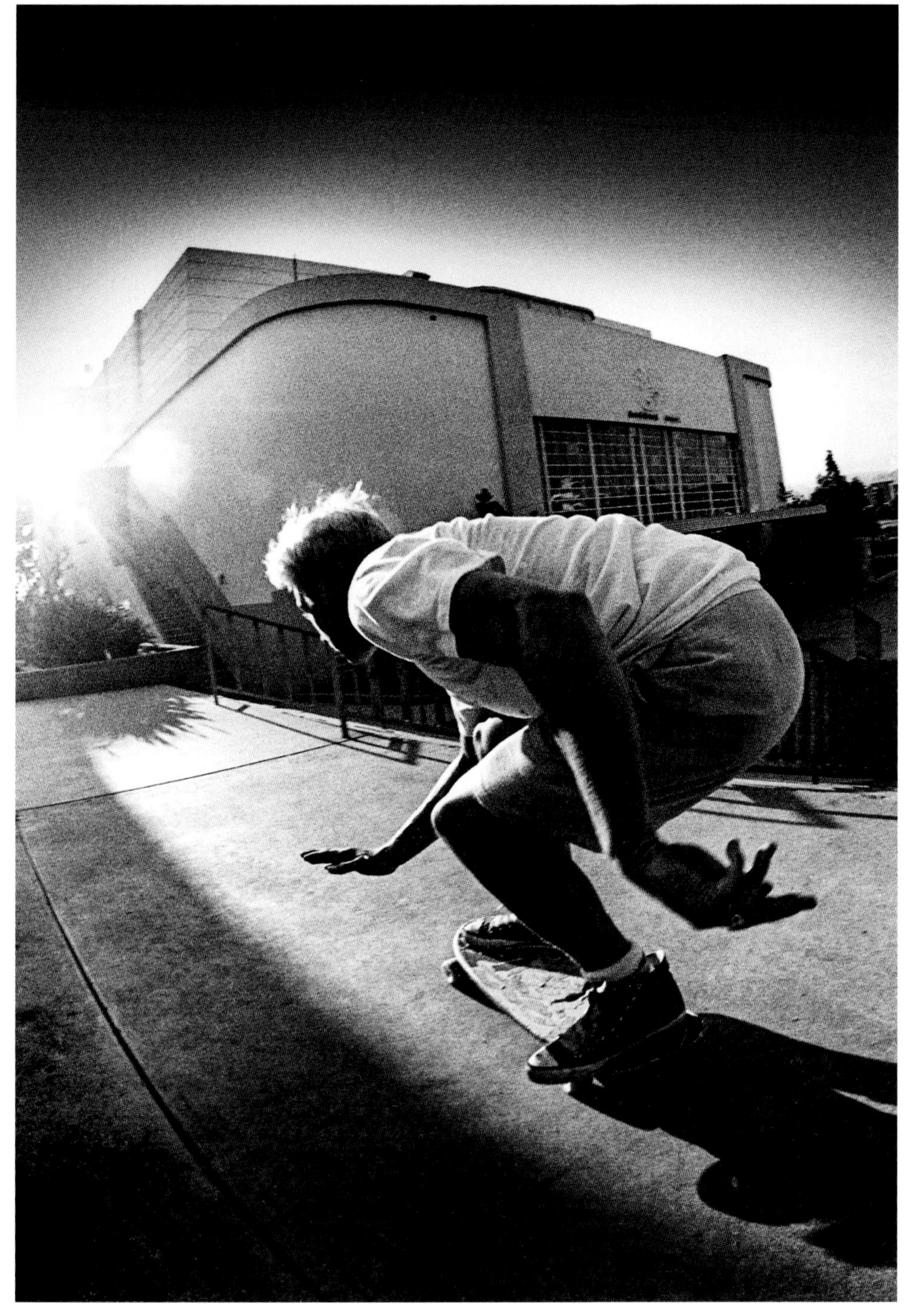

Natas Kaupas, The Landing, Santa Monica High School, Santa Monica, CA, 1985

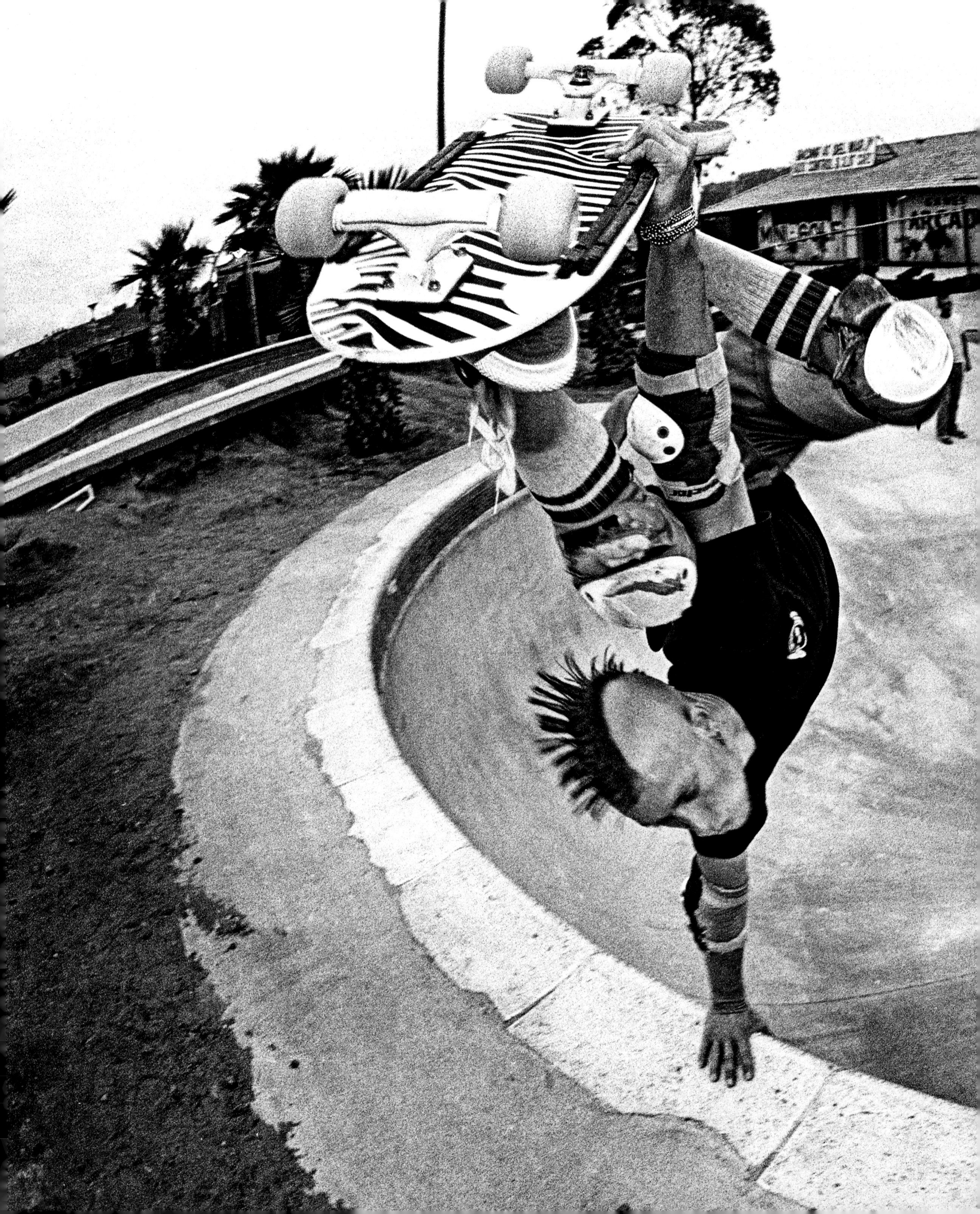

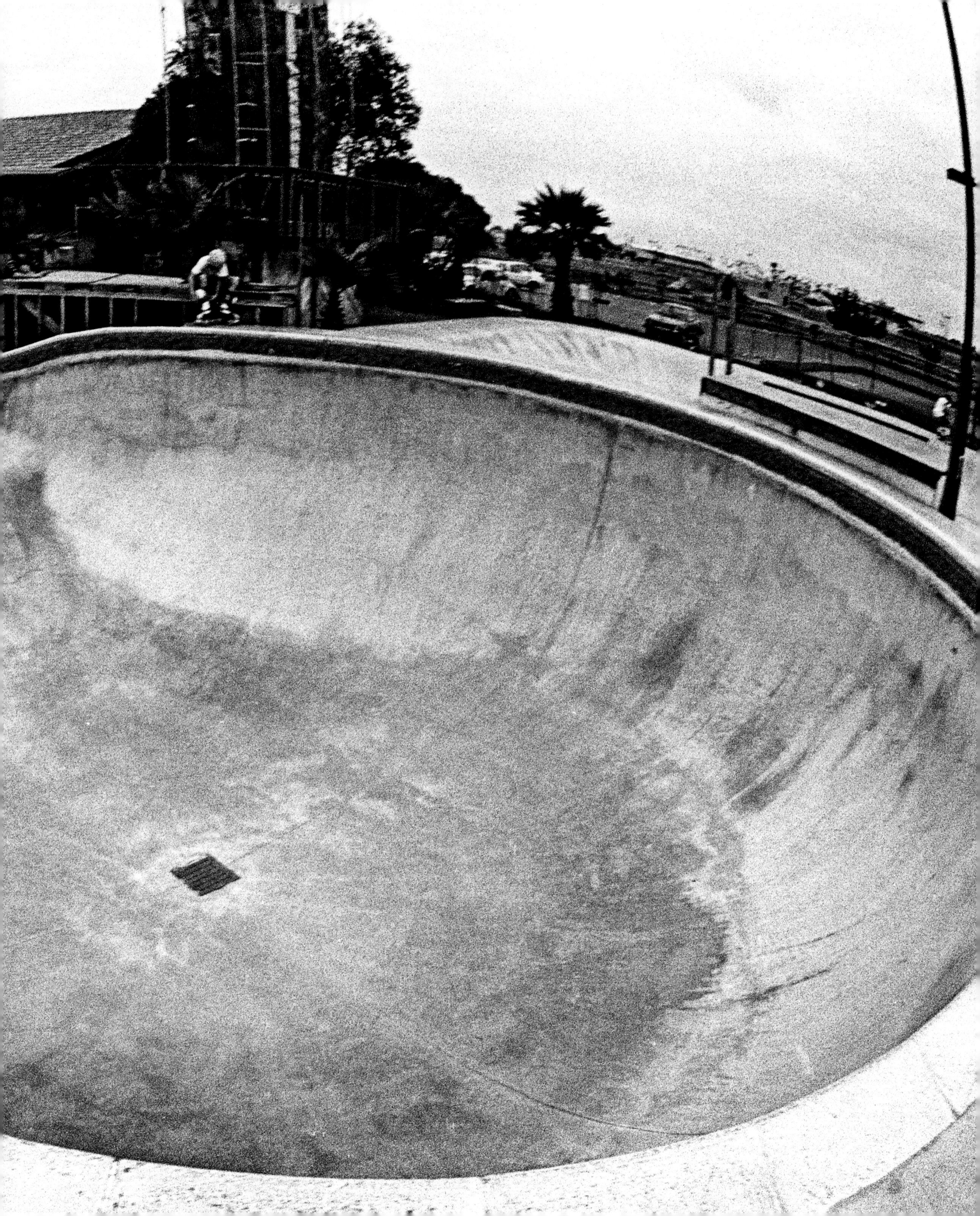

Previous spread: Owen Nieder, Layback air, Del Mar Skate Ranch, Del Mar, CA, 1983

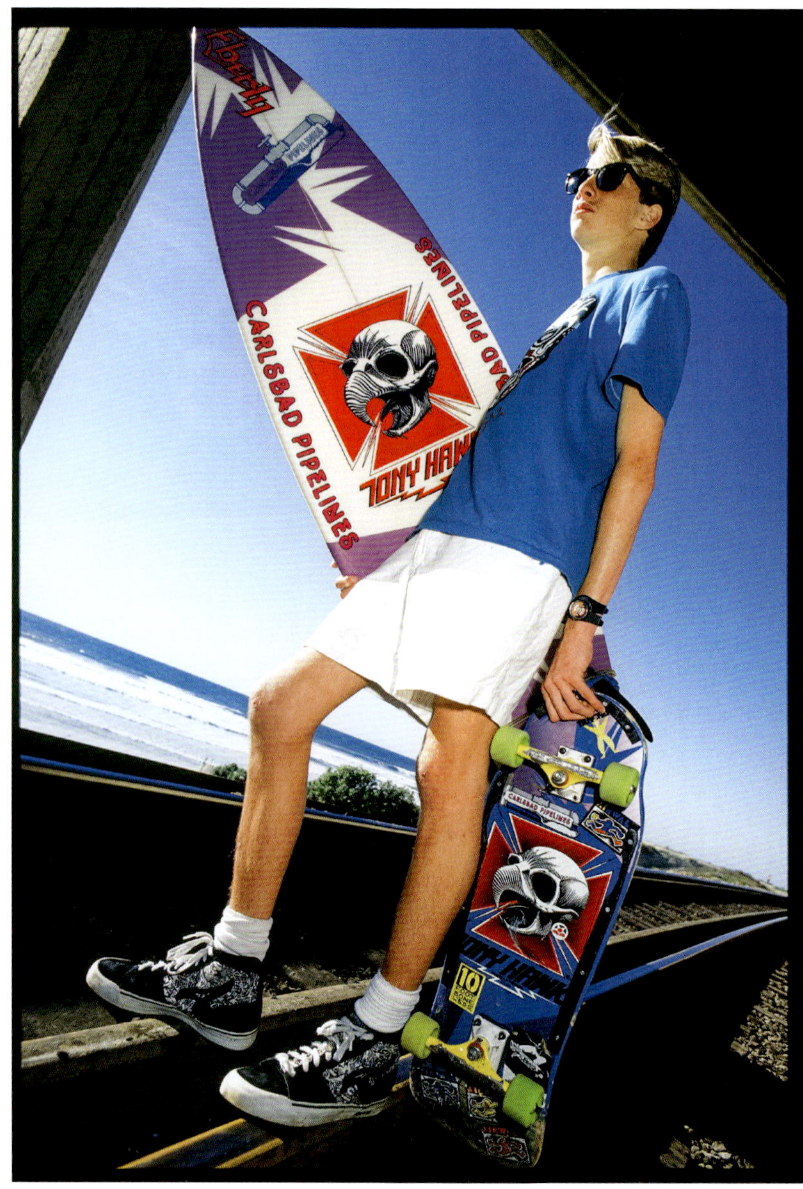

Tony Hawk, Portrait, Torrey Pines Beach, CA, 1987

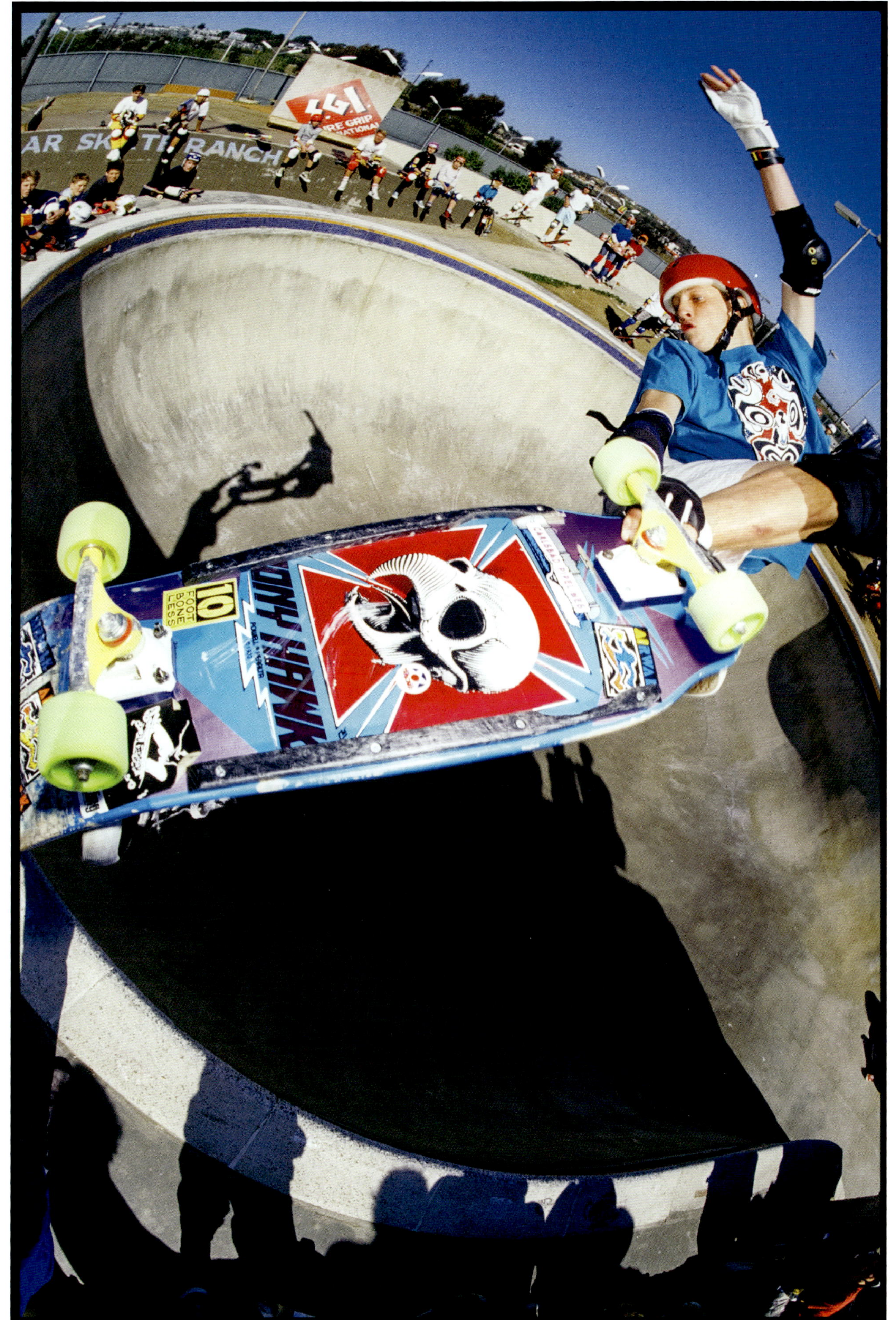

Tony Hawk, Crossbone lien air, Del Mar Skate Ranch, Del Mar, CA, 1987

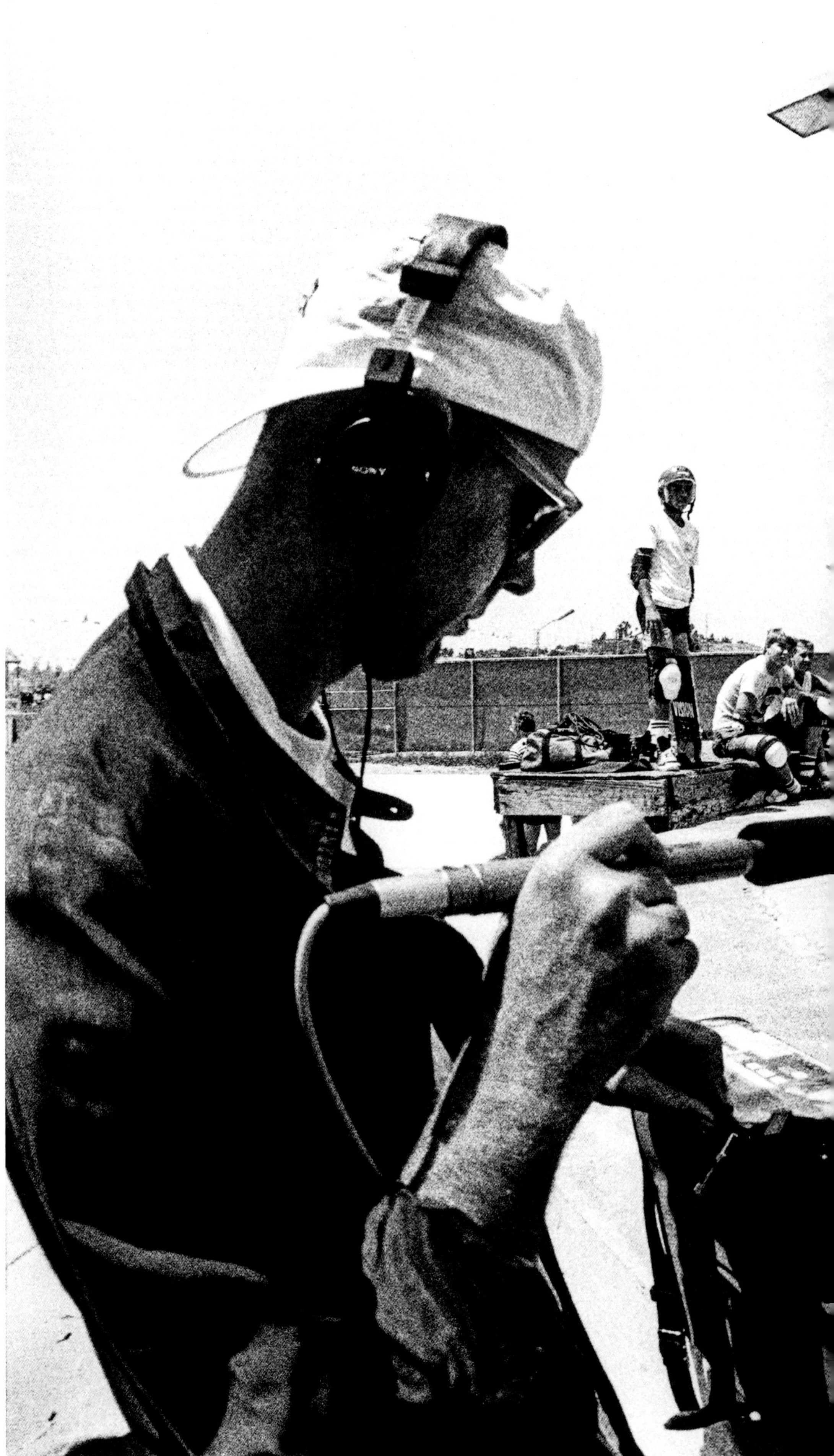

Tony Hawk, Craig Stecyk, and Stacy Peralta, Del Mar Skate Ranch, Del Mar, CA, 1985

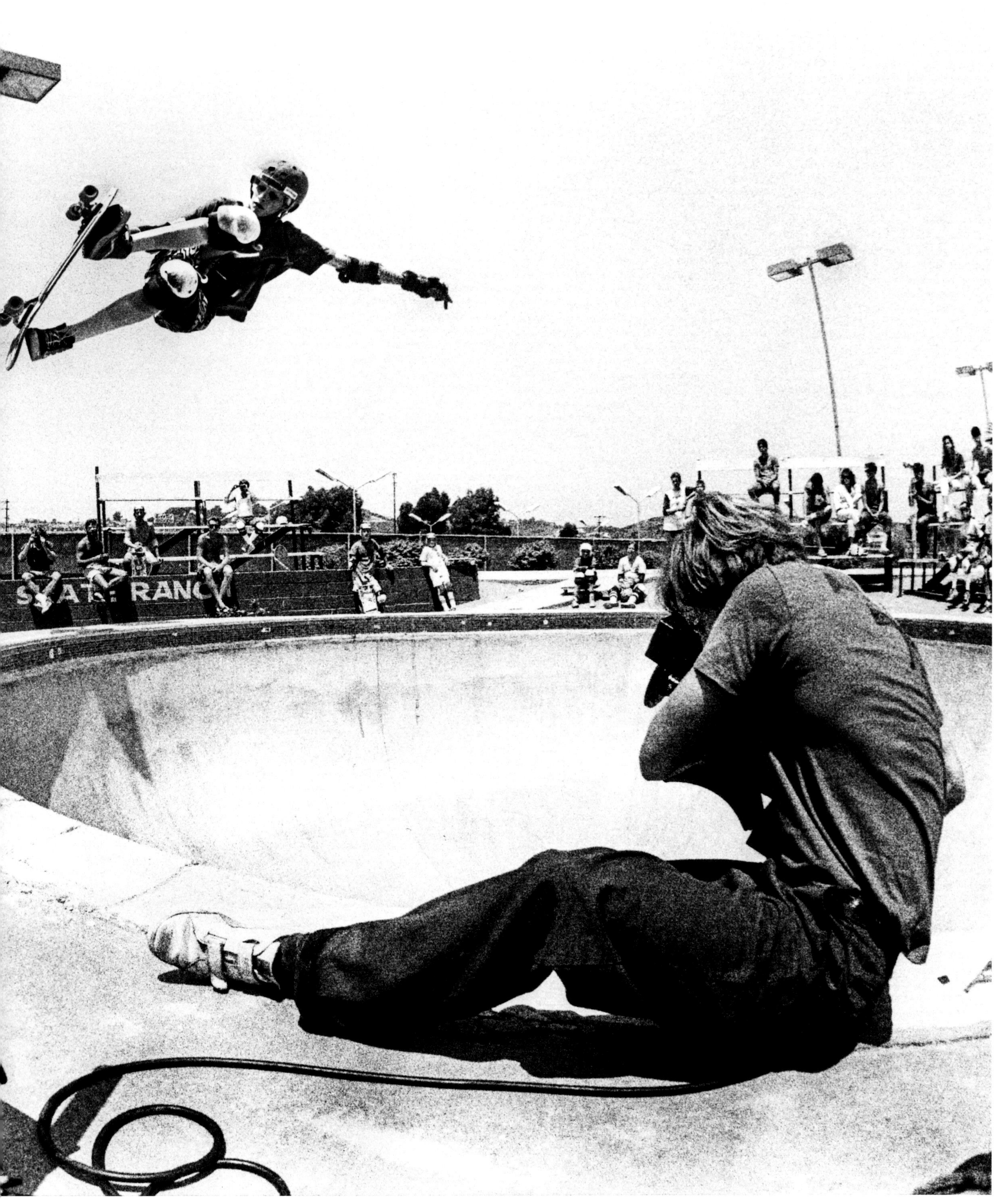

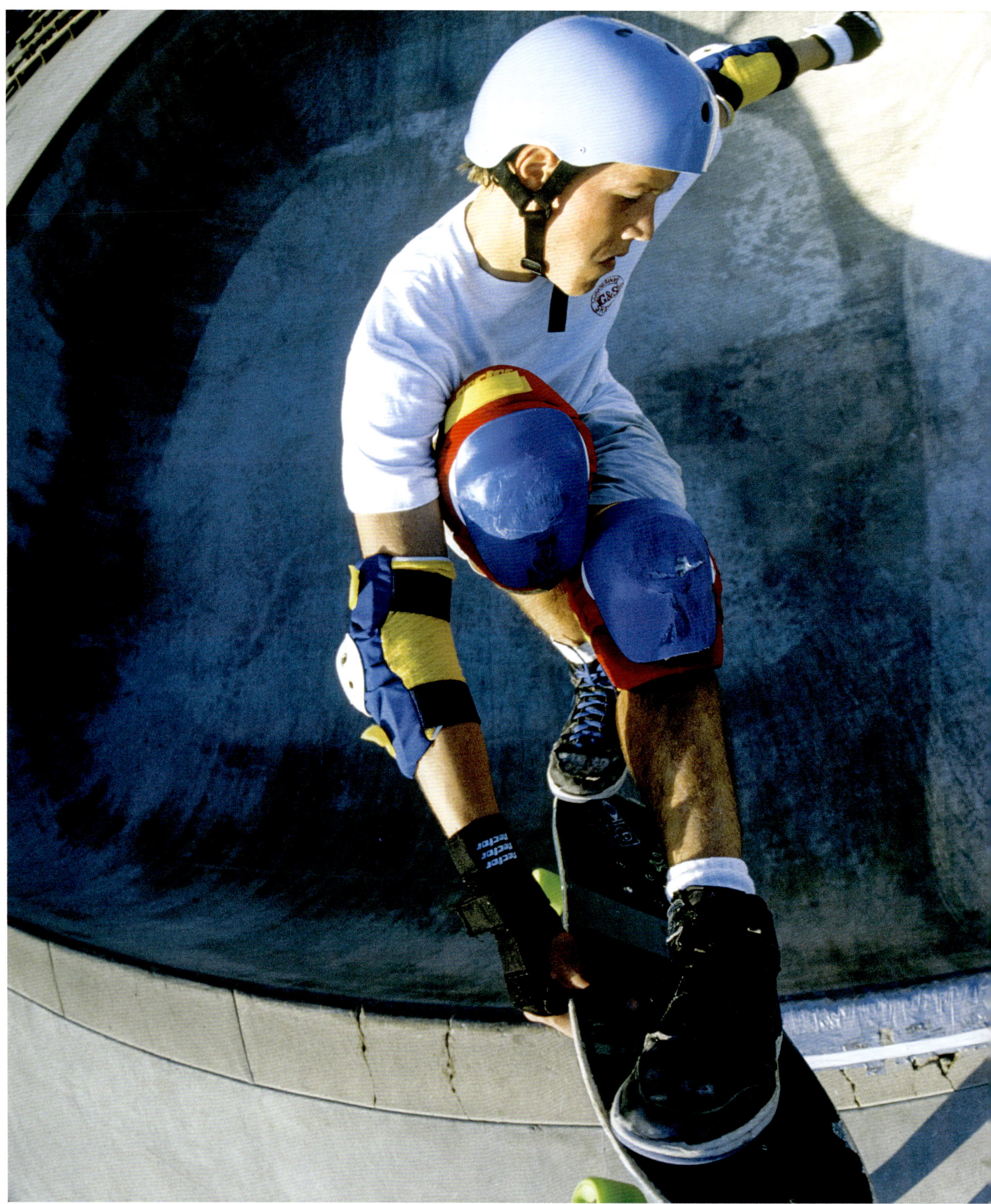
G&S

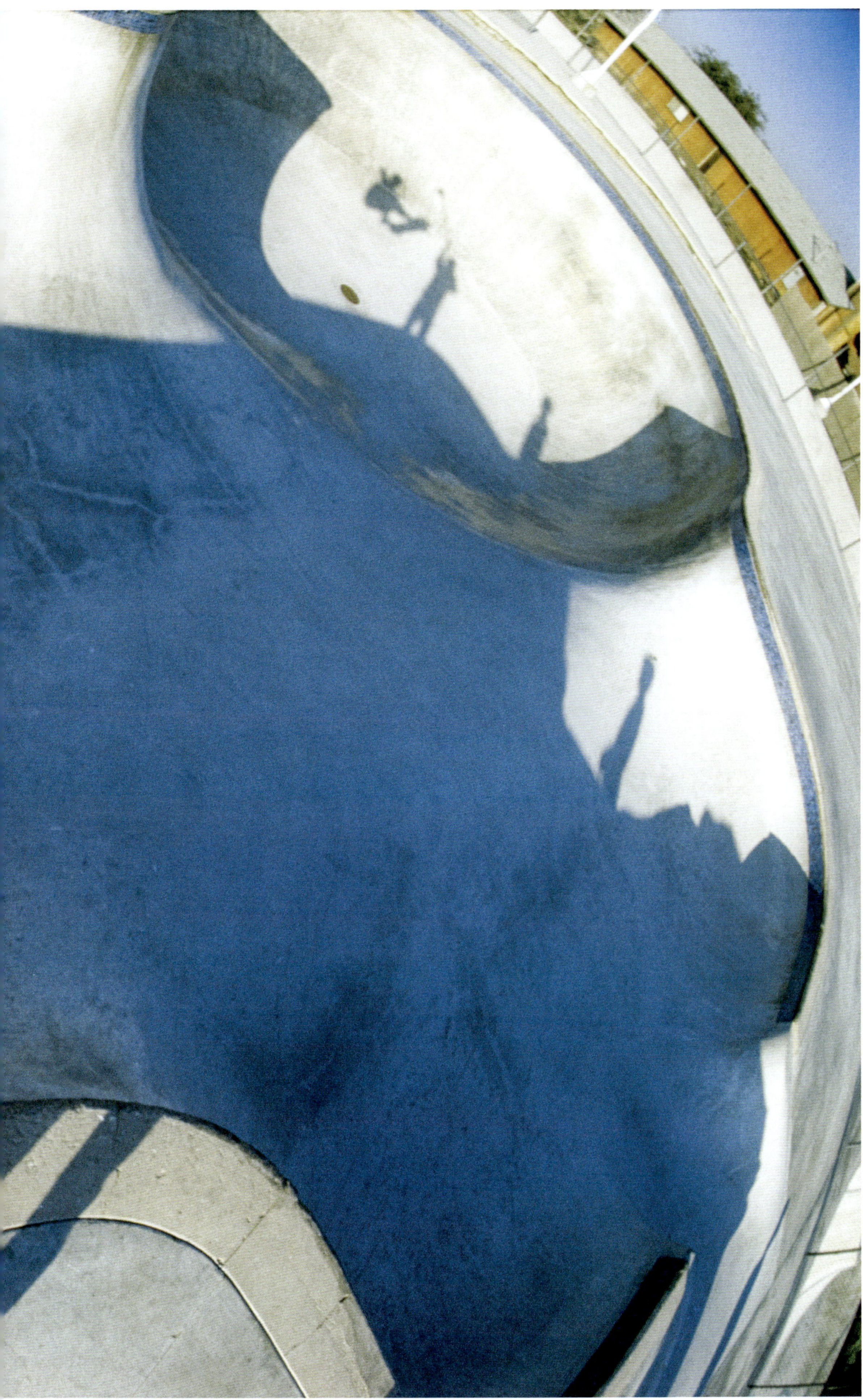

Chris Miller, Pole cam, Pipeline Skatepark, Upland, CA, 1986

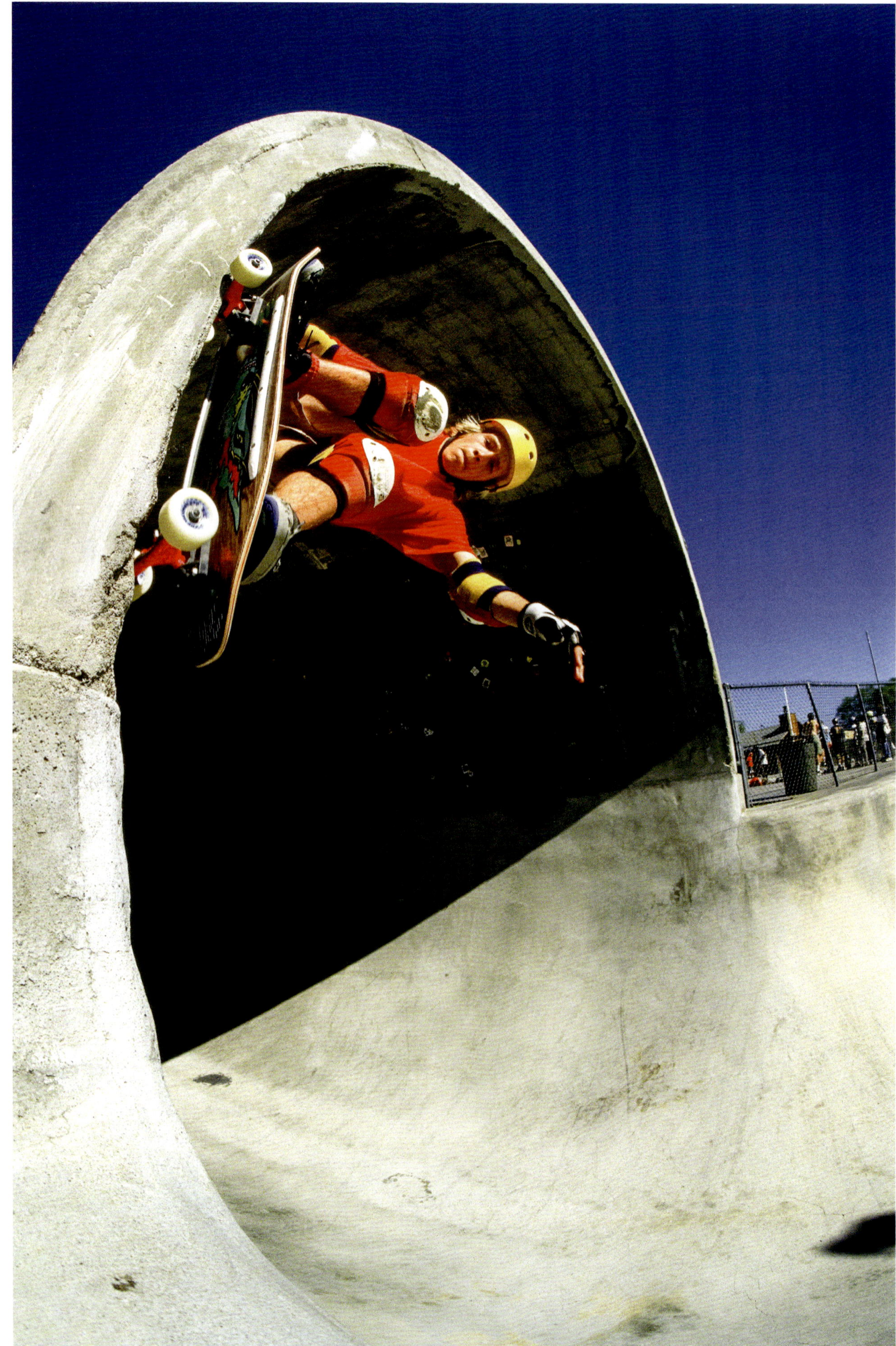

Chris Miller, fakie up and grind down, Pipeline Skatepark, Upland, CA, 1987

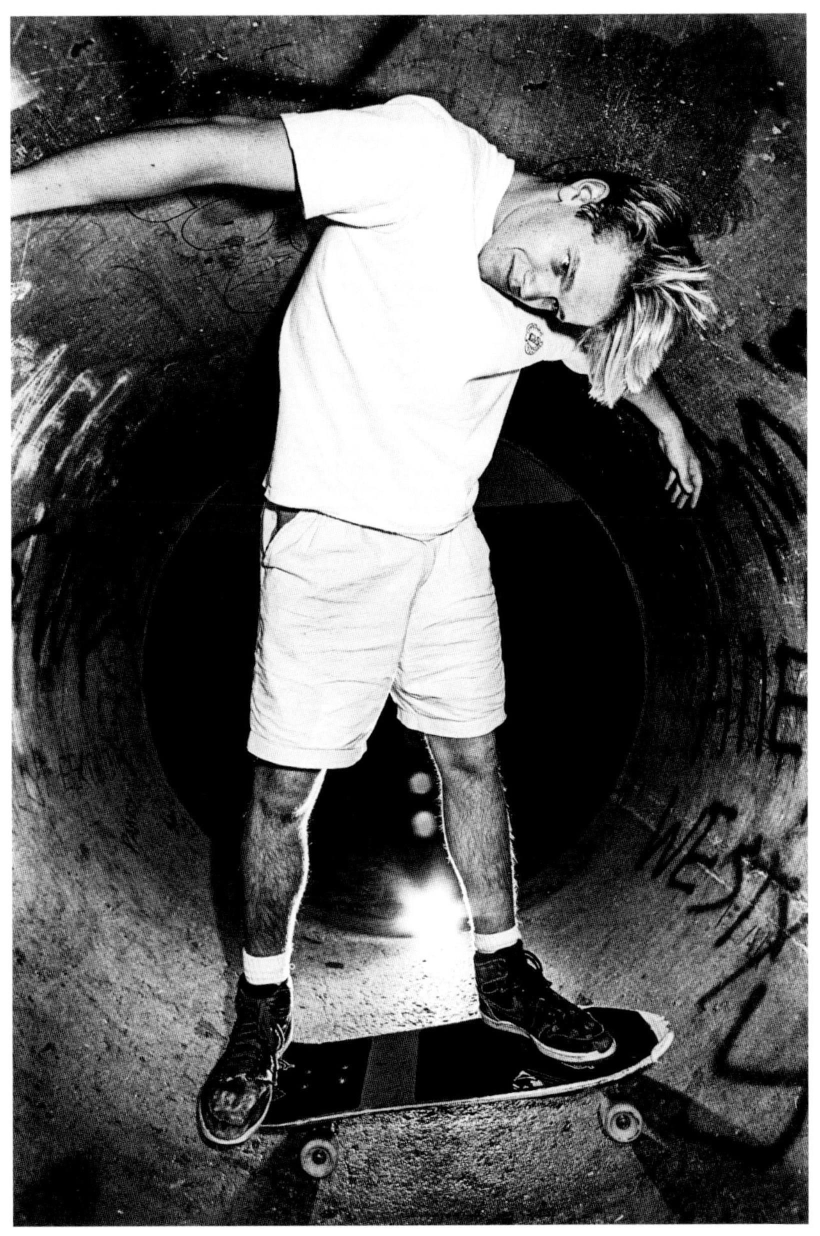

Chris Miller, Pipeline Skatepark, Upland, CA, 1986

Jeff Grosso, Crossbone lien air, Stone Mountain, Atlanta, GA, 1987

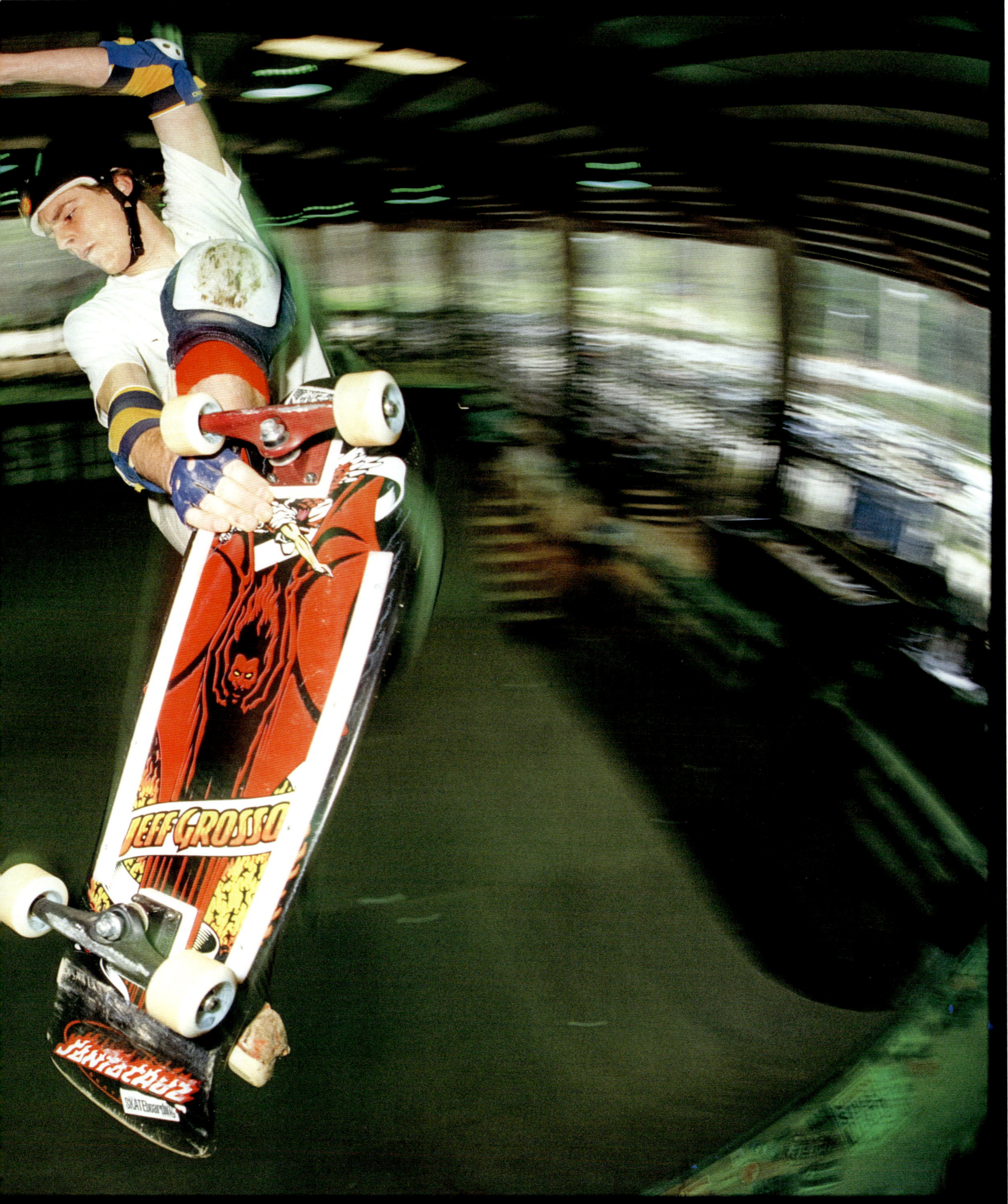
JEFF GROSSO
SANTA CRUZ

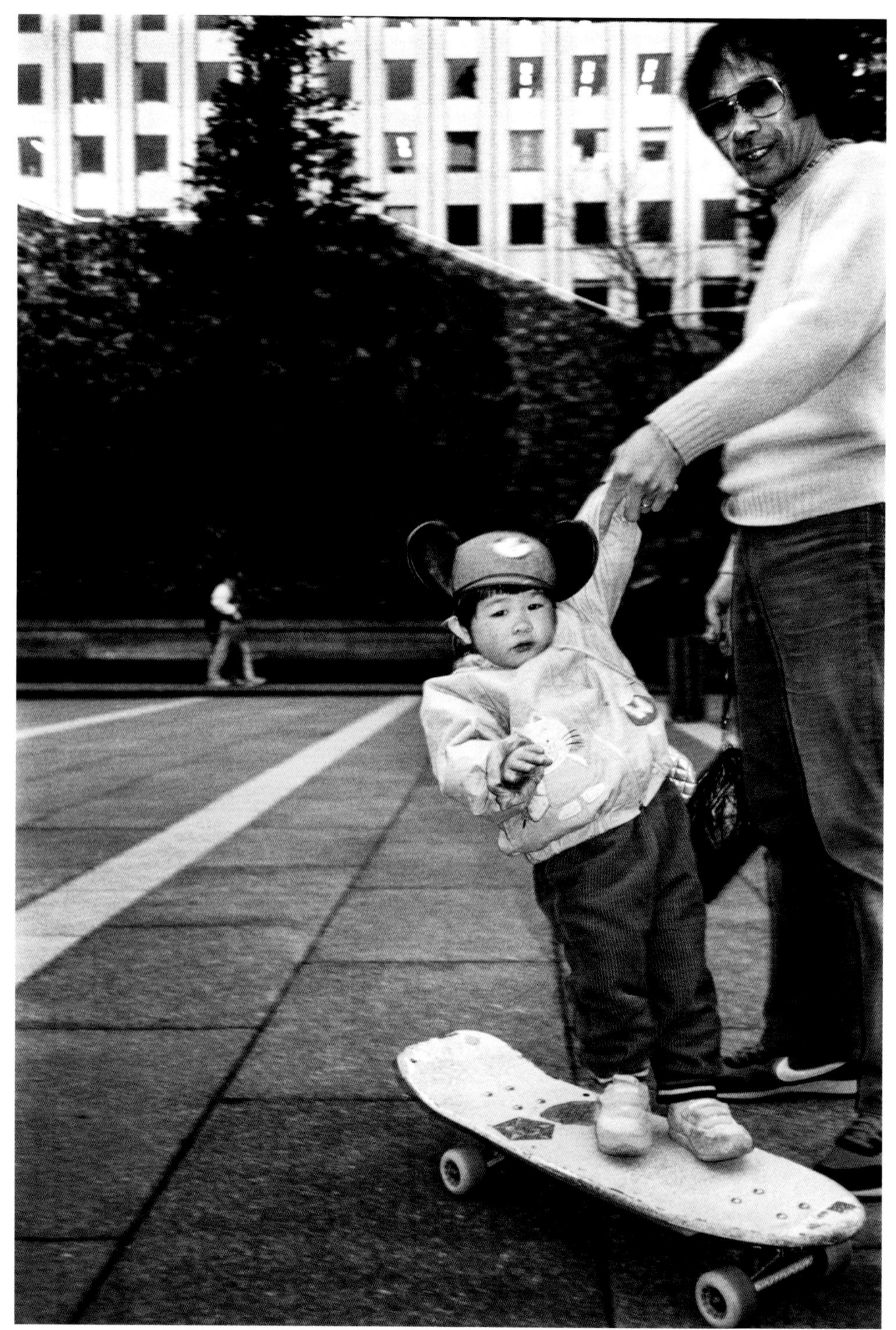

Minnie Mouse, Tokyo, Japan, 1988

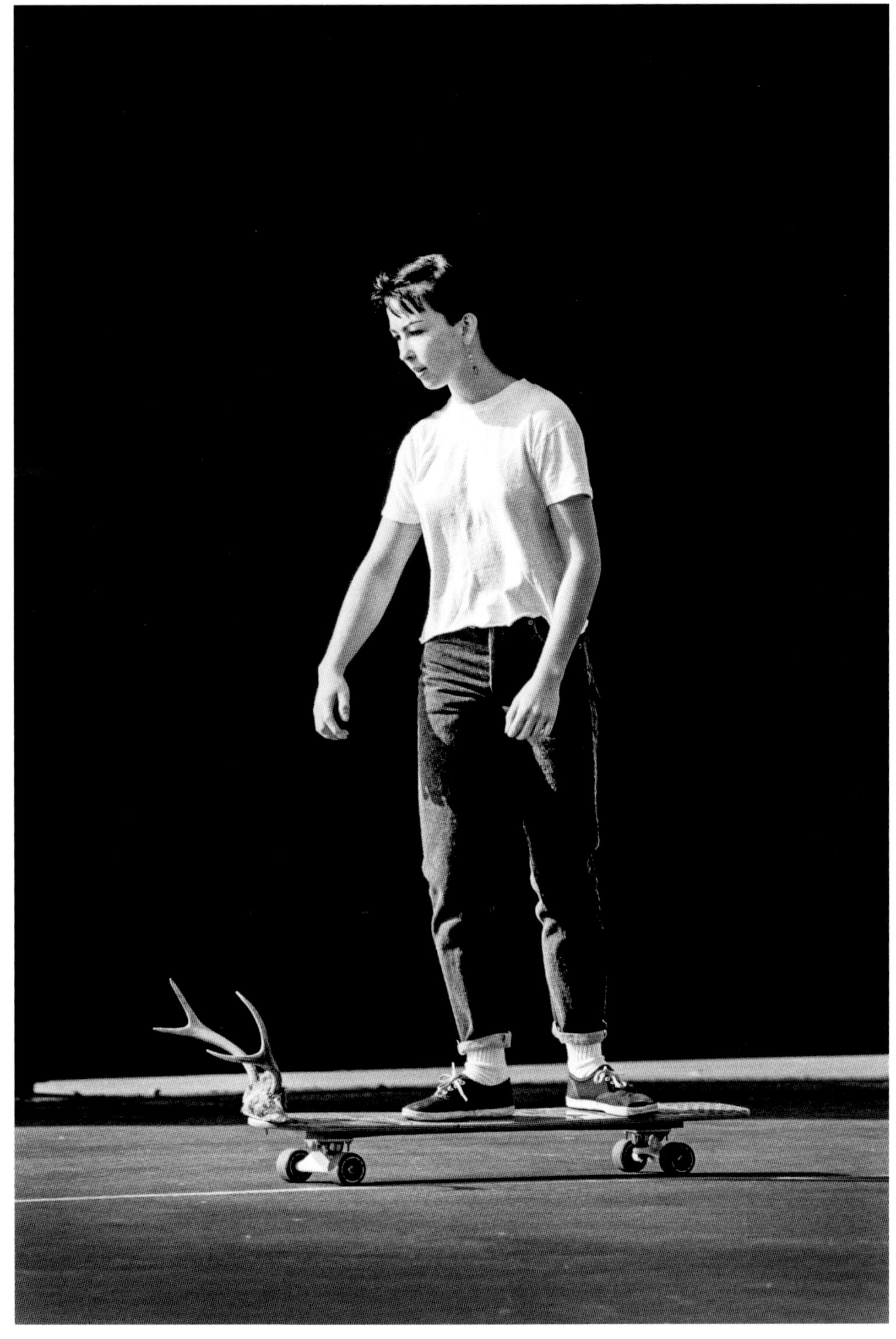

Danielle Soto, Deer horns, Oceanside, CA, 1988

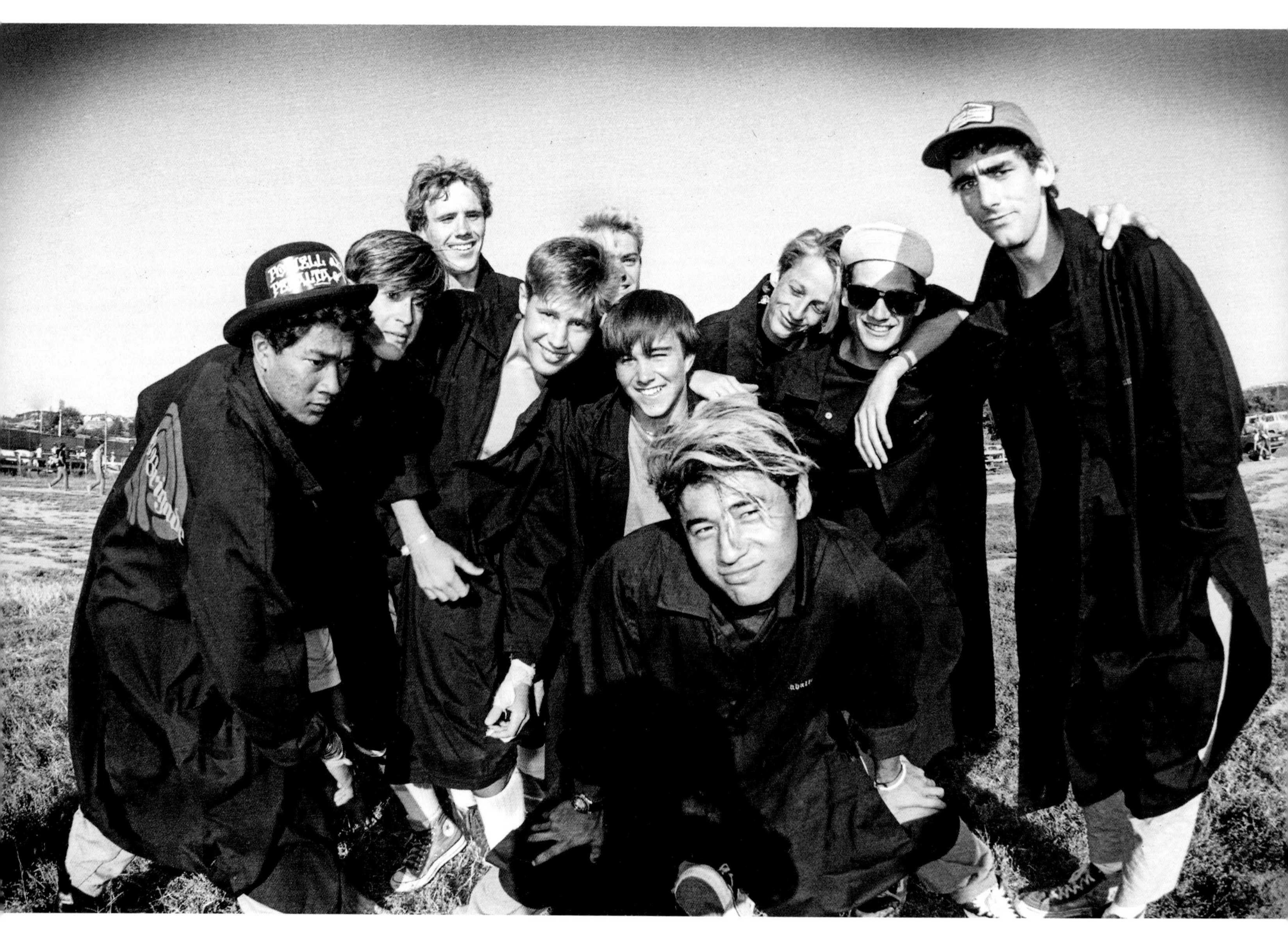

The Bones Brigade, Portrait JGB poached from Stecyk, Del Mar Skate Ranch, Del Mar, CA, 1986

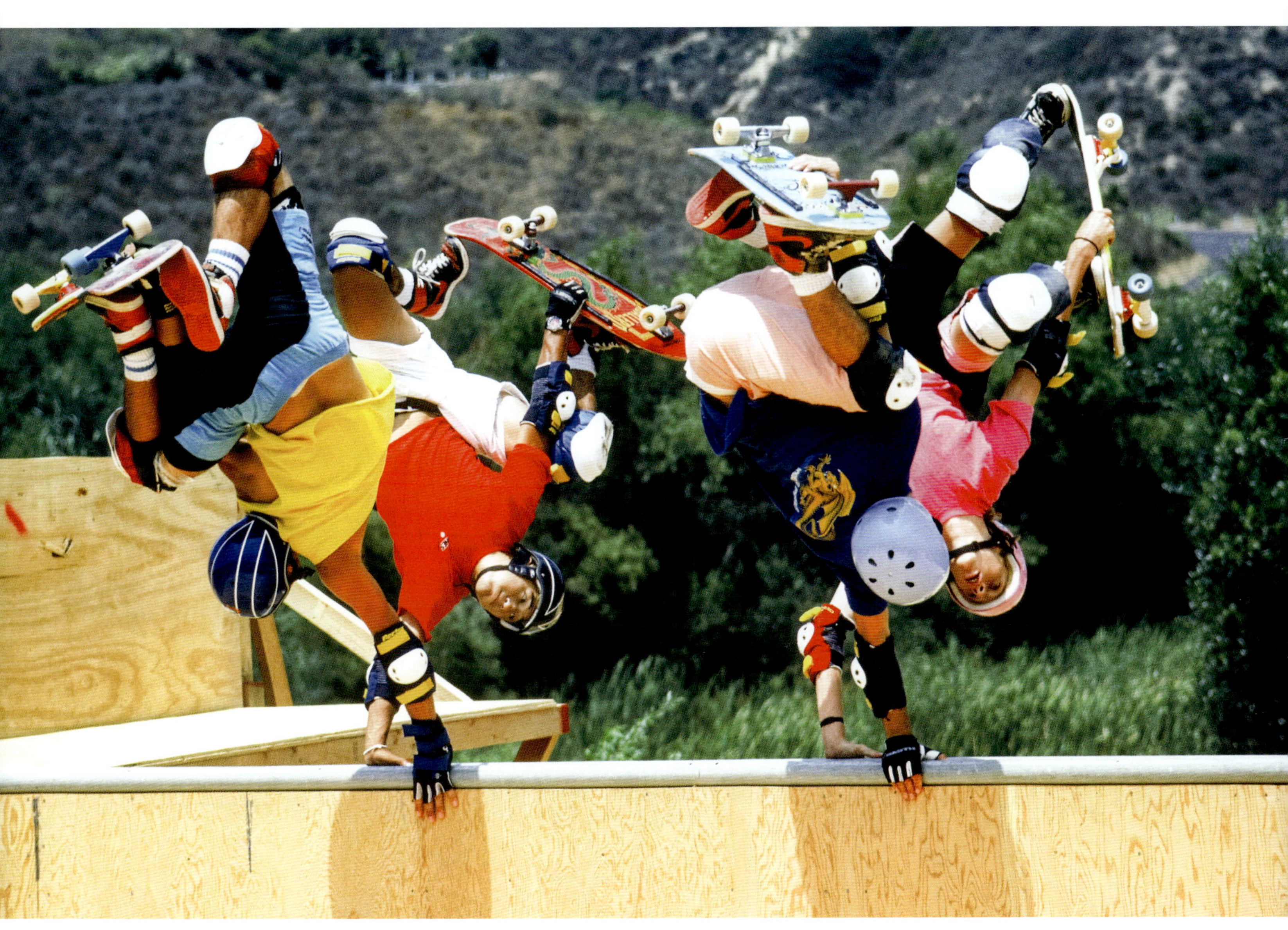

Mike McGill, Steve Caballero, Lance Mountain, and Tony Hawk, Chin Ramp, Oceanside, CA, 1986

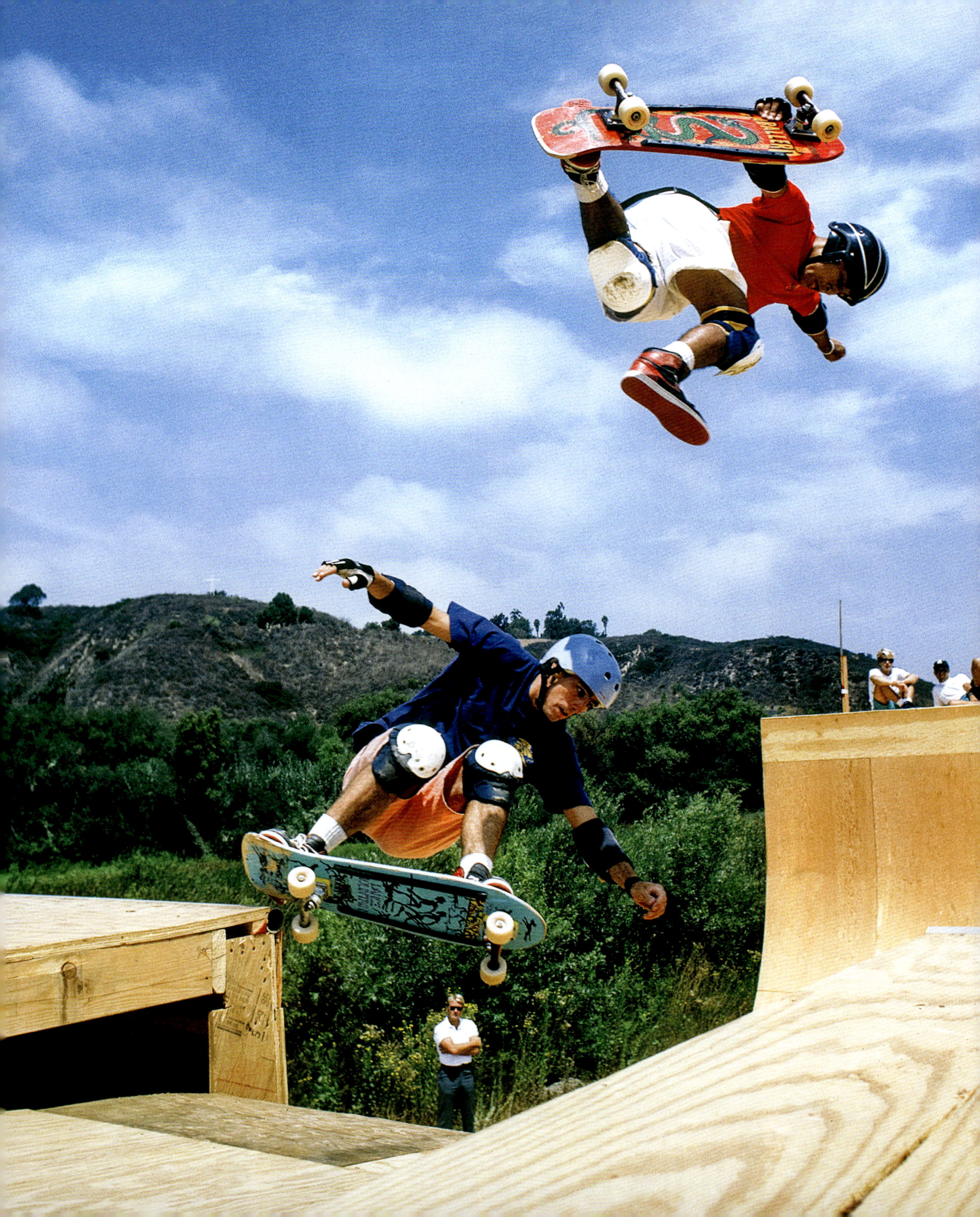

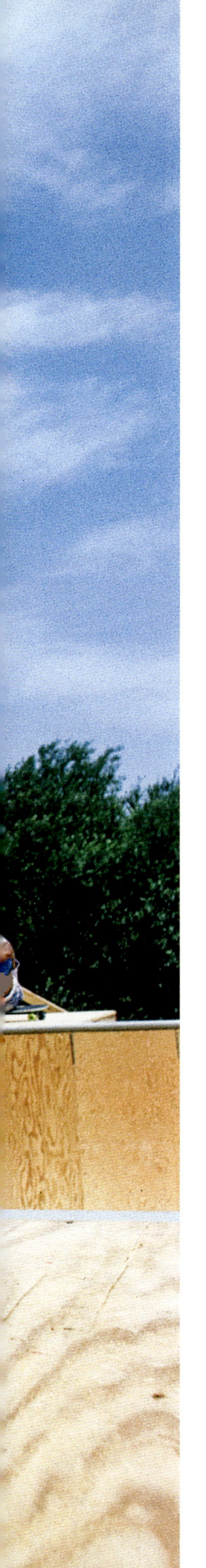

Steve Caballero and Lance Mountain, Doubles, Chin Ramp, Oceanside, CA, 1986

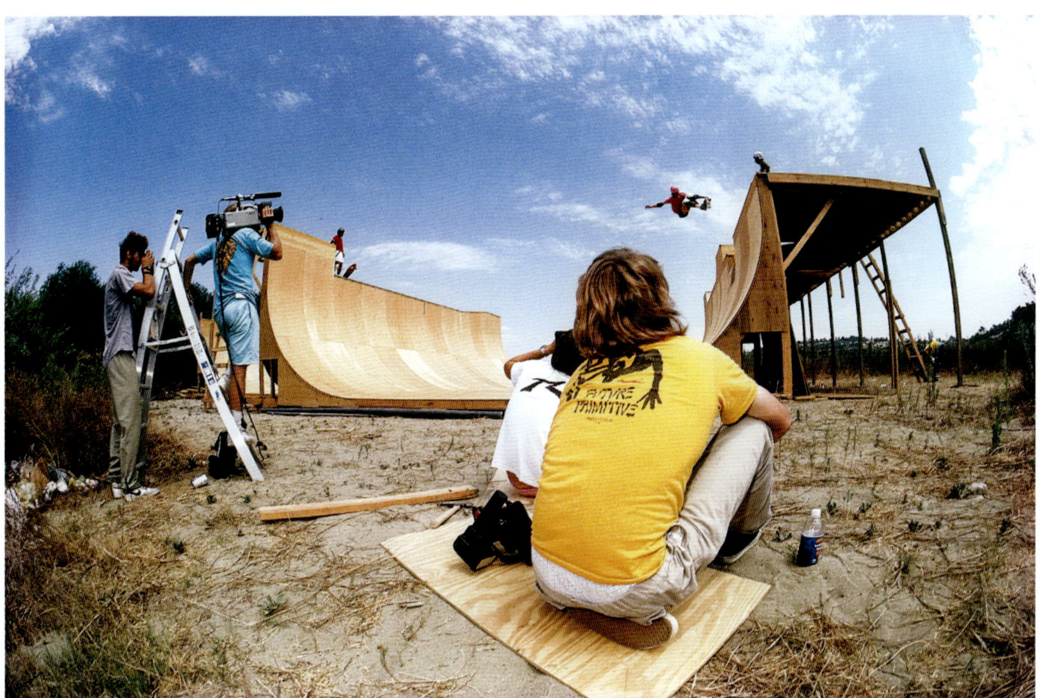

Tony Hawk, Frontside air over channel, Chin Ramp, Oceanside, CA, 1986

Helicopter View of the Chin Ramp, Oceanside, CA, 1986

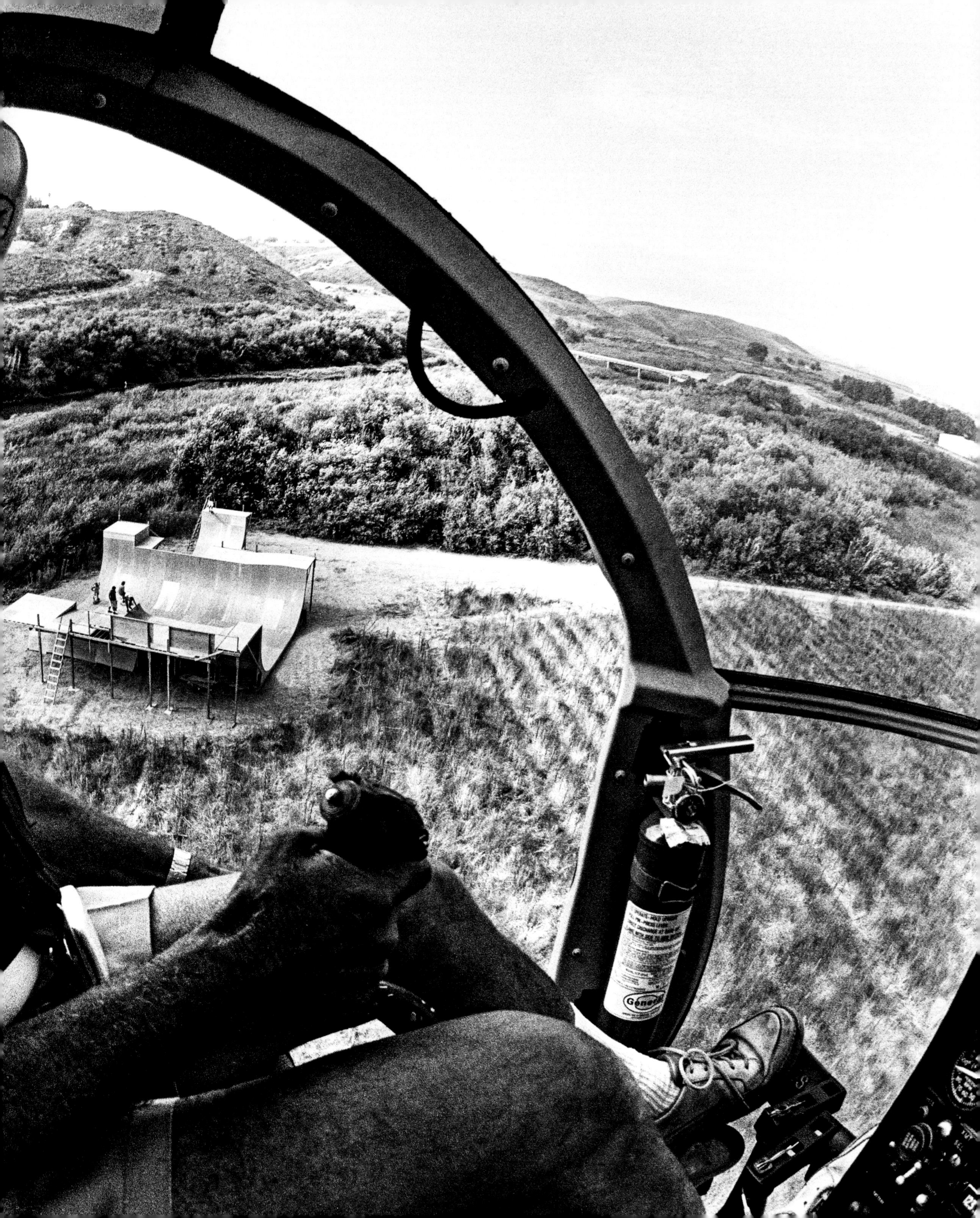

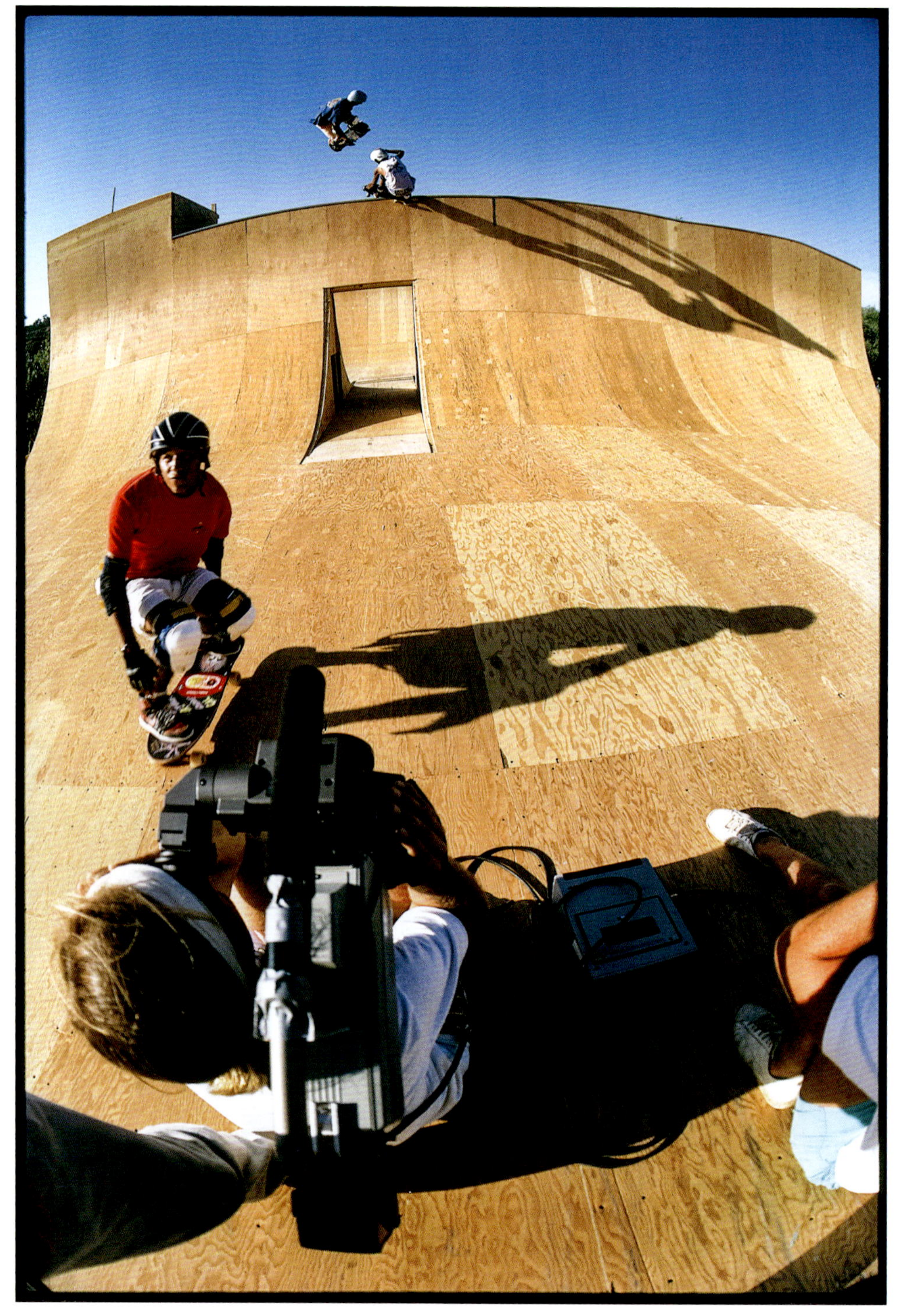

Lance Mountain, Tommy Guerrero, Steve Caballero, and Stacy Peralta, Chin Ramp, Oceanside, CA, 1986

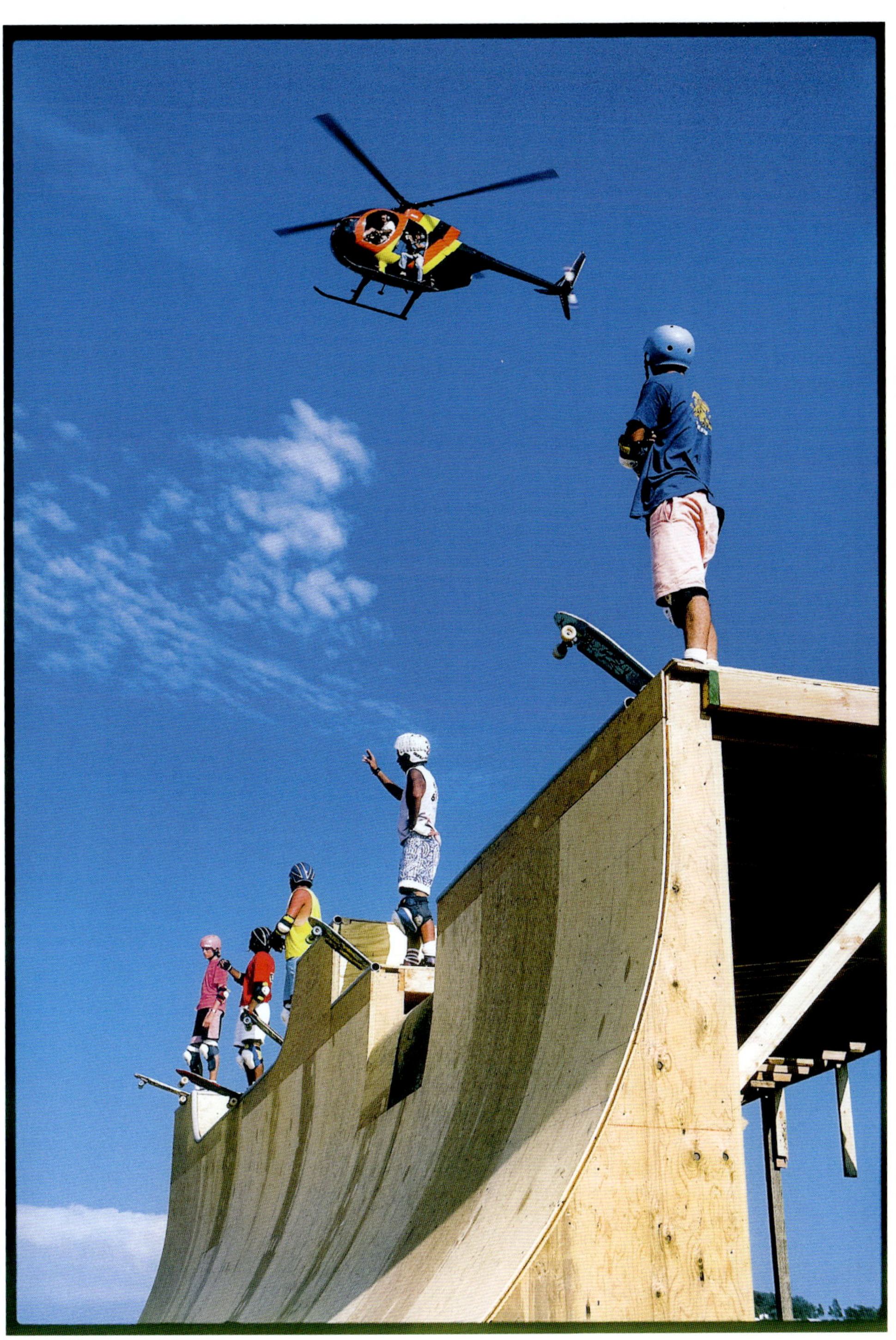

The Bones Brigade lineup, Chin Ramp, Oceanside, CA, 1986

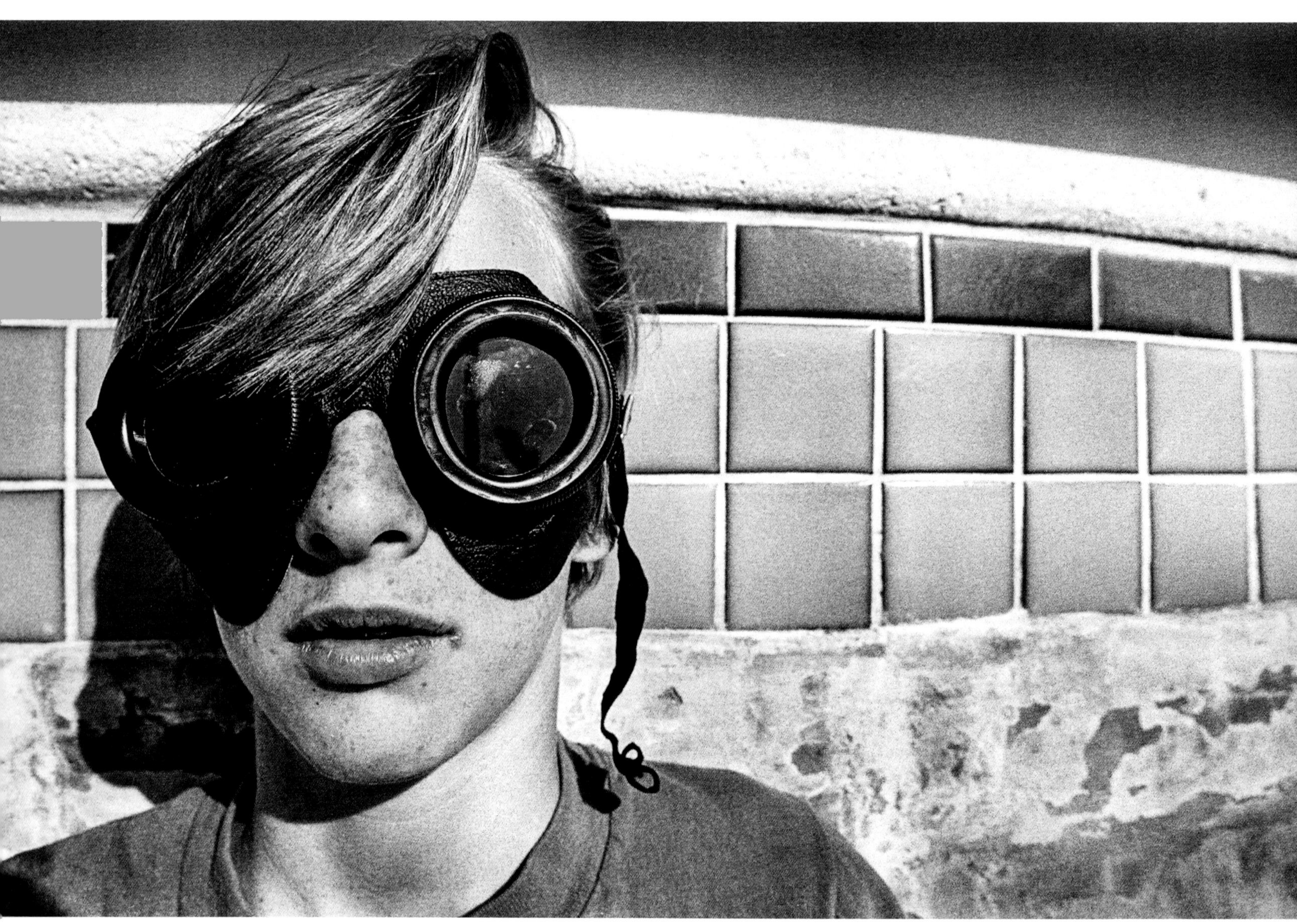

Tony Hawk, Goggles portrait, Del Mar Skate Ranch, Del Mar, CA, 1984

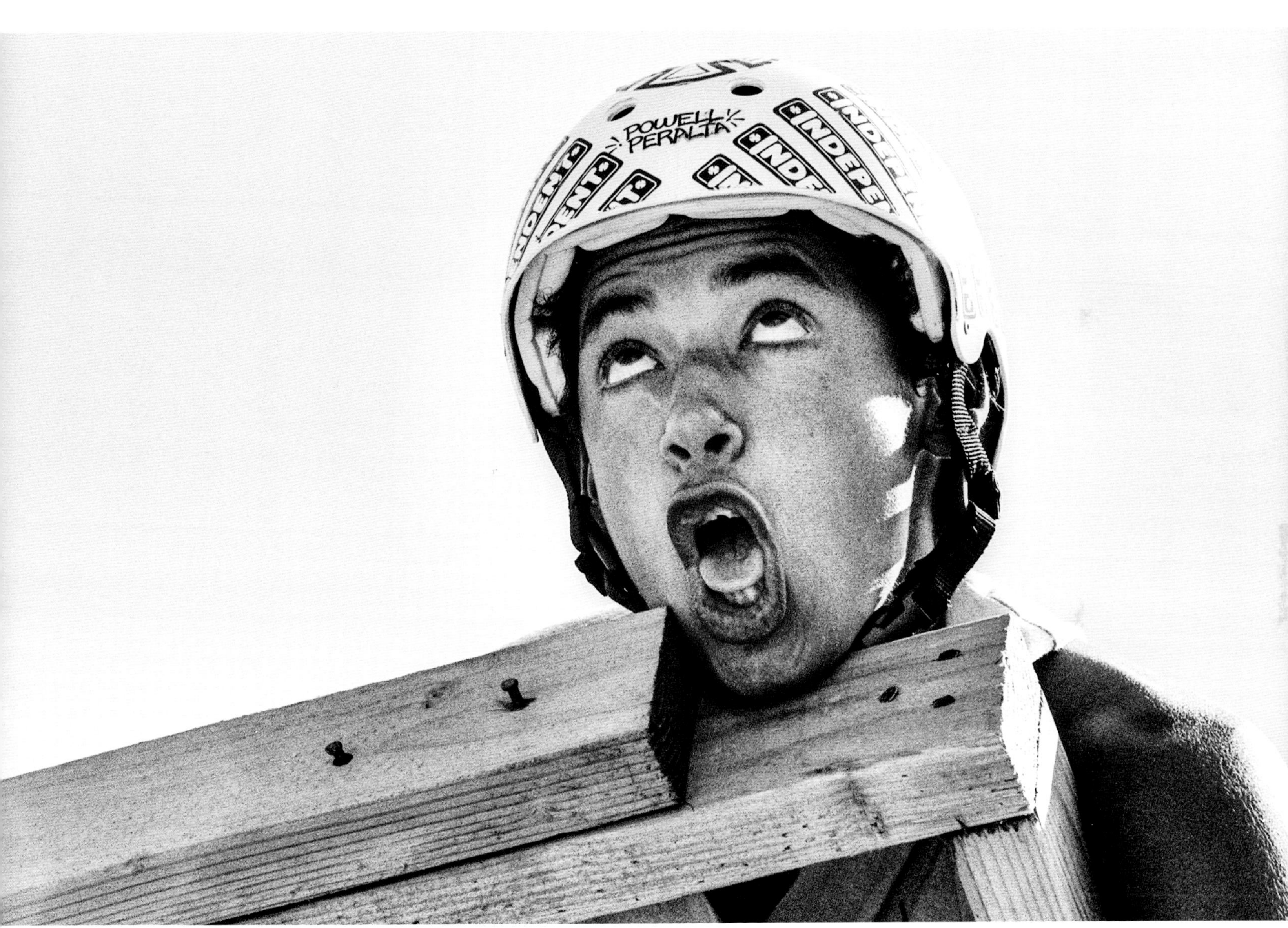

Tommy Guerrero, Portrait, Chin Ramp, Oceanside, CA, 1986

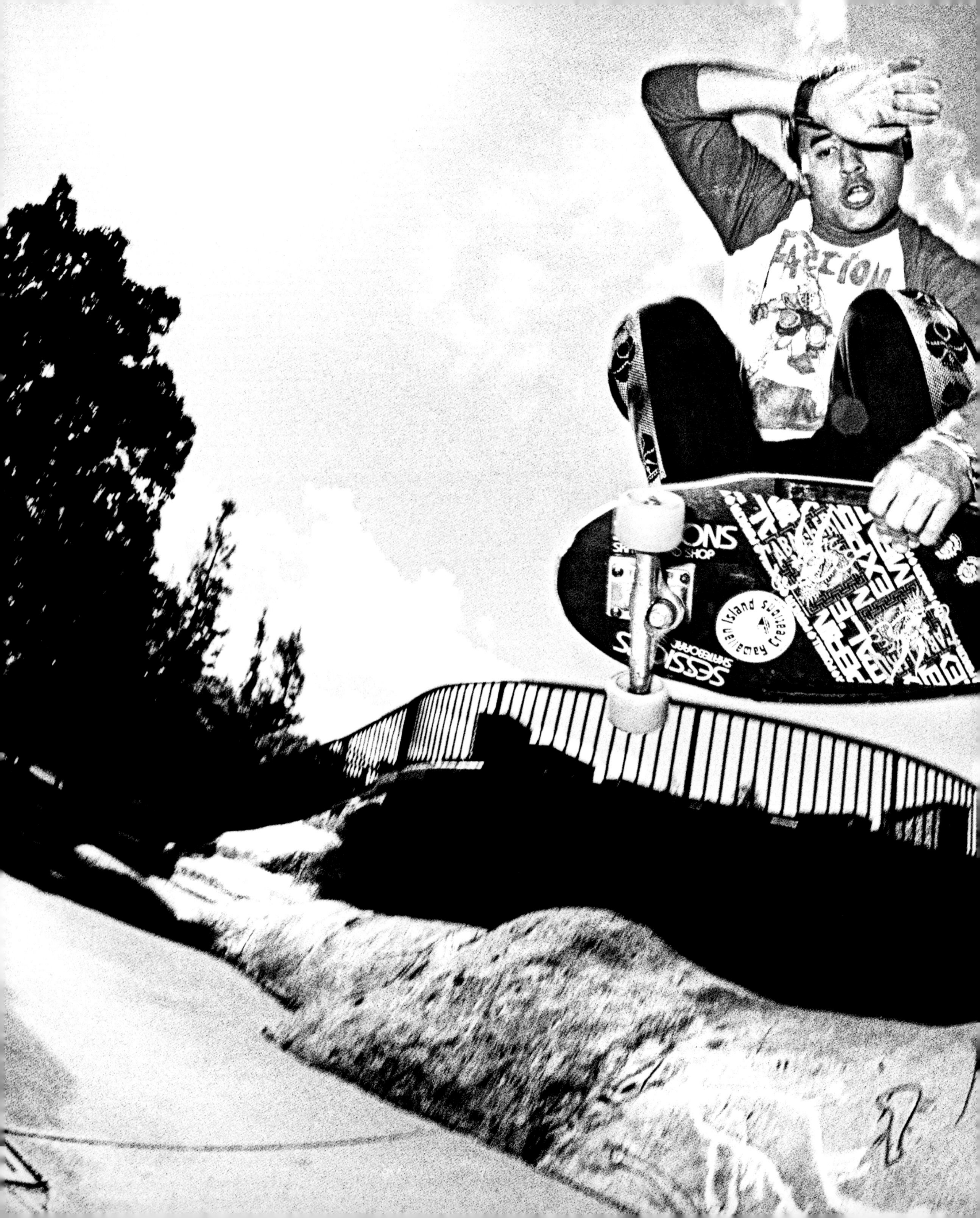

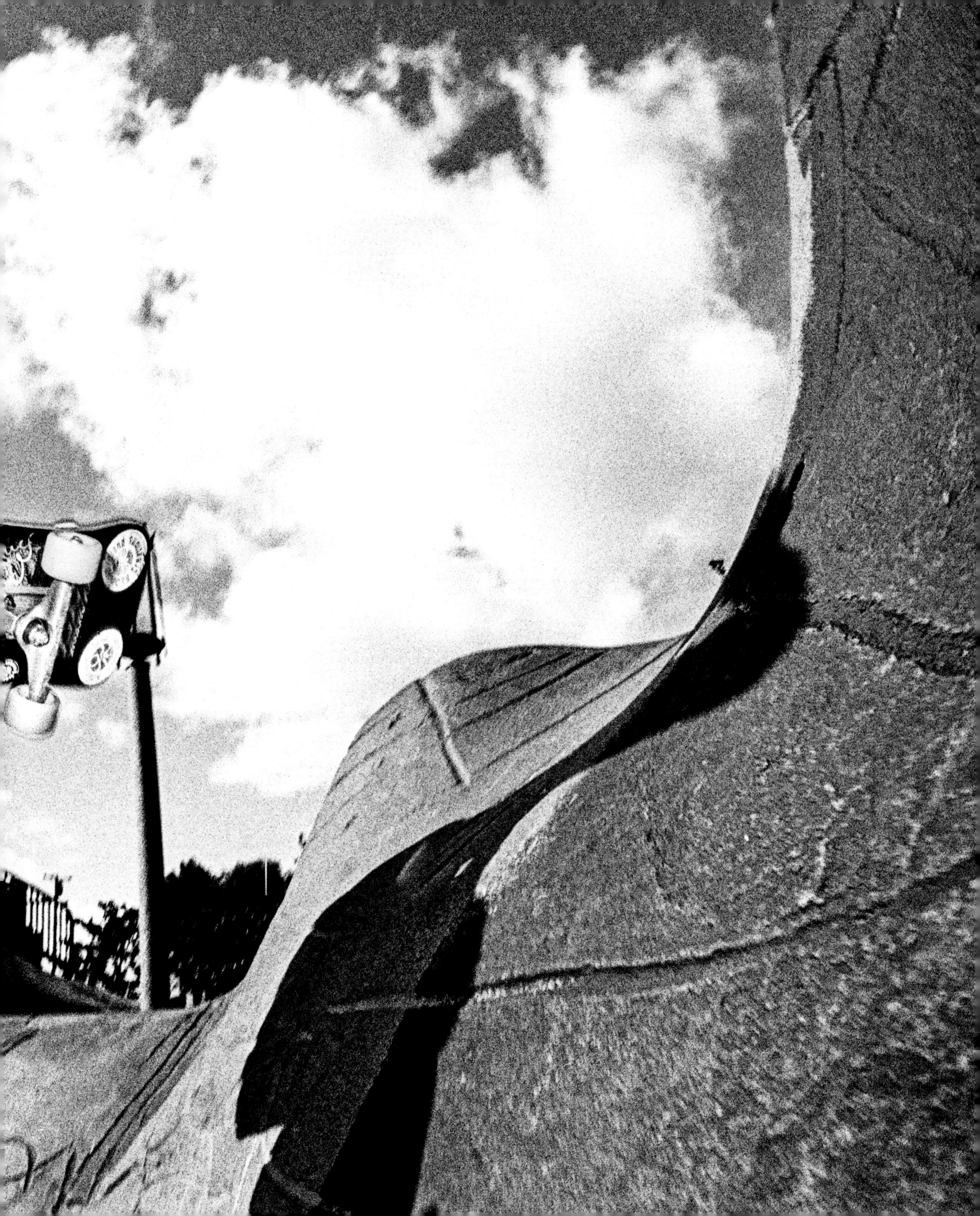

Previous spread: Steve Caballero, Frontside salute, Fish Banks, Sunnyvale, CA, 1987

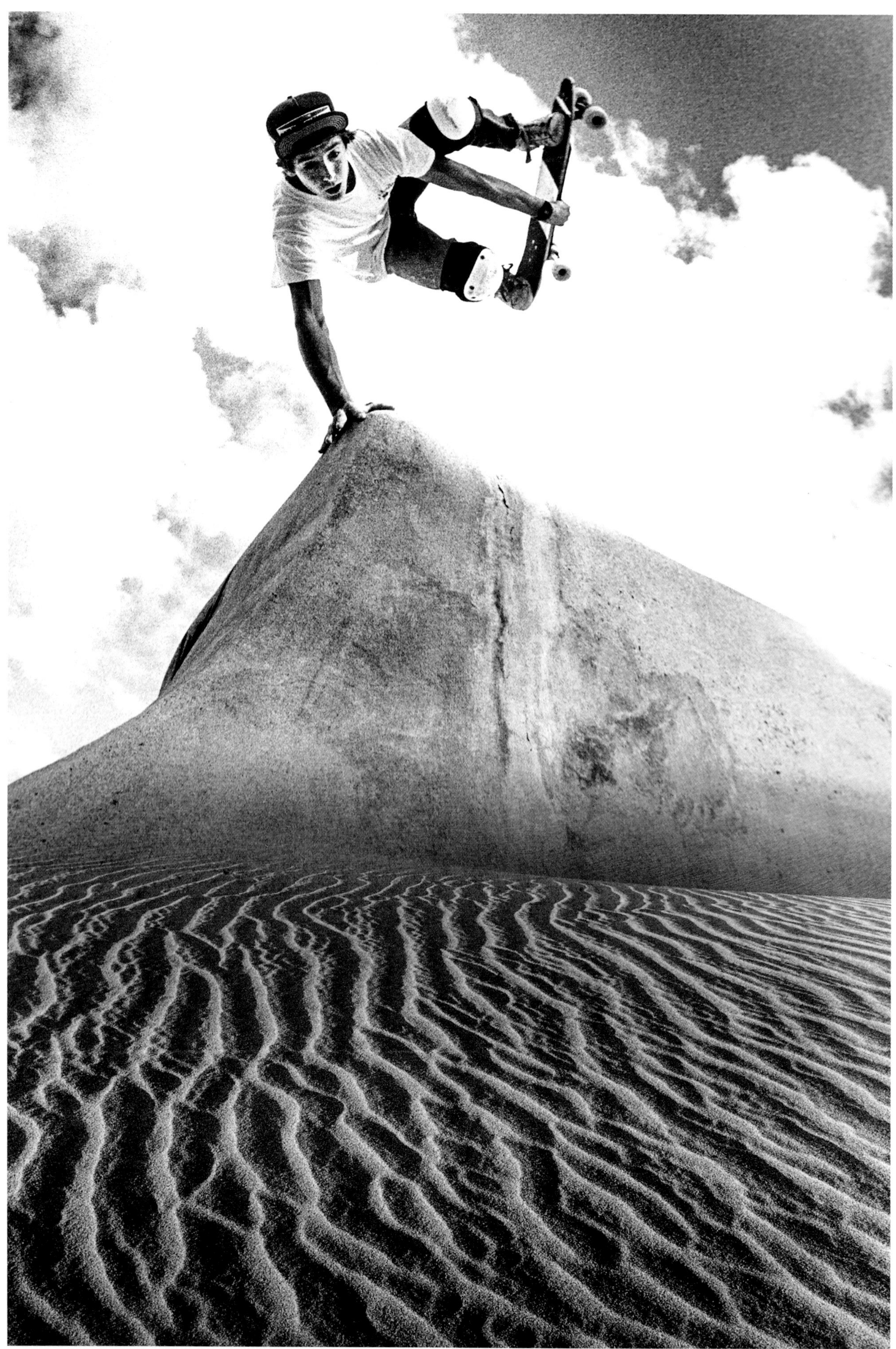

Billy Ruff, Darkroom image blend, Surf de Earth Park, Vista, CA, and Mesquite Dunes, Death Valley, CA, 1984

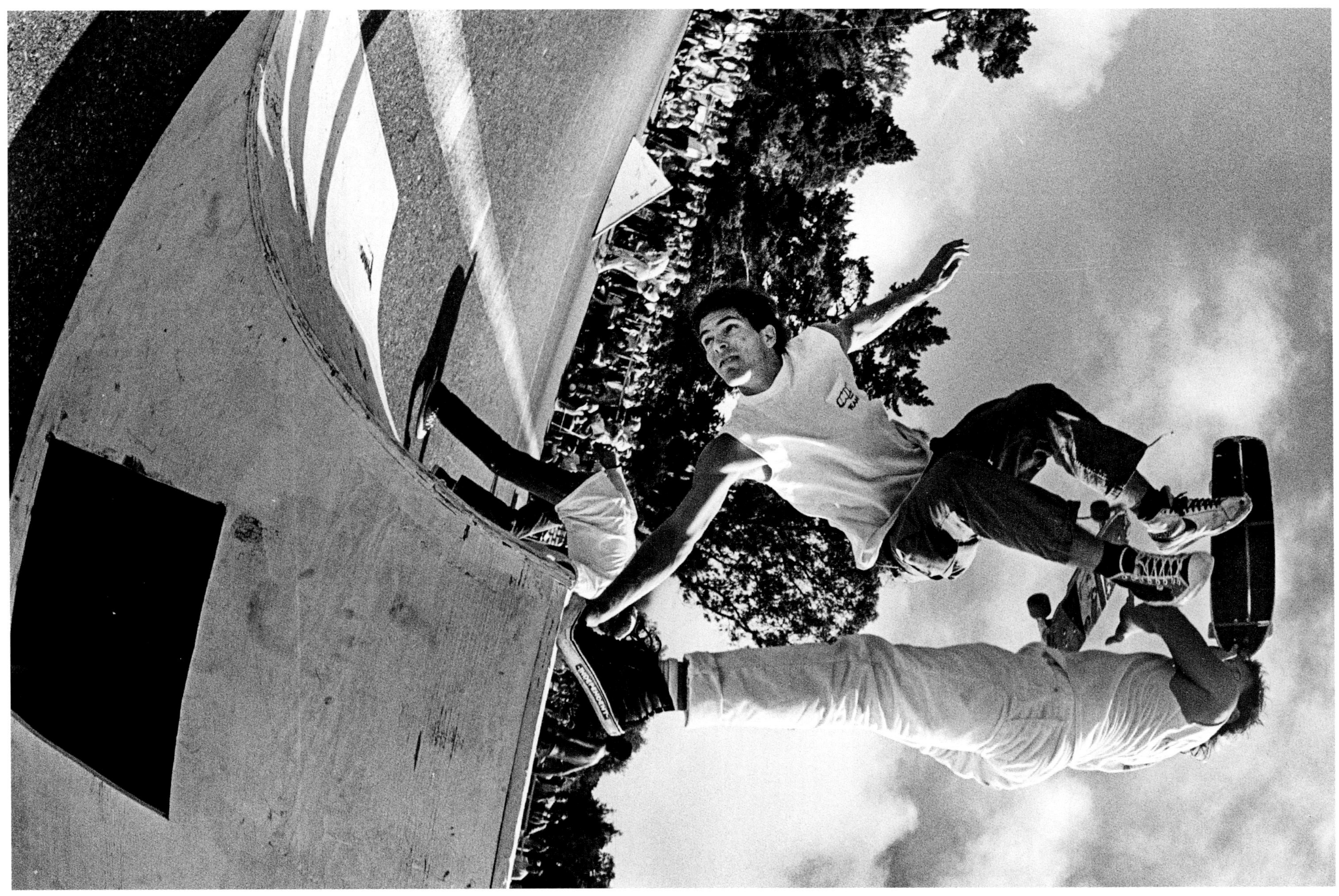

Neil Blender and Street Scott, Golden Gate Park, San Francisco, CA, 1984

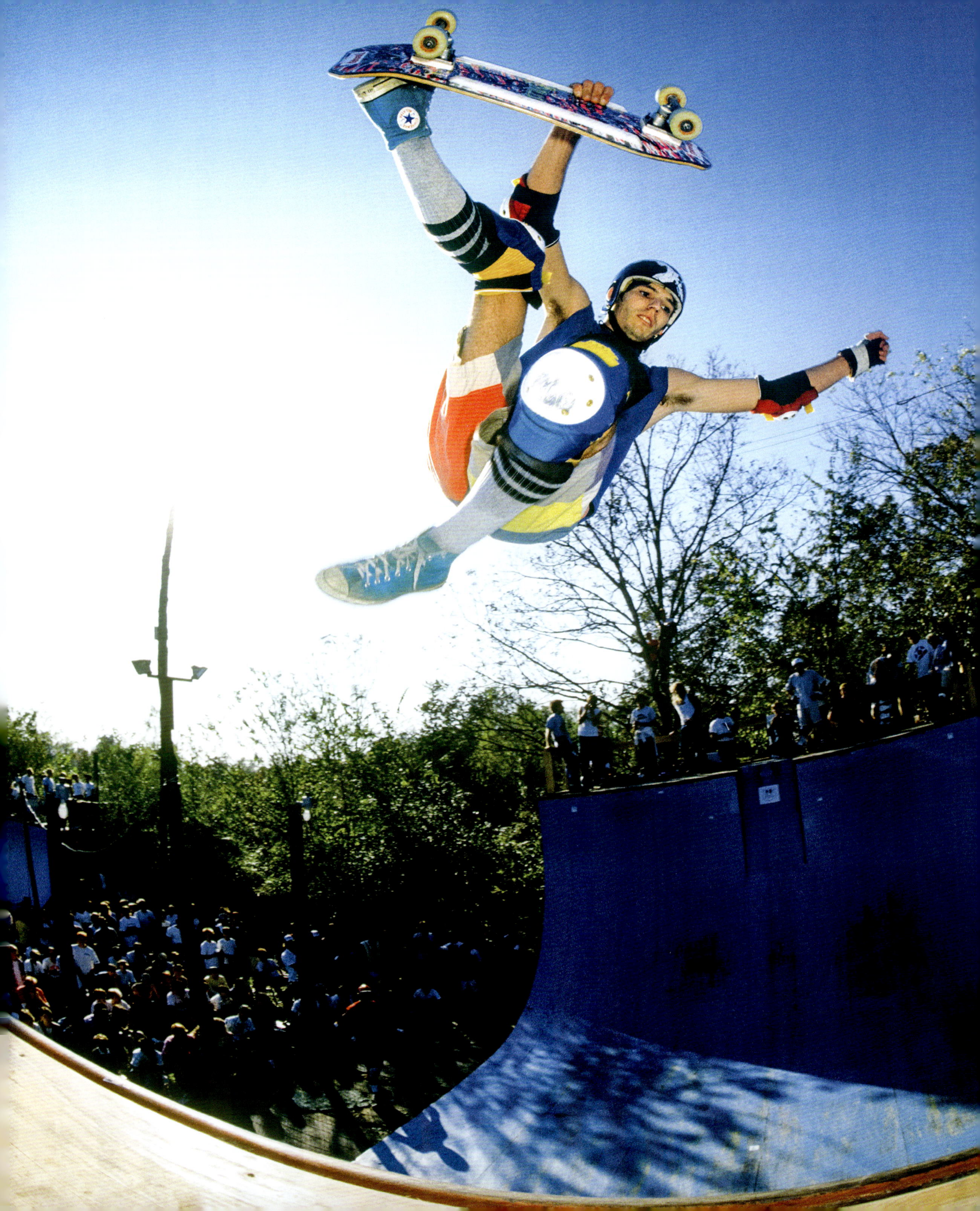

eff Phillips, Frontside boneless, Skatepark of Houston, TX, 1986

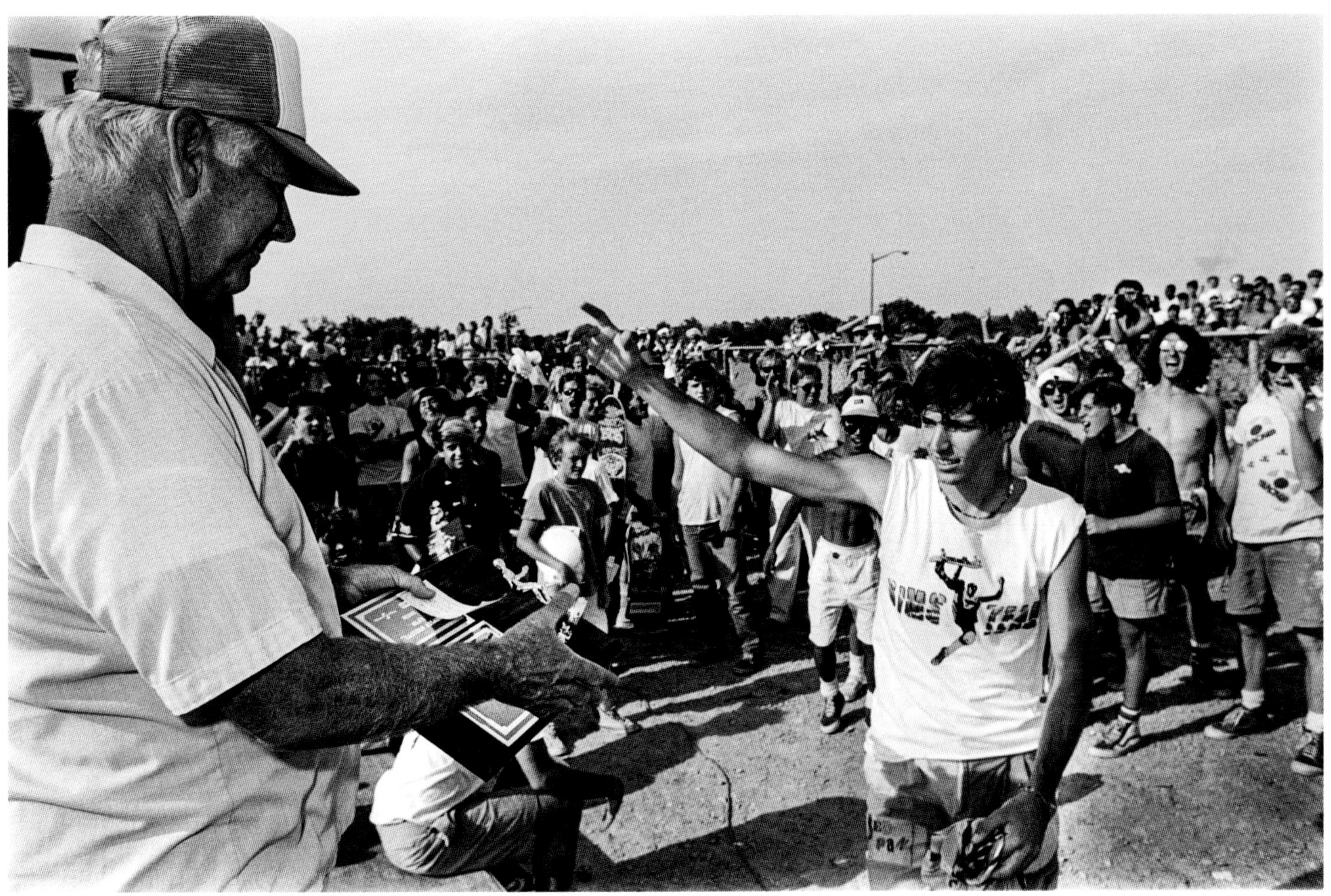

Jeff Phillips, The Winner, Mt. Trashmore, Virginia Beach, VA, 1986

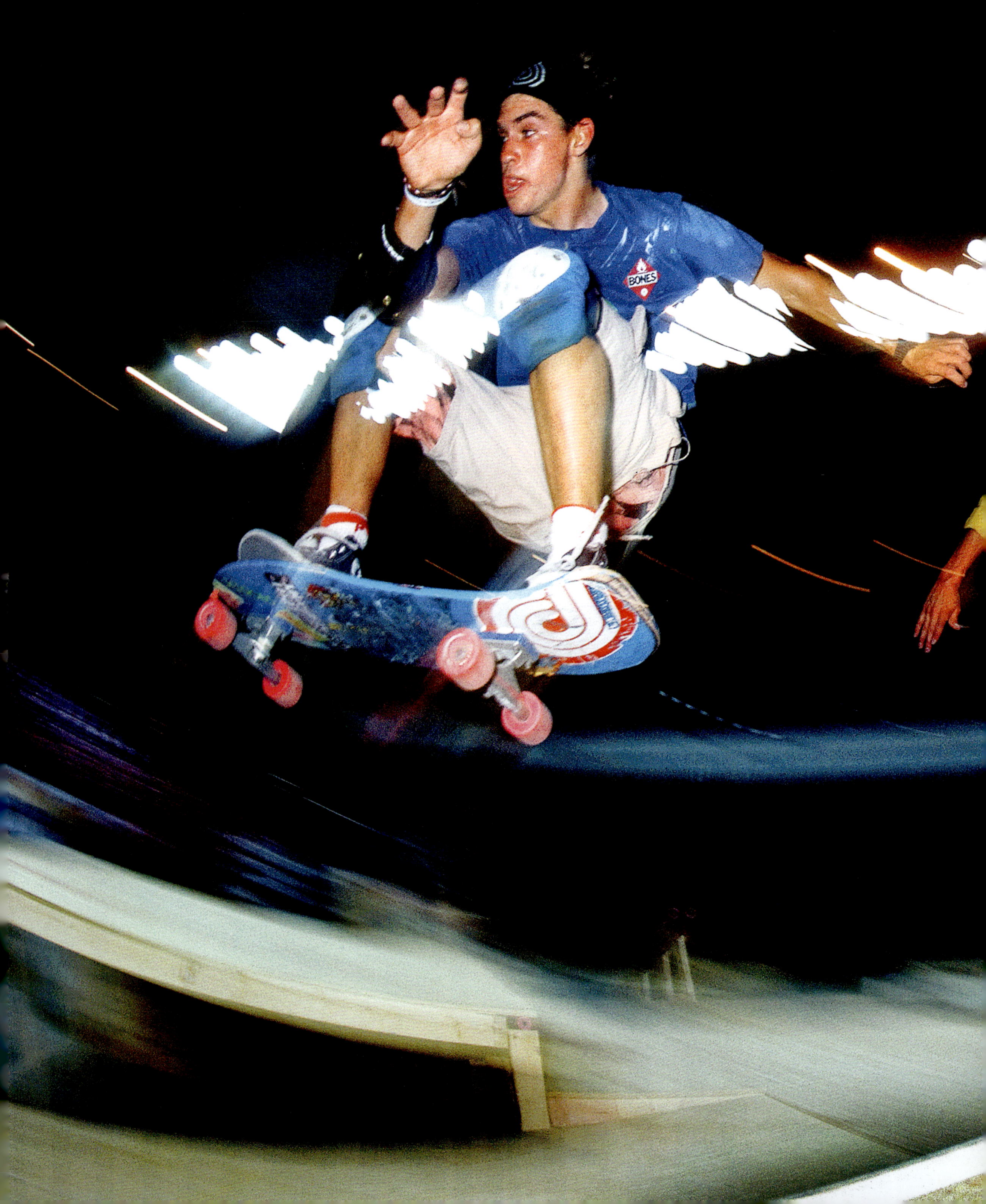
BONES

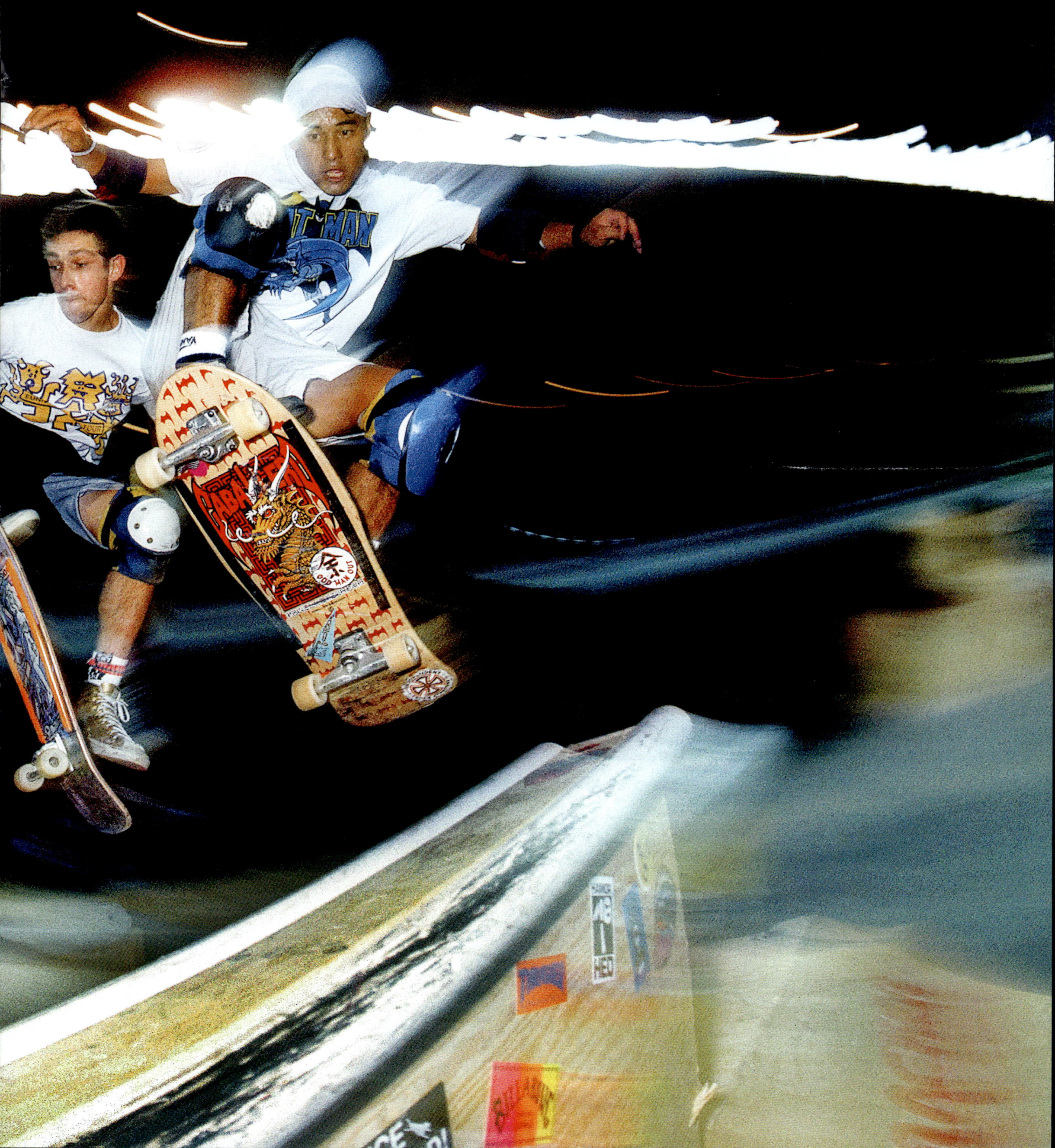

Previous spread: Doug Smith, Mark Gonzales, and Steve Caballero, Triple ollies, Louisville, KY, 1988

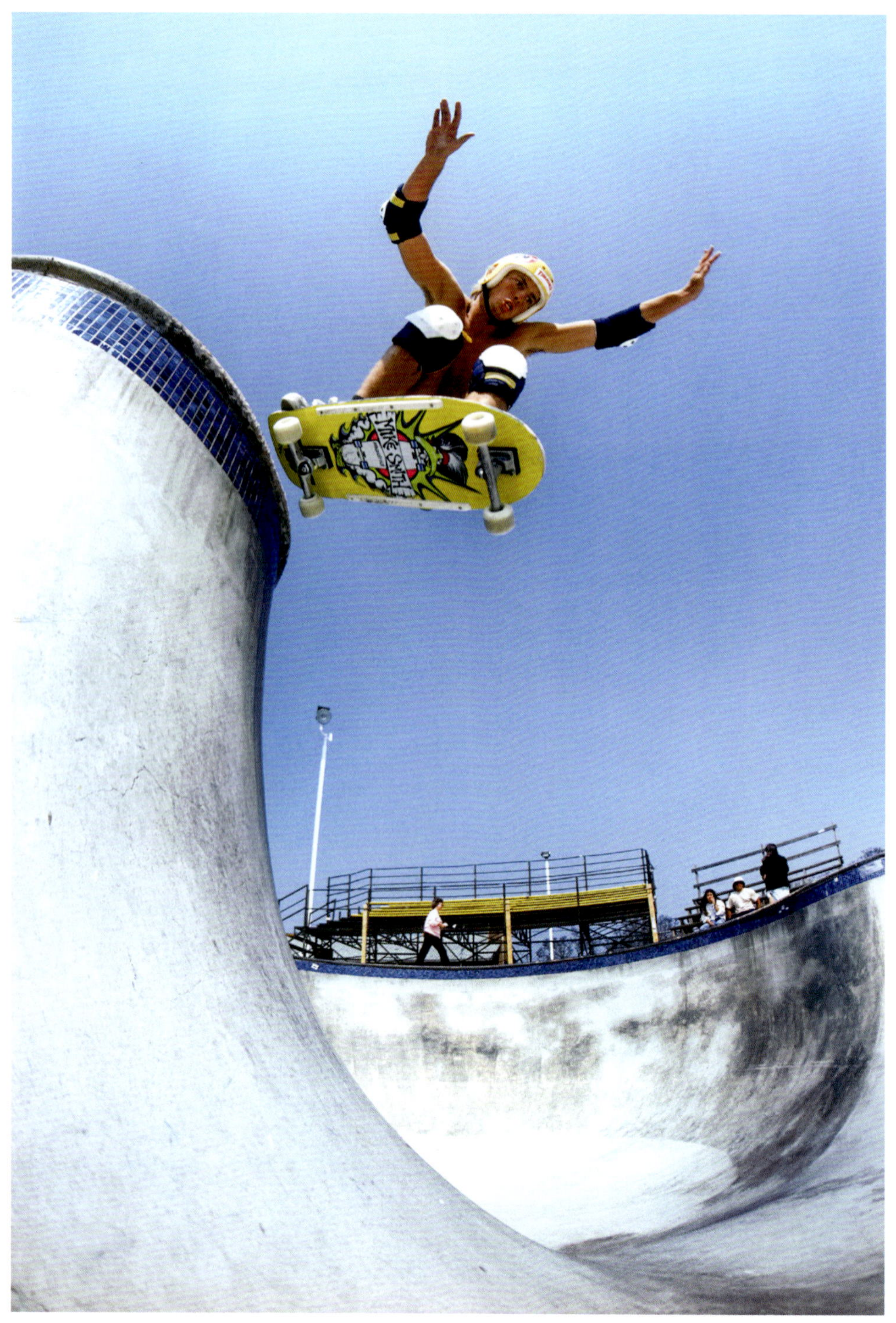

Mike Smith, Acid drop, Pipeline Skatepark, Upland, CA, 1985

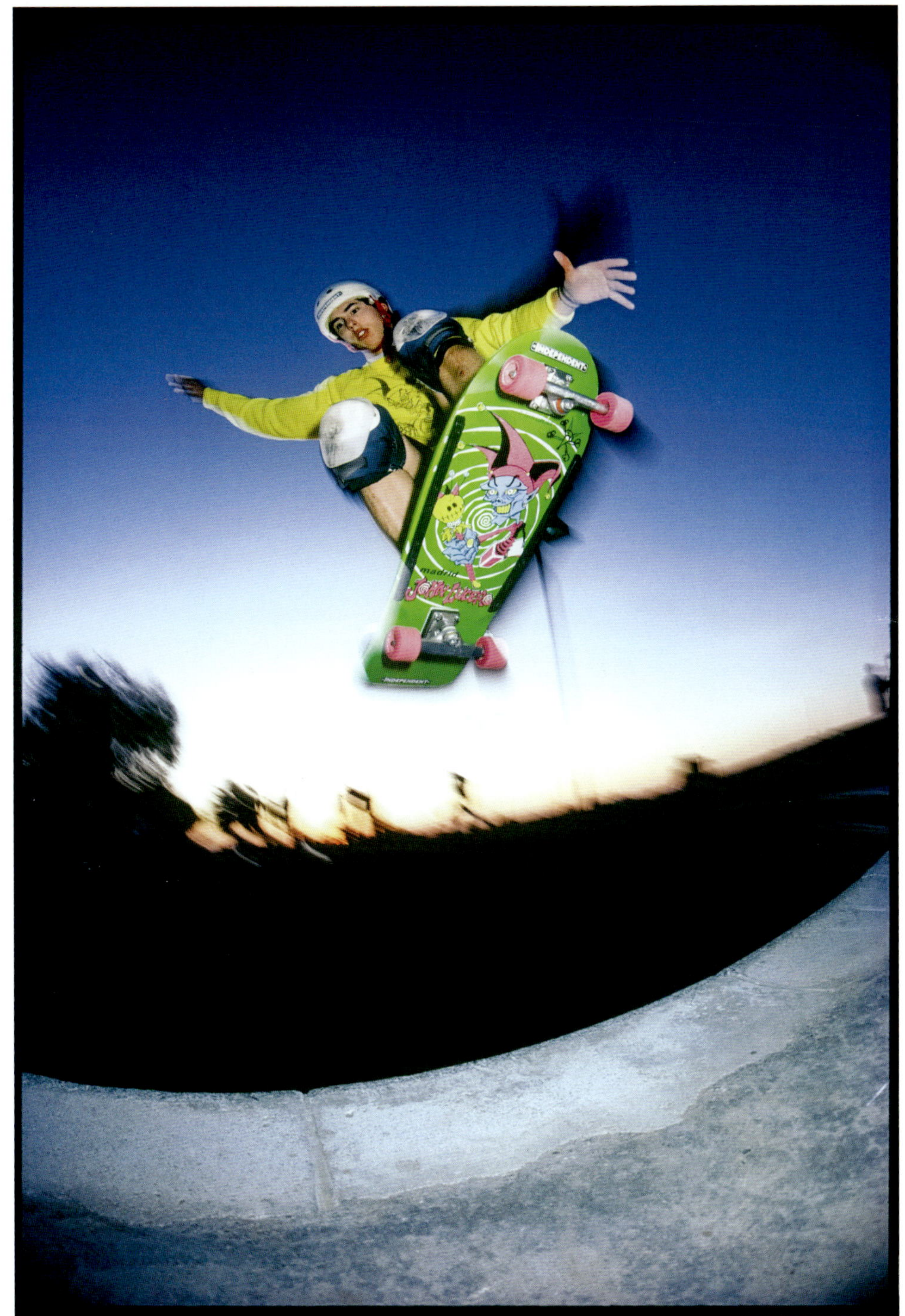

John Lucero, Pogo, Del Mar Skate Ranch, Del Mar, CA, 1985

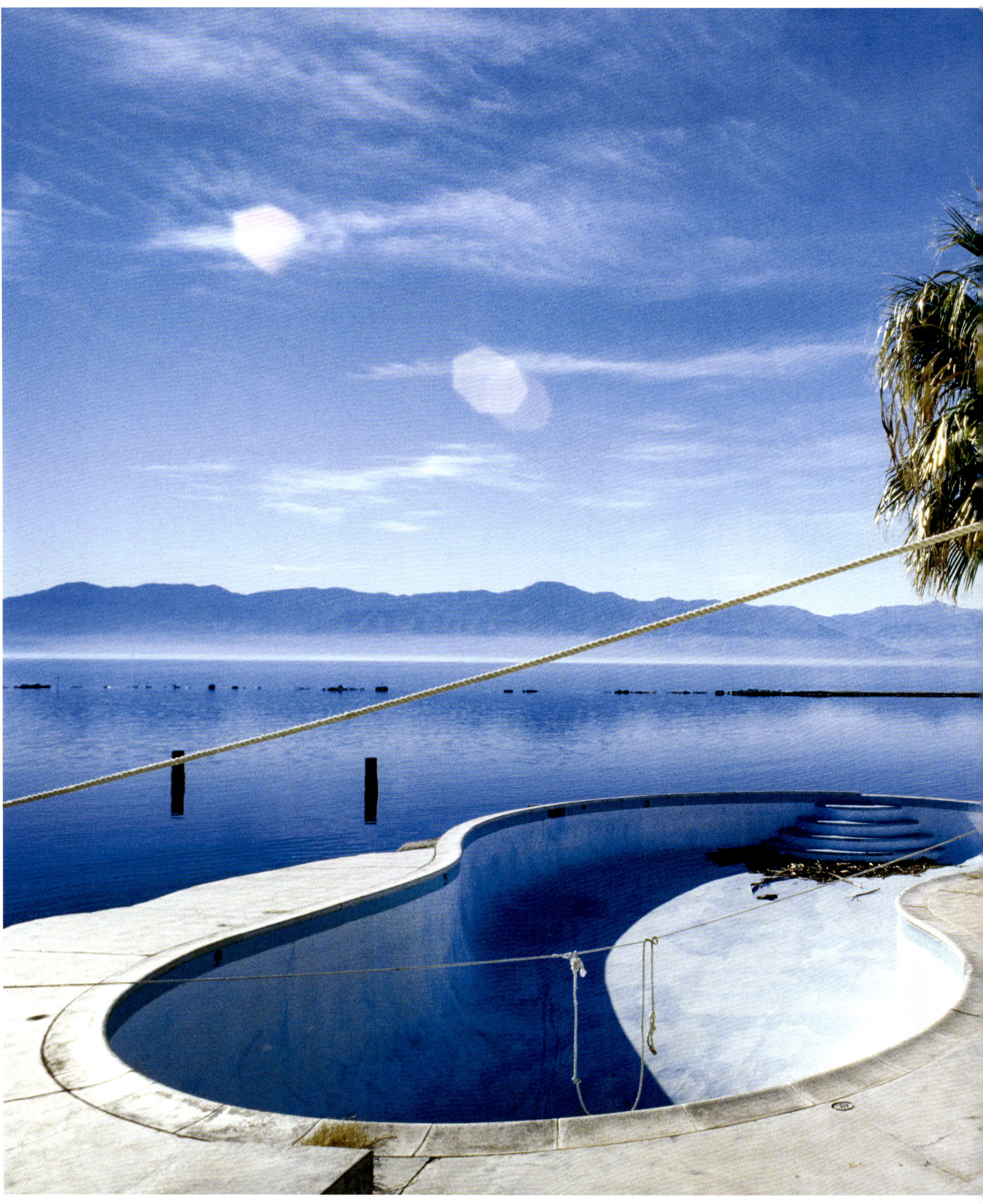

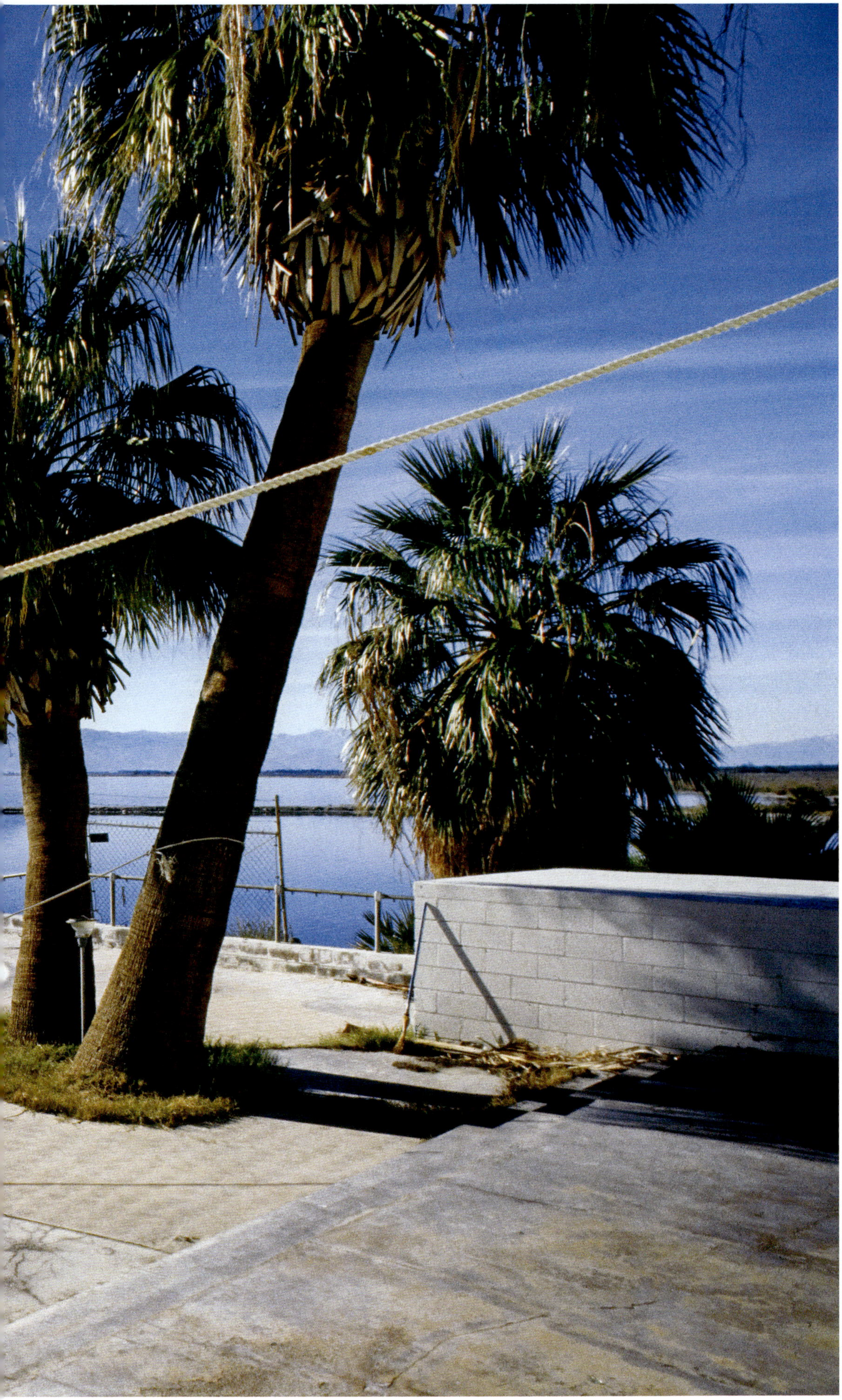

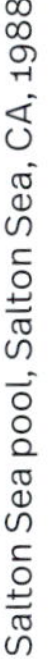

Salton Sea pool, Salton Sea, CA, 1988

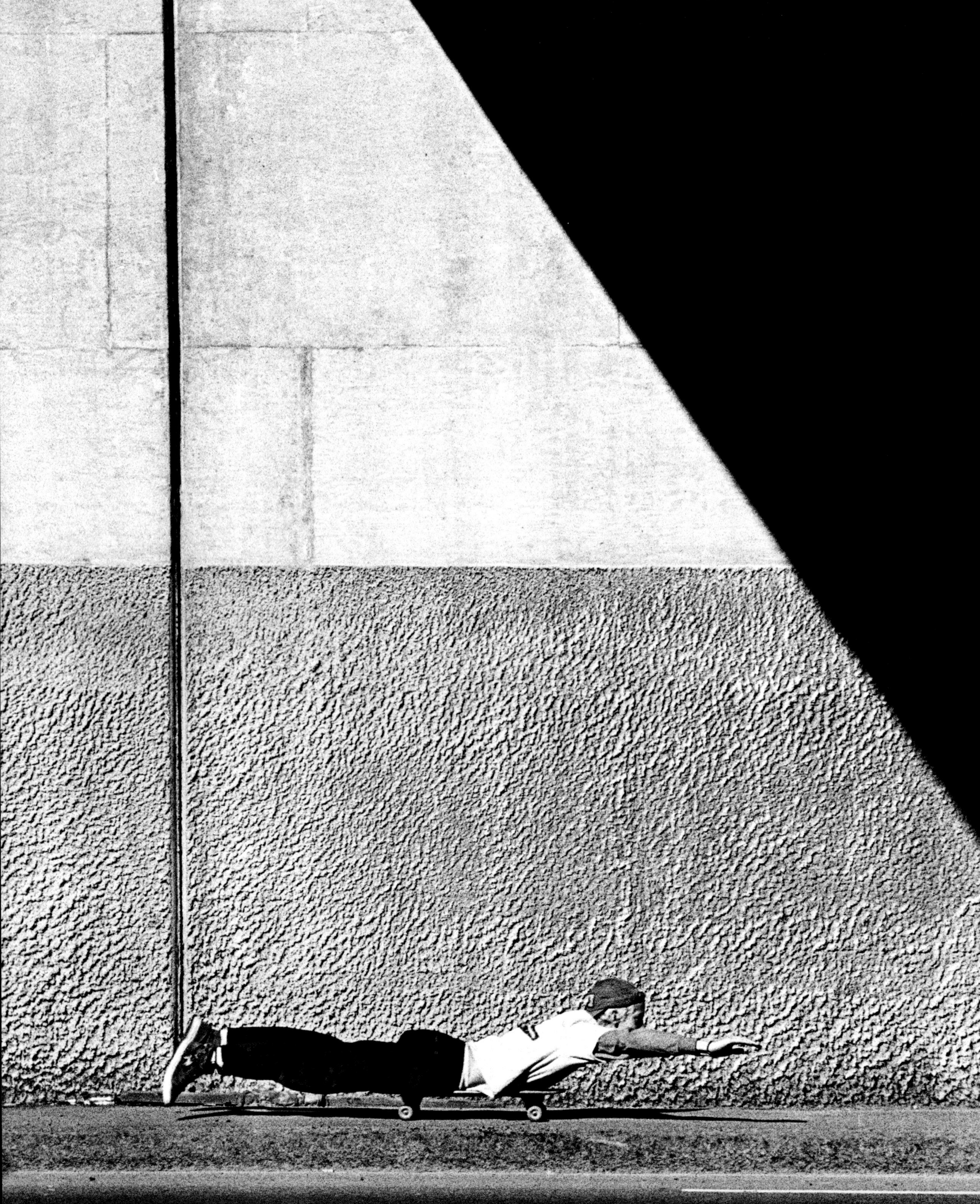

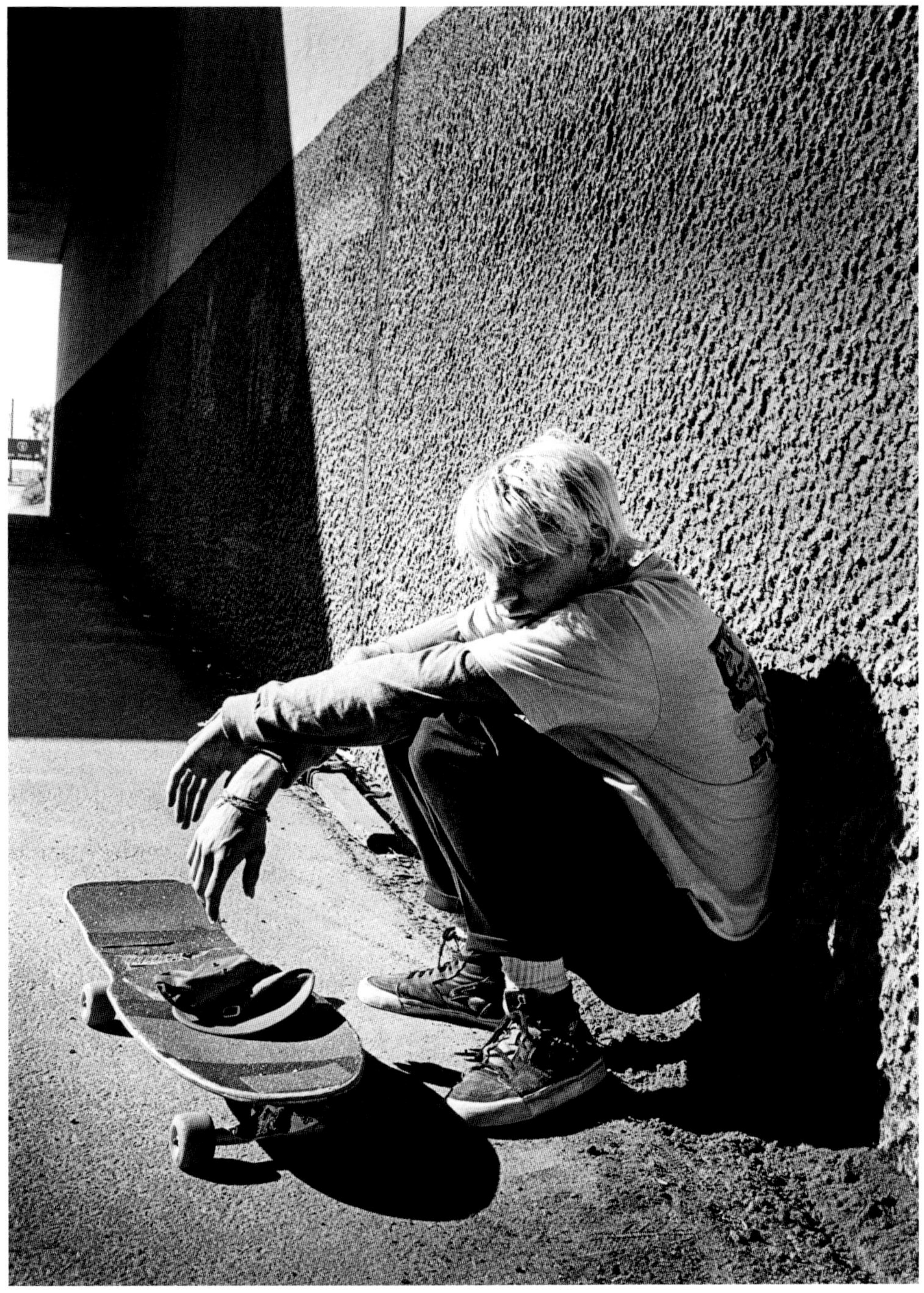

Tod Swank, The Sit, Del Mar, CA, 1987

Tod Swank, The Push, Del Mar, CA, 198

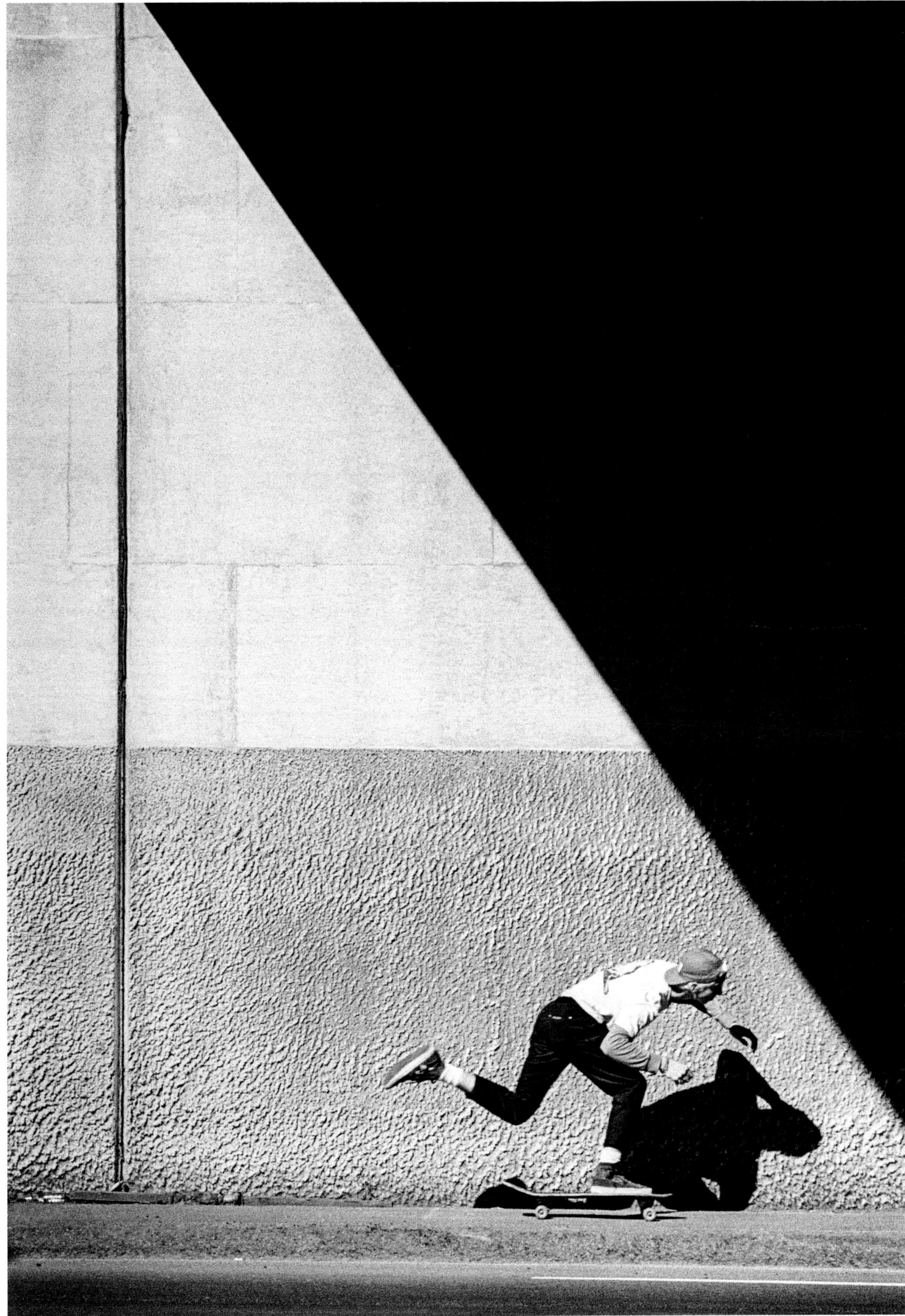

Christian Hosoi, Portrait, Westminster, CA, 1985

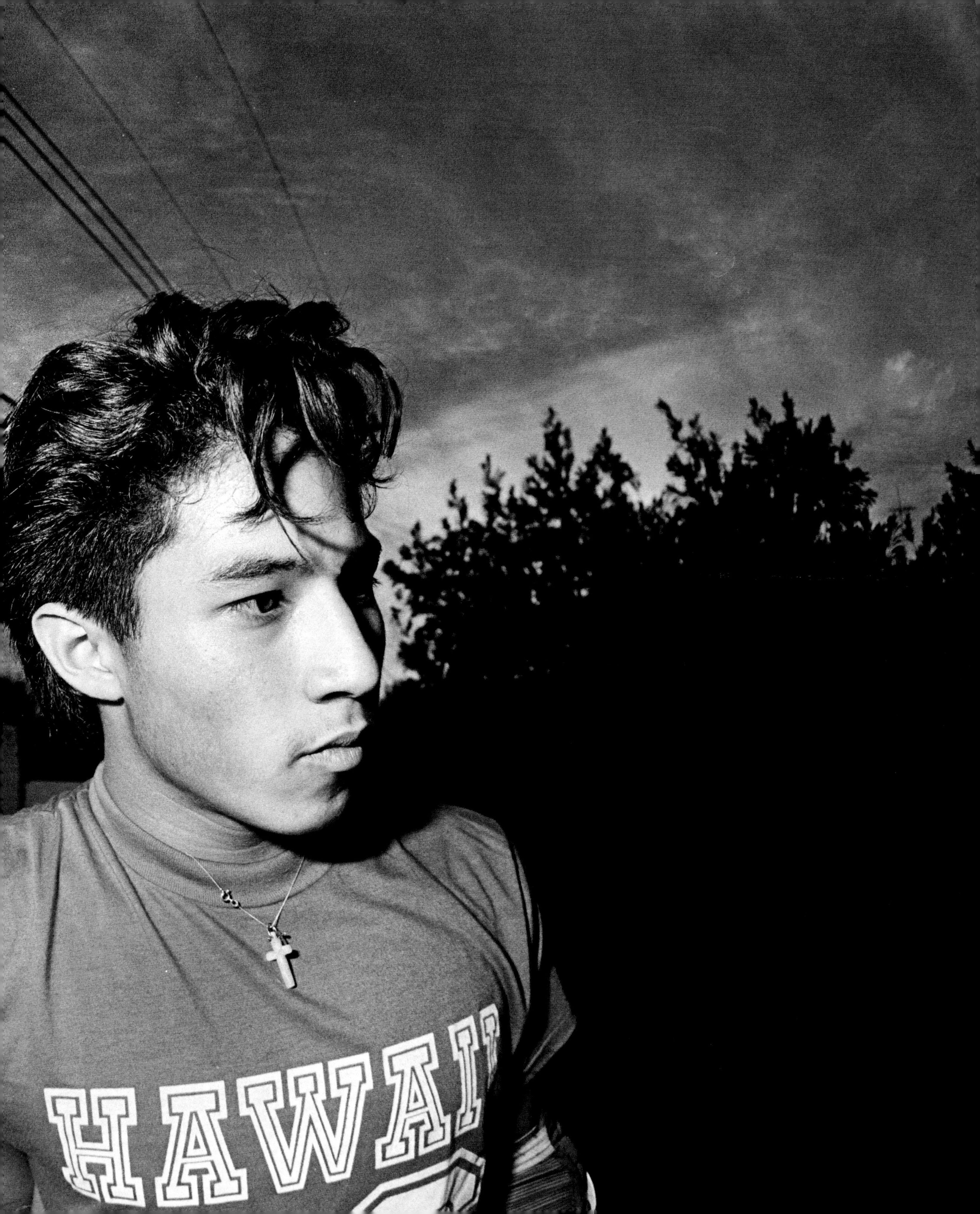
HAWAI

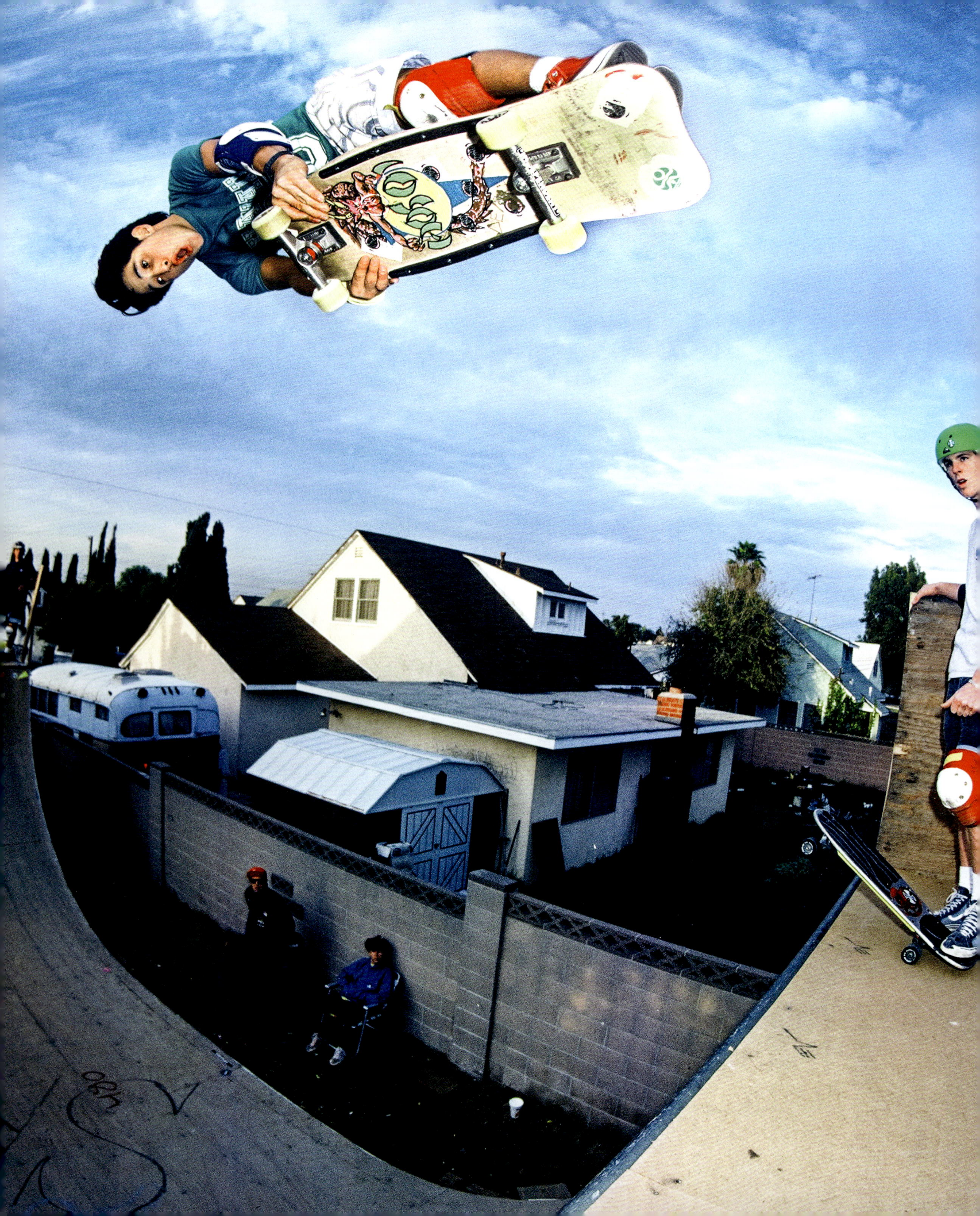

Christian Hosoi, Rocket air, Westminster, CA, 1985

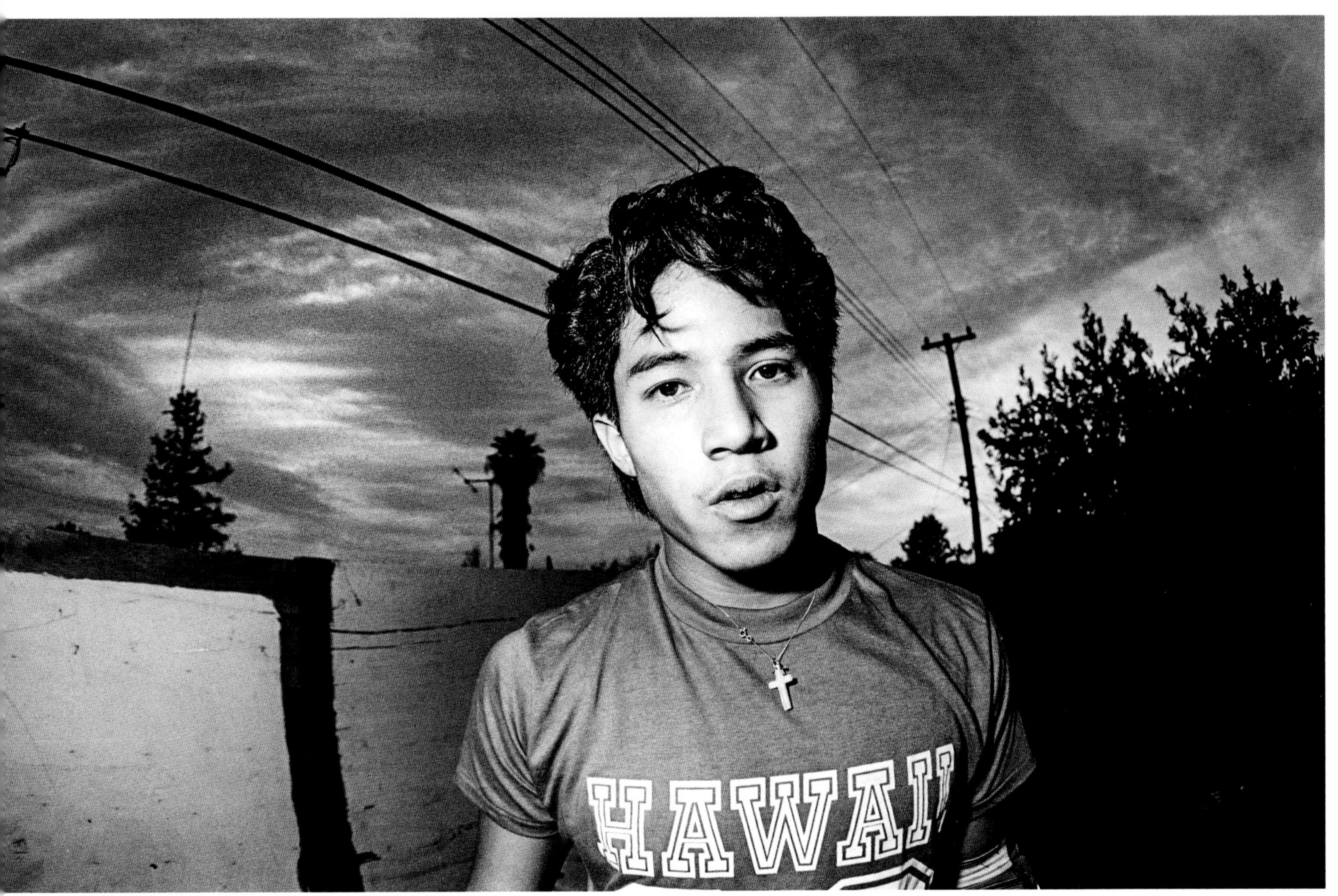

Christian Hosoi, Portrait, Westminster, CA, 1985

Garry Scott Davis (GSD), Frontside boneless, Shell Bowl, Oceanside, CA, 198

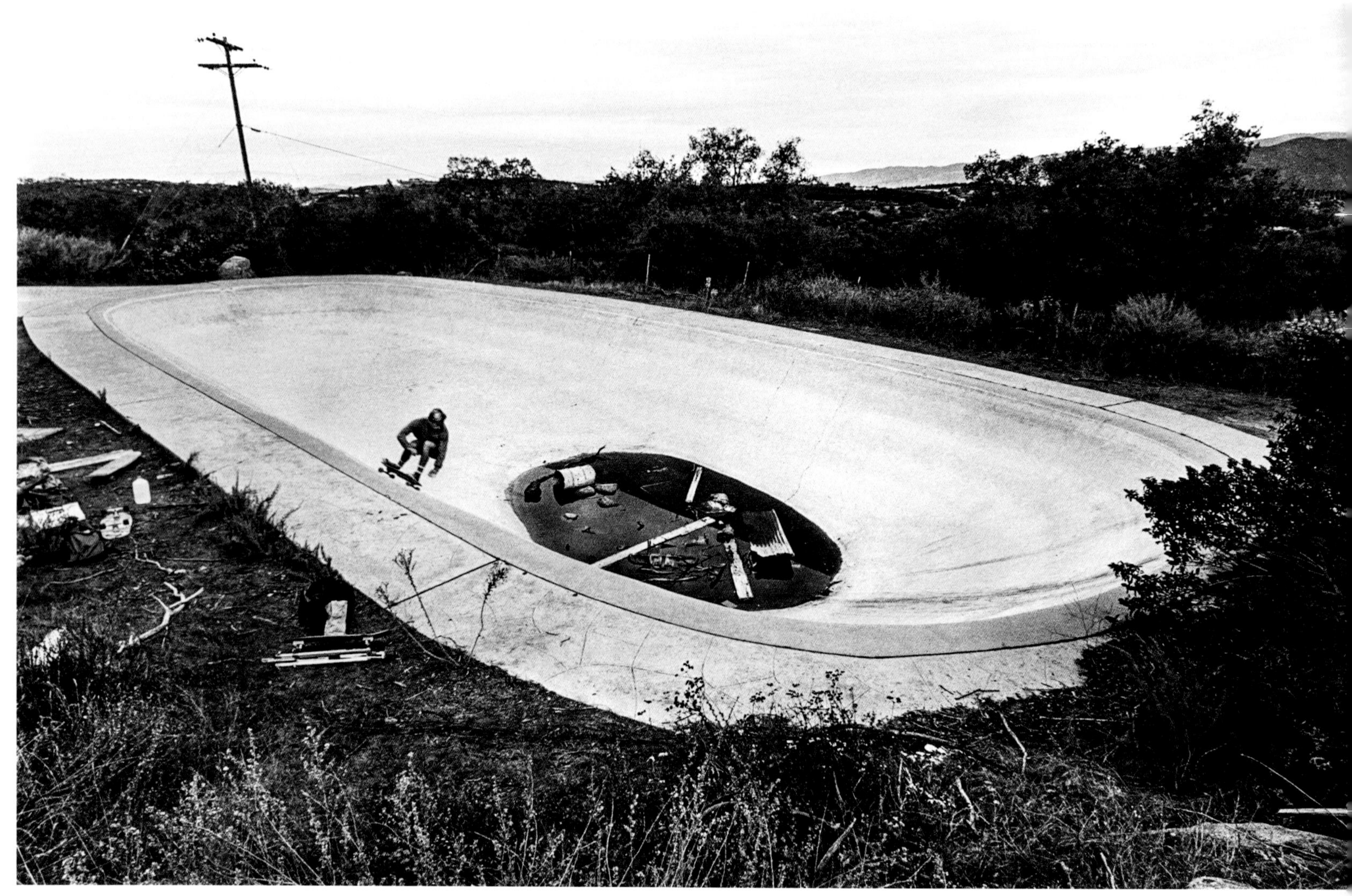

Bill Billing, VC Reservoir, Valley Center, CA, 1983

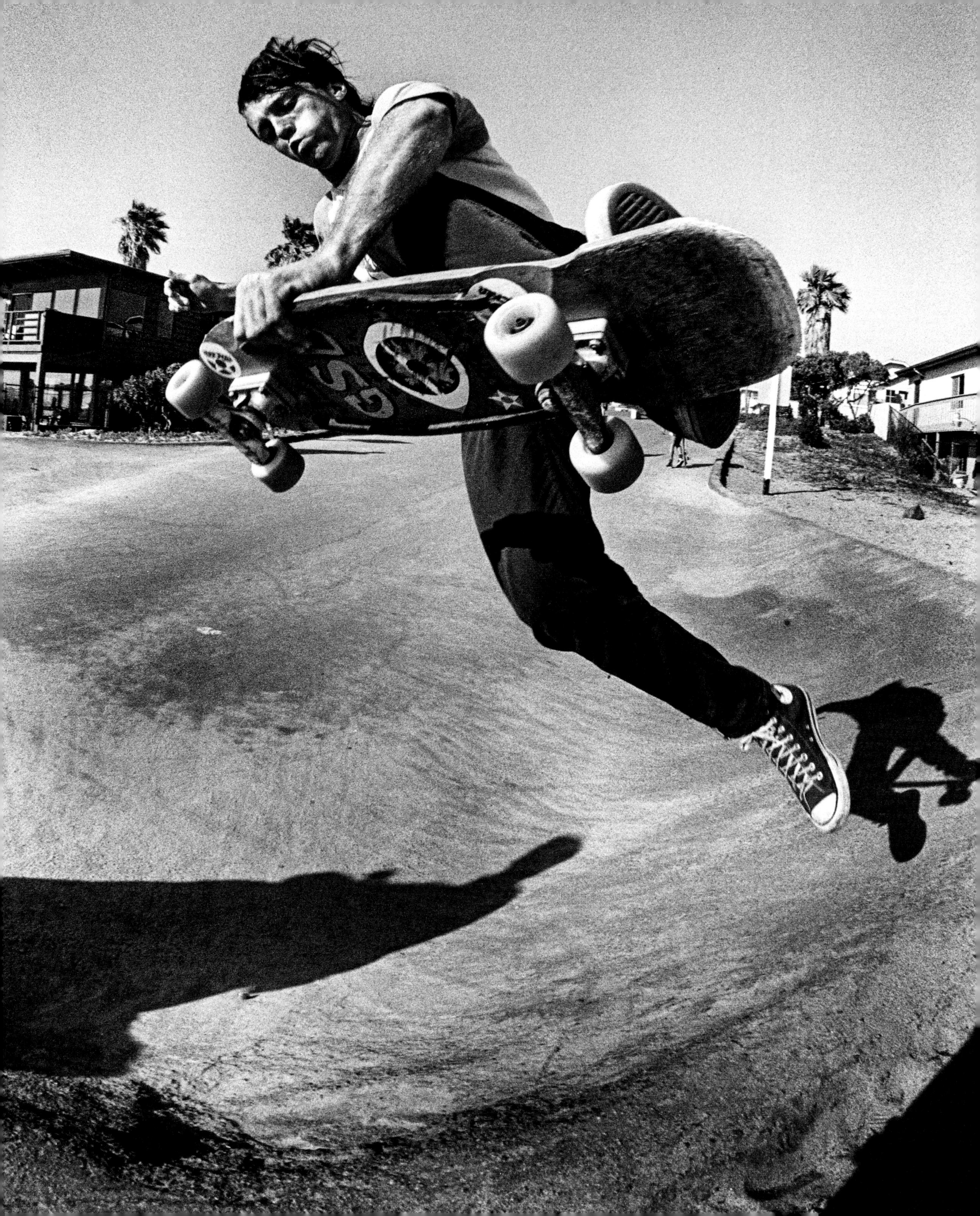

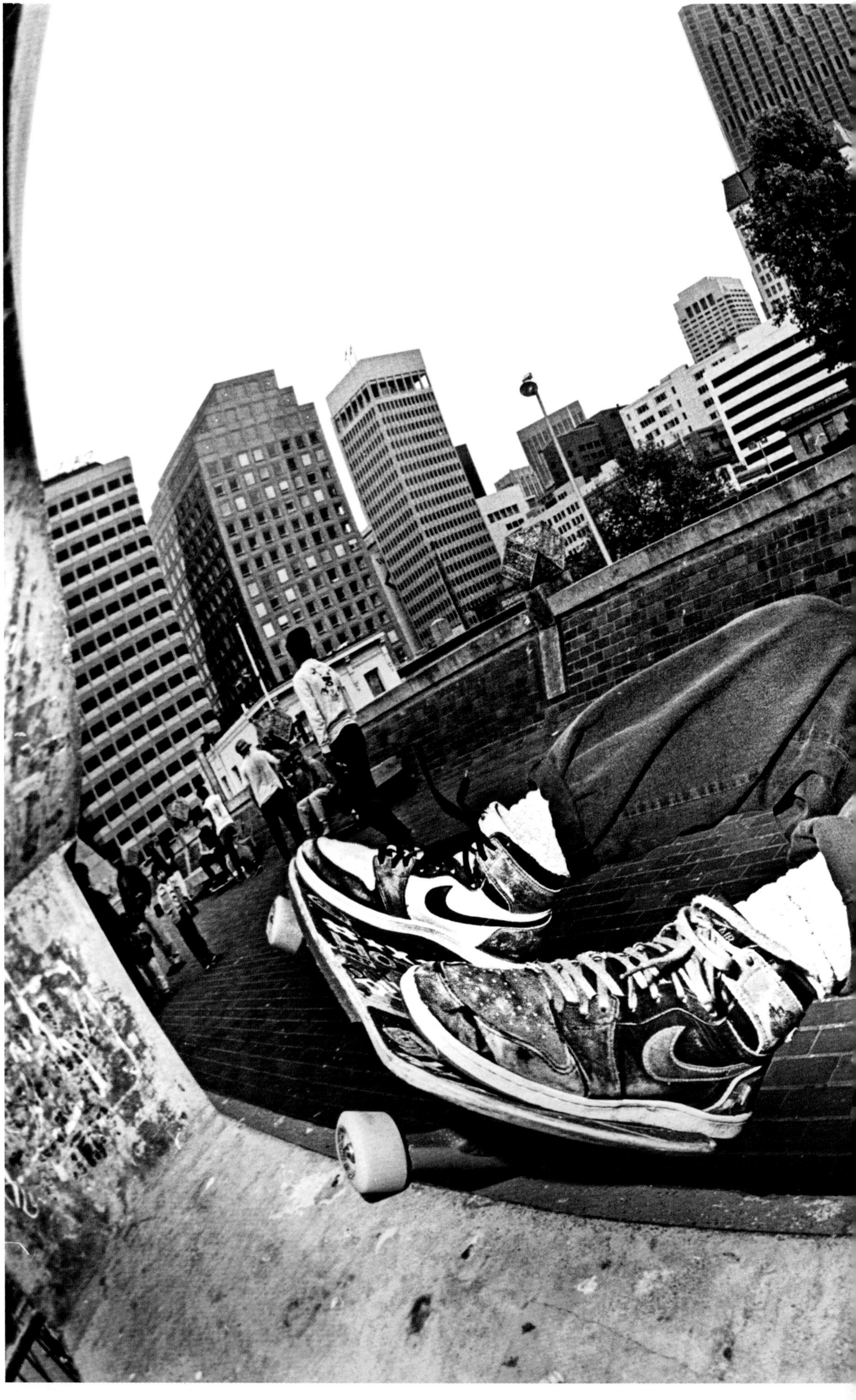

Bryce Kanights, Layback grind, China Banks, San Francisco, CA, 1986

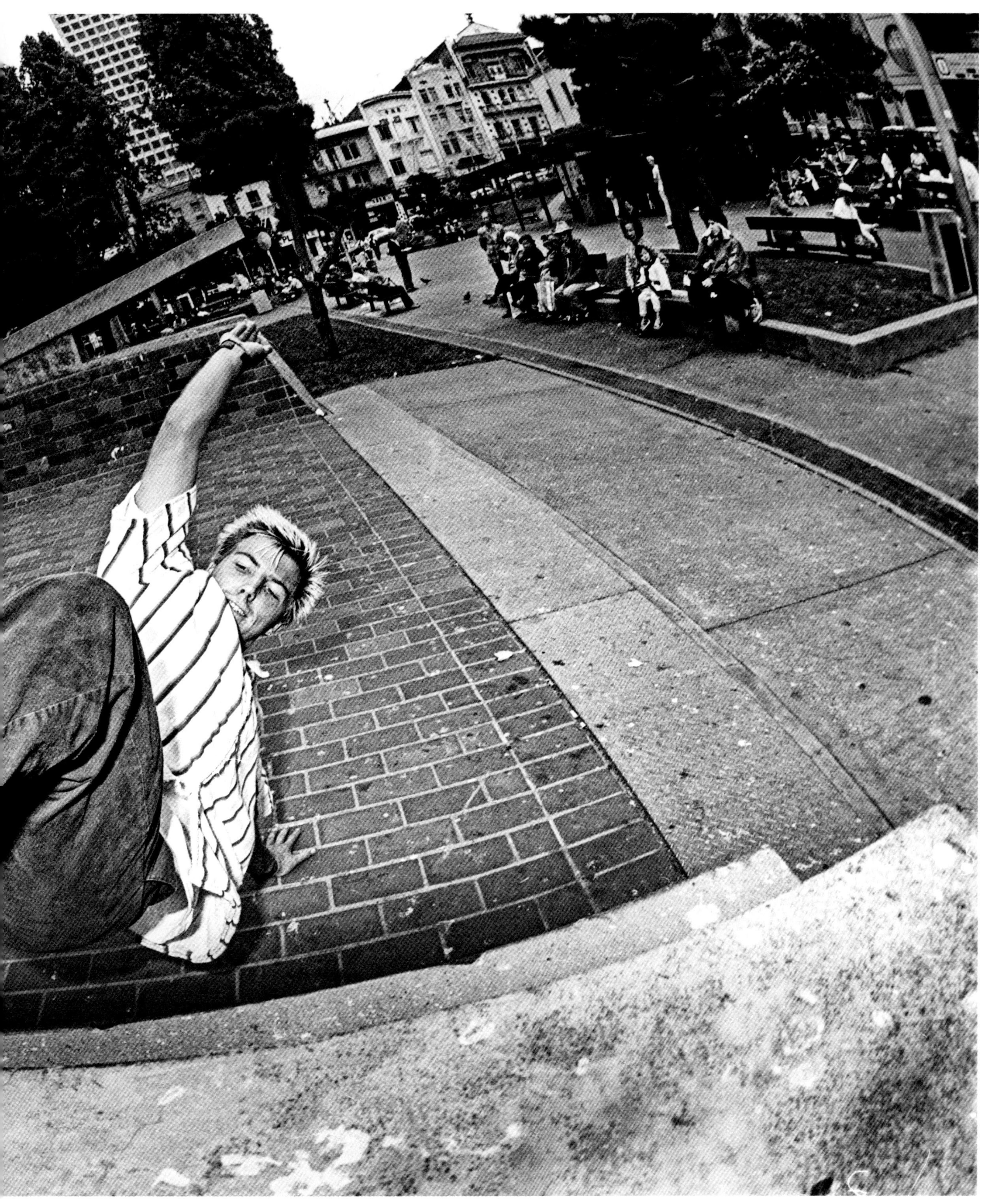

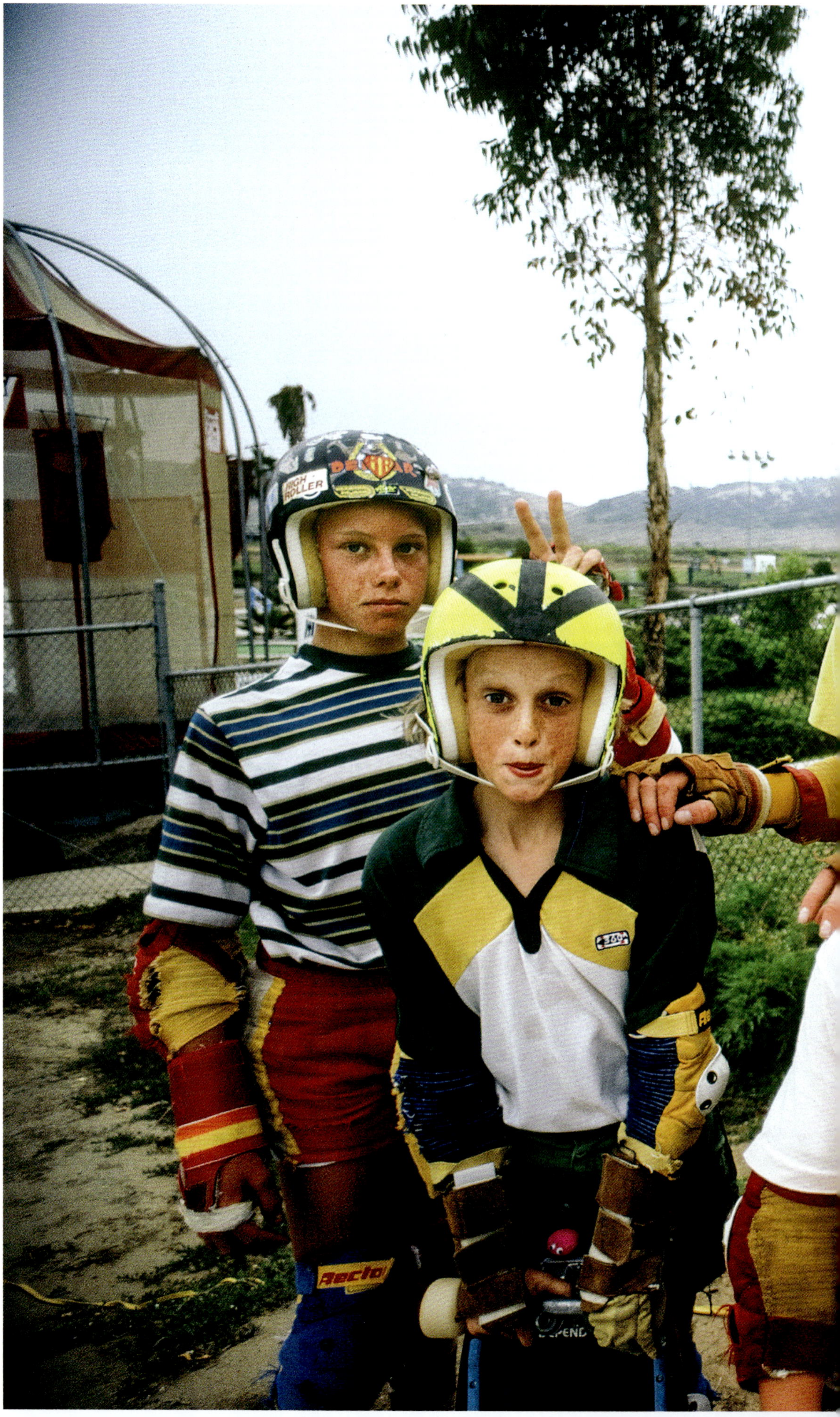

Del Mar Skate Ranch Locals David Eckles, Tony Hawk, Owen Nieder, Kenny Stalmasky, Mike Stalmasky Sr., and Mike Stalmasky Jr., Del Mar, CA, 1980

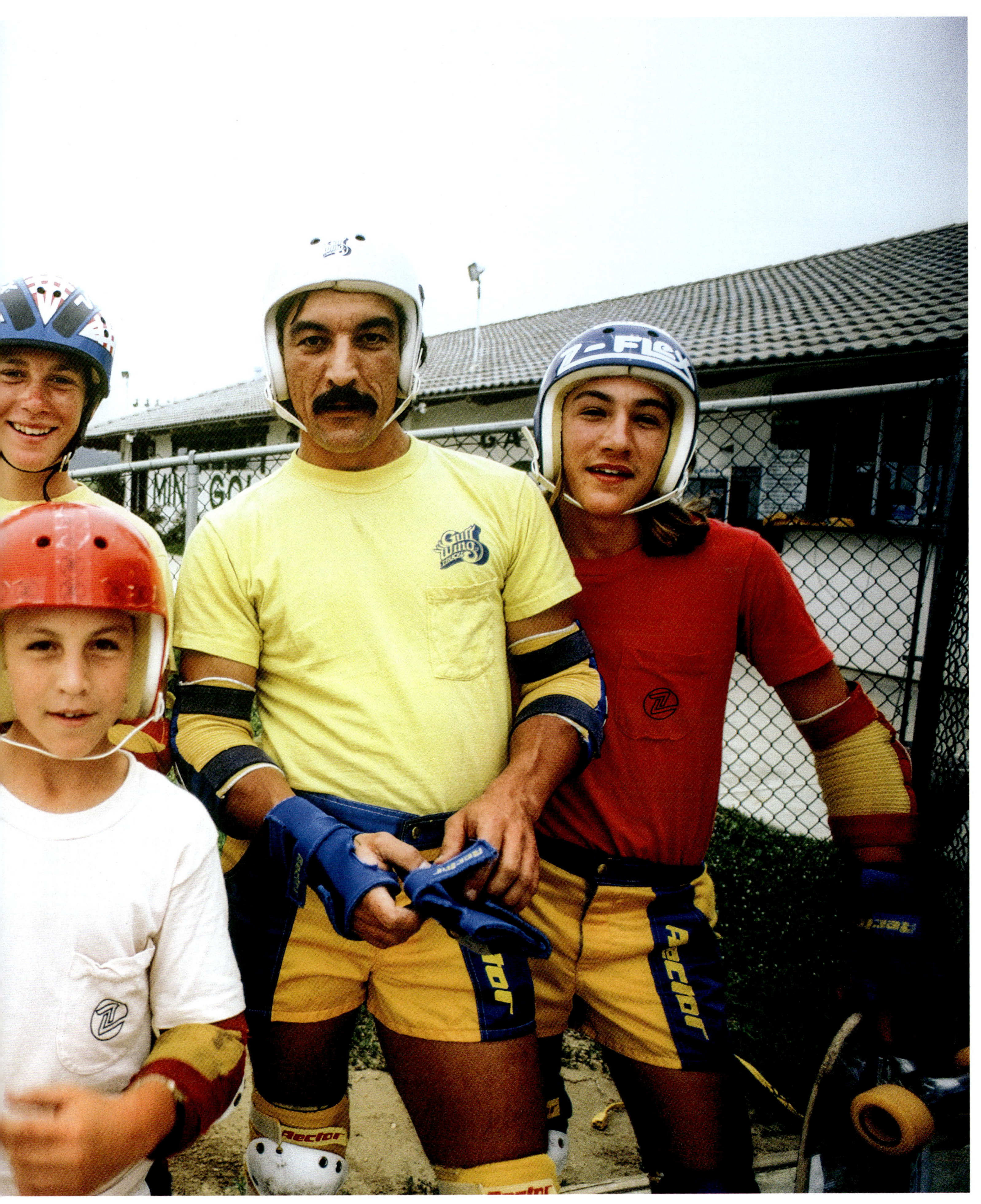

Z-FLEX
Gull Wing
Rector
Rector
Rector

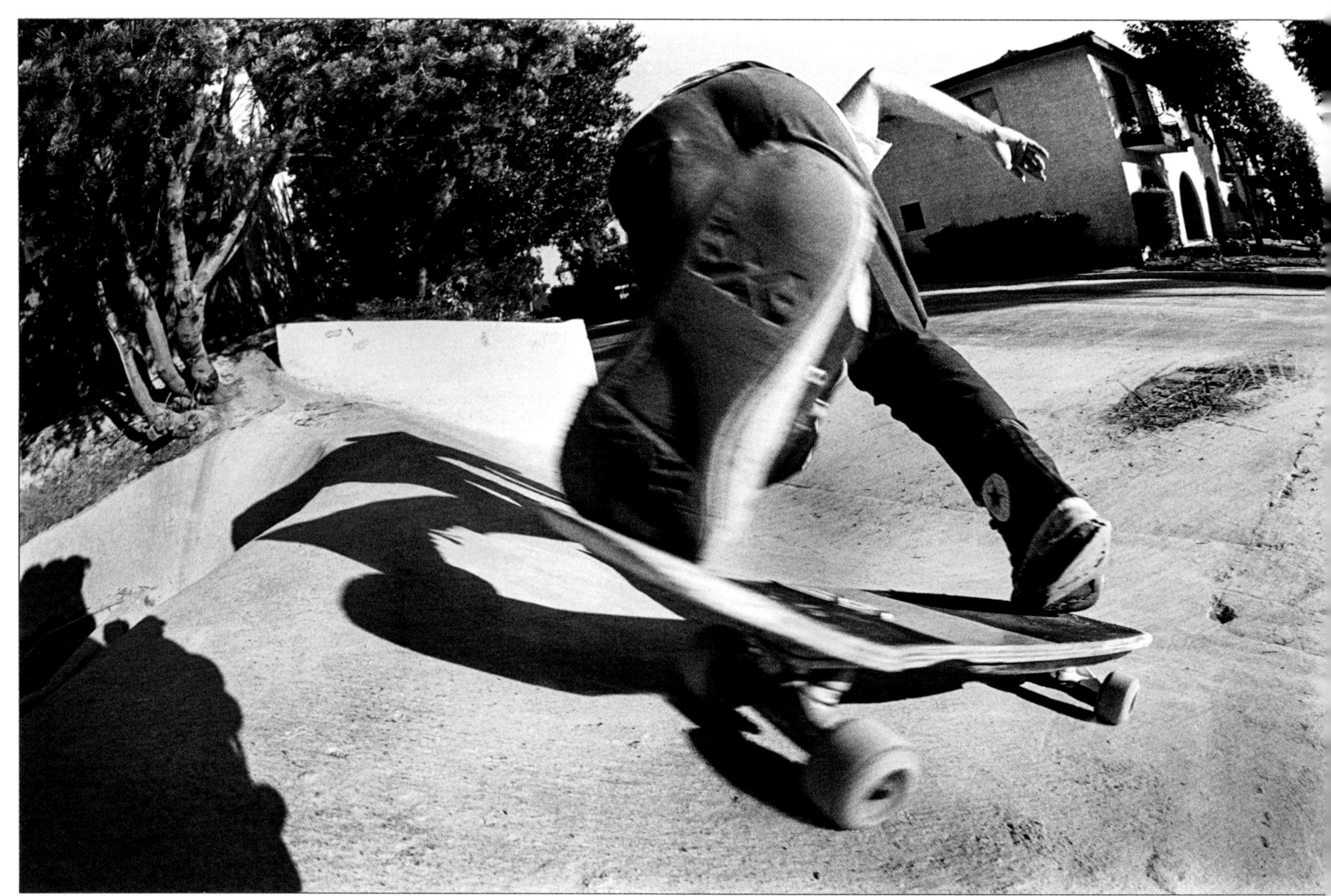

GSD, Backside Bertlemann, Gemco Bank, Oceanside, CA, 1985

Jesse Martinez, Picnic table launch, Huntington Beach, CA, 198

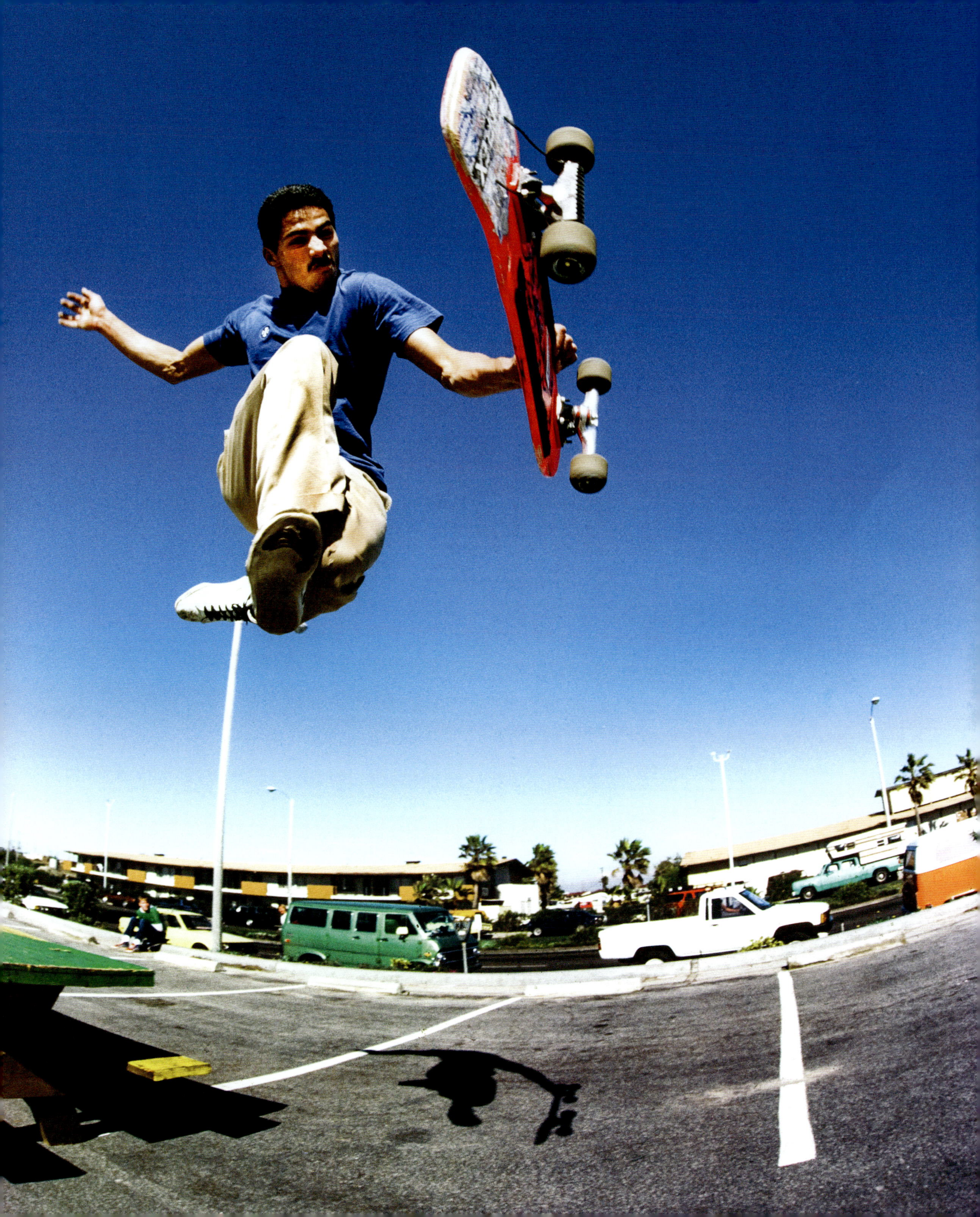

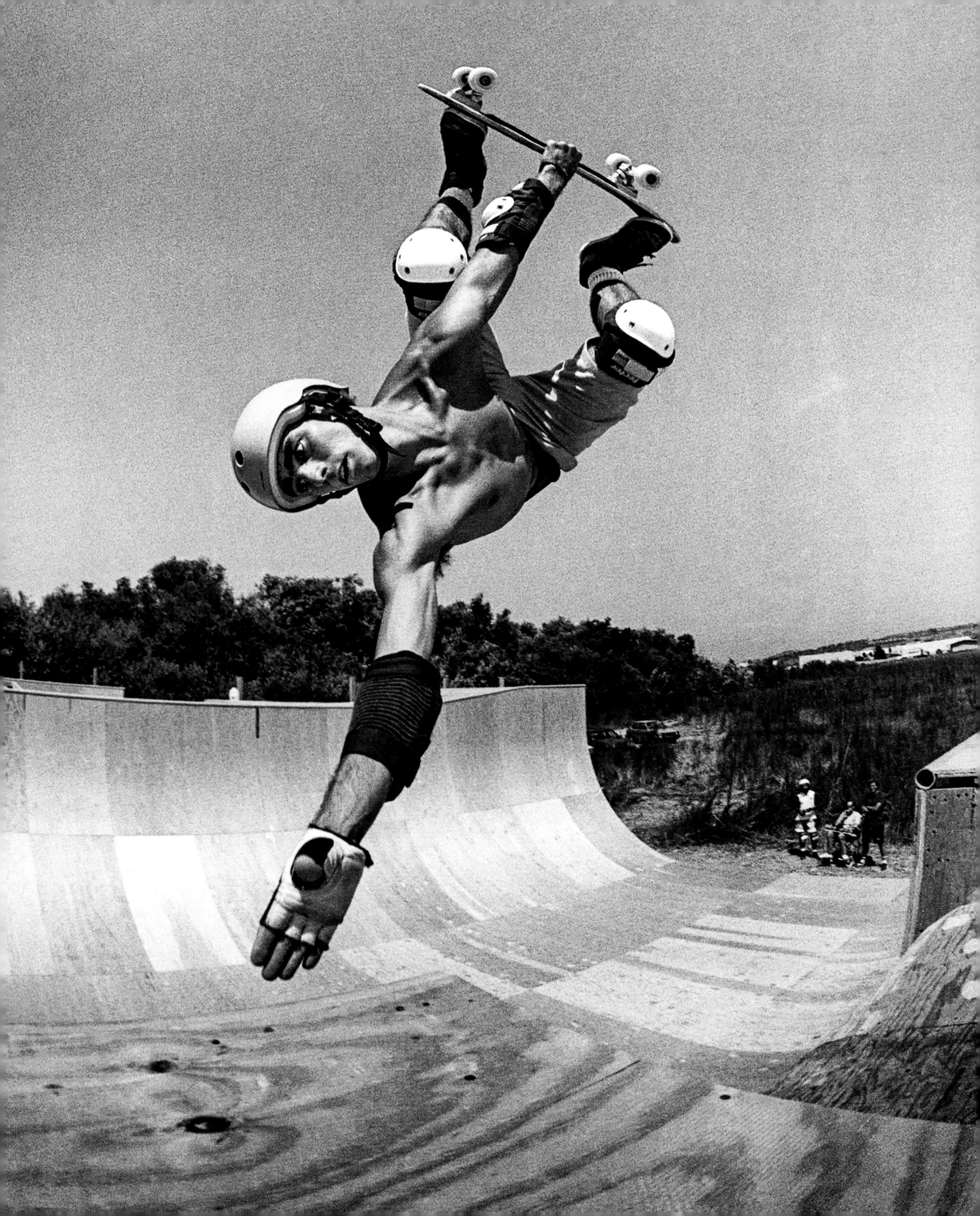

_ance Mountain, Channel invert, Chin Ramp, Oceanside, CA, 1986

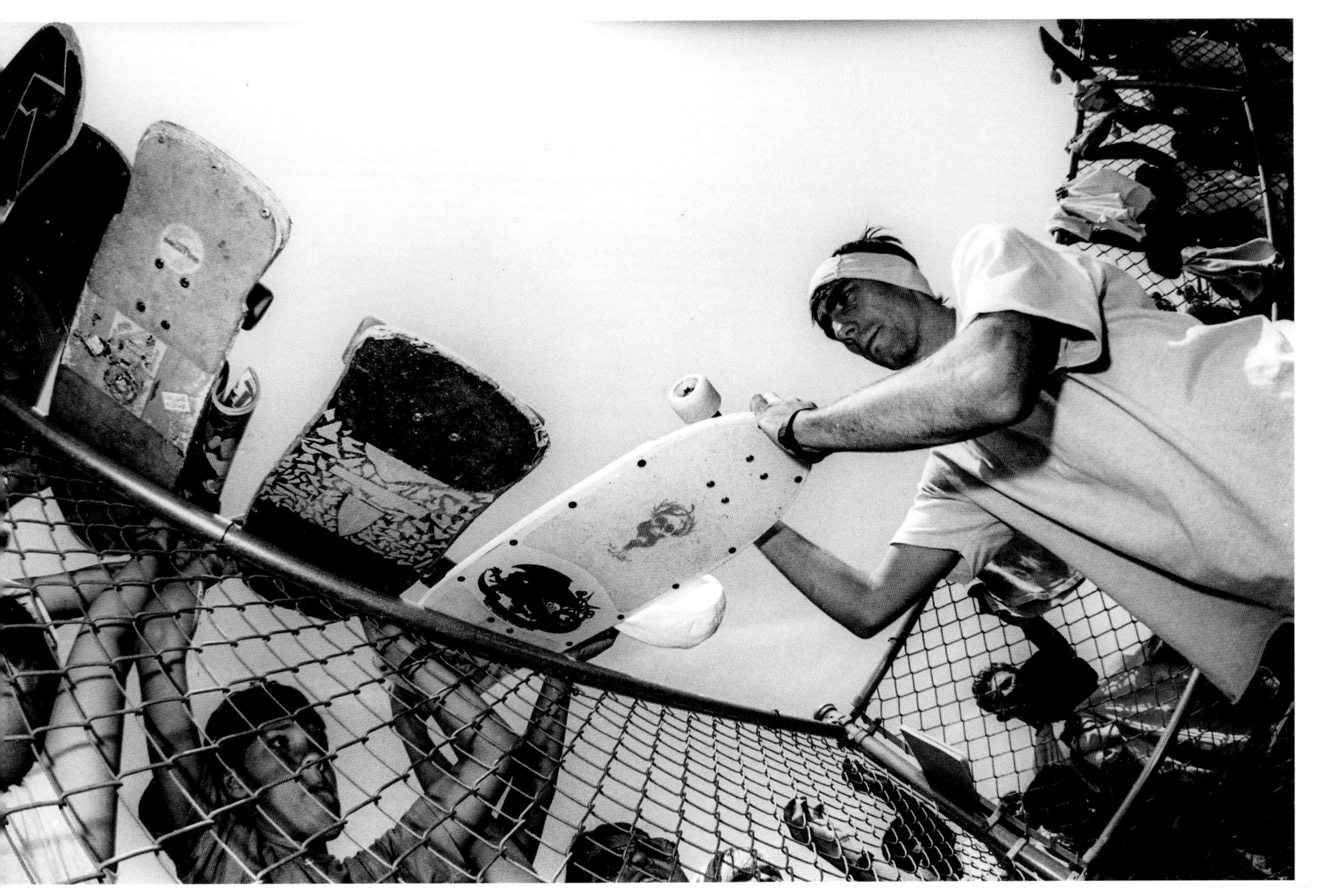

Lance Mountain and skate fans, Mt. Trashmore, Virginia Beach, VA, 1986

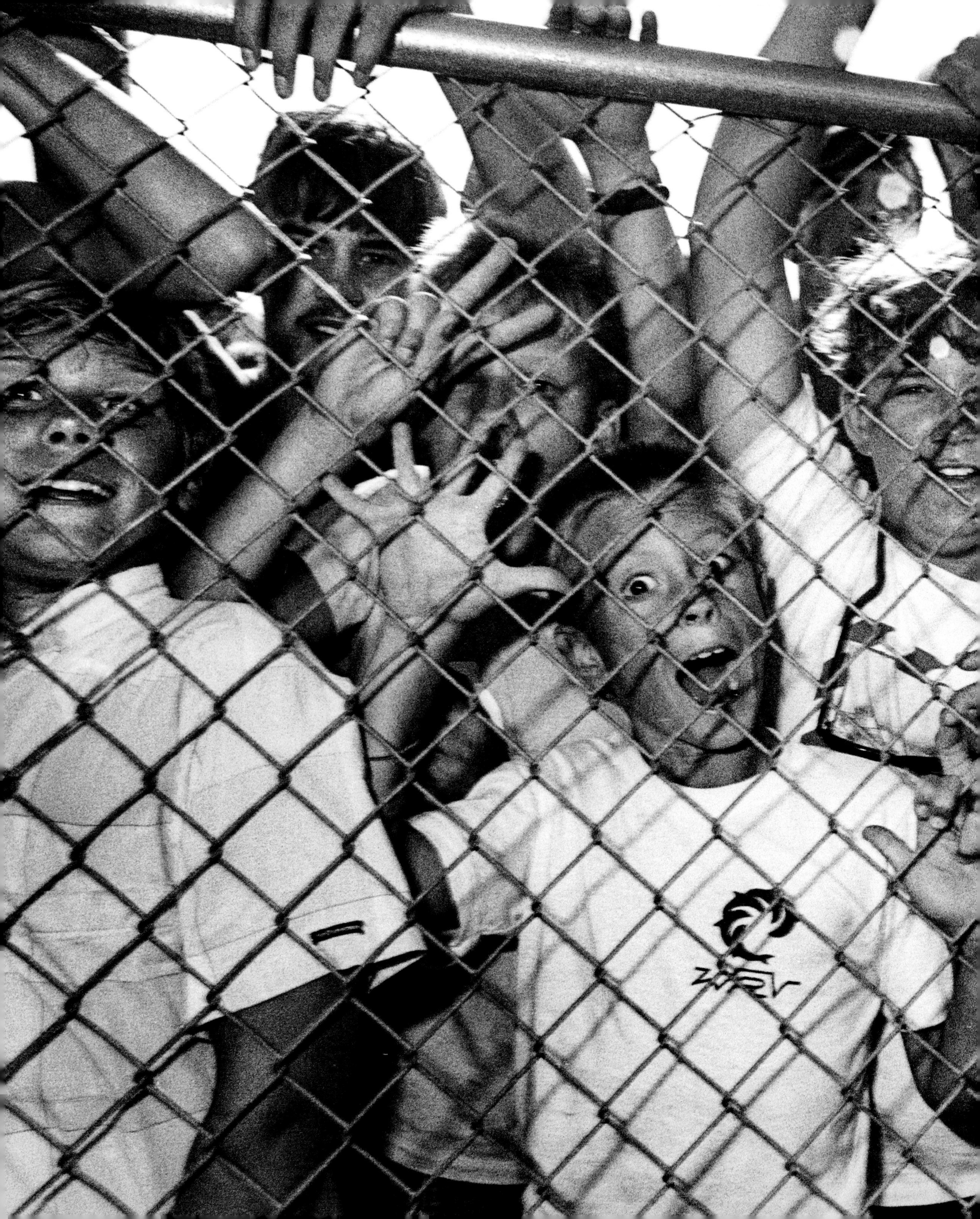

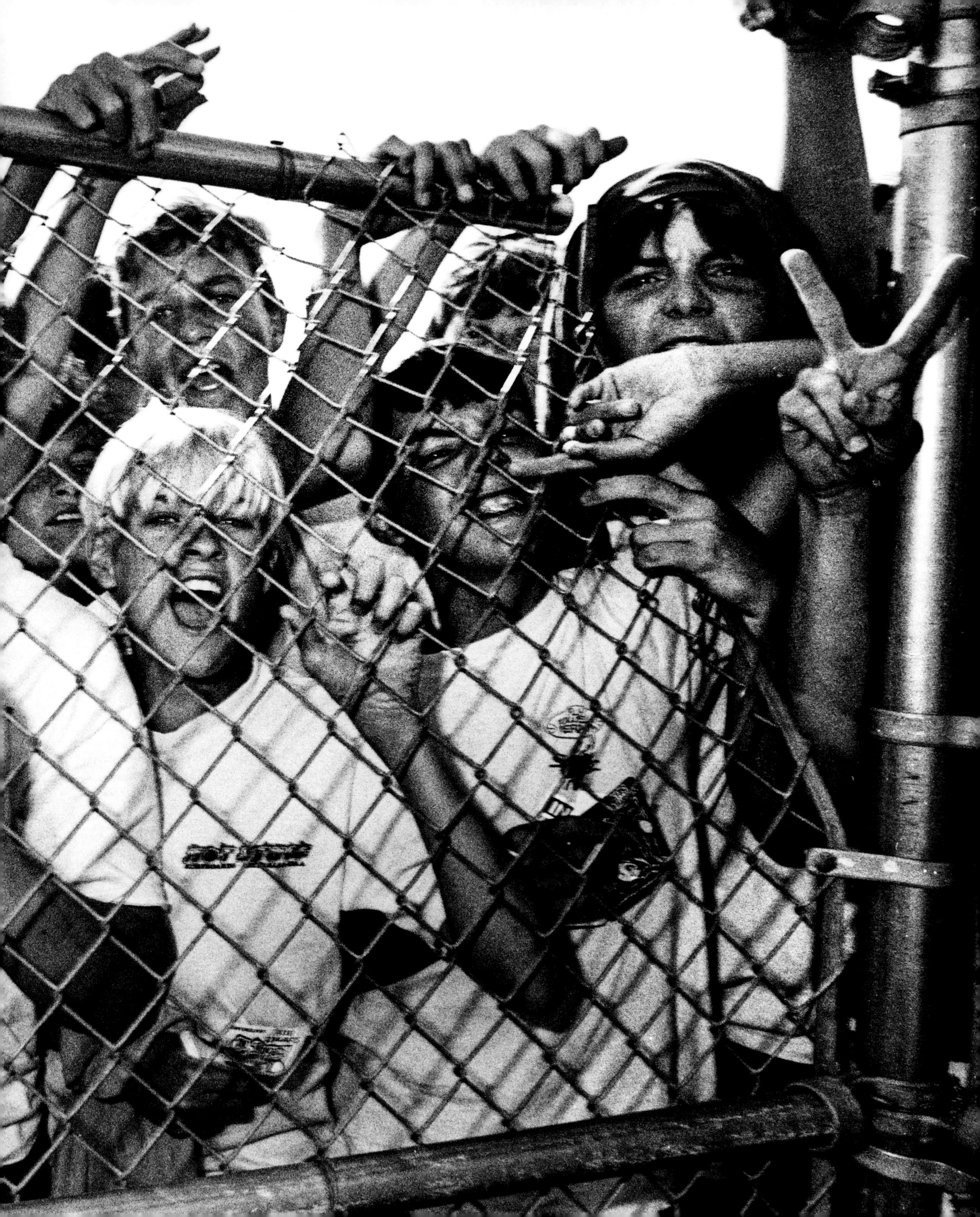

Previous spread: Skate Fans, Mt. Trashmore, Virginia Beach, VA, 1986

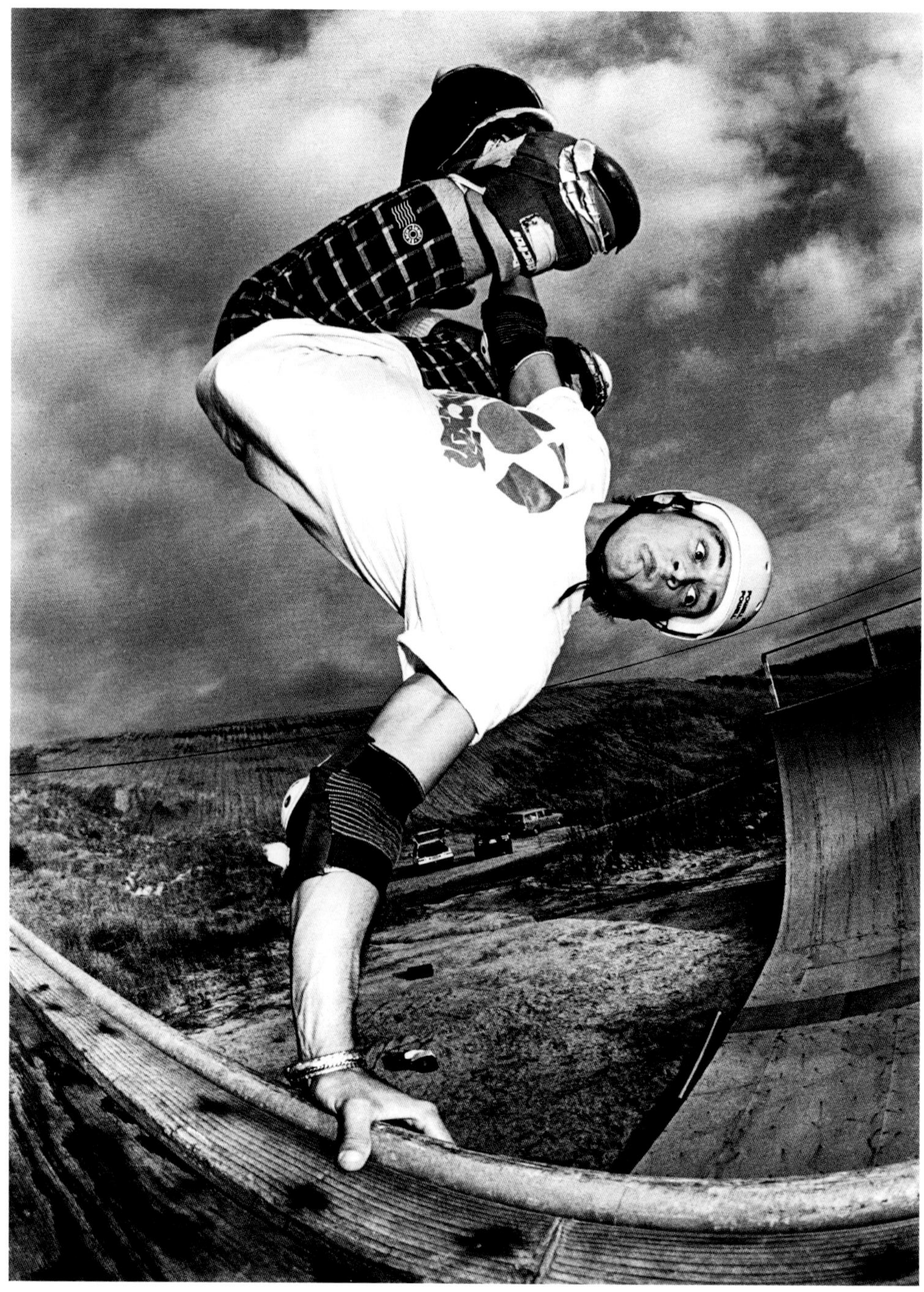

Ray Underhill, Frontside invert, Ken Park's Ramp, Fairbanks Ranch, CA, 1986

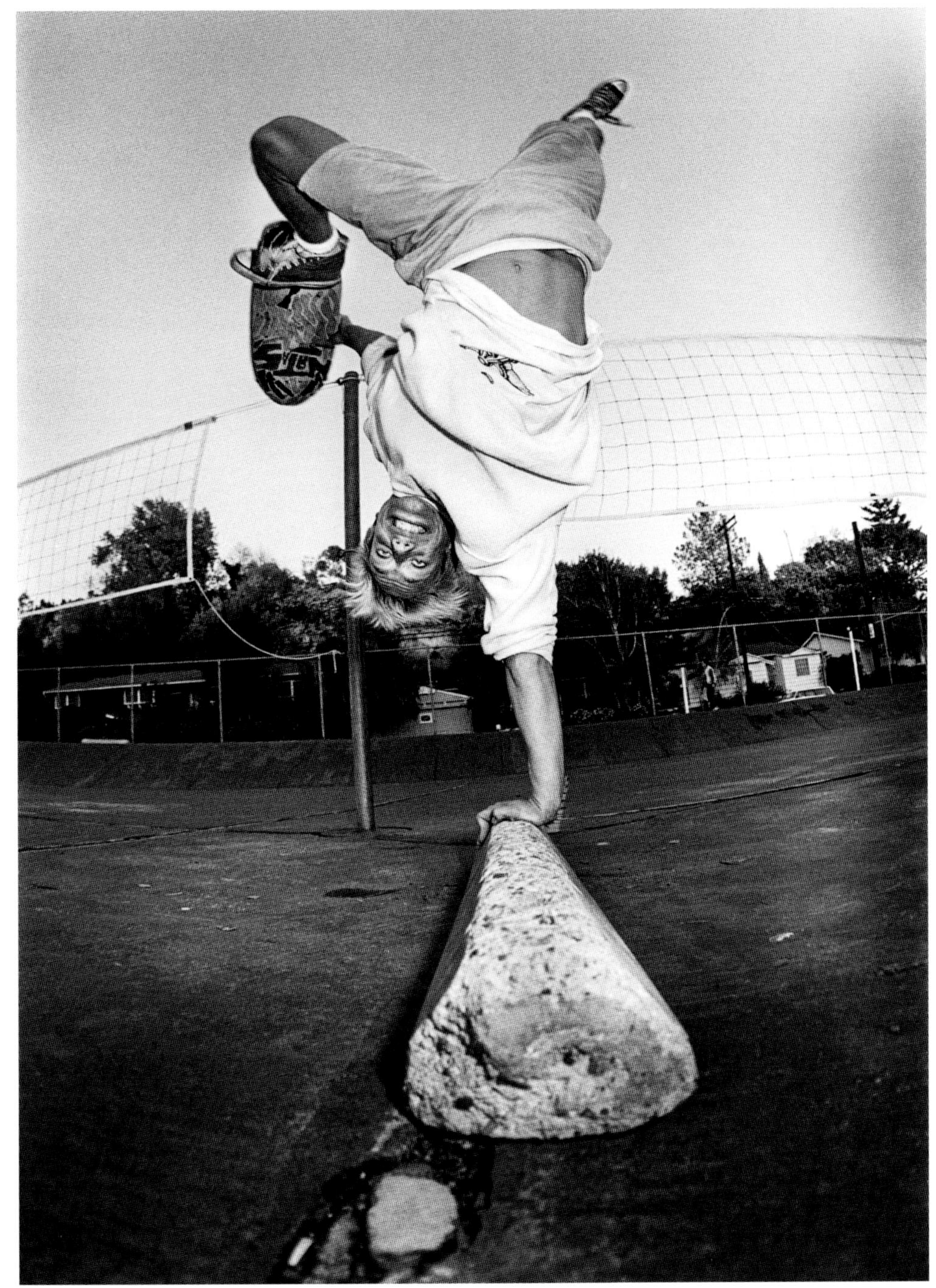

Natas Kaupas, Curb plant, Kenter Banks, Brentwood, CA, 1985

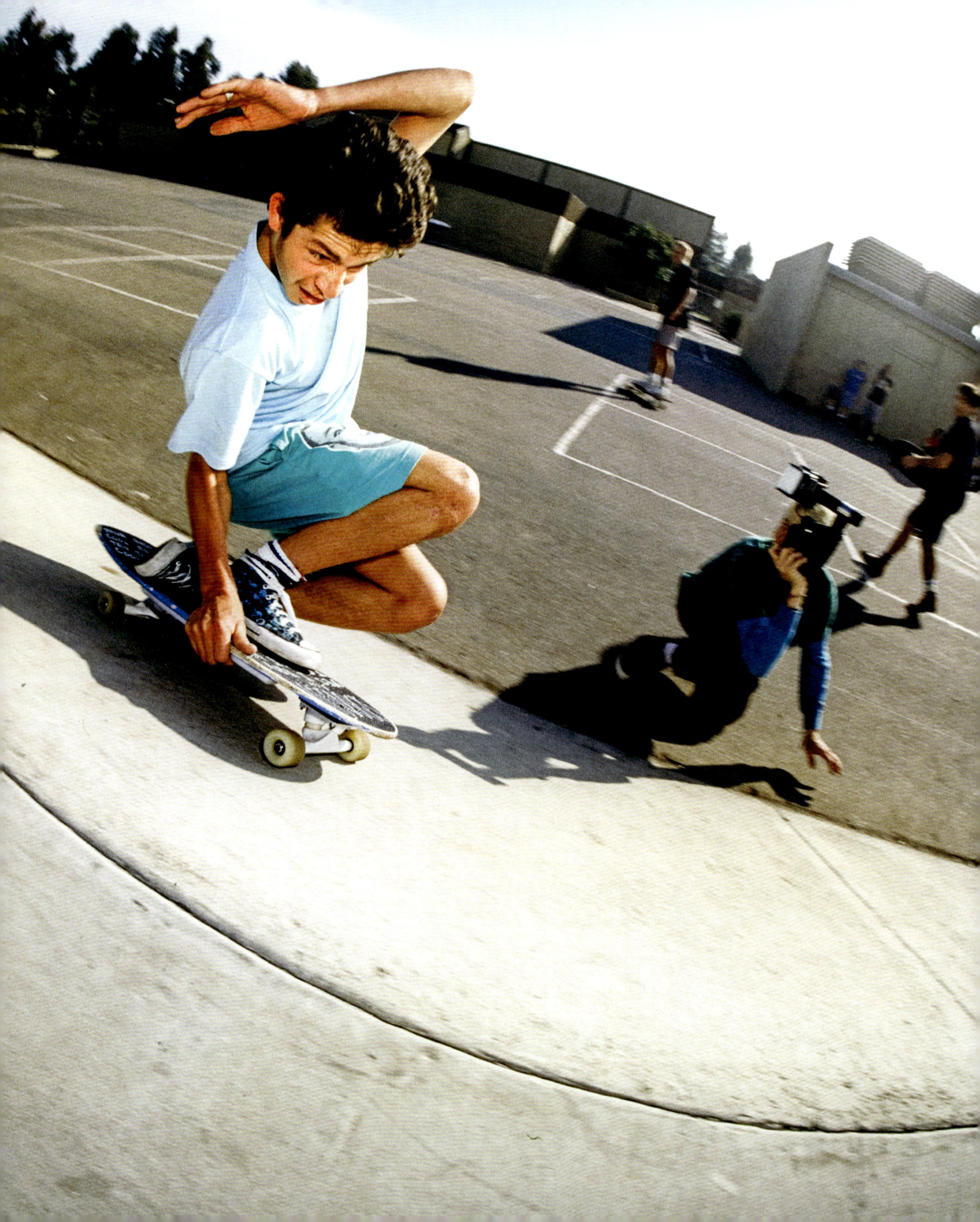

ark Gonzales, Rail grab, School W, San Diego, CA, 1987

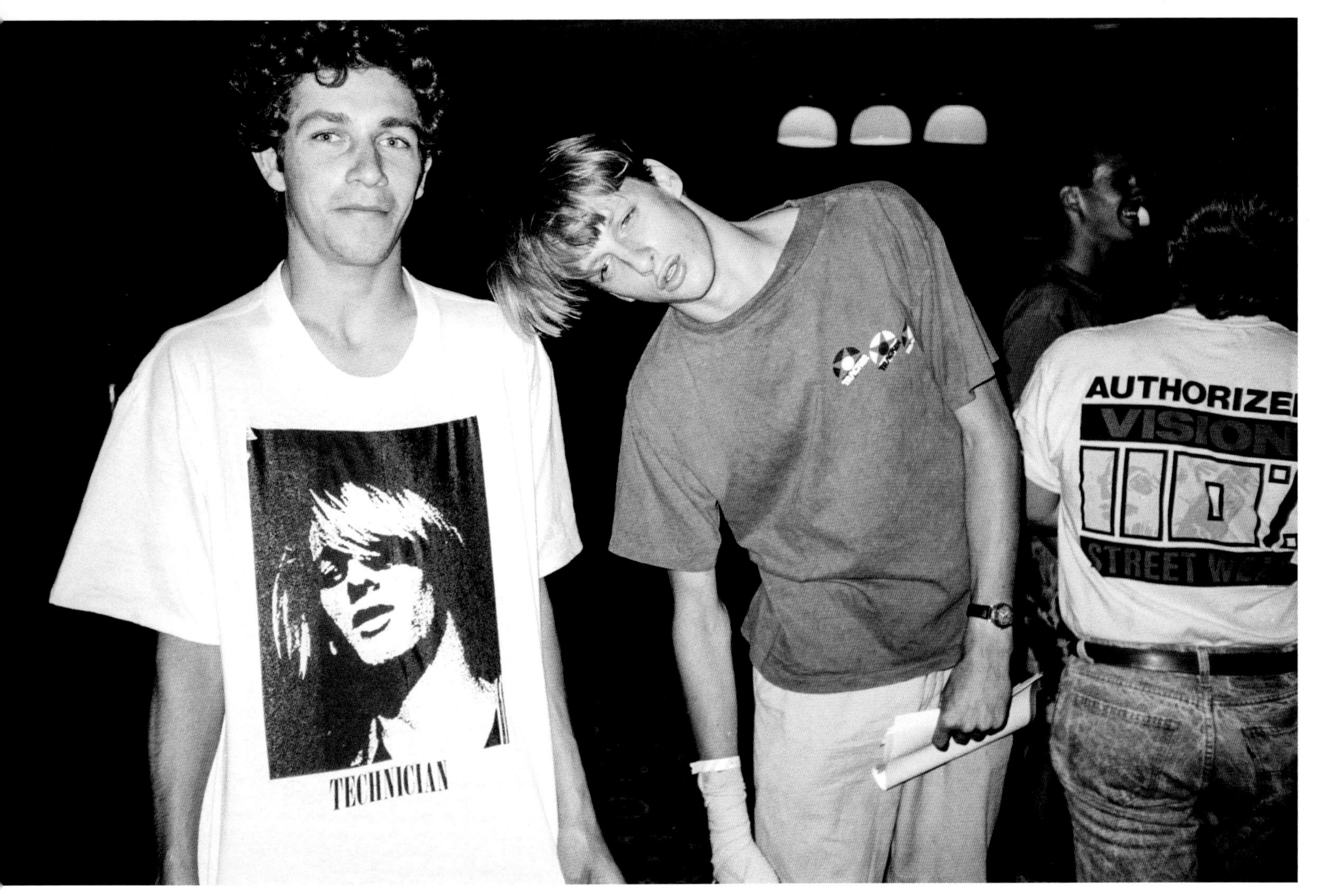

Mark Gonzales and Tony Hawk, Portrait, Anaheim, CA, 1988

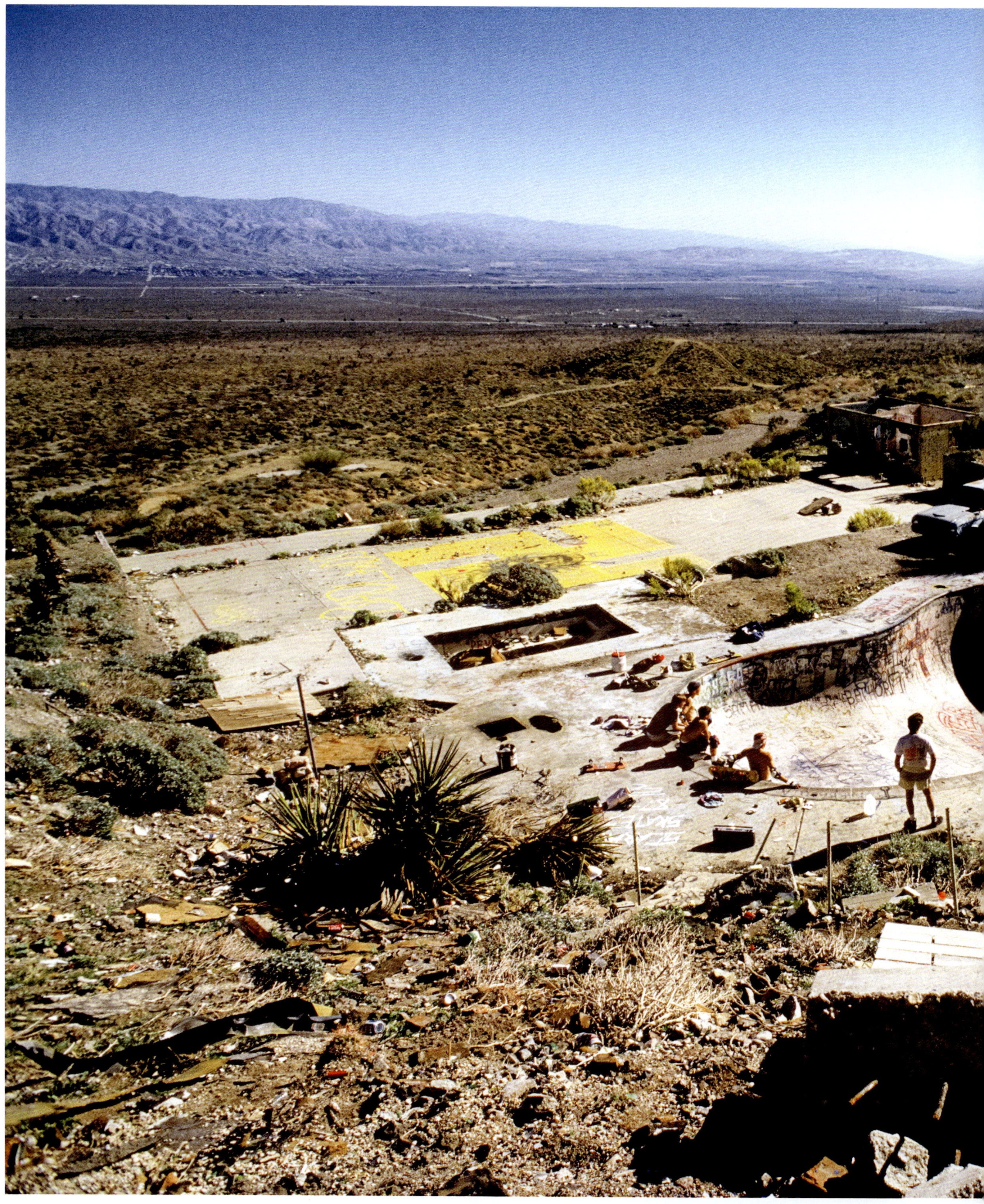

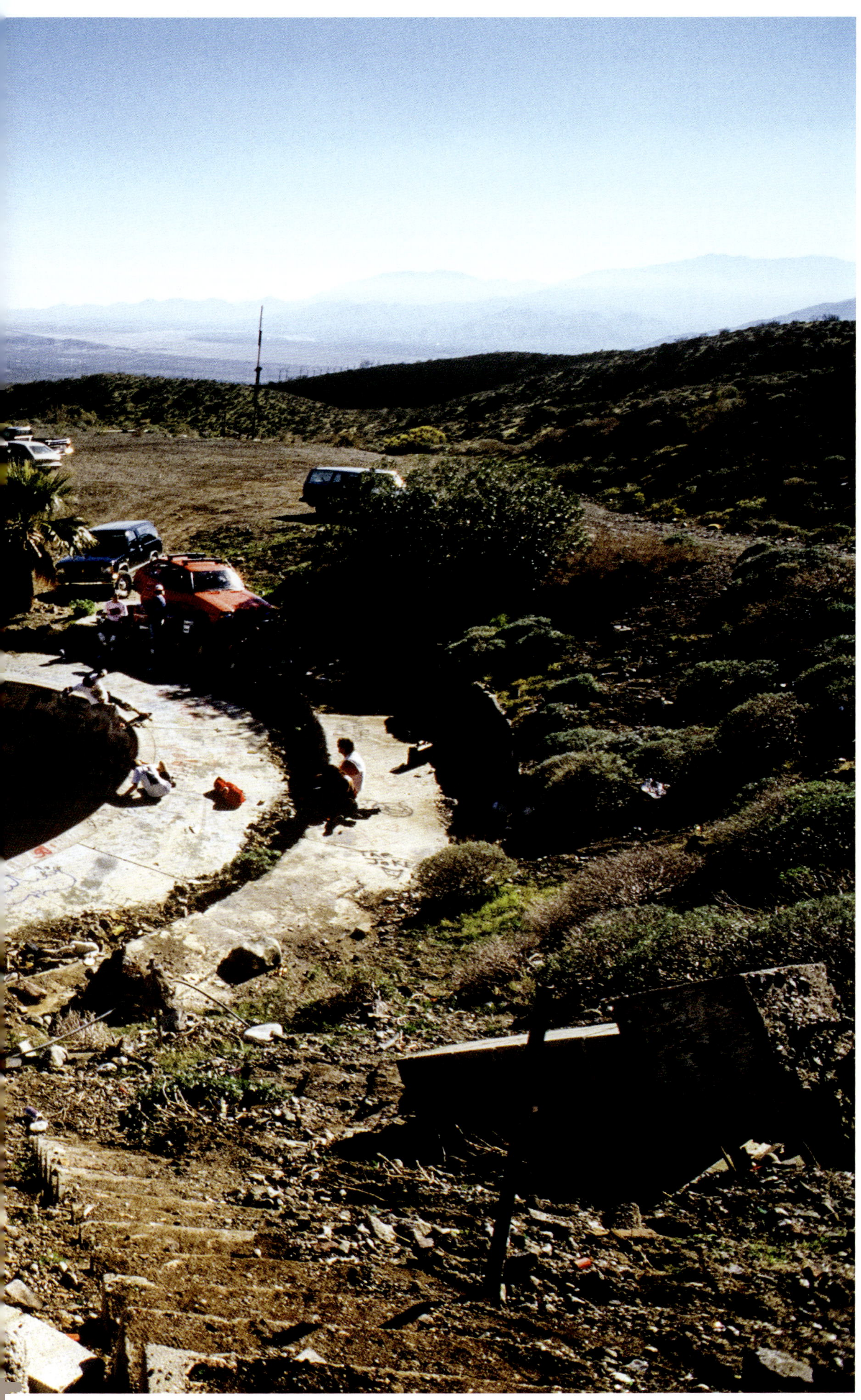

Steve Alba, Nude Bowl, Desert Hot Springs, CA, 1987

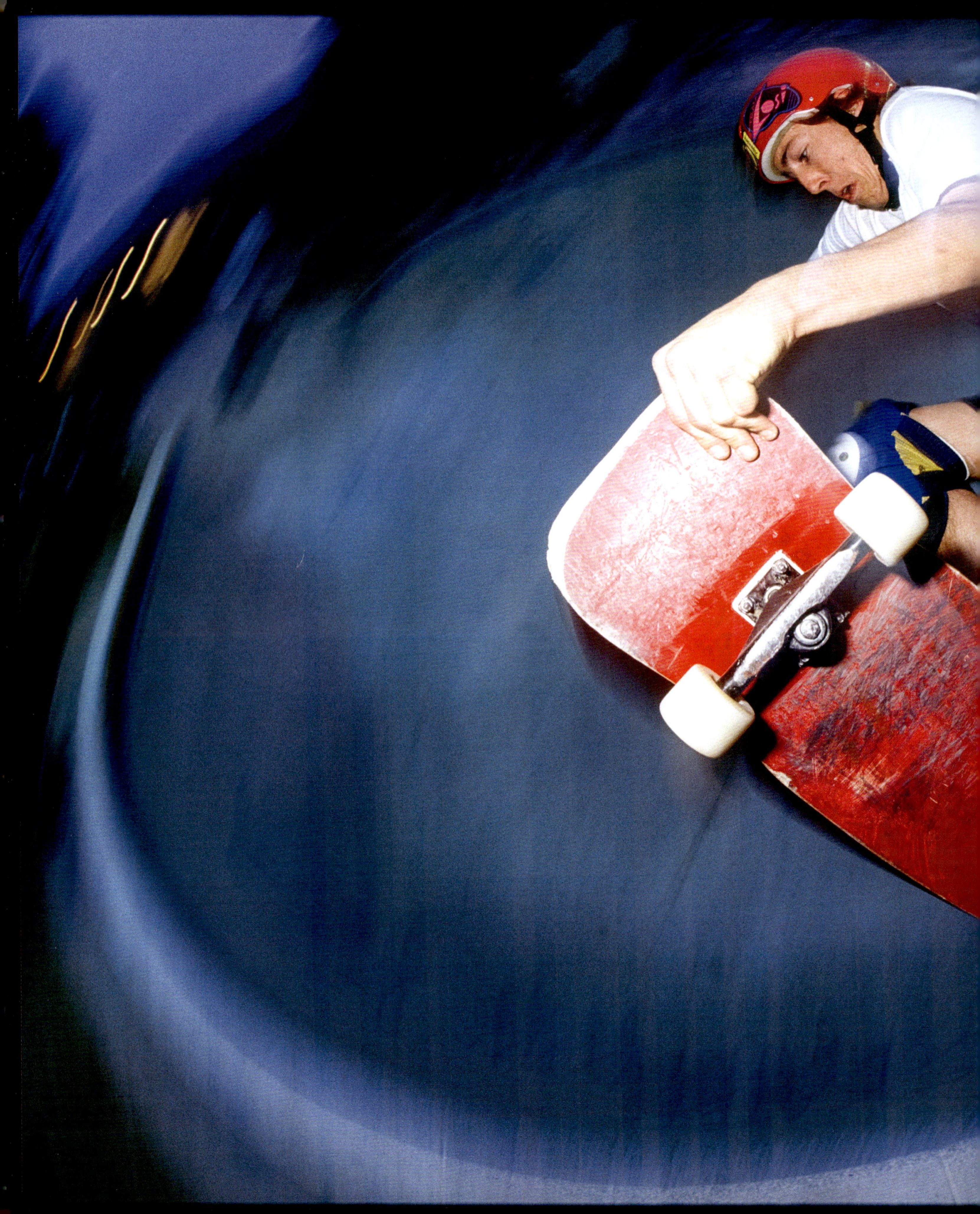

Reese Simpson, Fakie Thruster, Del Mar Skate Ranch, Del Mar, CA, 1987

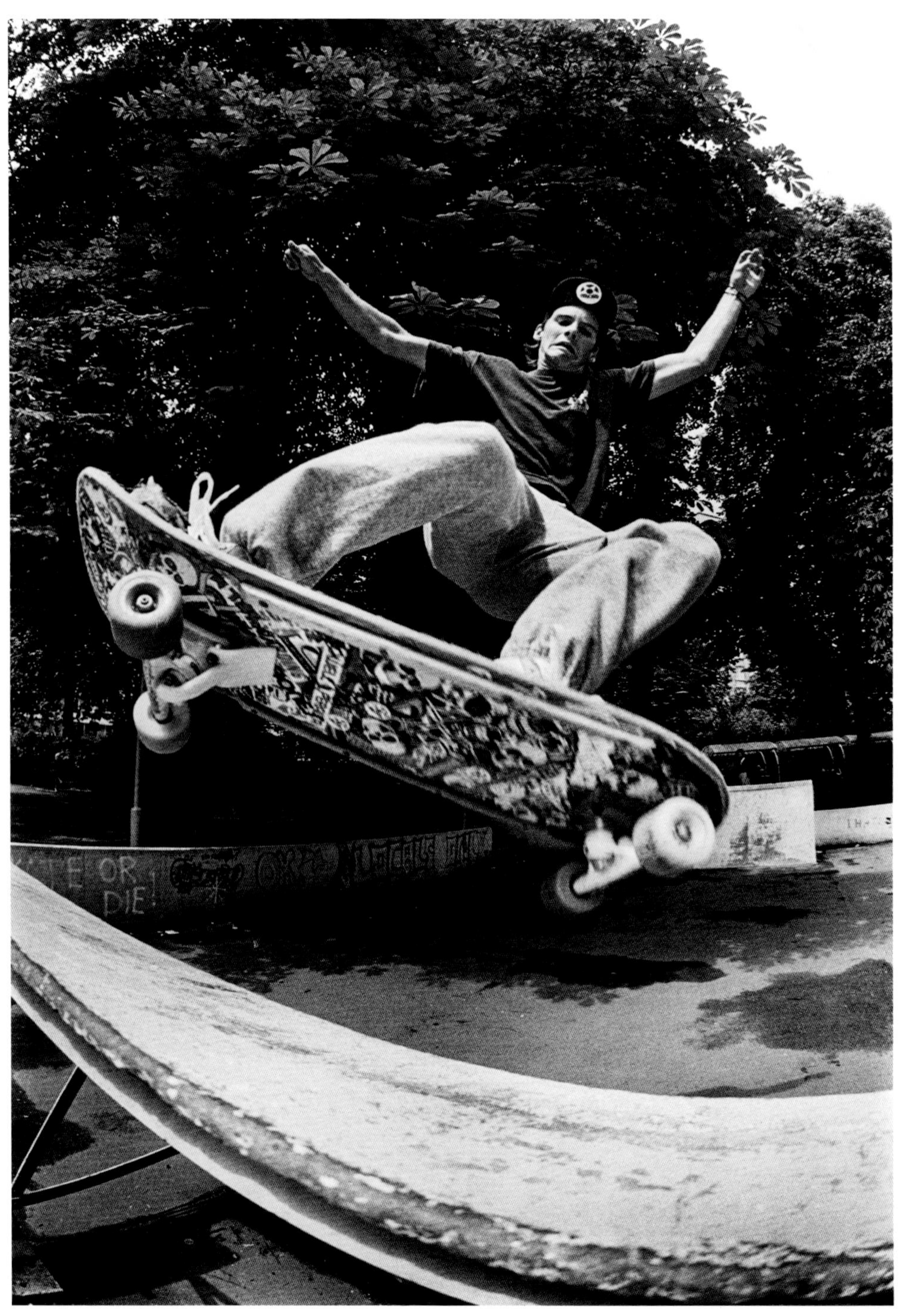

Kevin Staab, Ollie, Antwerp, Belgium, 1985

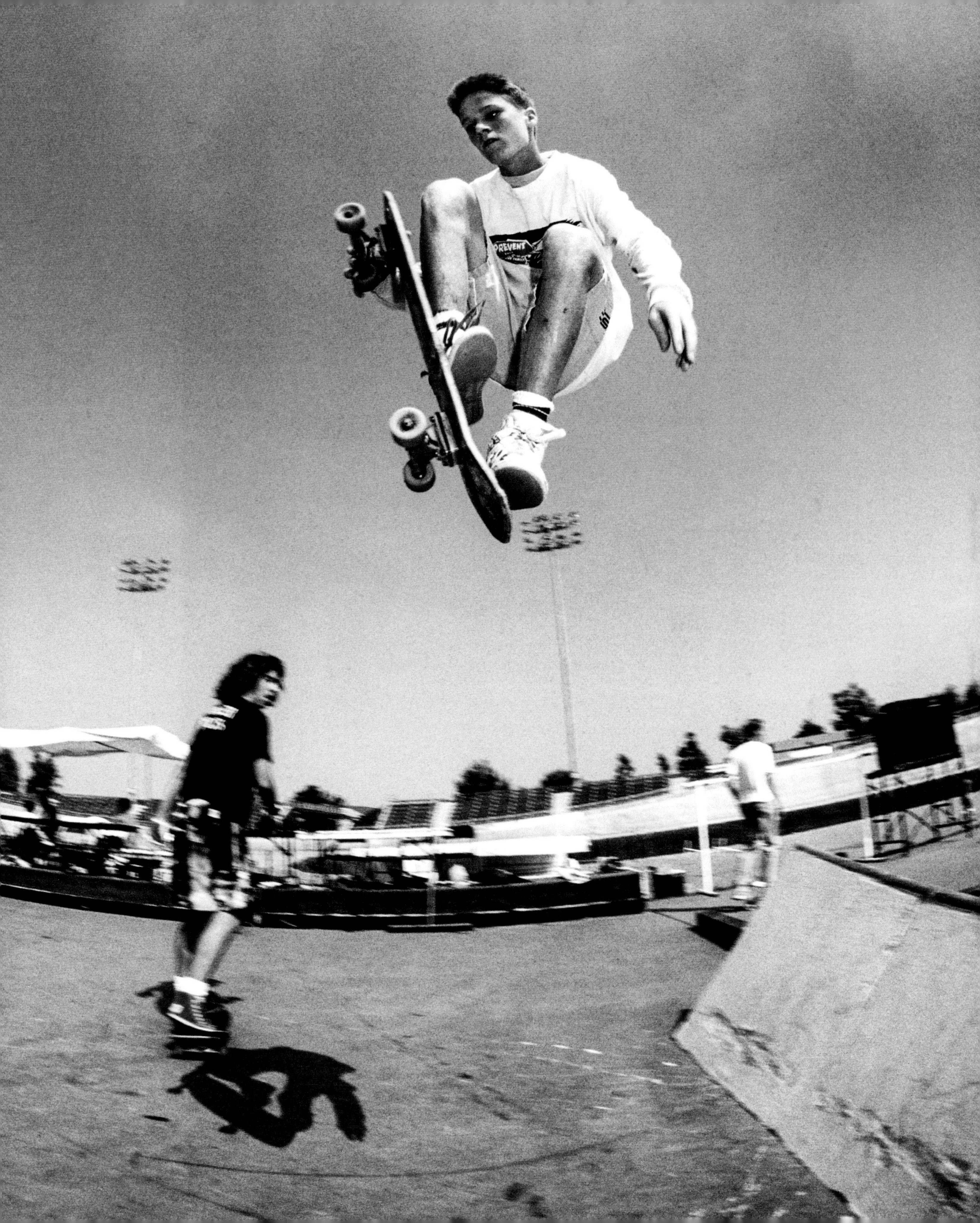
PREVENT

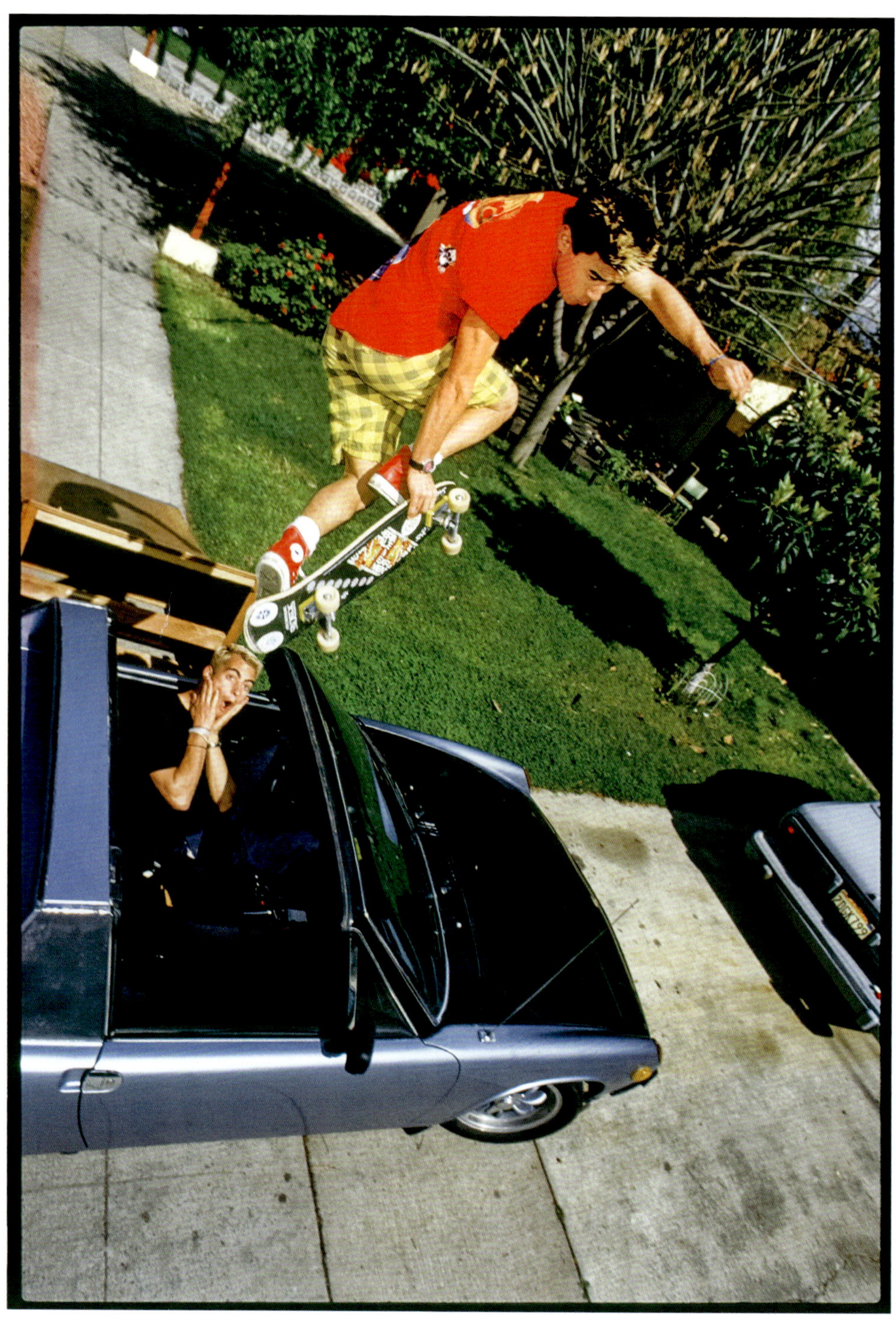

Steve Caballero, Air over his Porsche, San Jose, CA, 1987

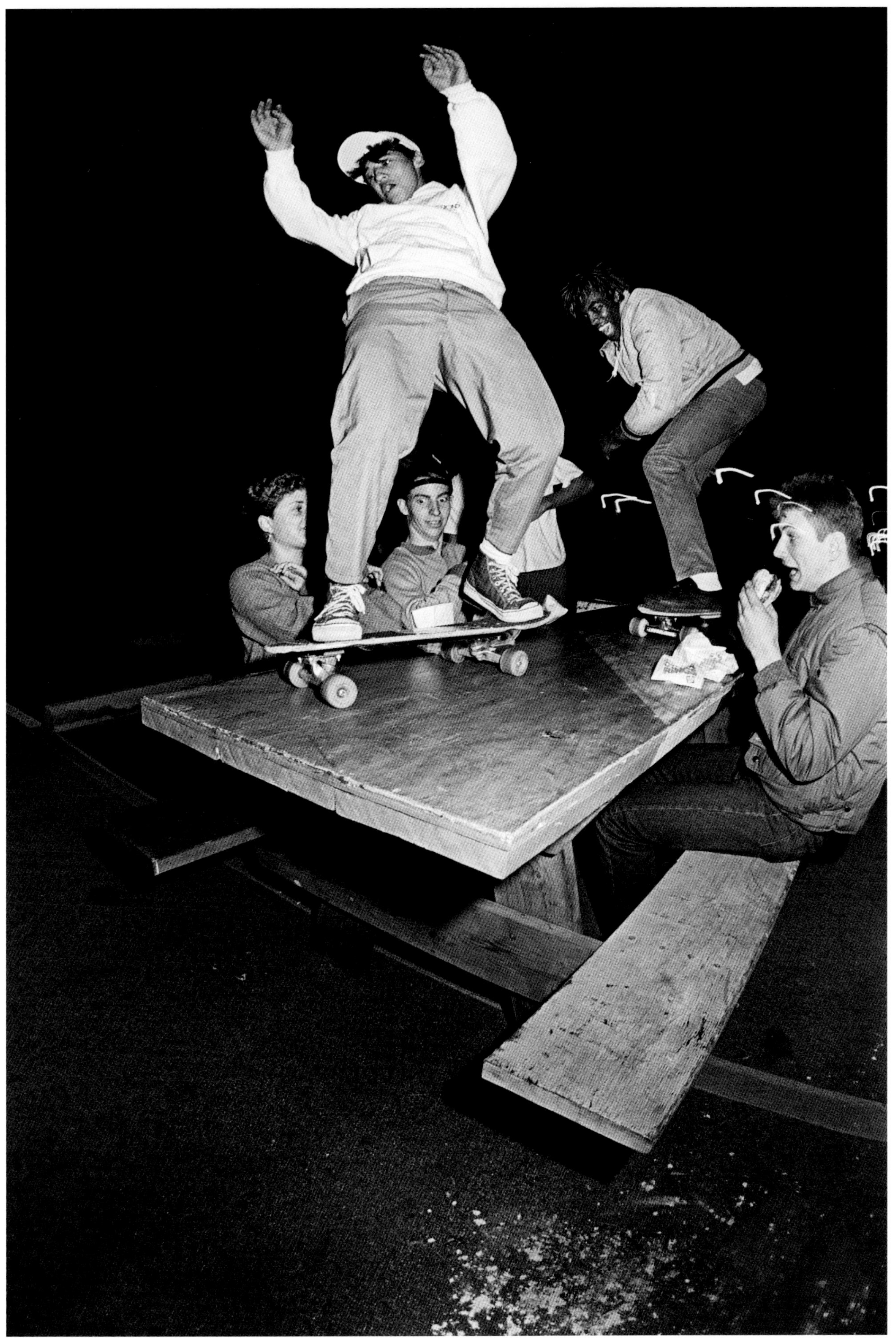

Steve Caballero and Steve Steadham, Barging, Huntington Beach, CA, 1984

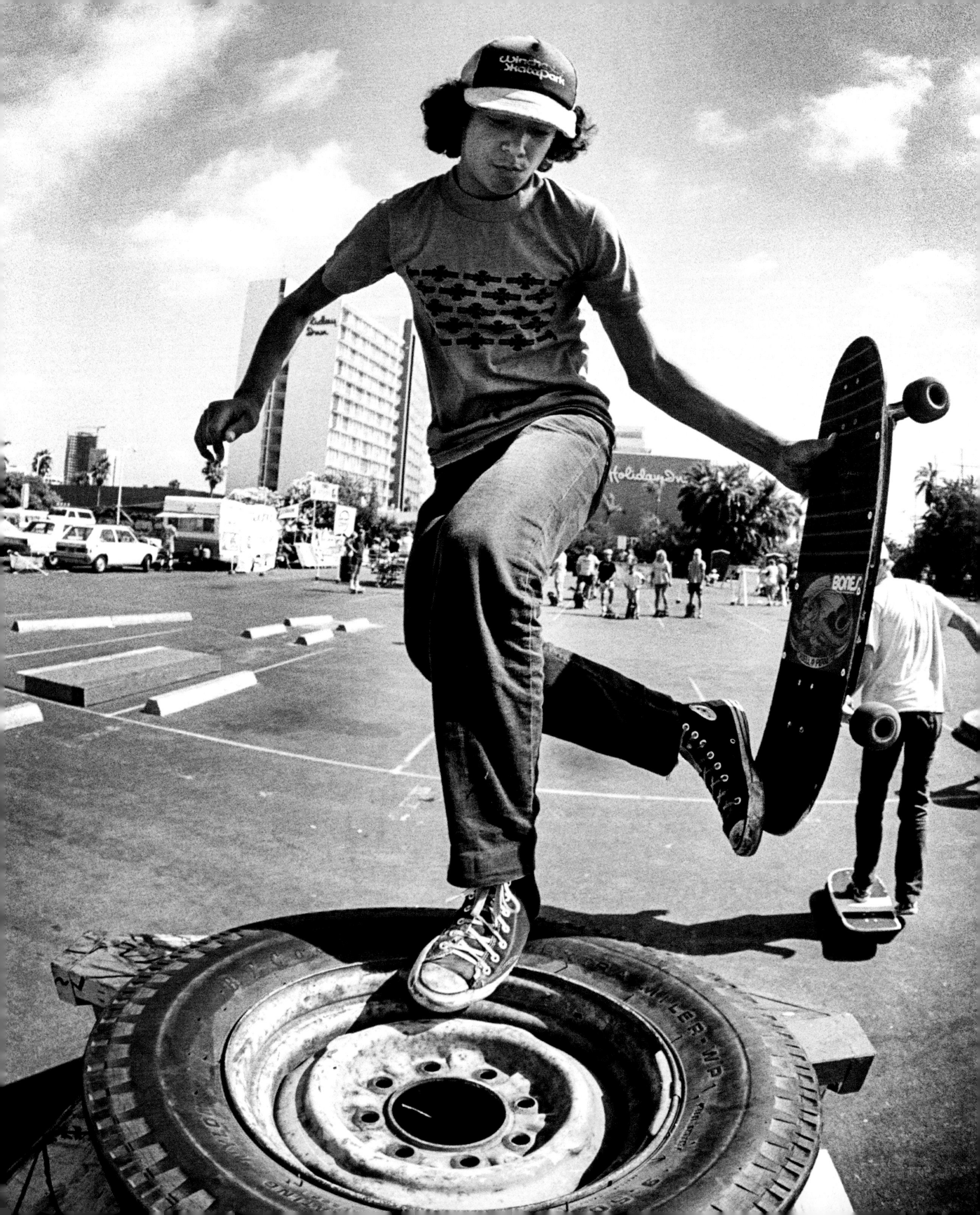
Skatepark
BONES

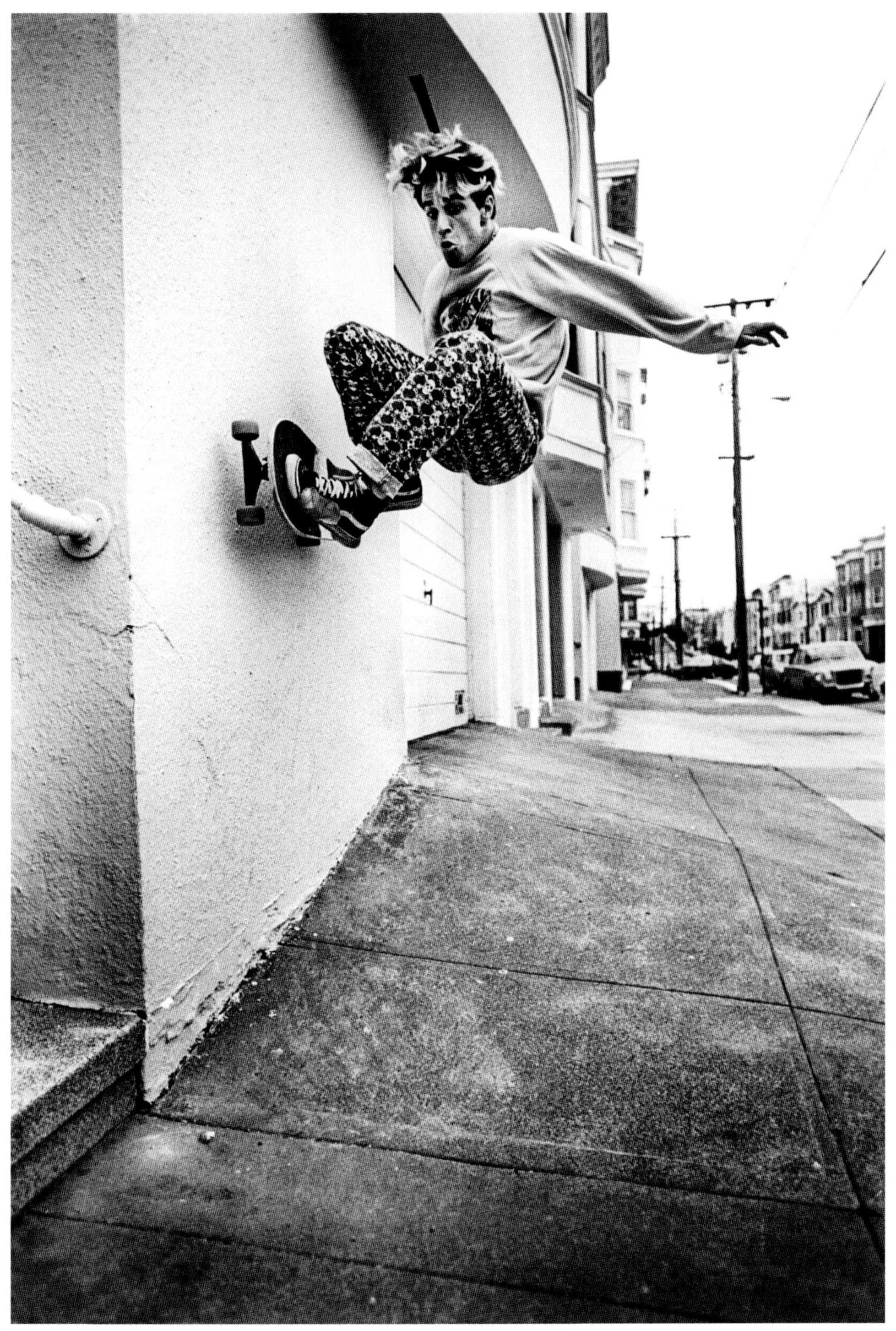

Jim Thiebaud, Wallride, San Francisco, CA, 1986

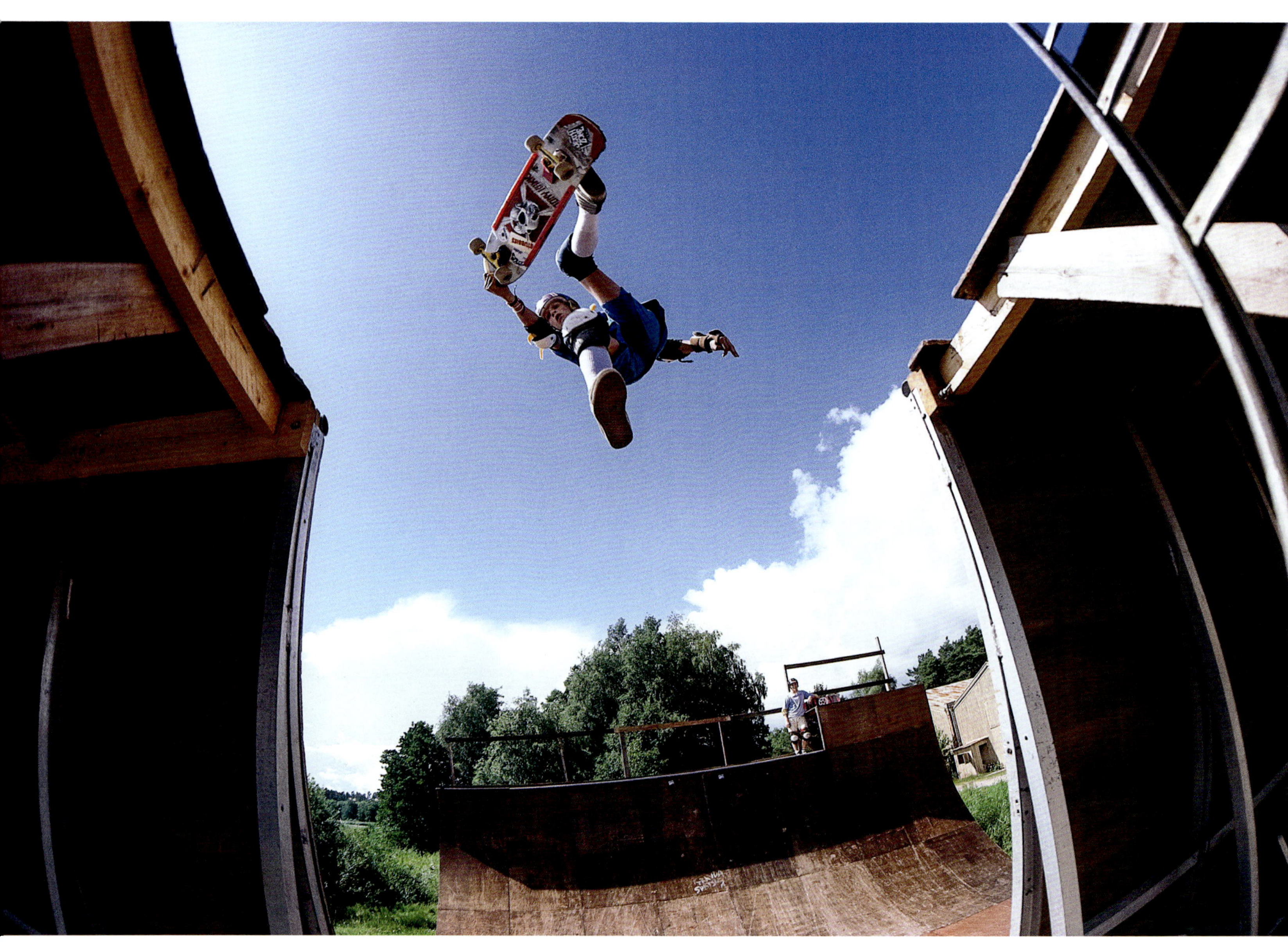

Tony Hawk, Madonna over the channel, Swedish Skateboard Summer Camp, Hägernäs, Sweden, 1985

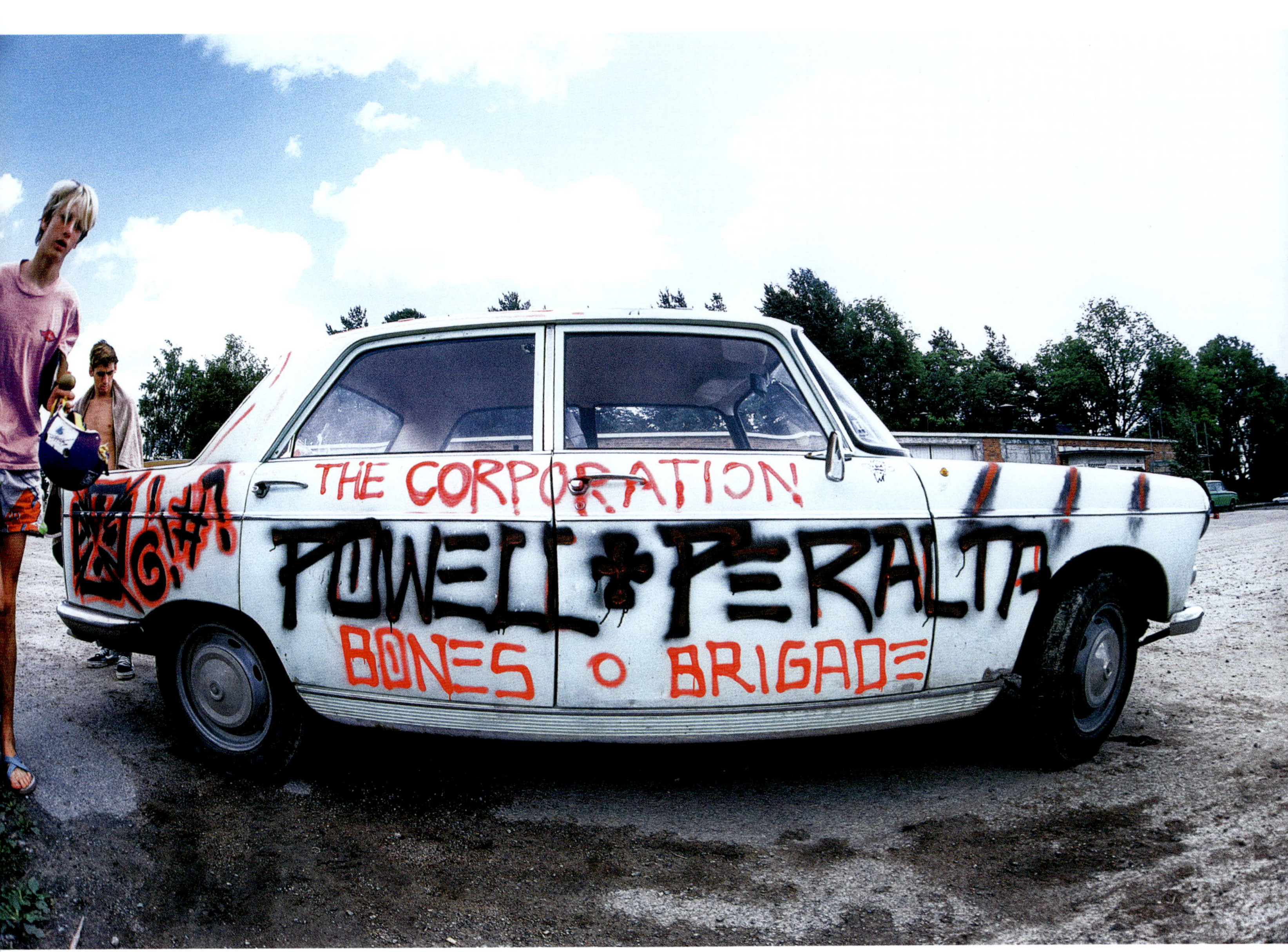

Tony Hawk and Lance Mountain's Peugeot, Swedish Skateboard Summer Camp, Hägernäs, Sweden, 1985

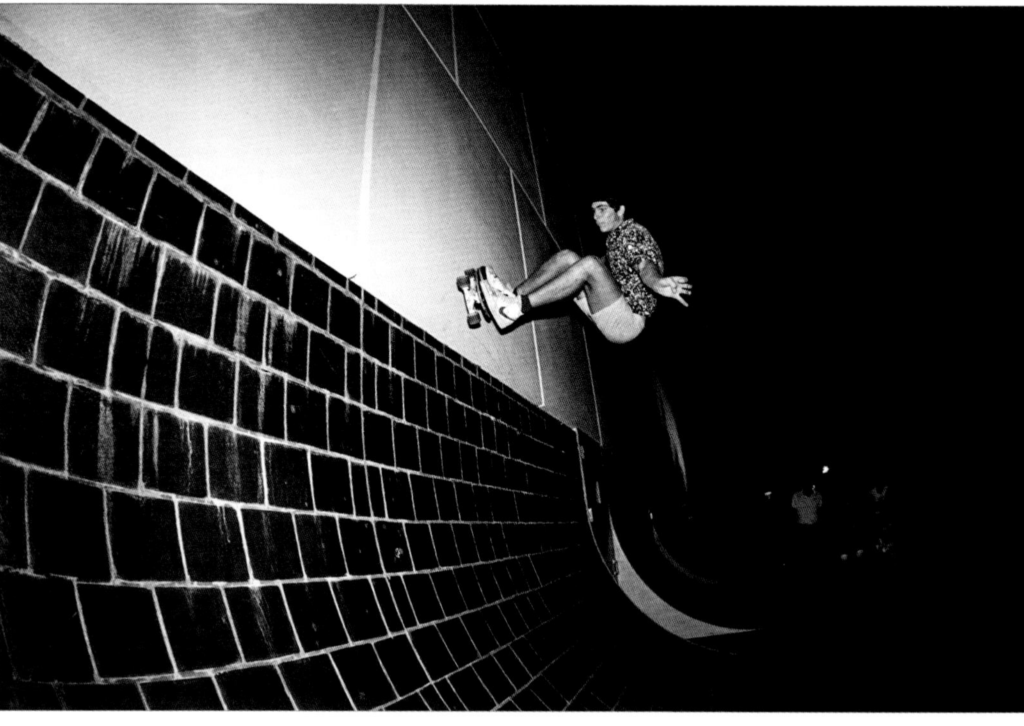

Neil Blender, Late night Burdines session, Orlando, FL, 1983

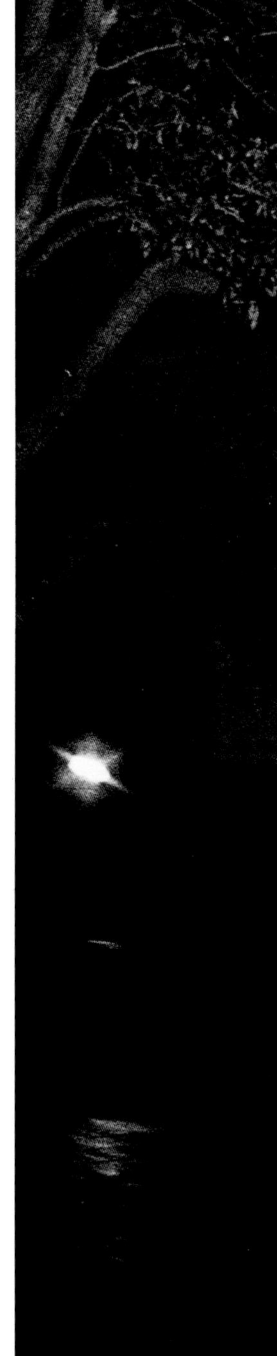

Billy Ruff, Carve over Neil Blender, Burdines, Orlando, FL, 1983

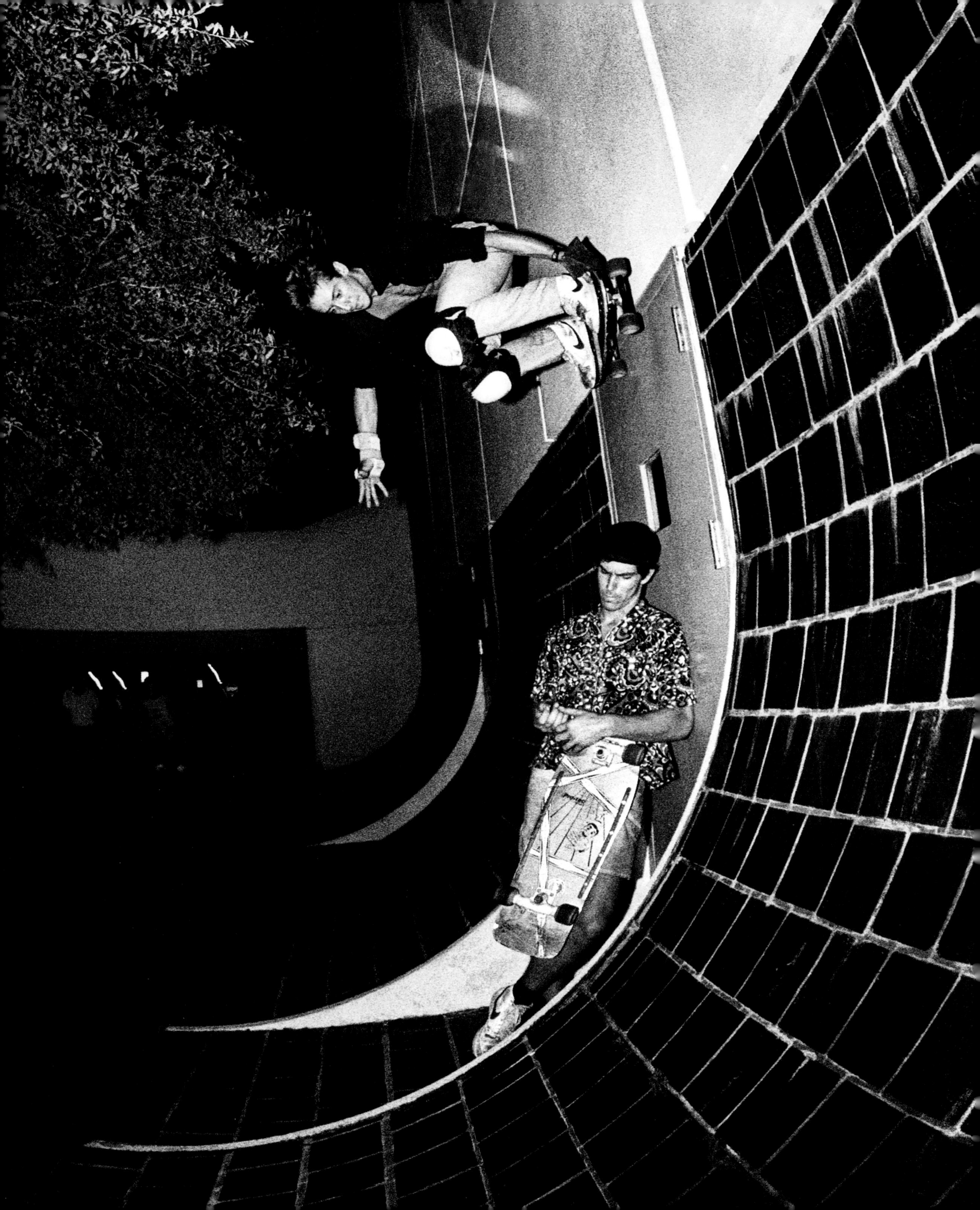

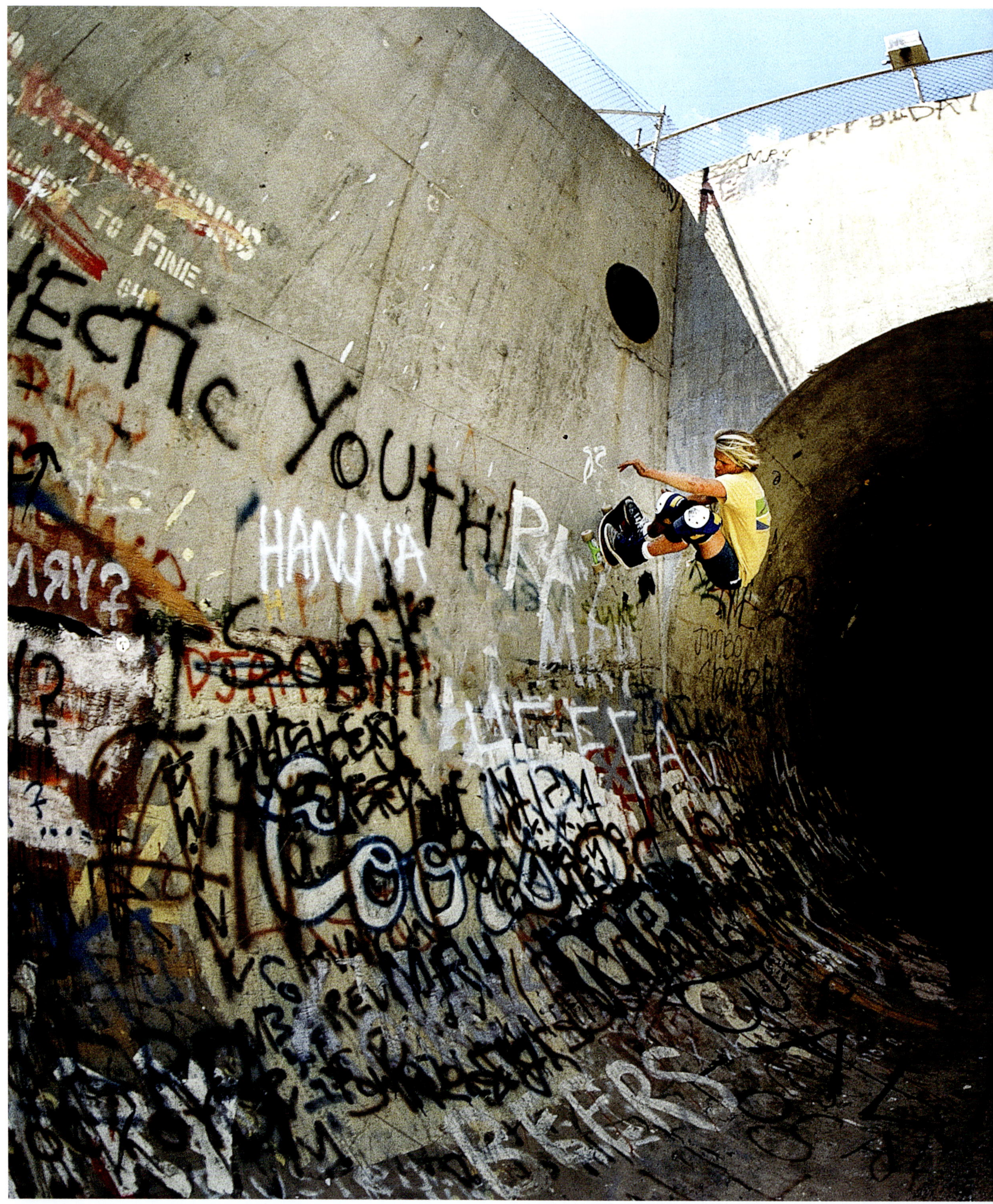
TO FINE
ECTIC YOUTH
HANNA

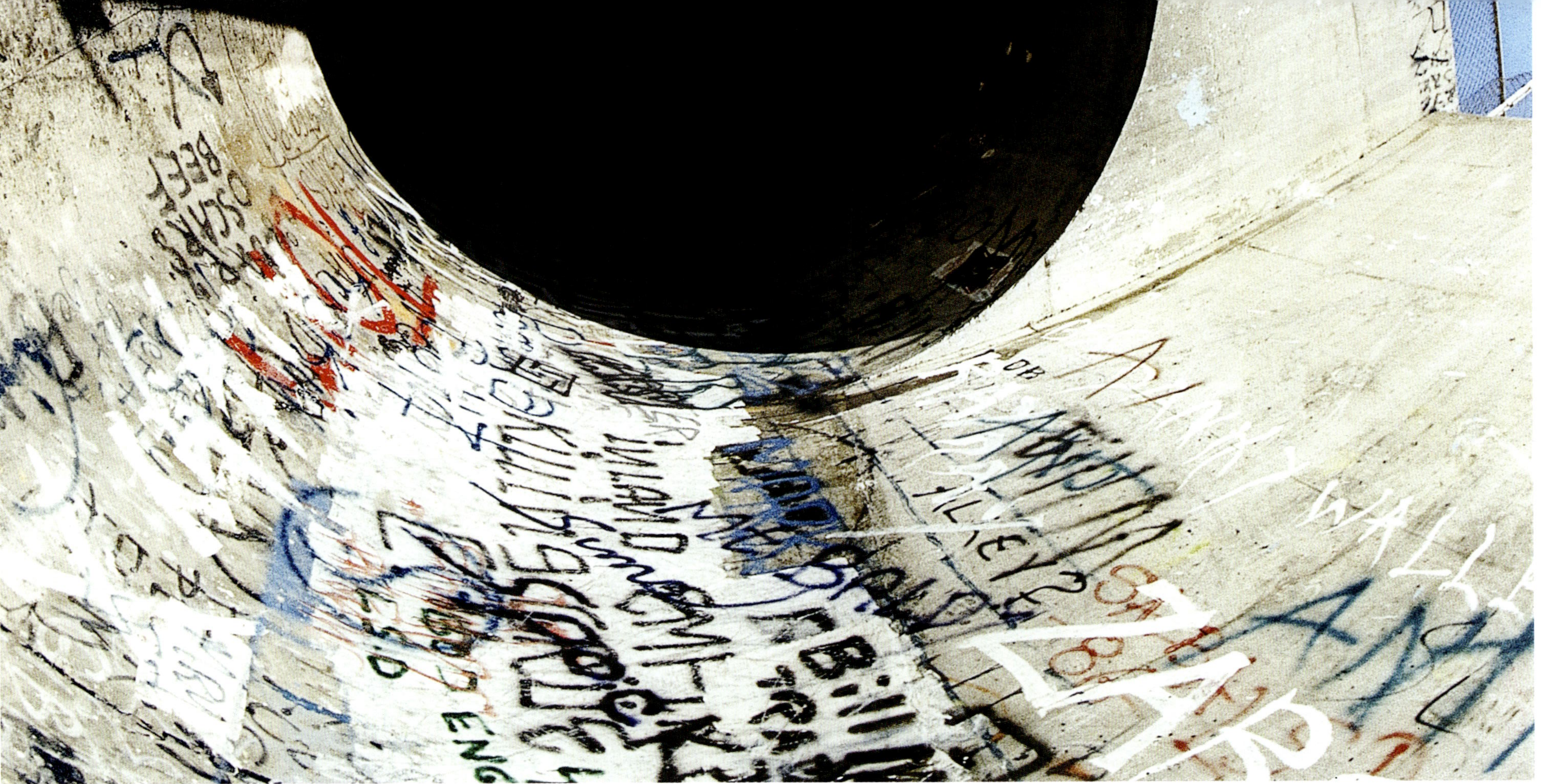

Chris Miller, Baldy Pipe, Upland, CA, 1987

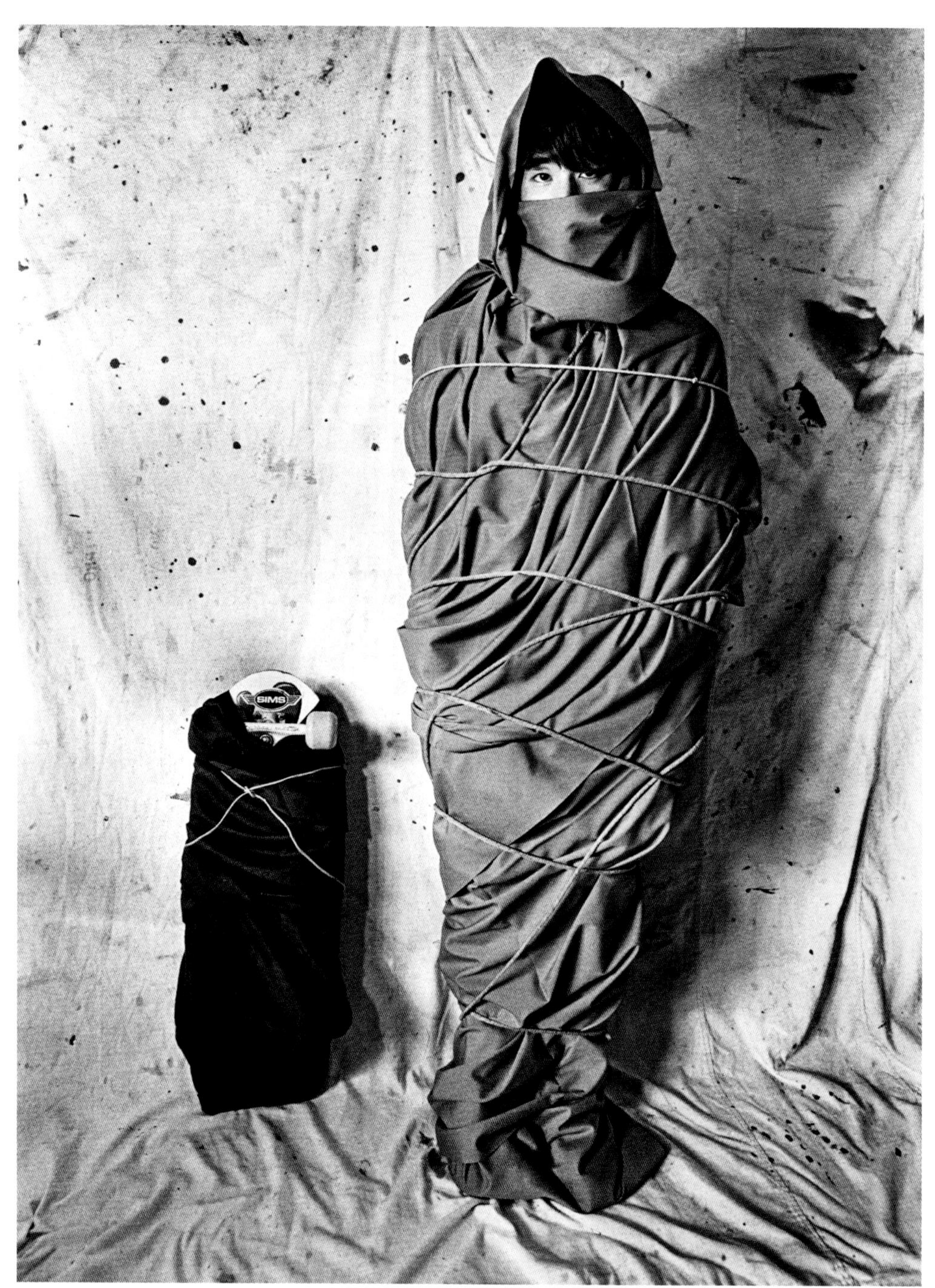

Lester Kasai, Homage to Christo, Leucadia, CA, 1985

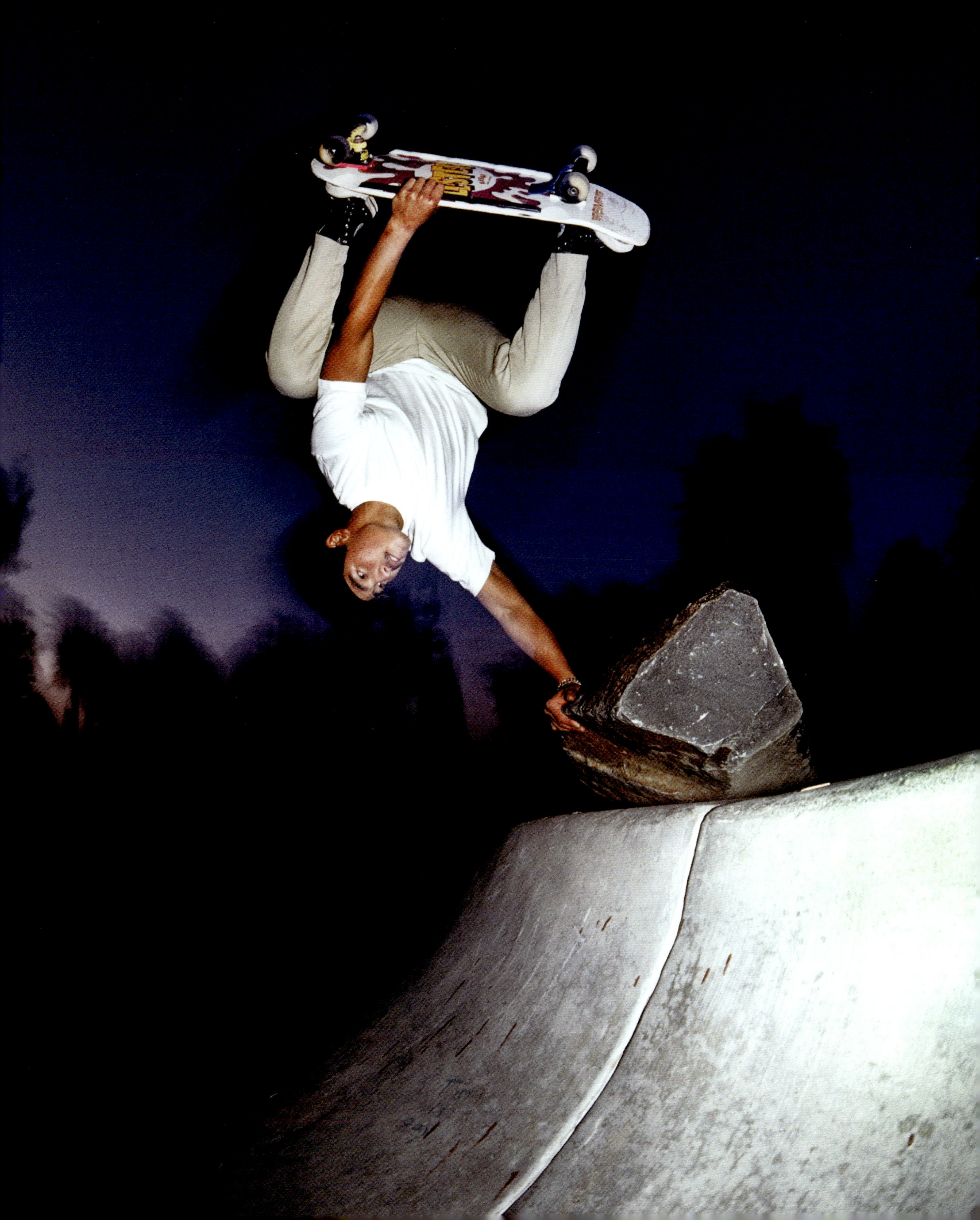

Steve Caballero, Backside air, Caballero's Ramp, San Jose, CA, 1986

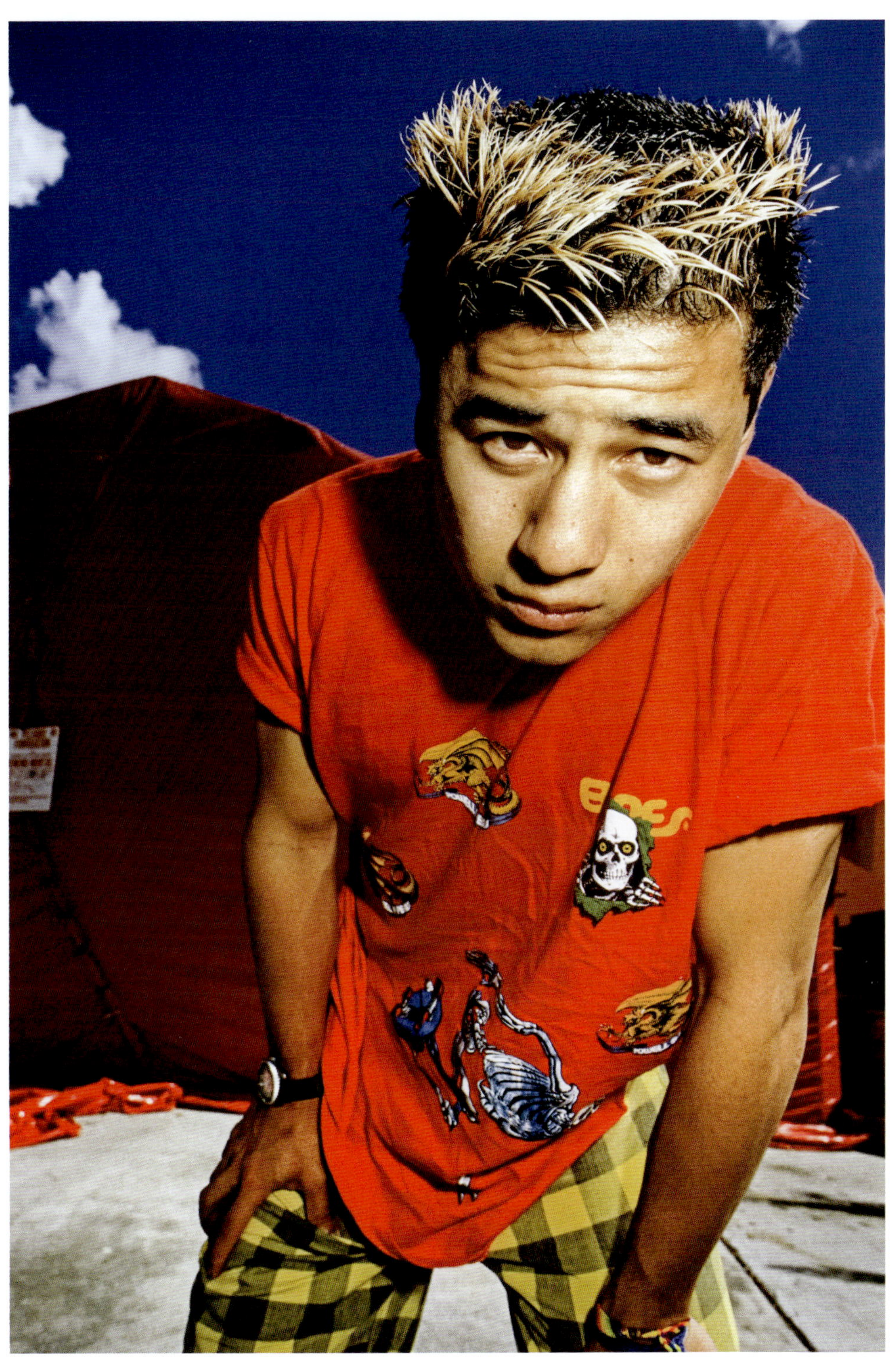

Steve Caballero, Portrait, San Jose, CA, 1987

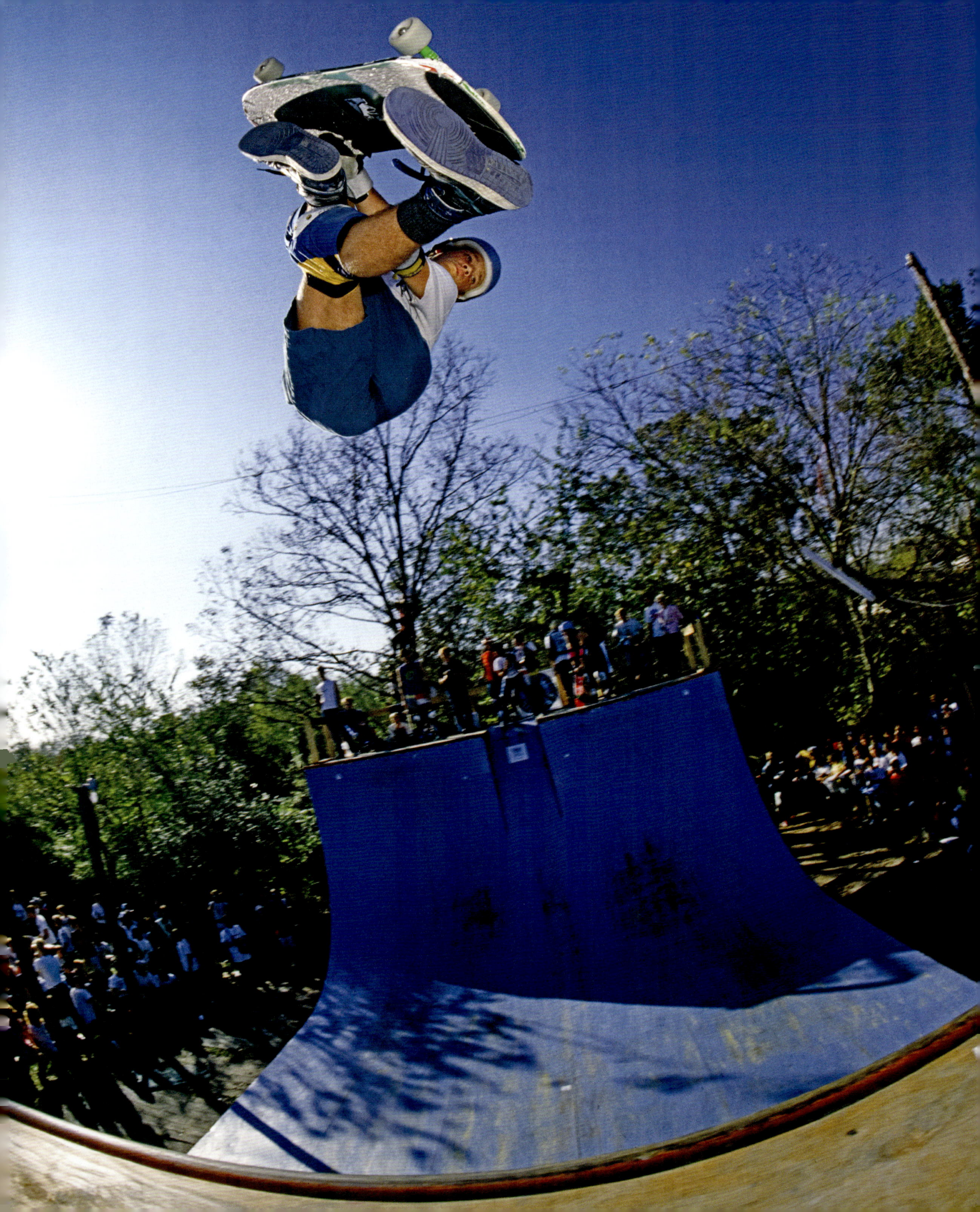

hris Miller, Crossbone lien air, Skatepark of Houston, Houston, TX, 1986

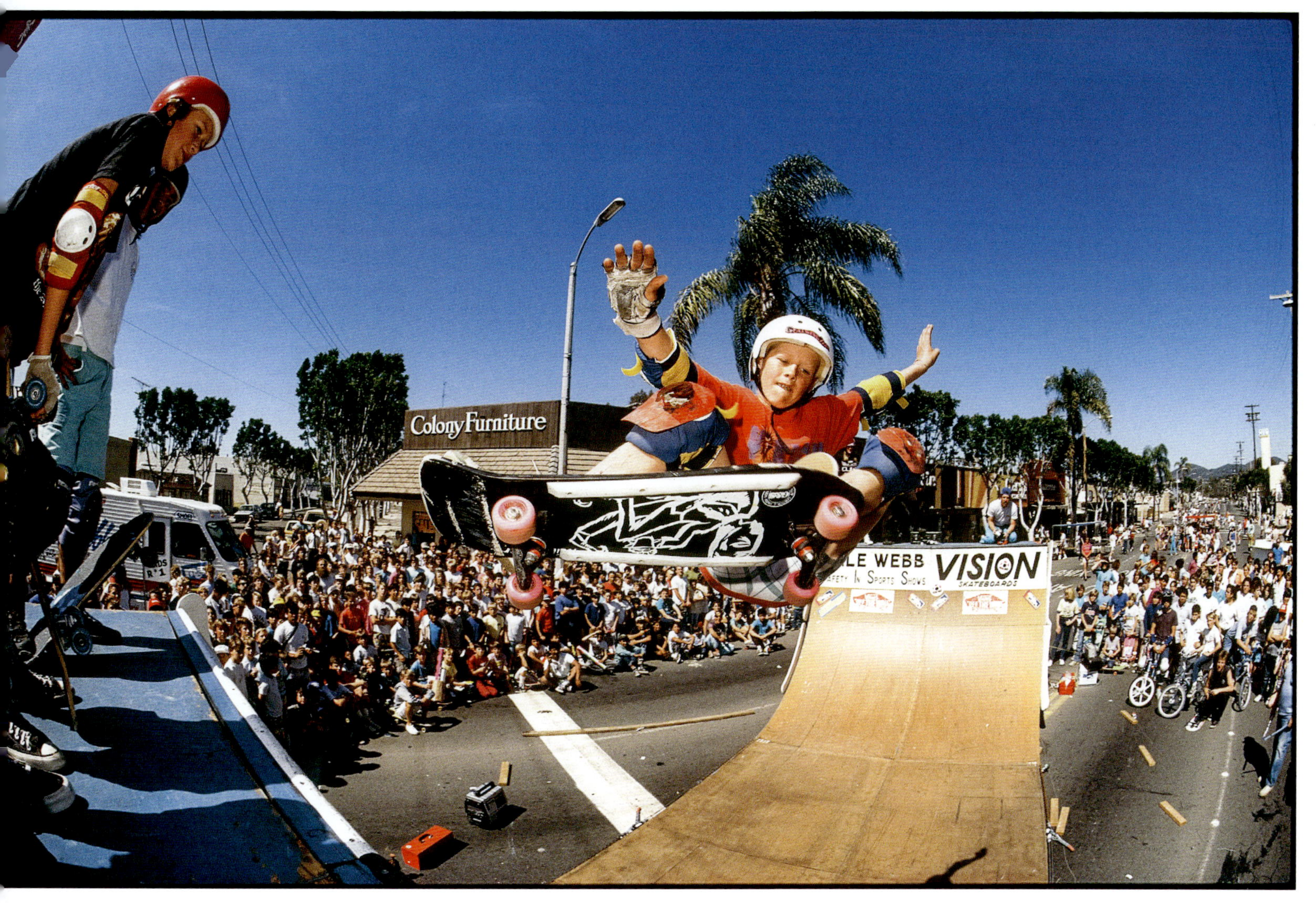

Danny Way, Frontside ollie at Gail Webb demo, Vista, CA, 1987

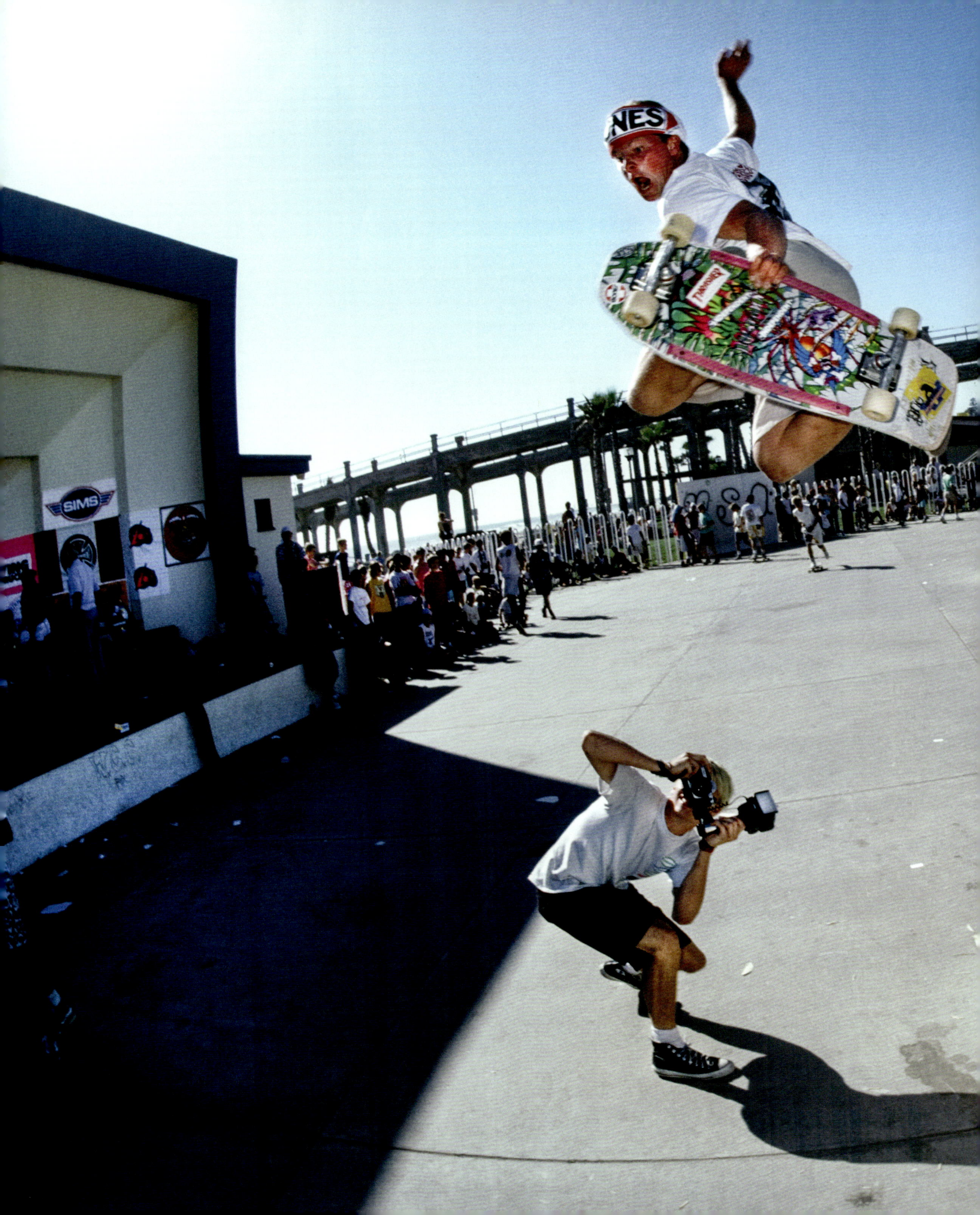
NES
SIMS

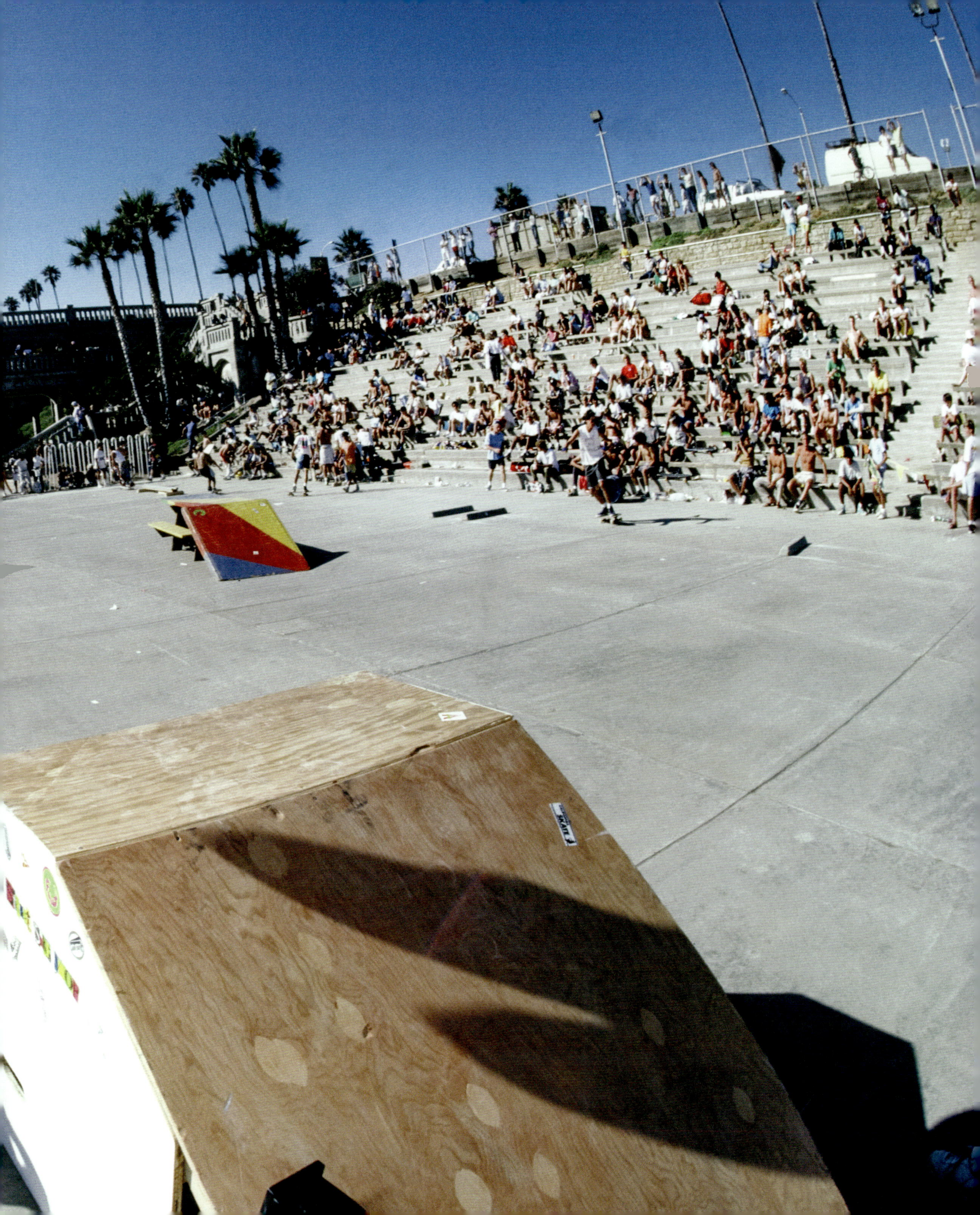

Previous spread: Eric Dressen, Contest jump ramp launch, Oceanside, CA, 1986

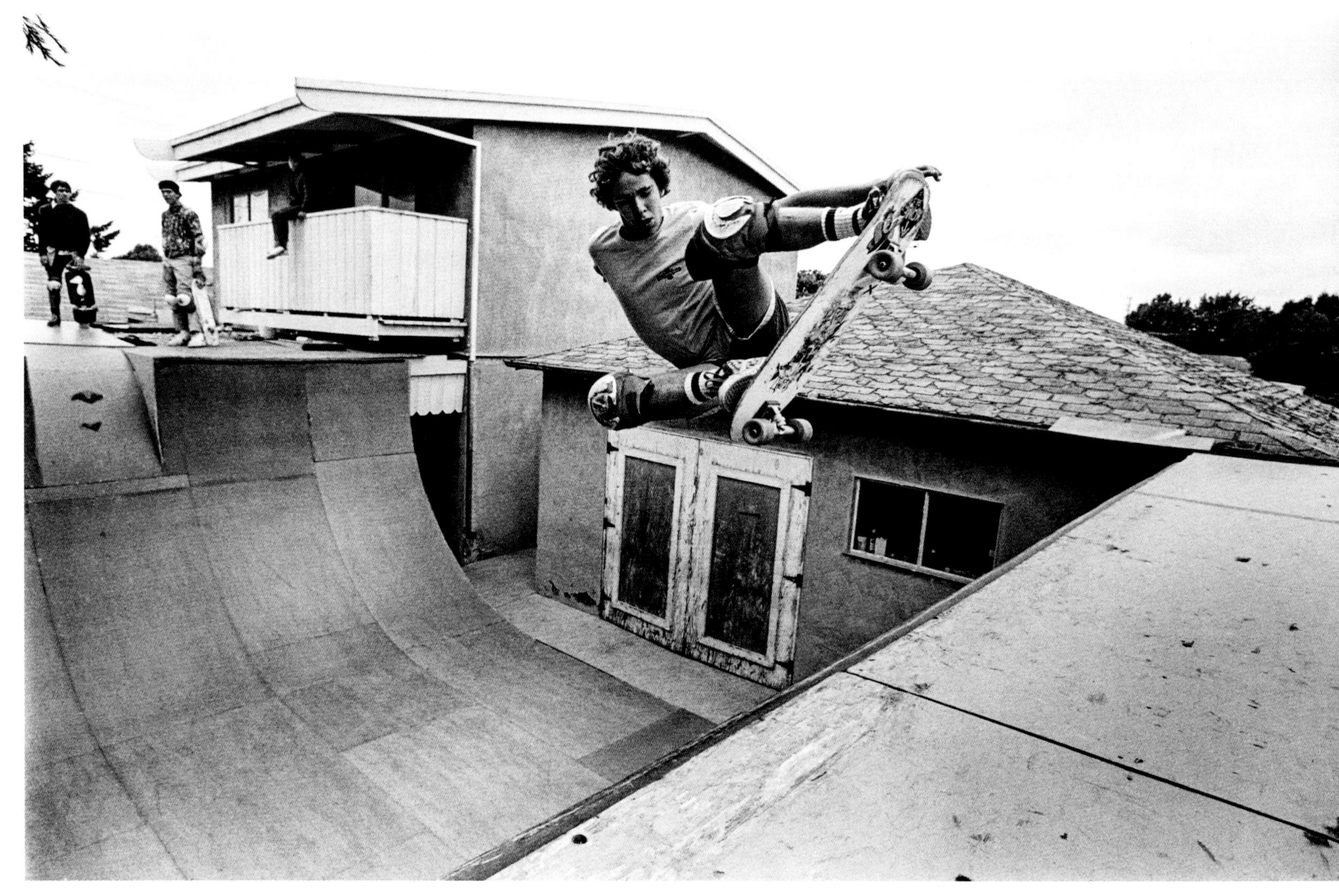

Joe Lopes, Ollie, Lopes' Ramp, San Leandro, CA, 1983

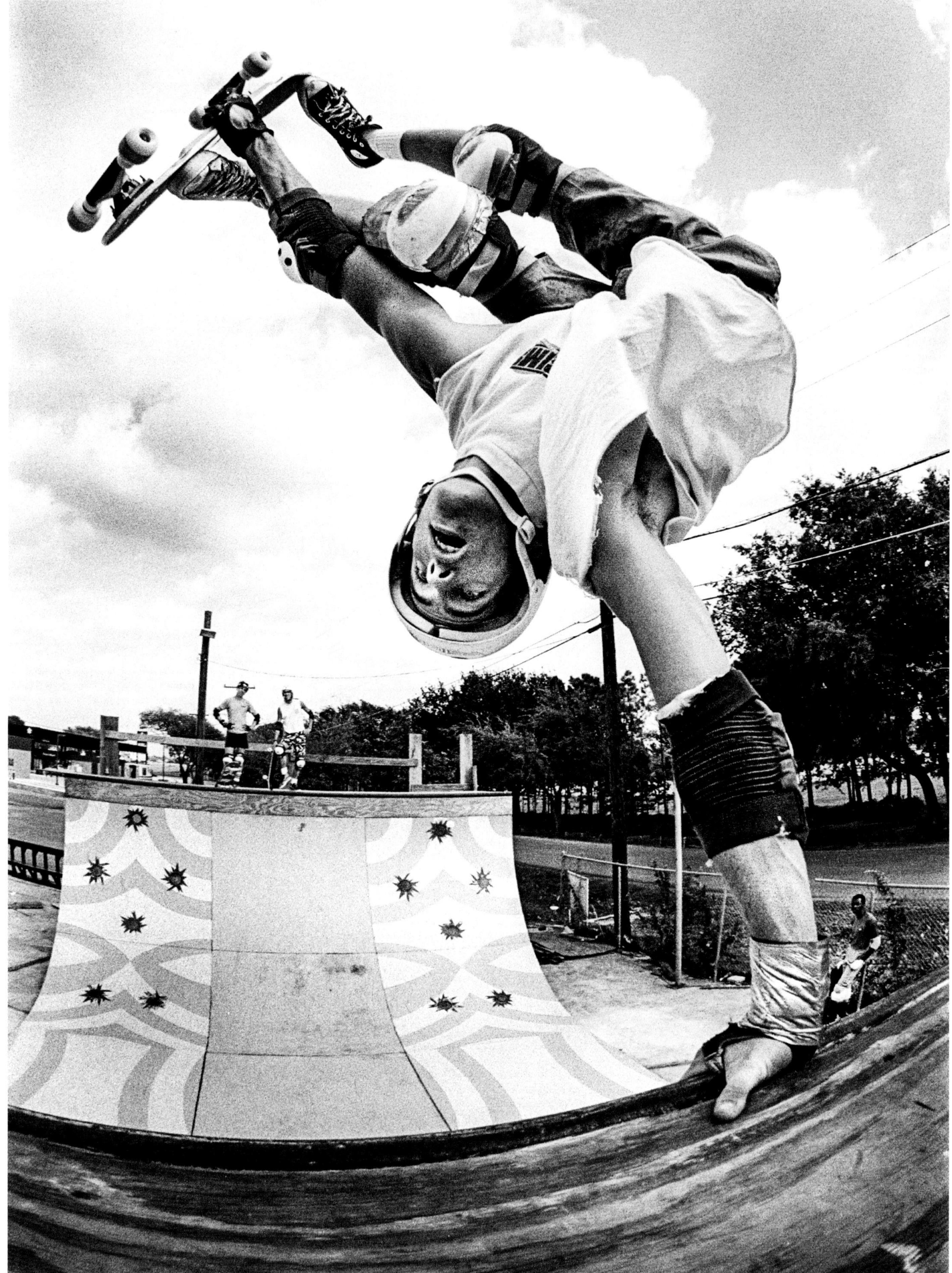

John Grigley, Contorted handplant, Clown Ramp, Dallas, TX, 1984

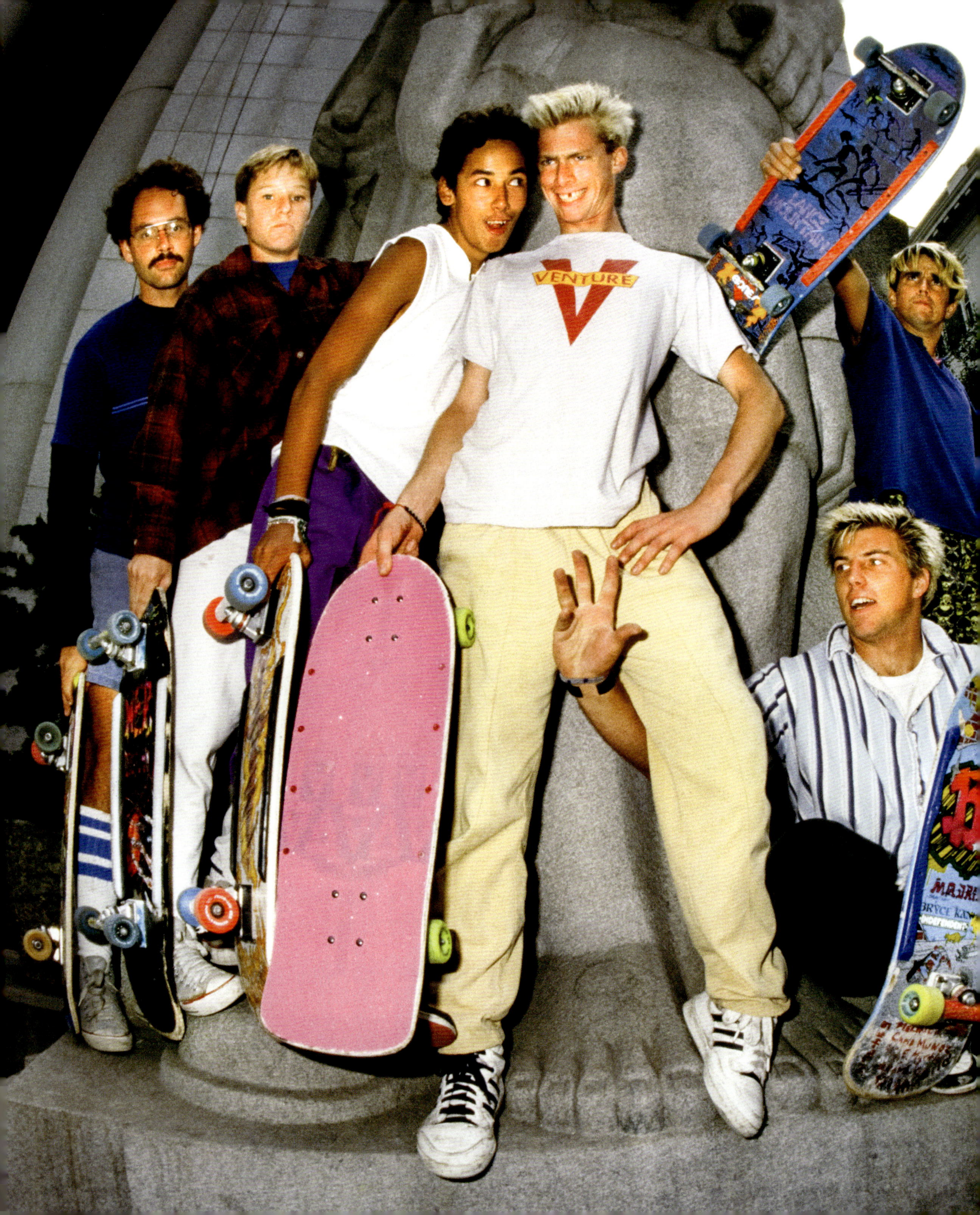
VENTURE

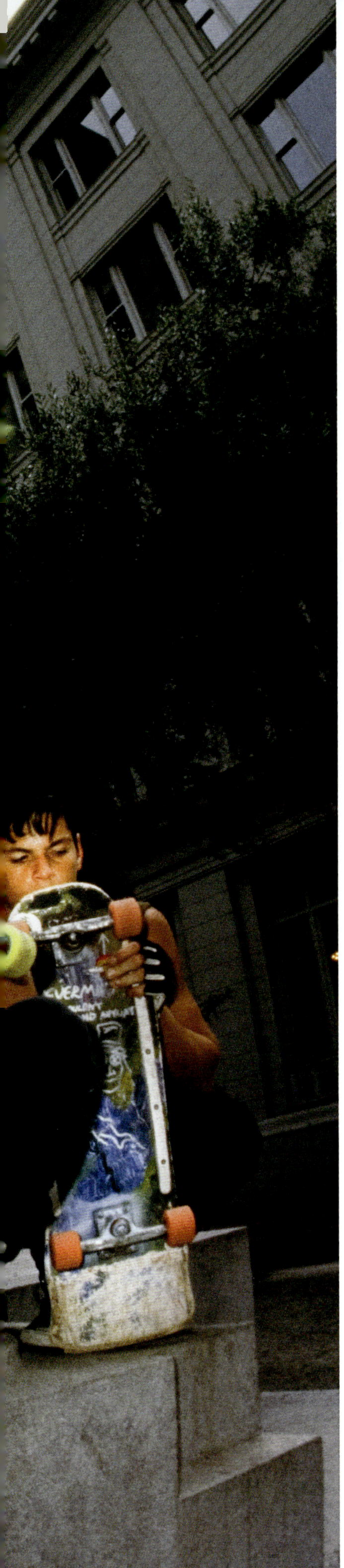

Ray Meyer, Julien Stranger, Tommy Guerrero, Orb, Bryce Kanights, Jim Thiebaud, and Jeff Whitehead, San Francisco, CA, 1986

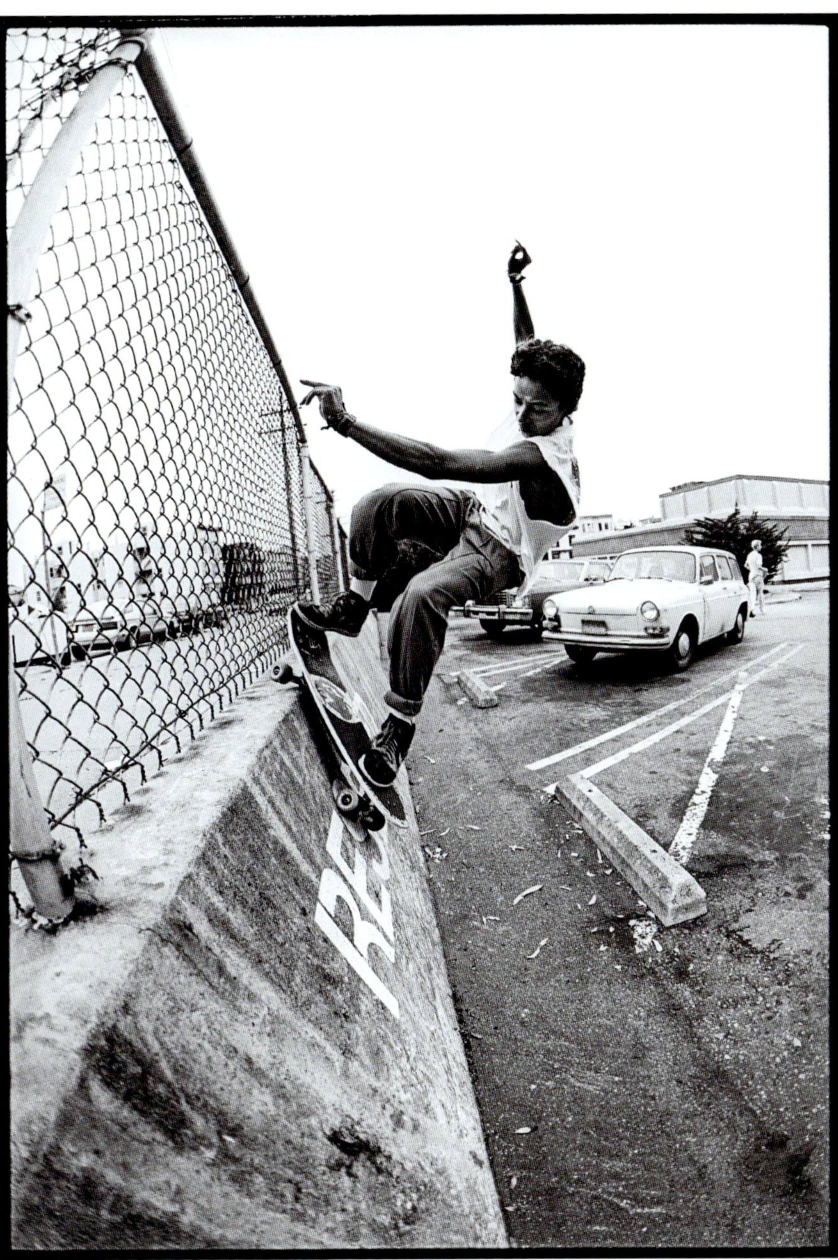

Tommy Guerrero, Whale wall, San Francisco, CA, 1986

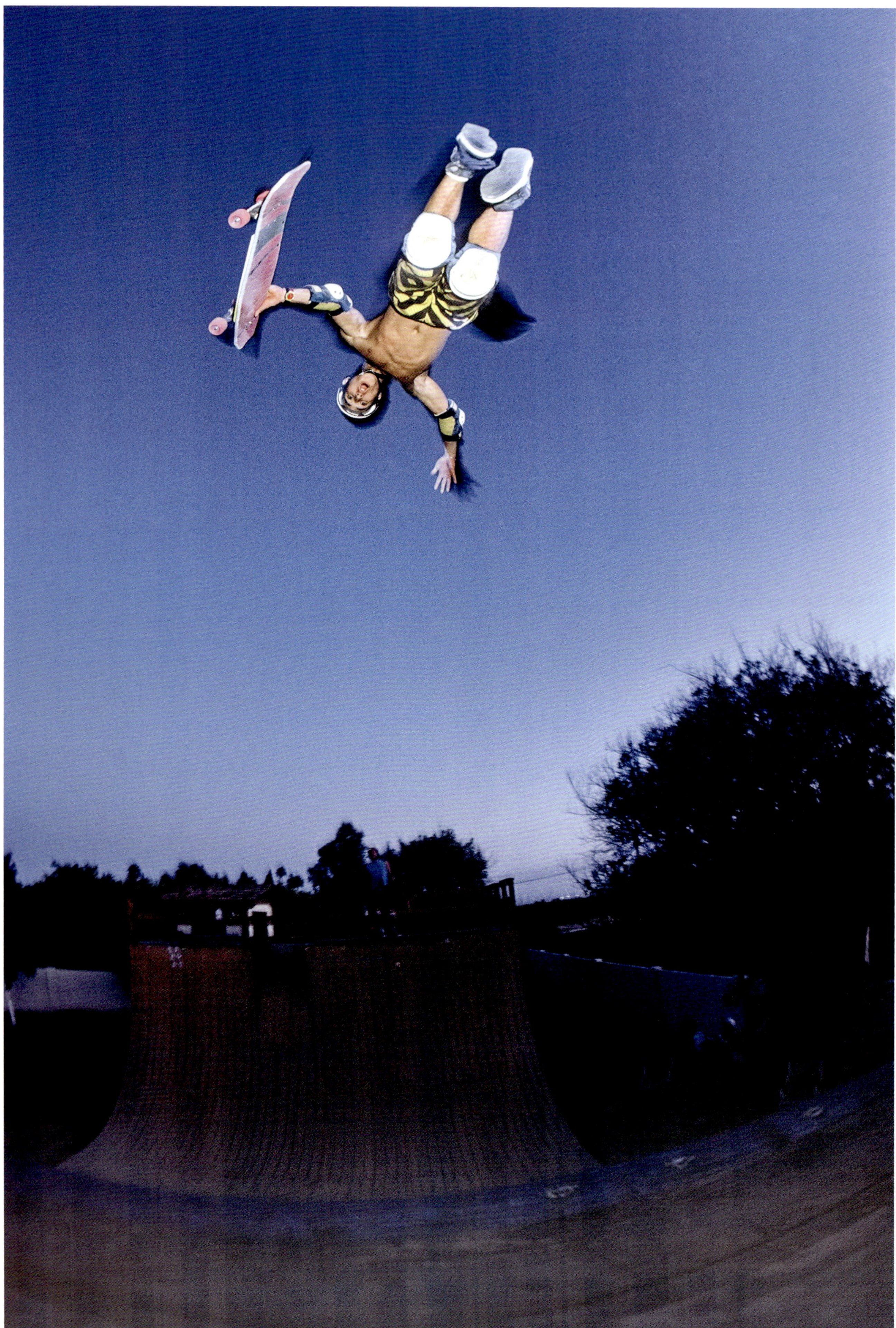

Christian Hosoi, Christ air, Sellars' Ramp, Mesa, AZ, 1986

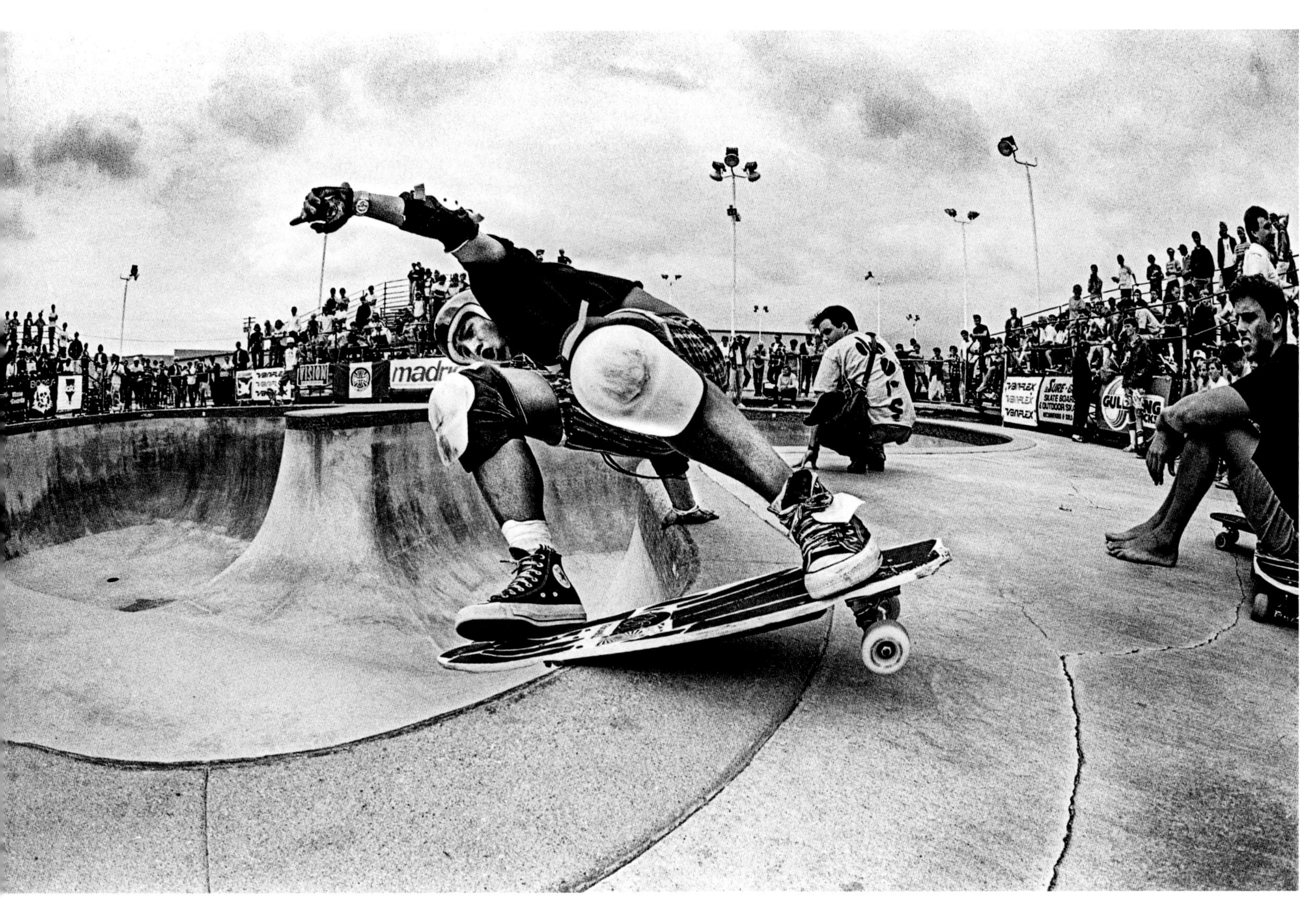

Christian Hosoi, Backside layback boardslide, Pipeline Skatepark, Upland, CA, 1985

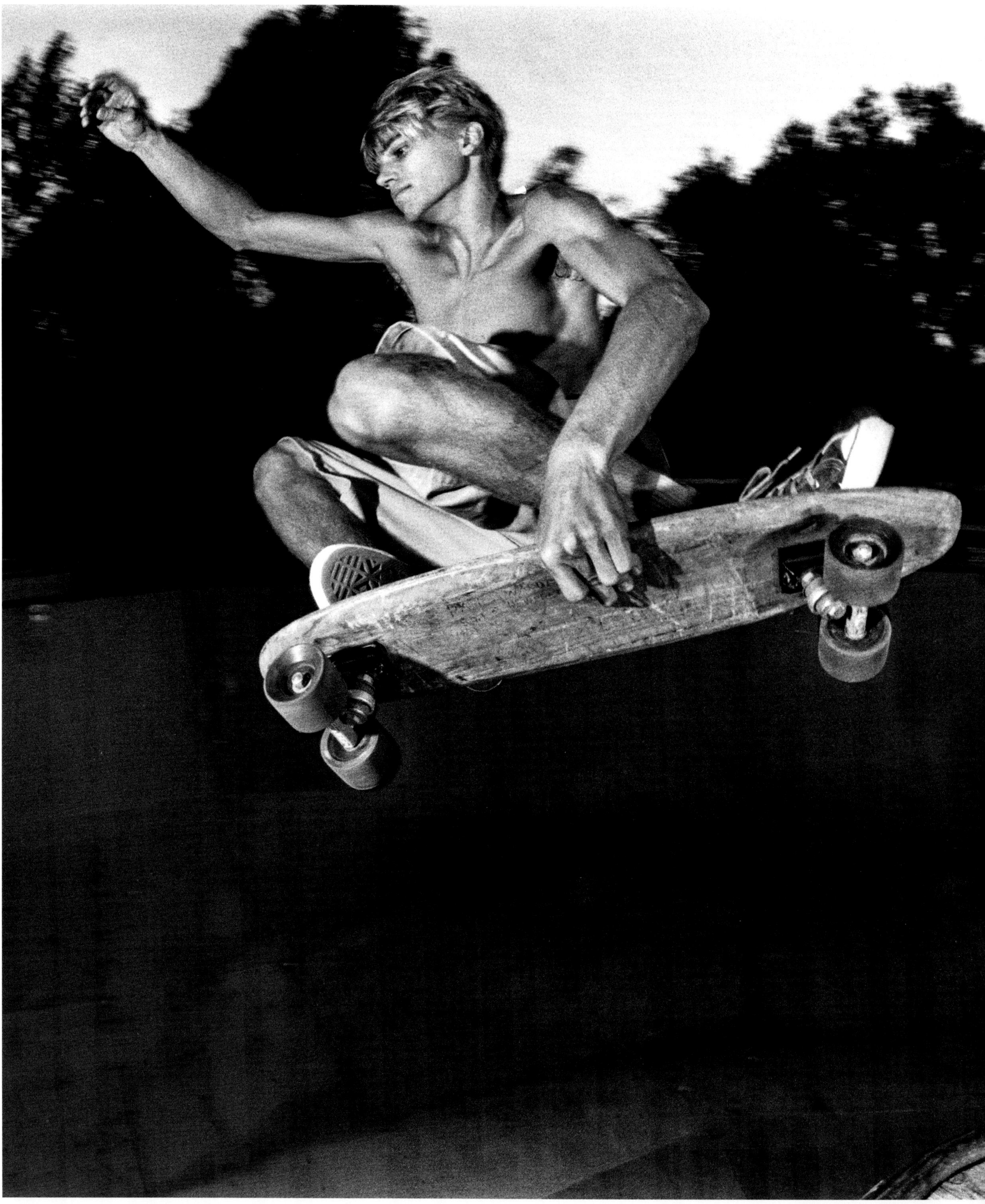

Ron Cameron, Frontside air over hip, Blockhead Ramp, Bonsall, CA, 1989

Previous spread: Pierre André Senizergues, Tsunami wall, Fuji, Japan, 1988

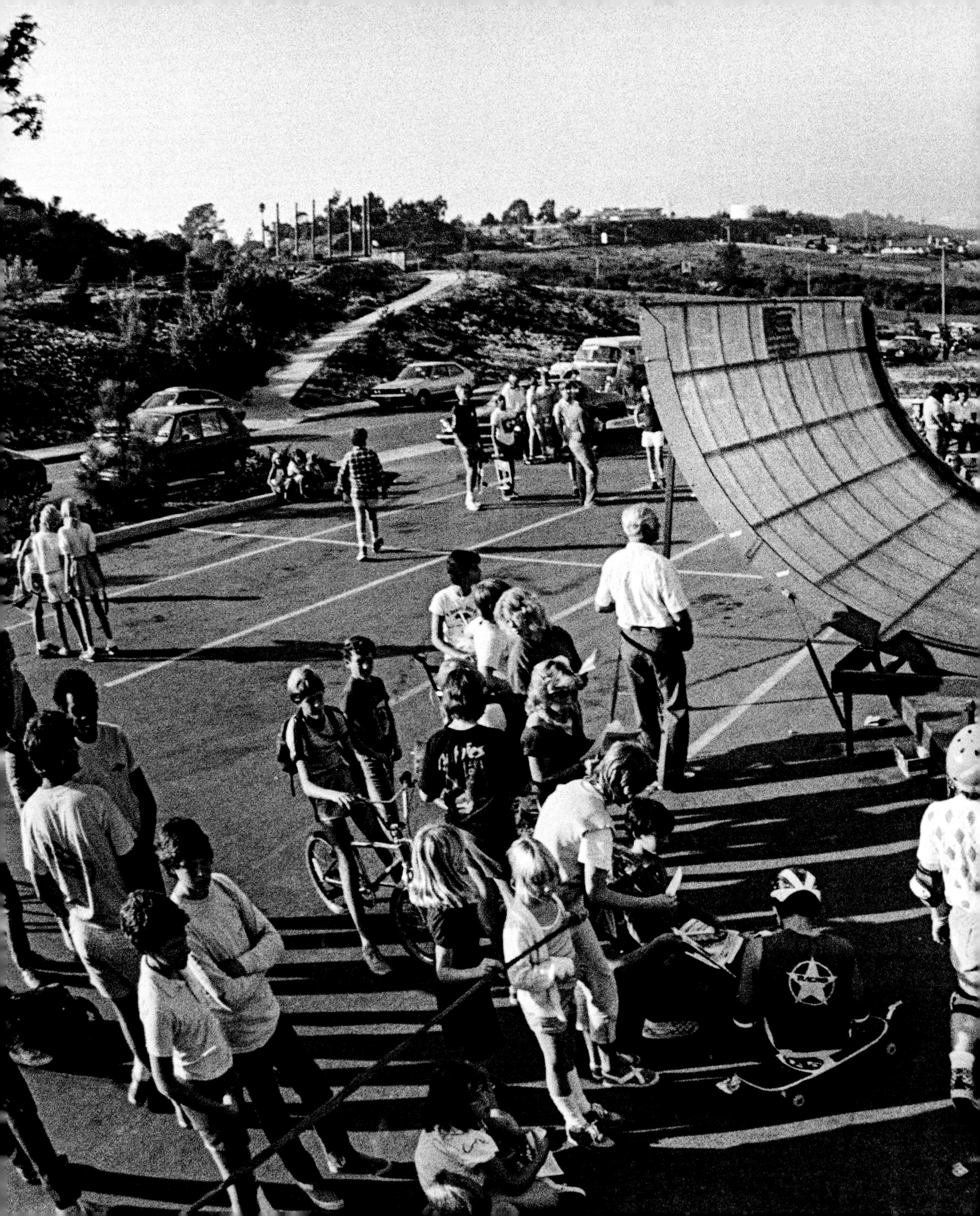

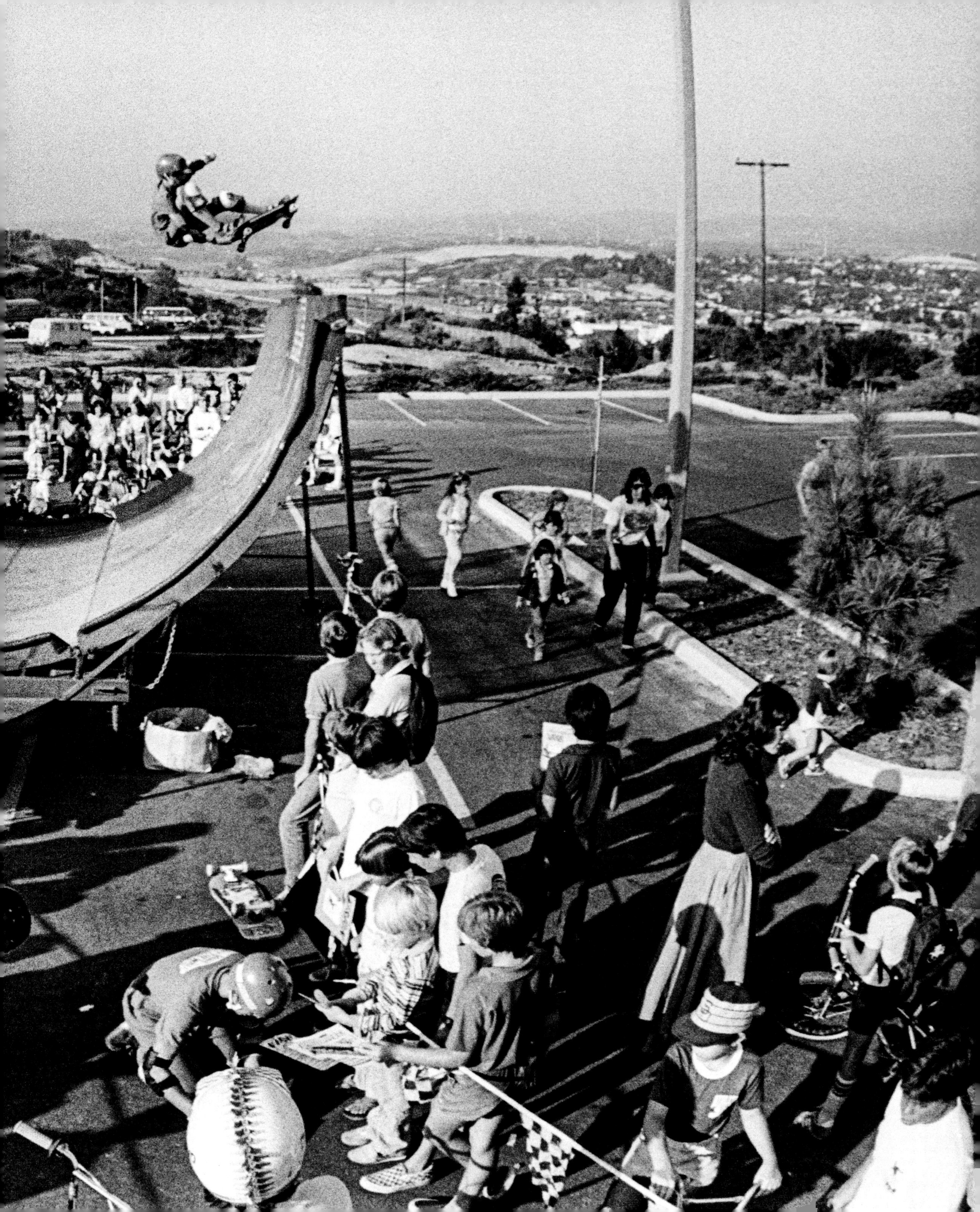

Previous spread: Tony Hawk, Boys & Girls Club demo, Encinitas, CA, 1984

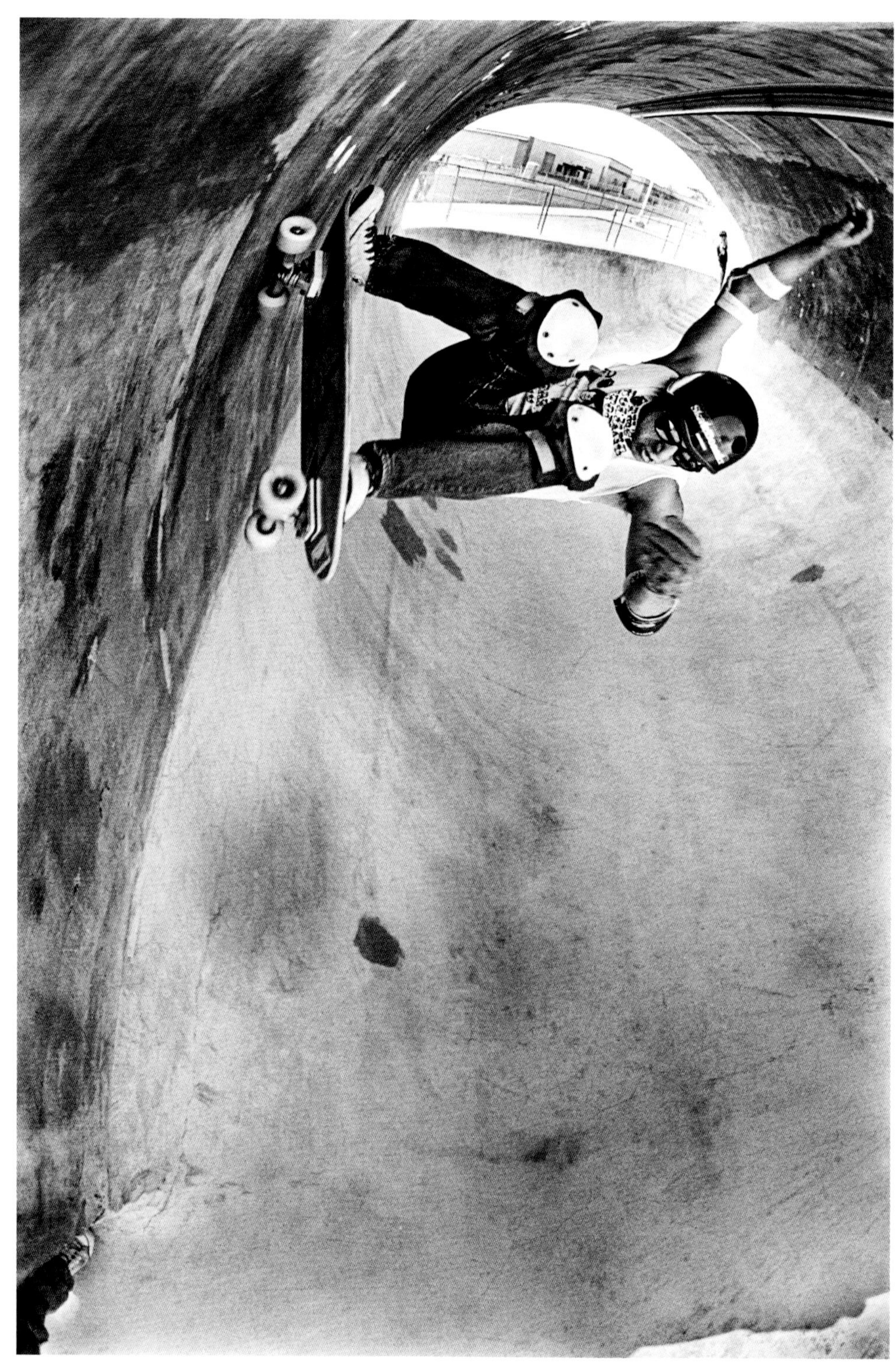

Steve Alba, Pipeline Skatepark, Upland, CA, 1985

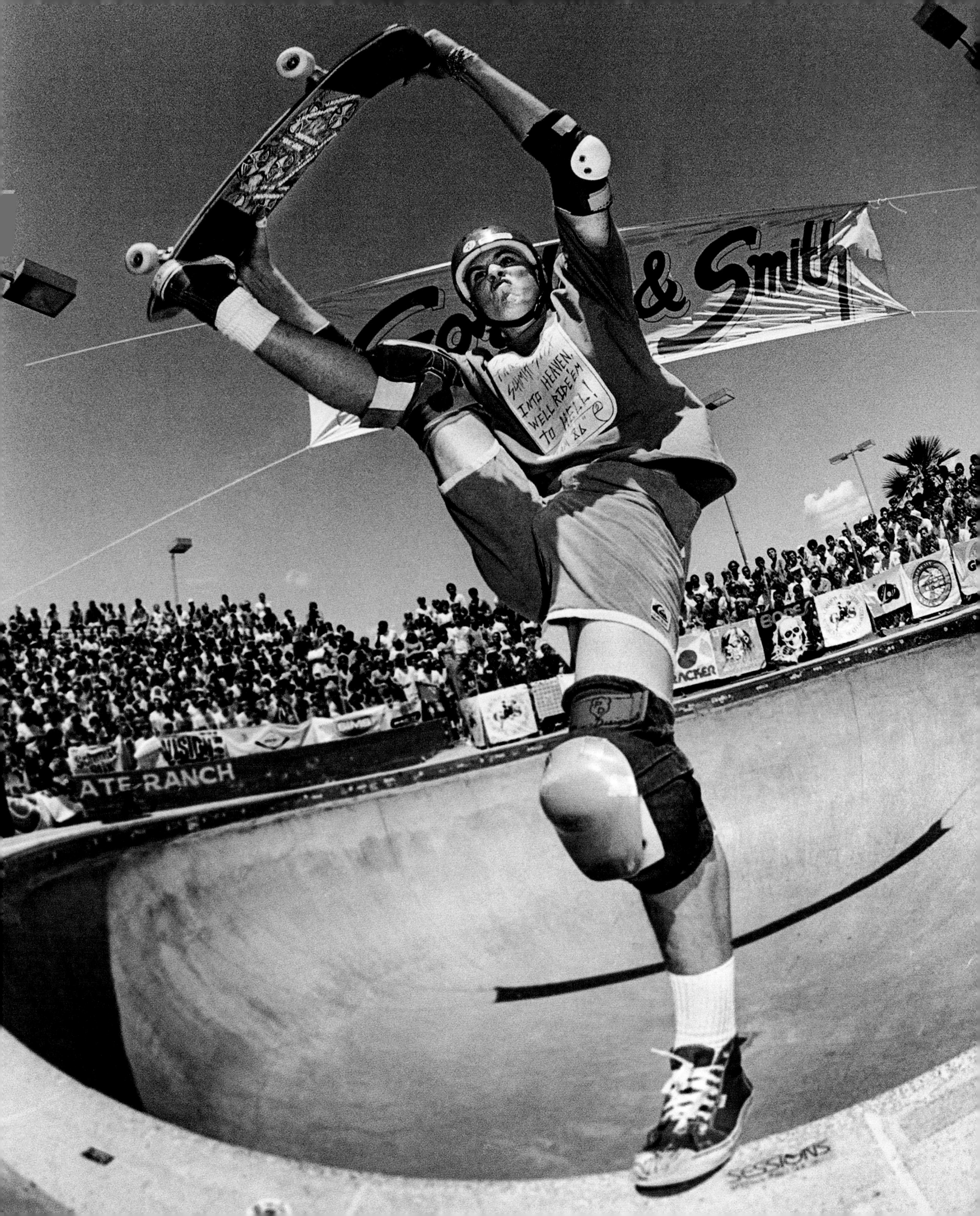

& Smith
INTA HEAVEN, WELL RIDE EM TO HELL!
ATE RANCH

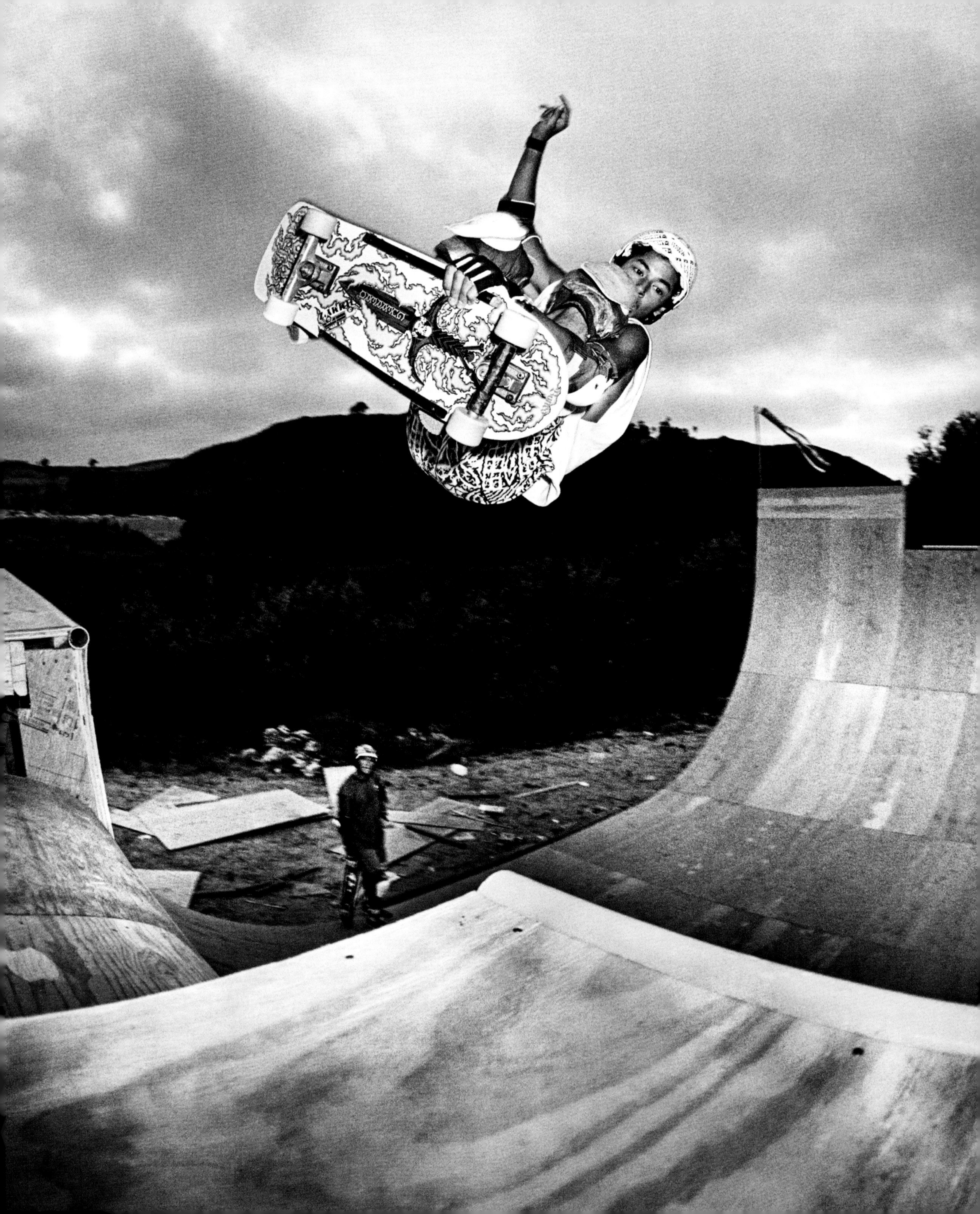

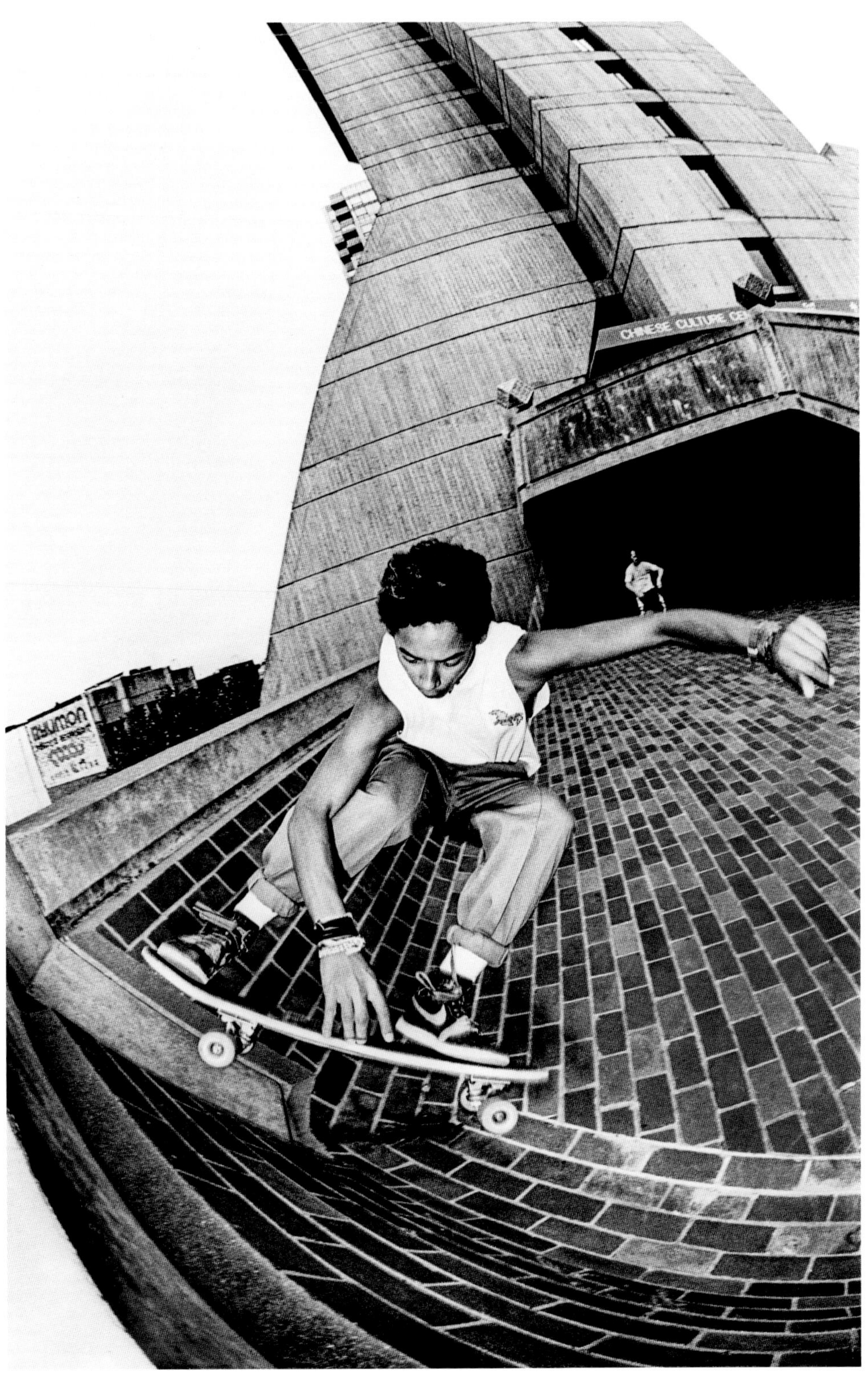

Tommy Guerrero, China Banks, San Francisco, CA, 1986

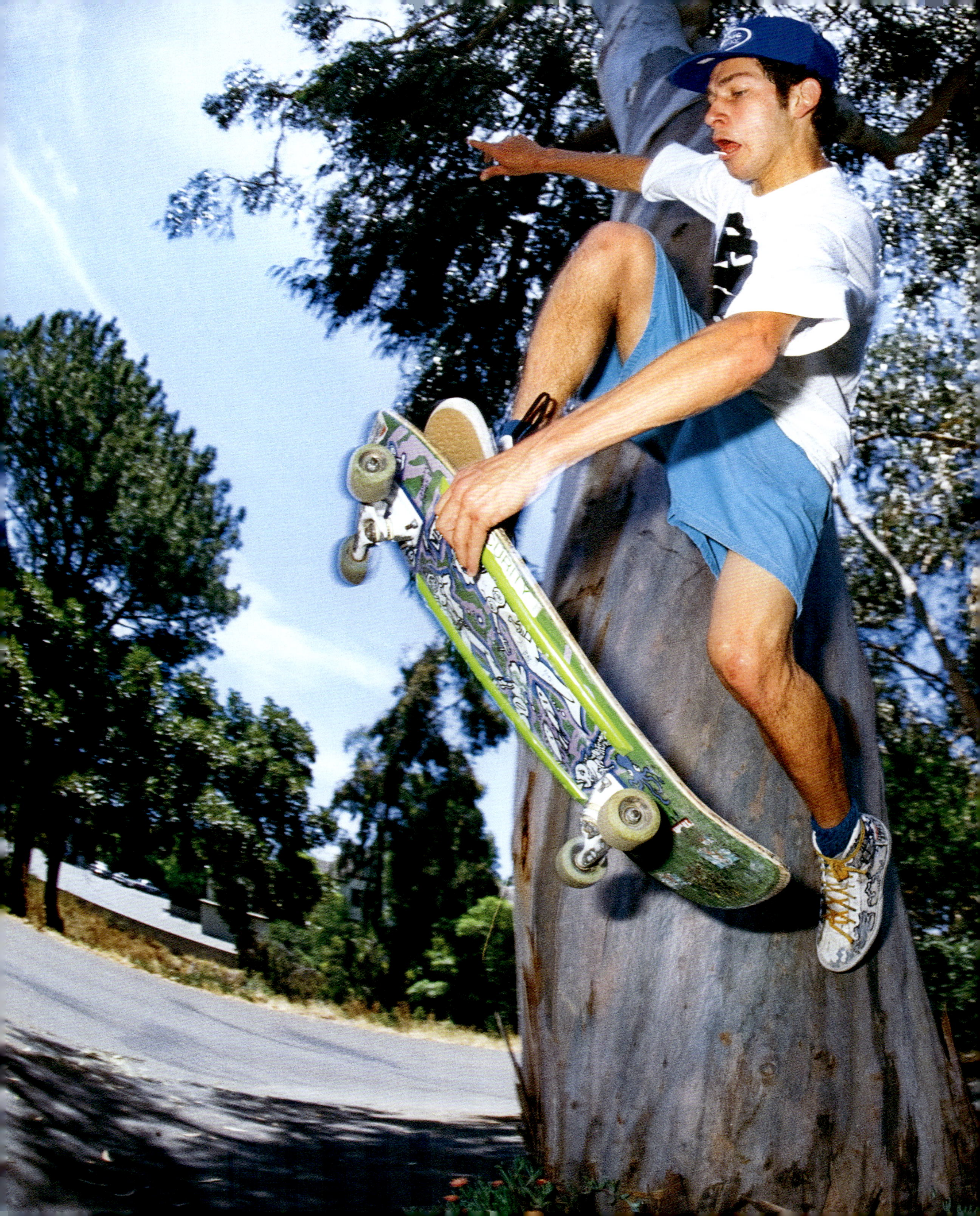

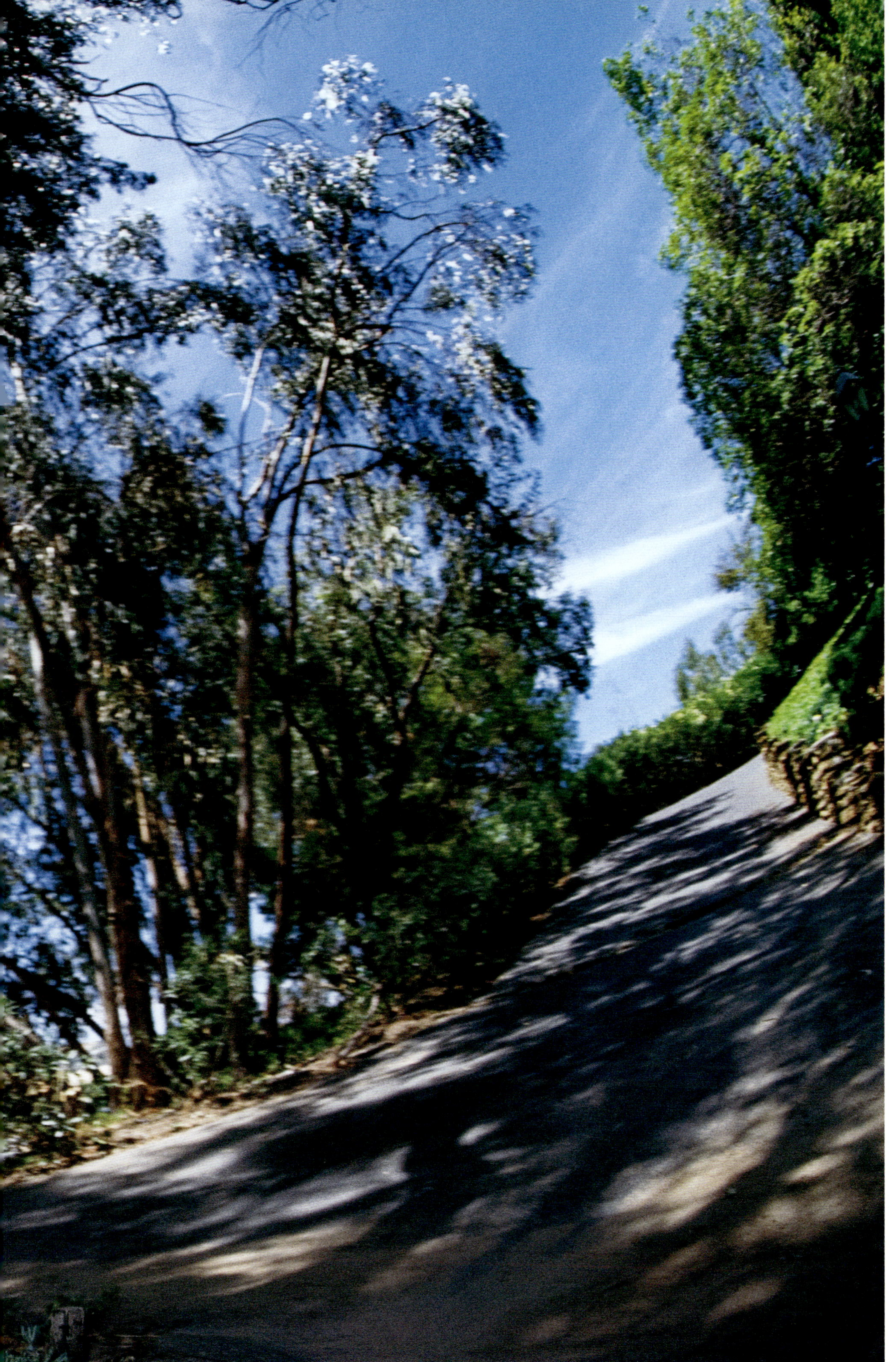

Mark Gonzales, Tree footplant, Laguna Beach, CA, 1988

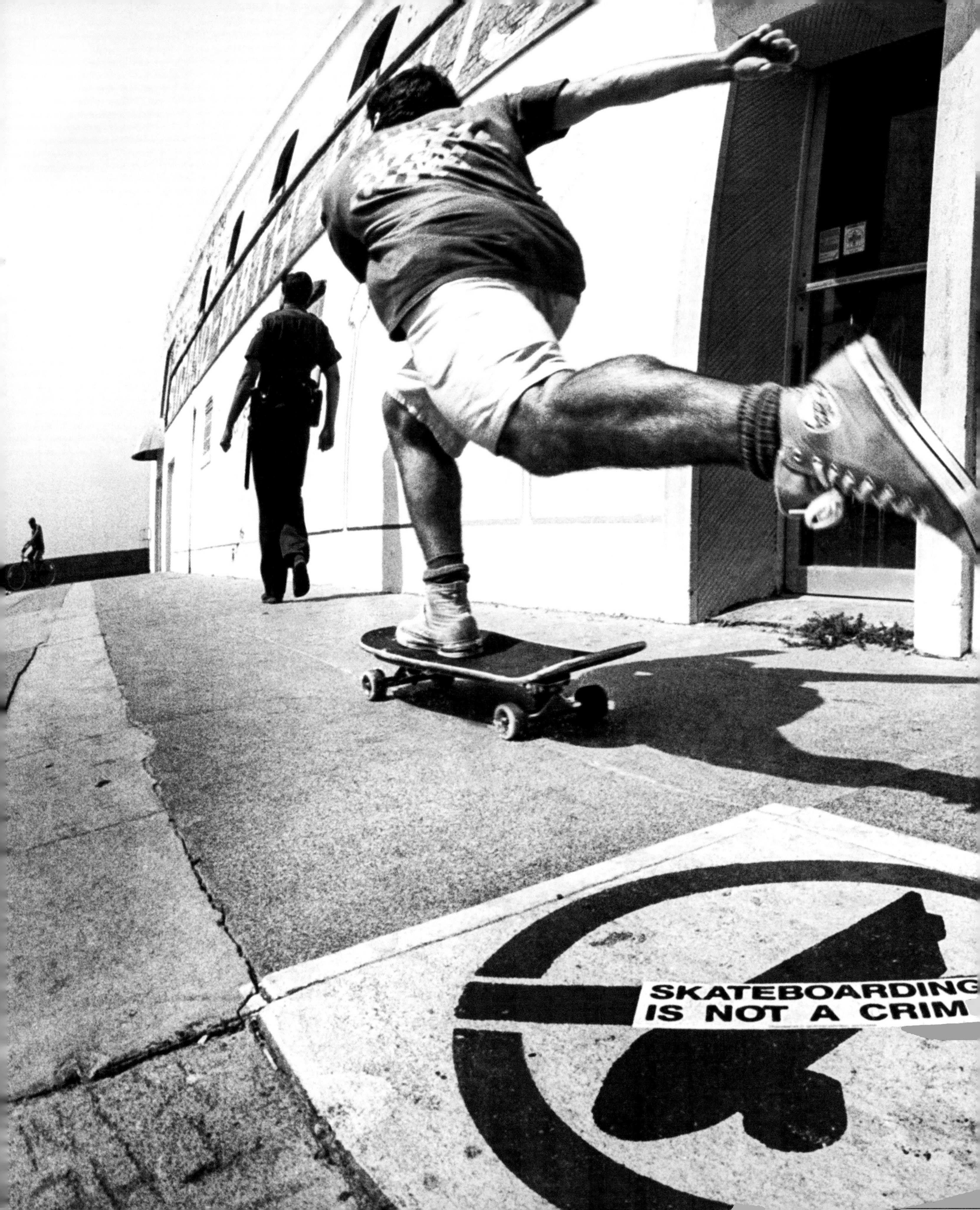
SKATEBOARDING
IS NOT A CRIM

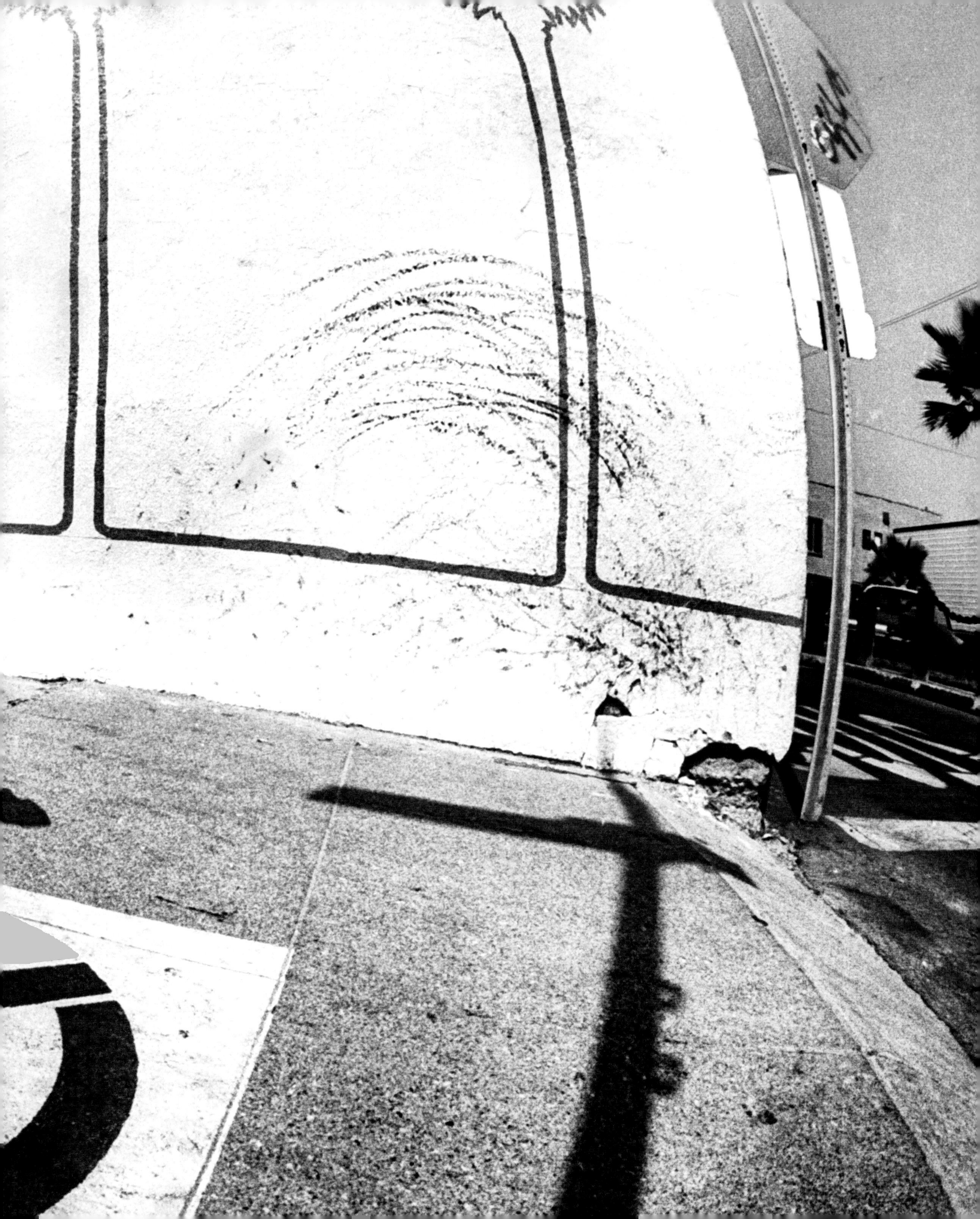

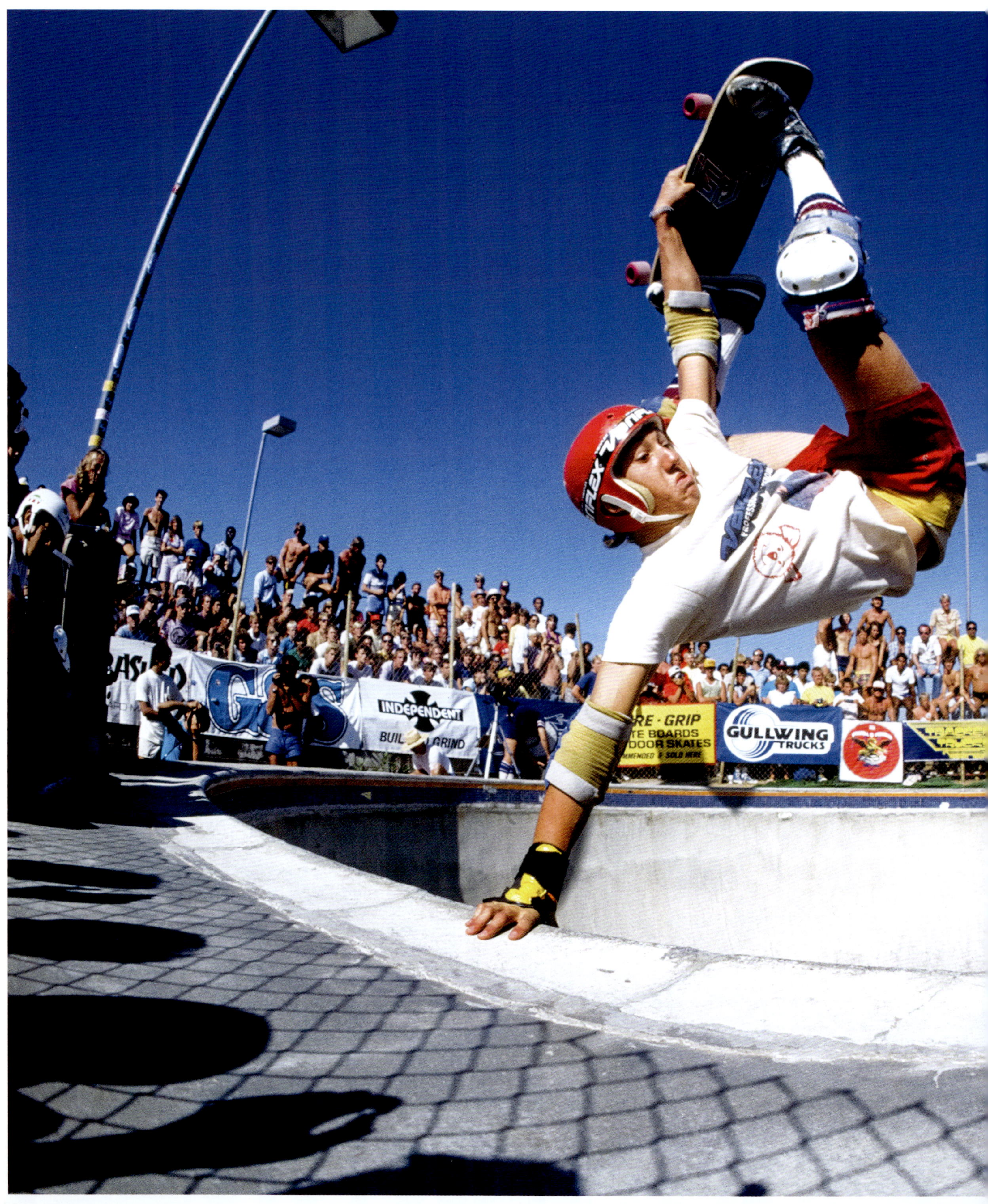
INDEPENDENT
GULLWING
TRUCKS

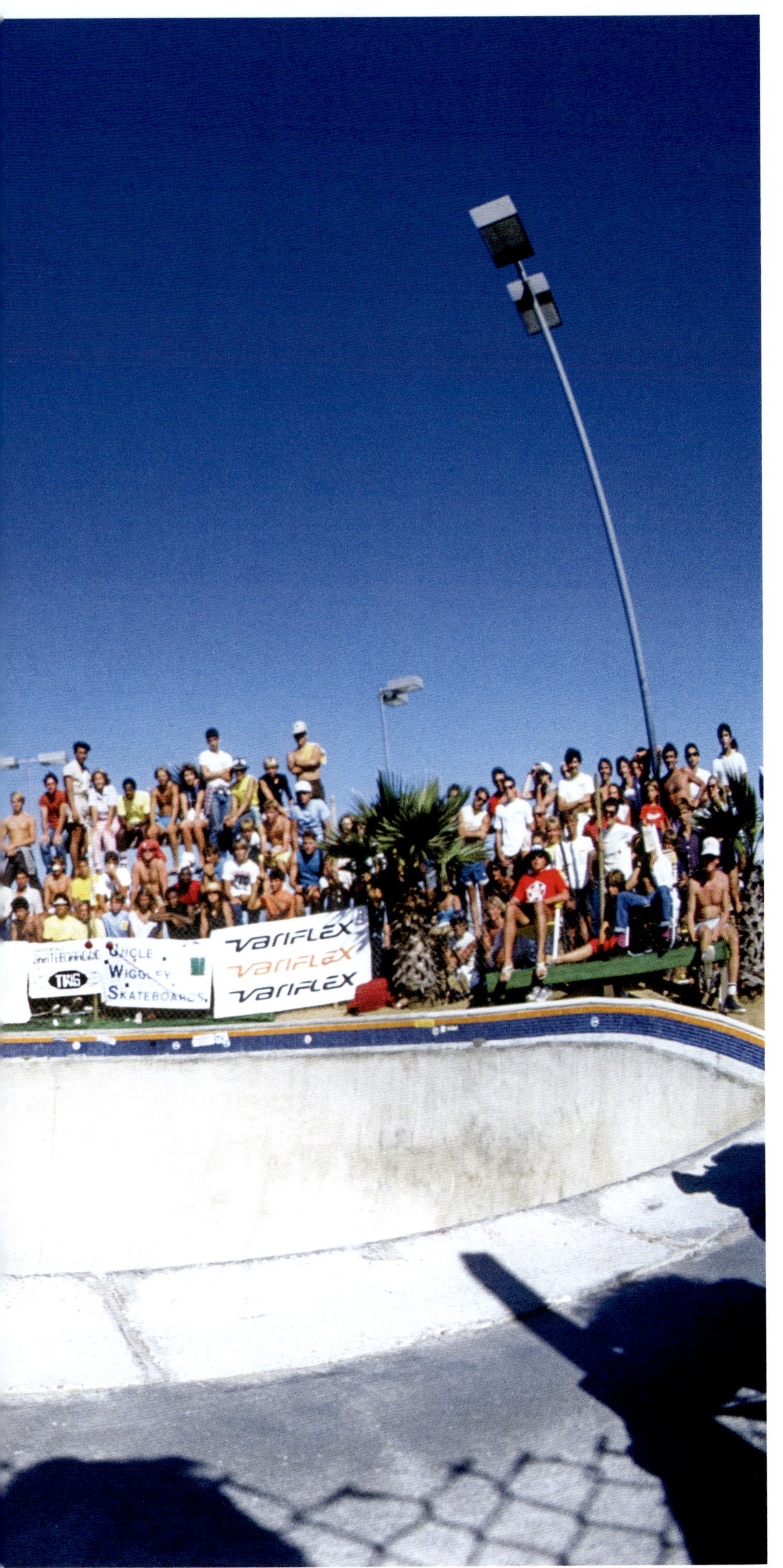

Allen Losi, Layback air, Del Mar Skate Ranch, Del Mar, CA, 1983

Previous spread: Steve Rocco, Pushing, Hermosa Beach, CA, 1987

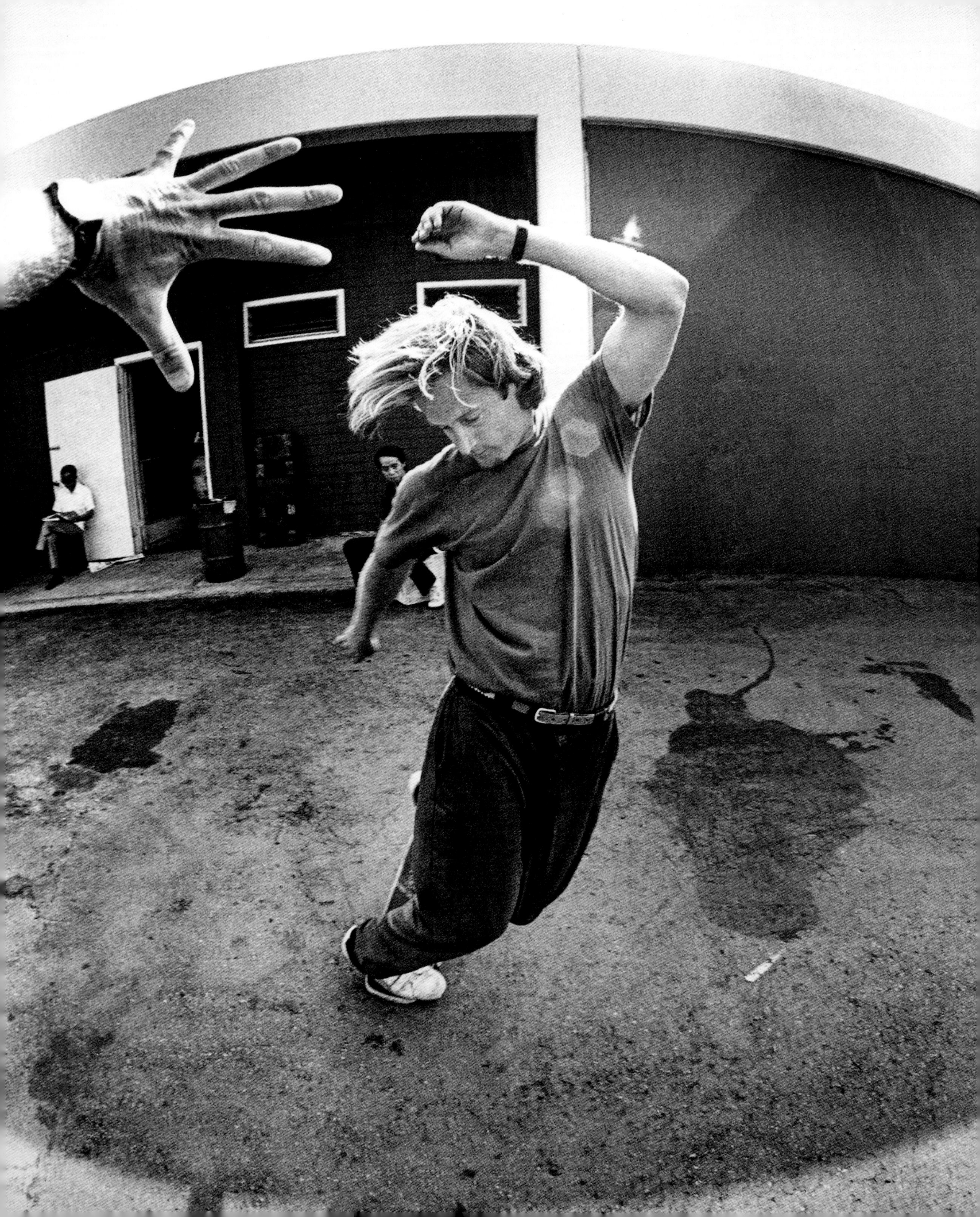

Stacy Peralta, Behind taco shop, Solana Beach, CA, 1985

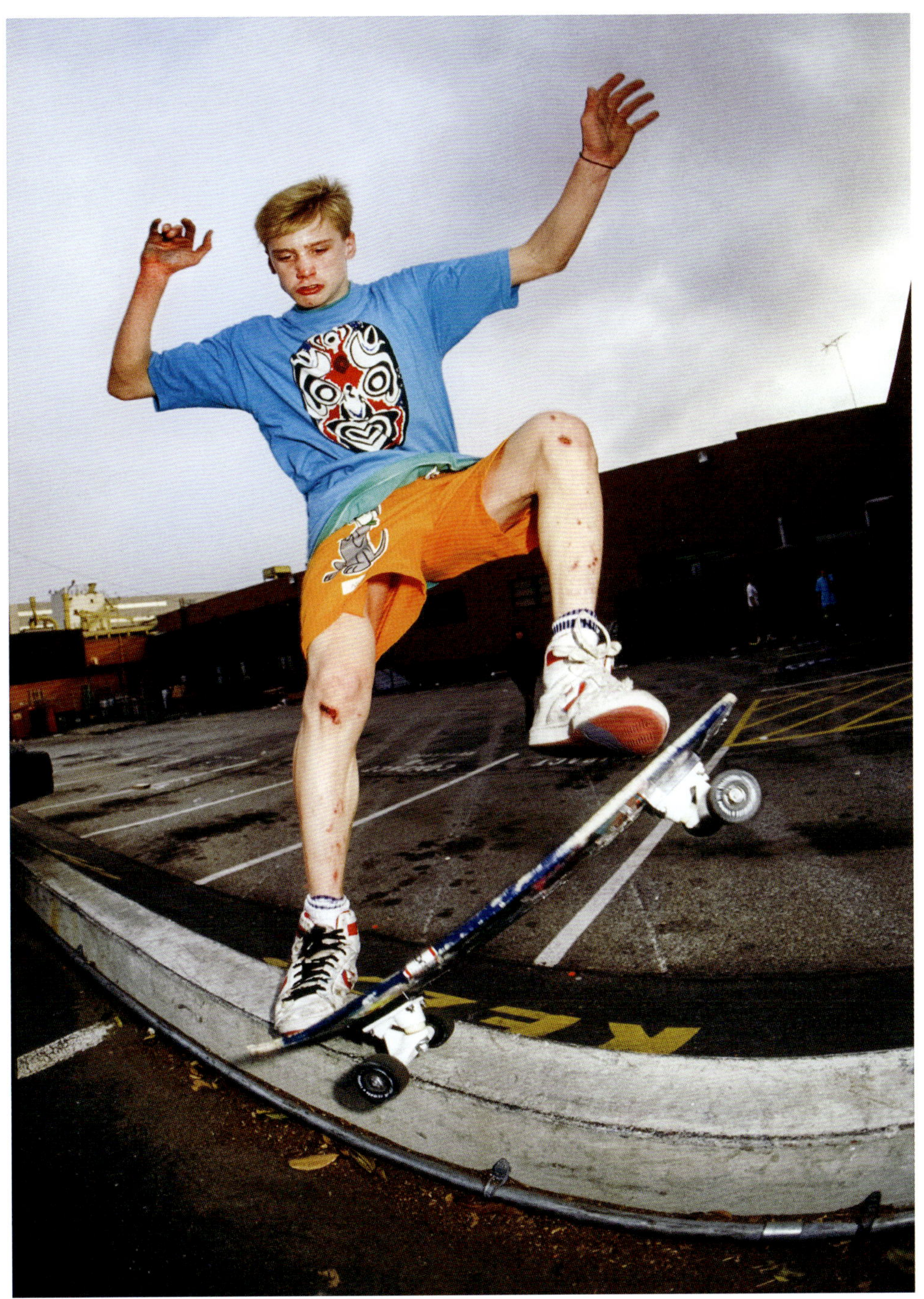

Mike Vallely, LAX Banks, Los Angeles, CA, 1987

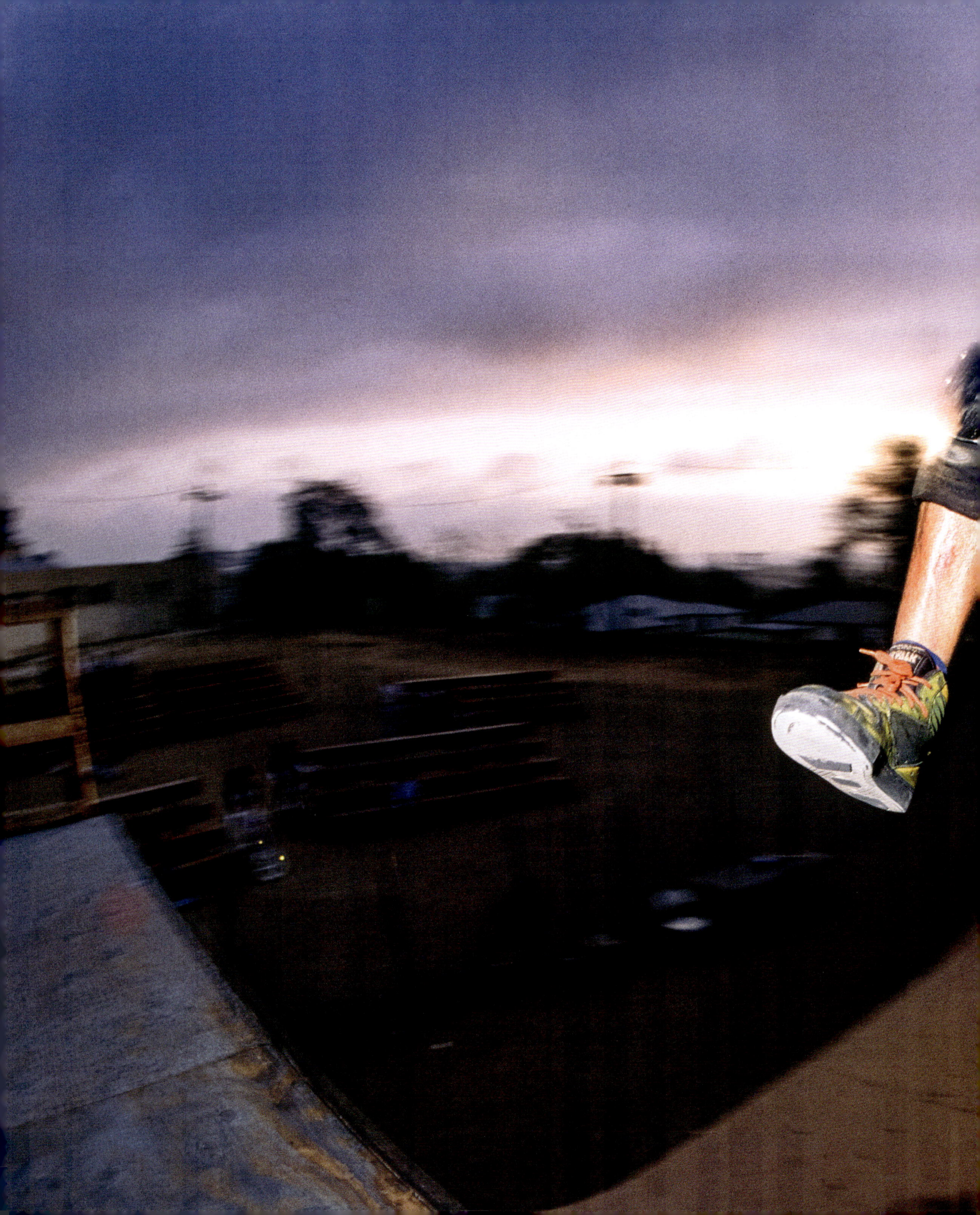

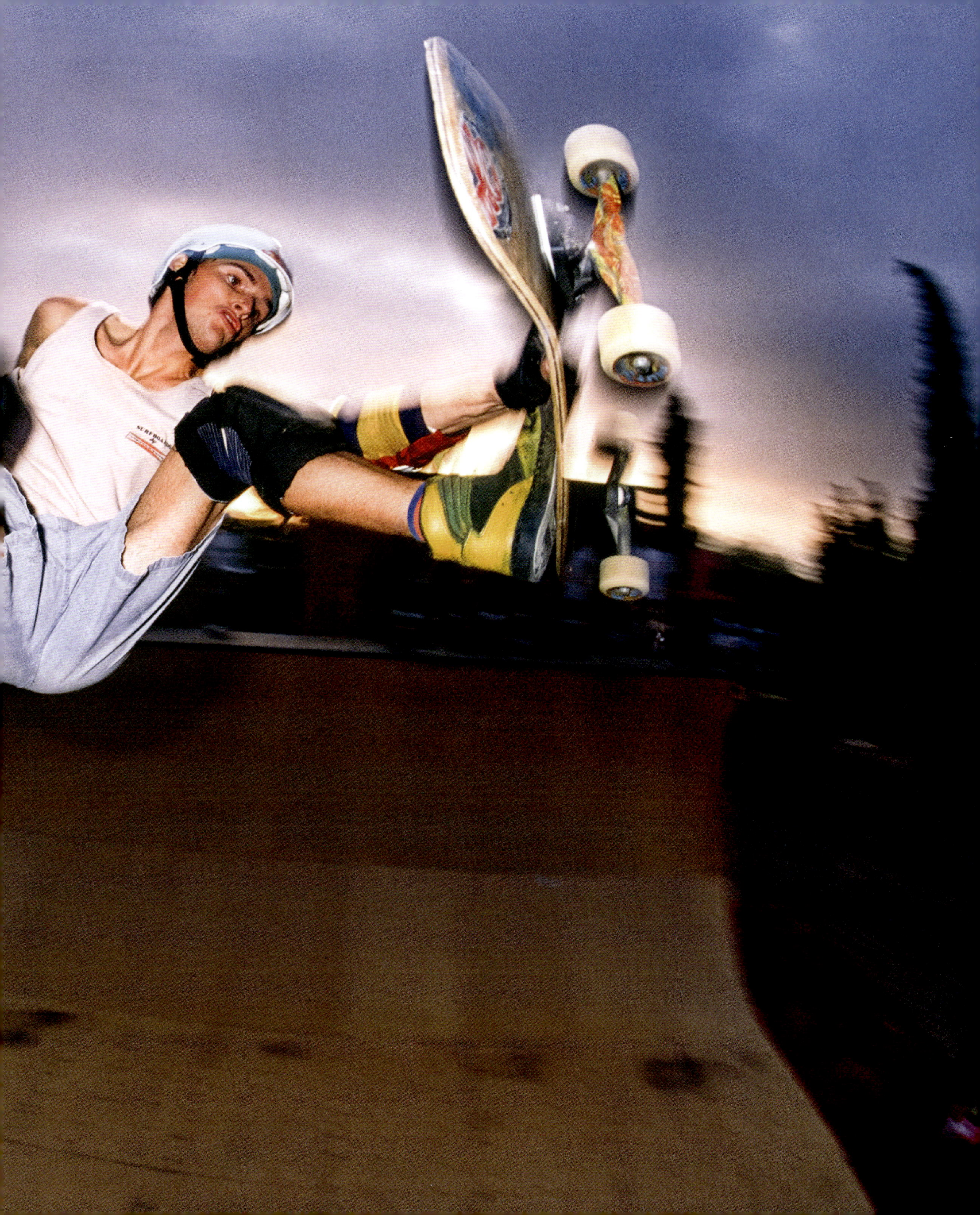

Previous spread: Steve Claar, Slob fastplant, Linda Vista, CA, 1988

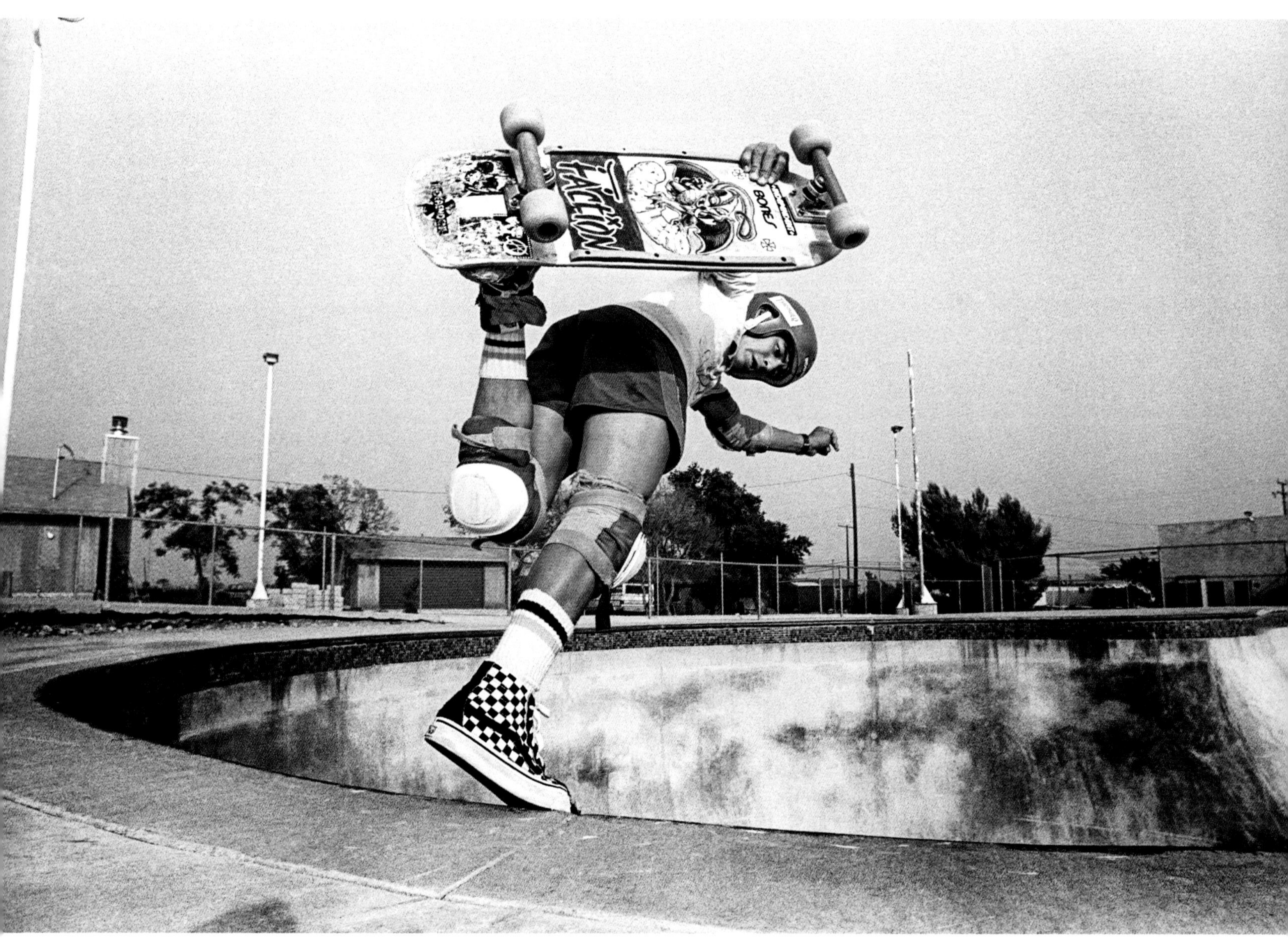

Steve Caballero, Backside boneless, Pipeline Skatepark, Upland, CA, 1983

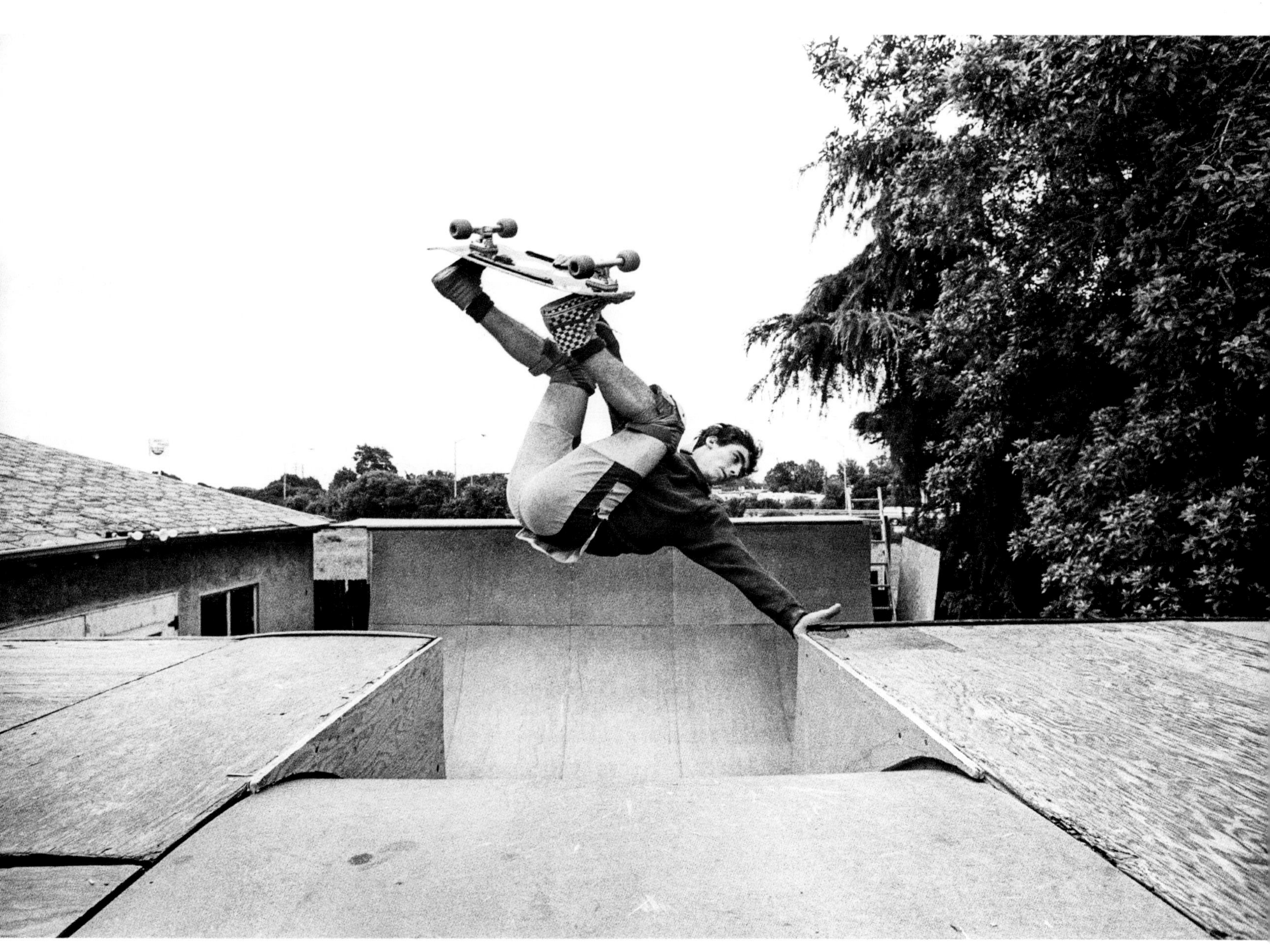

Lance Mountain, Frontside invert, Lopes' Ramp, San Leandro, CA, 1984

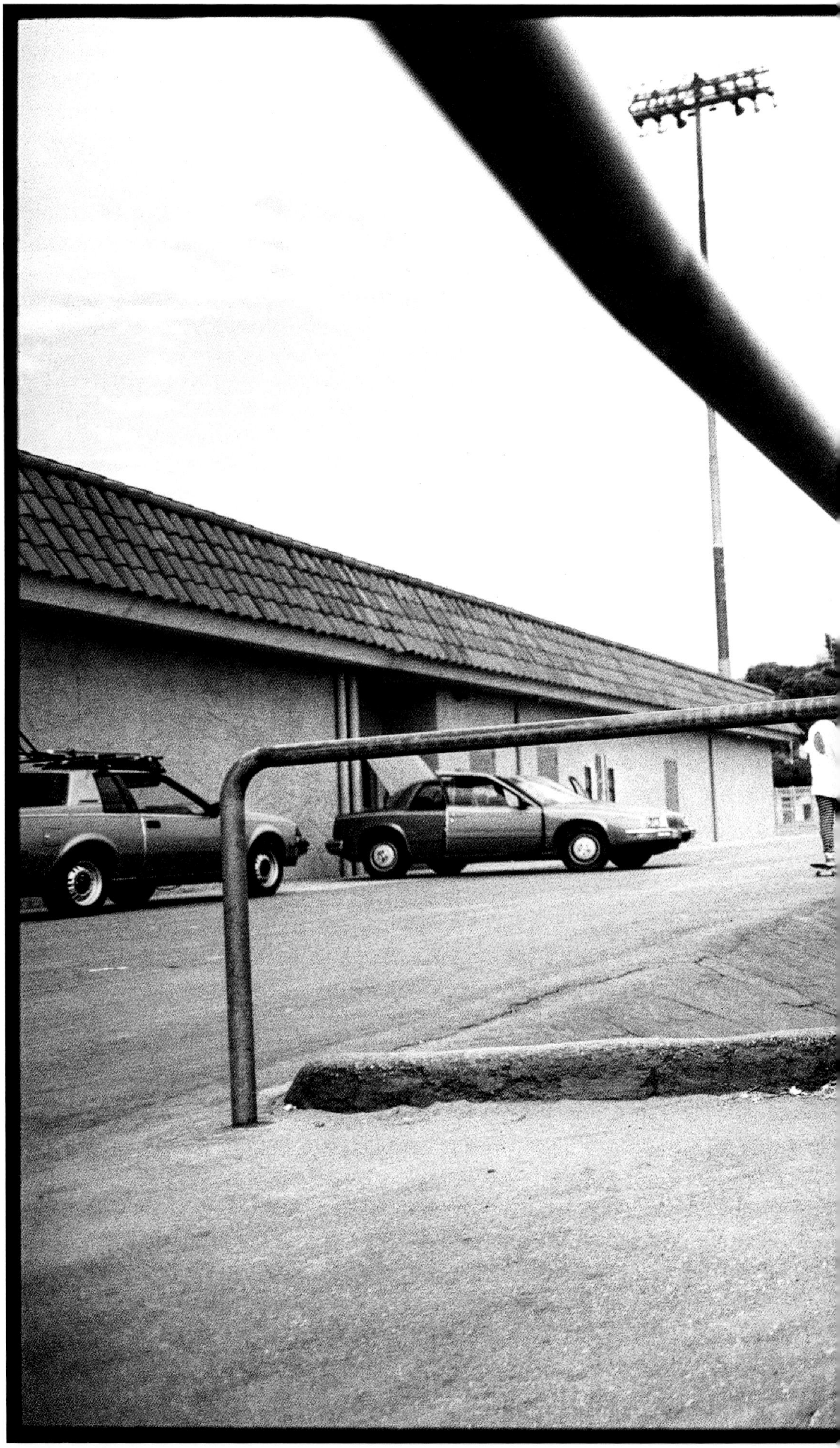

Tommy Guerrero, Tuck knee over hip, San Pasqual High, San Pasqual, CA, 1987

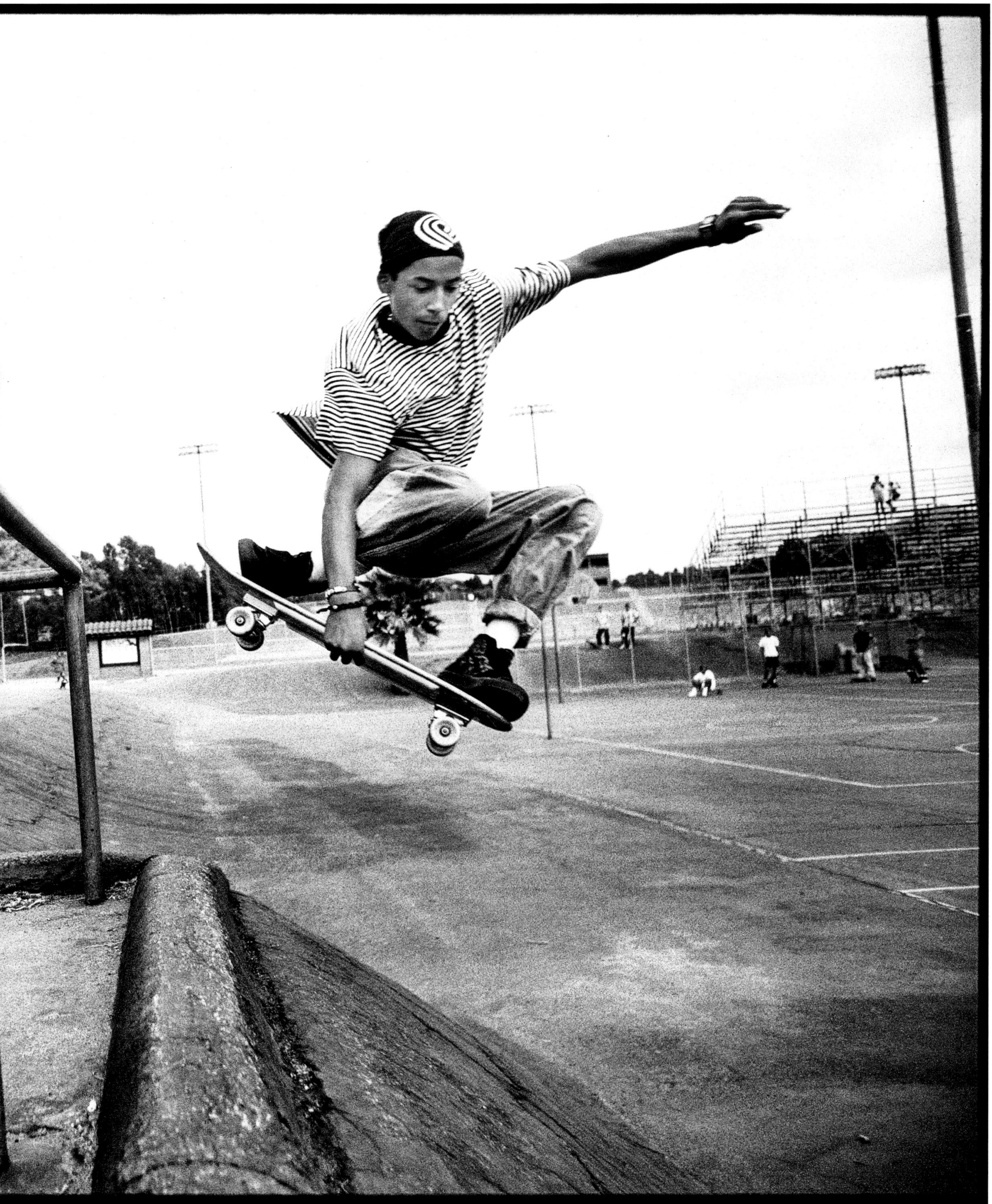

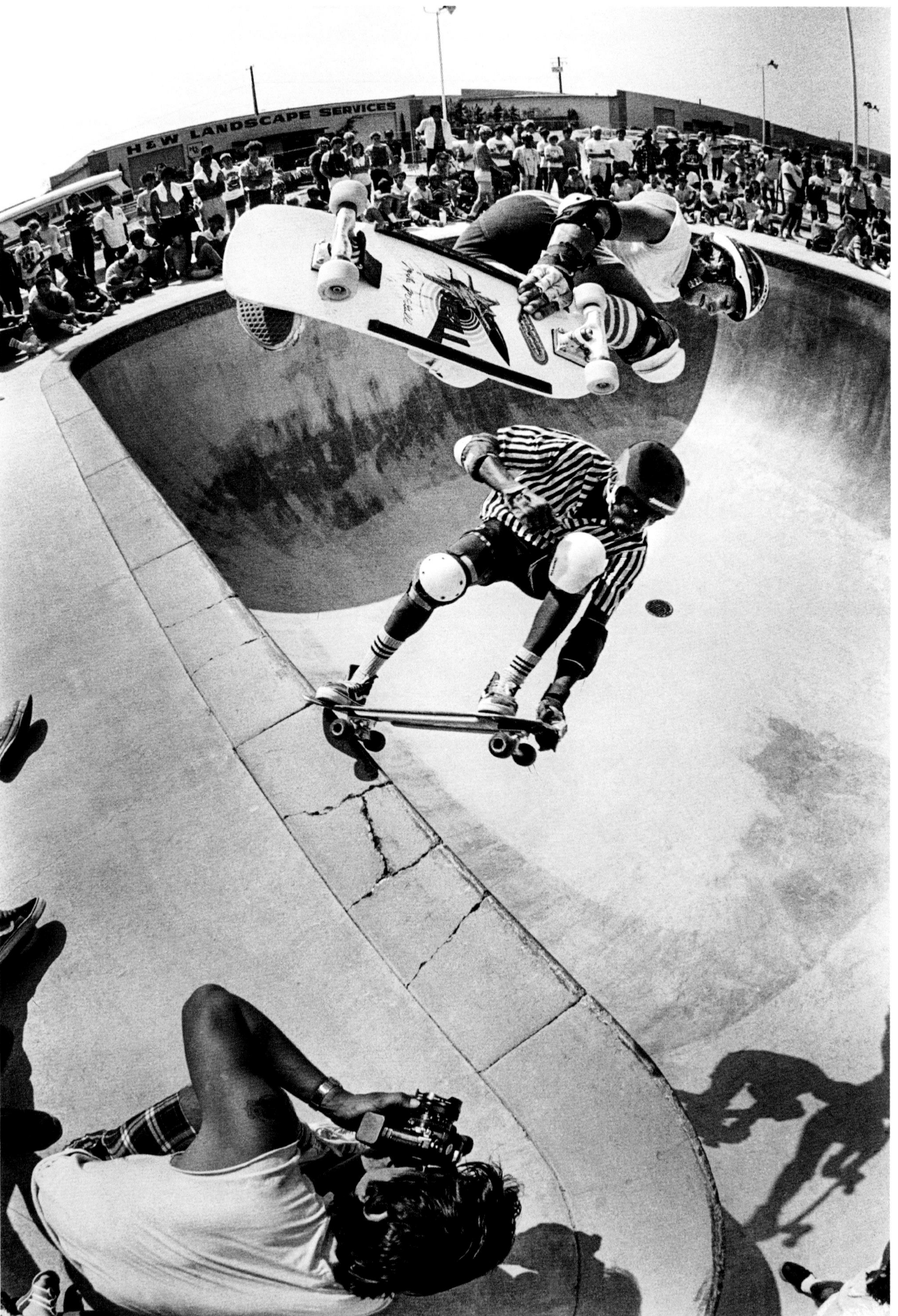

Mofo shooting Mike McGill and Steve Steadham, Pipeline Skatepark, Upland, CA, 1984

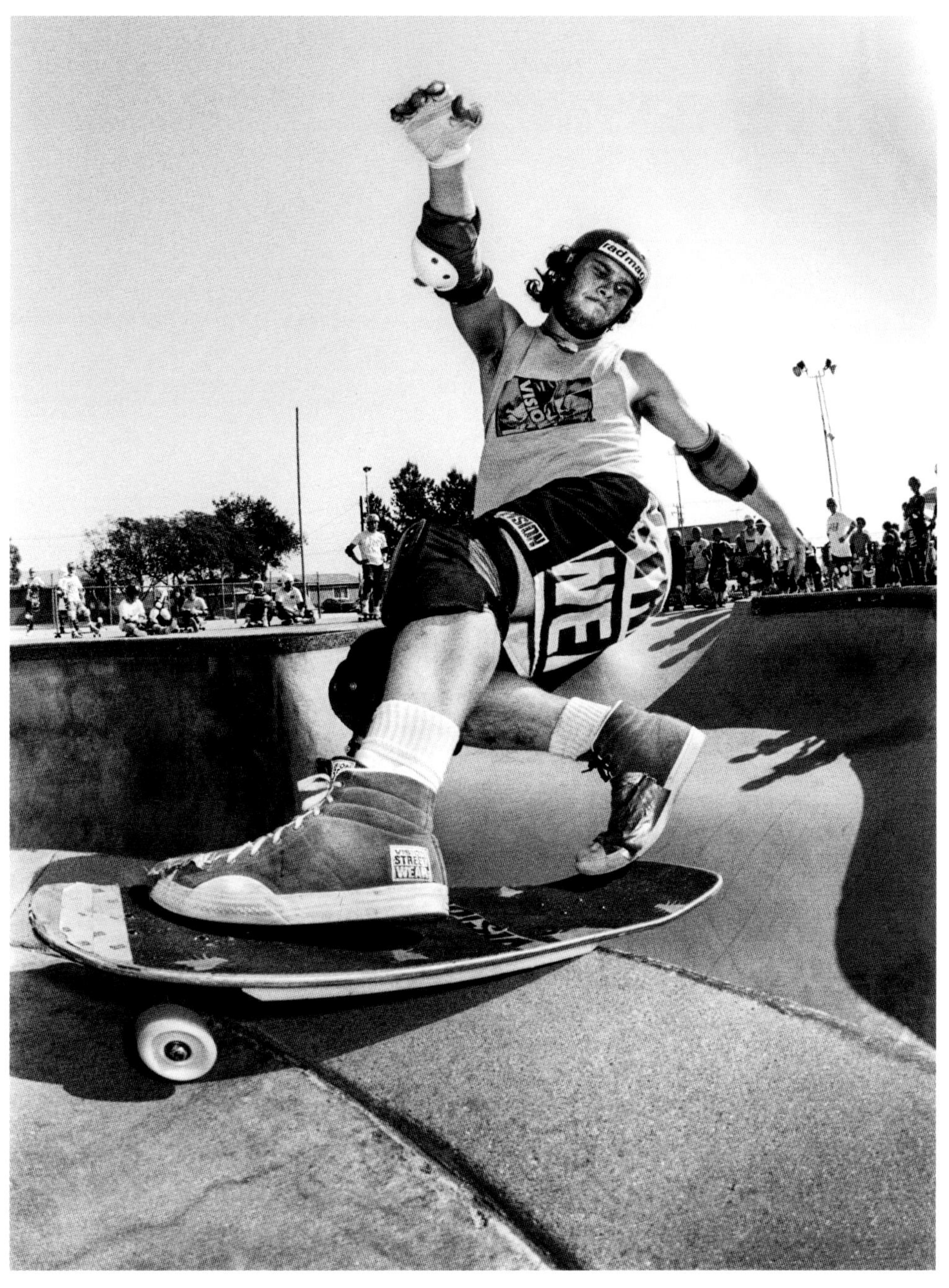

Lee Ralph, Frontside rock on the hip, Pipeline Skatepark, Upland, CA, 1988

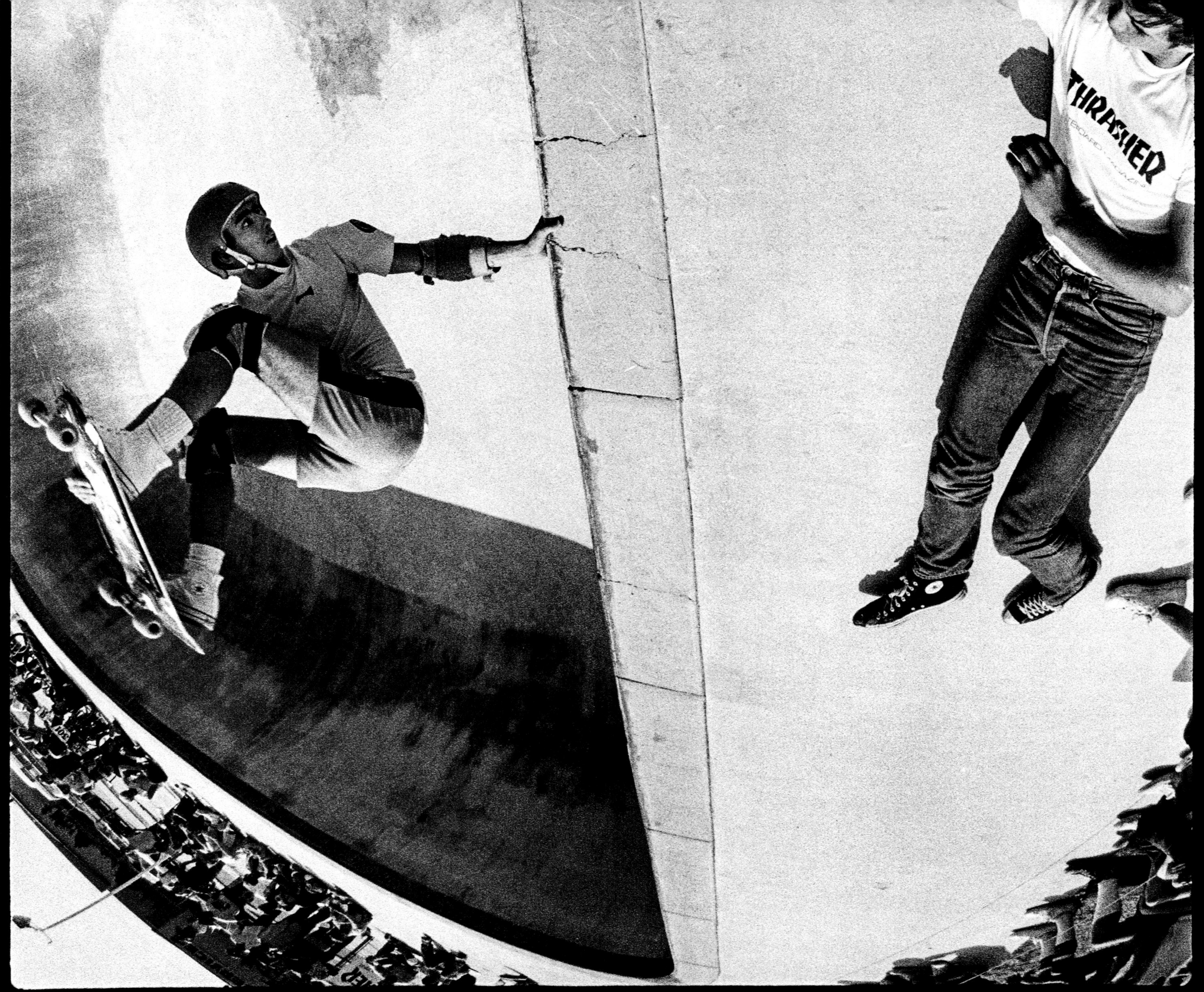
THRASHER

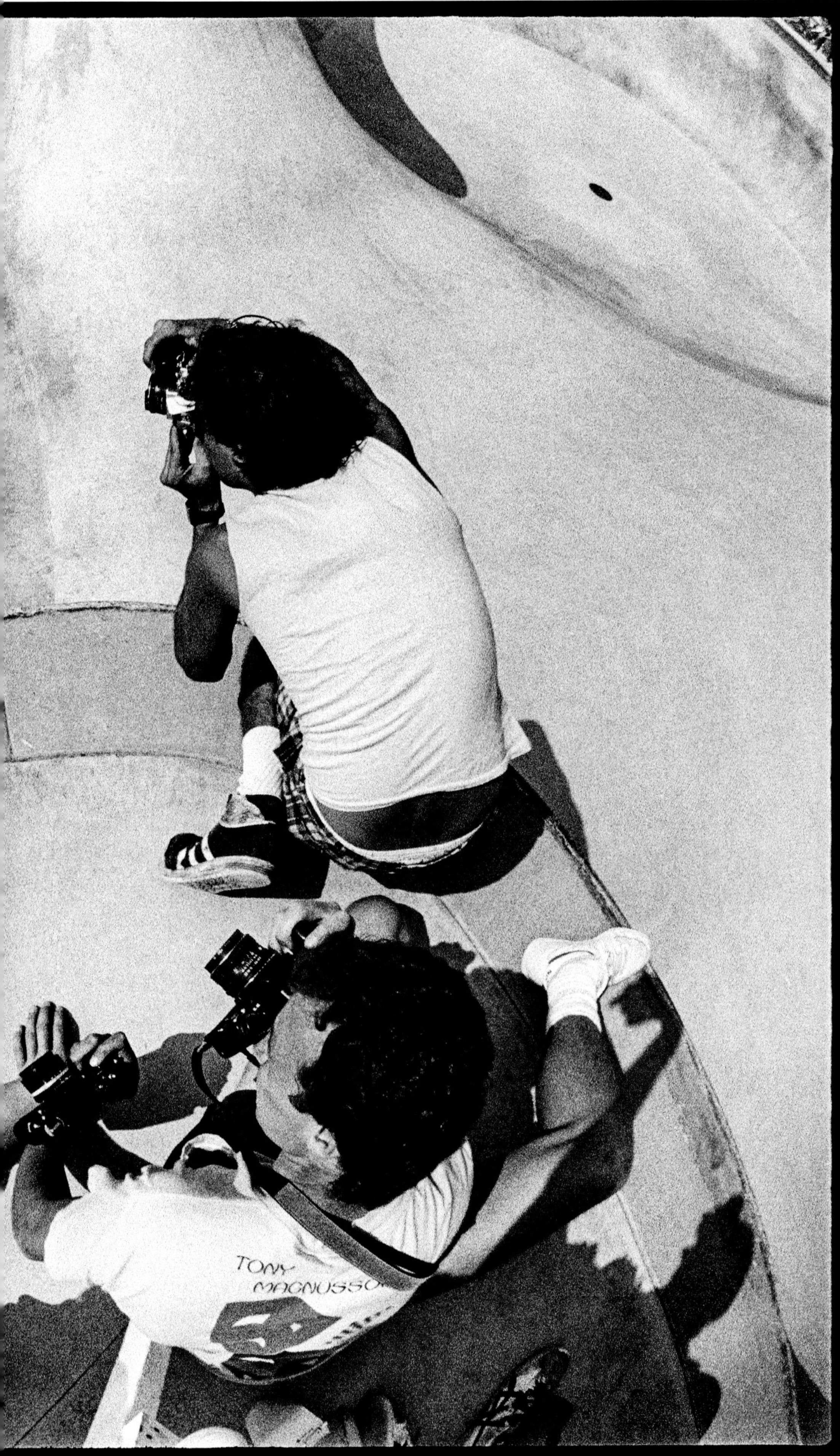

Glen Friedman and Dave Omer shooting Lance Mountain, Frontside invert, Pipeline Skatepark, Upland, CA, 1984

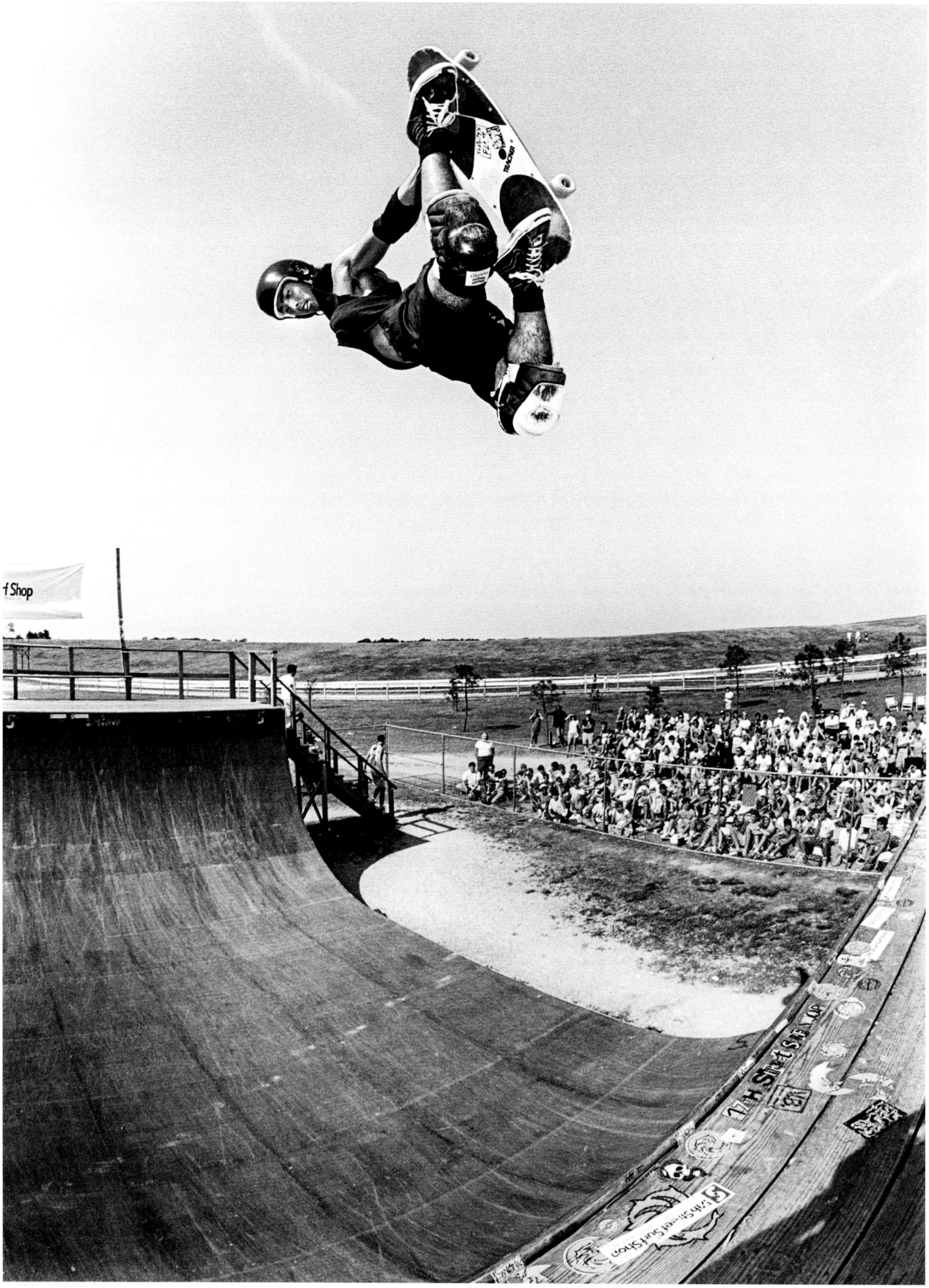

Lester Kasai, Crooked cop, Mt. Trashmore, Virginia Beach, VA, 1986

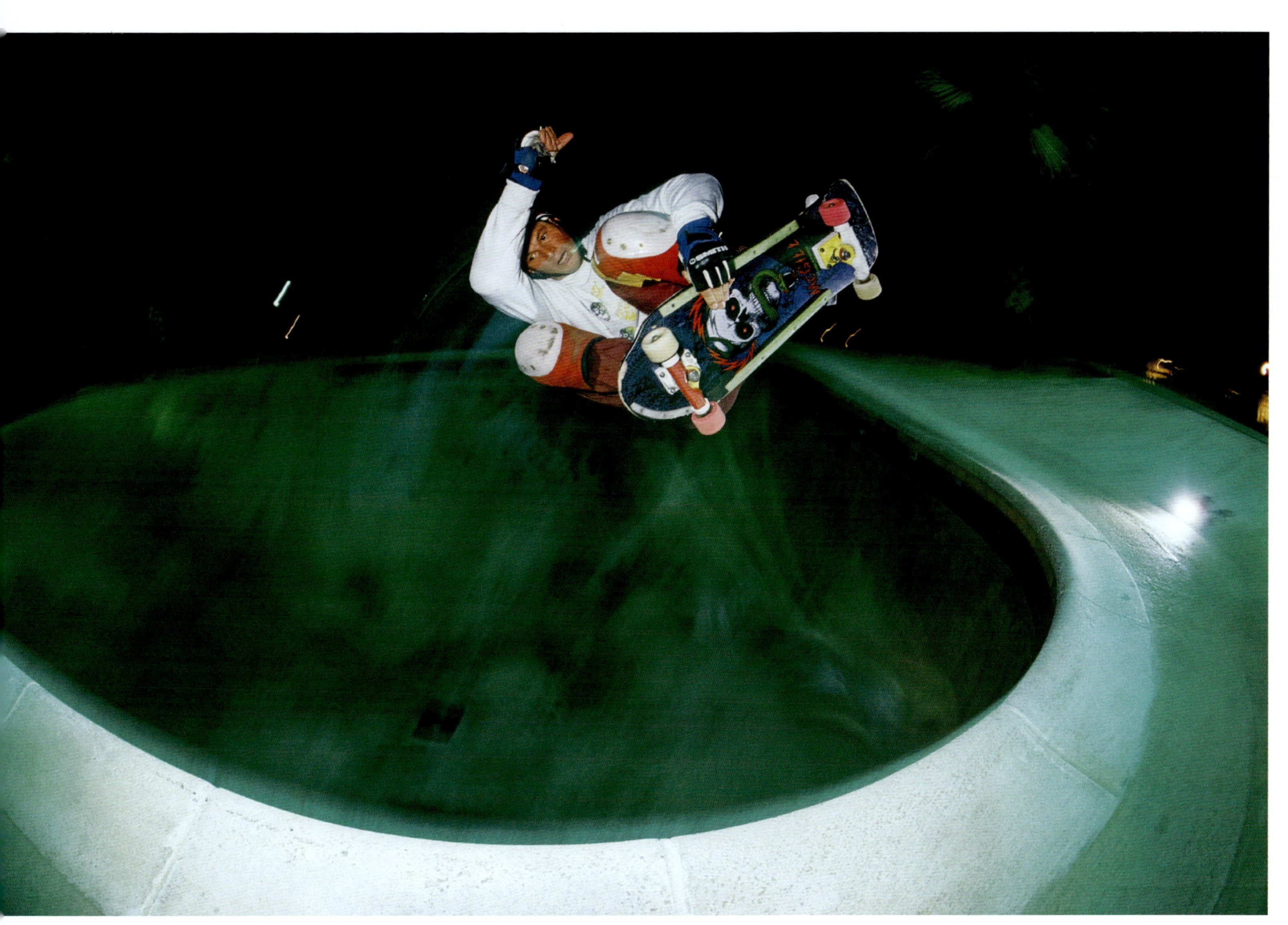

ike McGill, Corner air in square pool, Del Mar Skate Ranch, Del Mar, CA, 1985

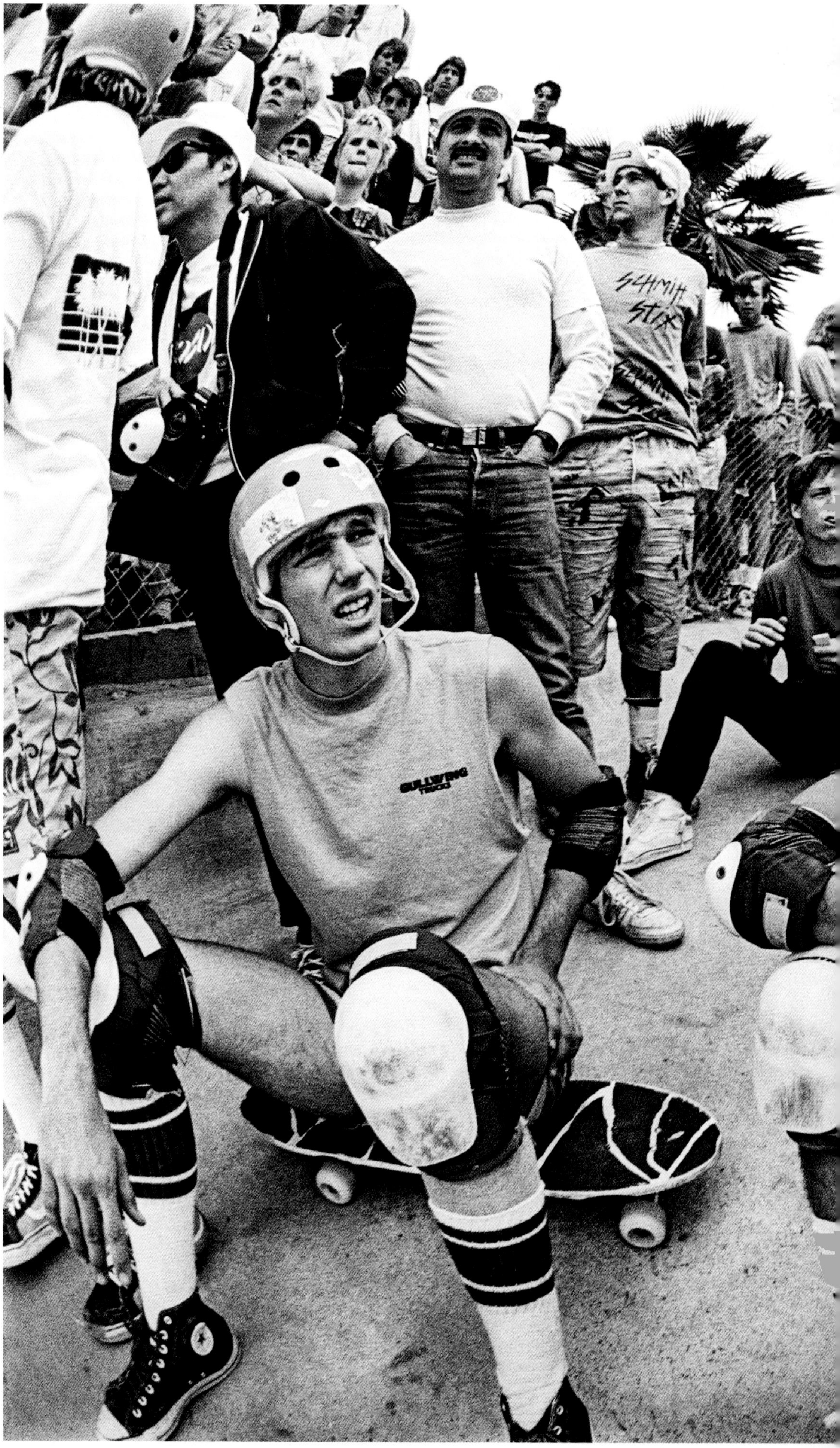

Pro contest skaters in keyhole pool entrance, Del Mar Skate Ranch, Del Mar, CA, 1985

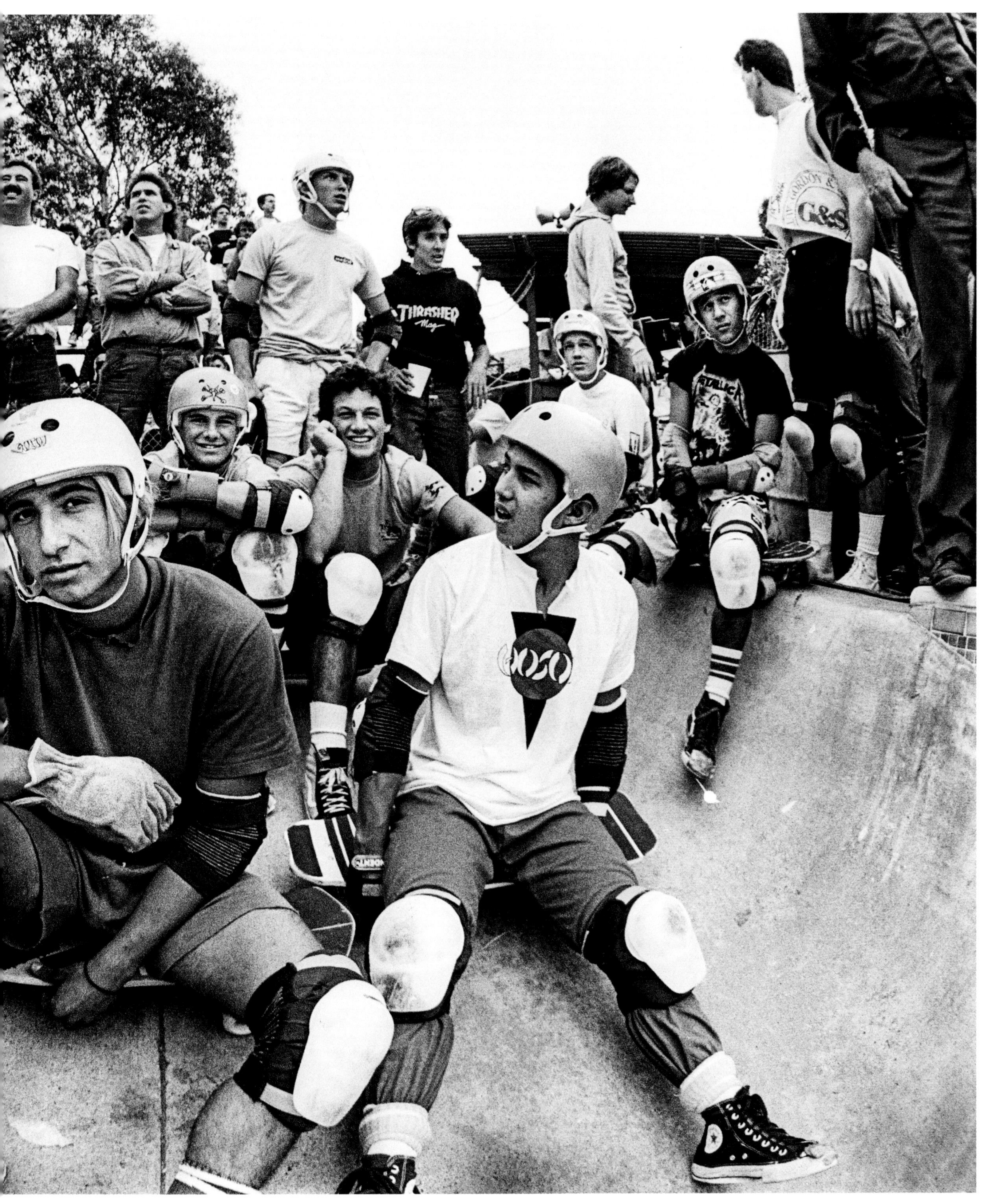
THRASHER
Mag
G&S

Sinisa Egelja, Portrait for TWS contents page, Del Mar, CA, 1985

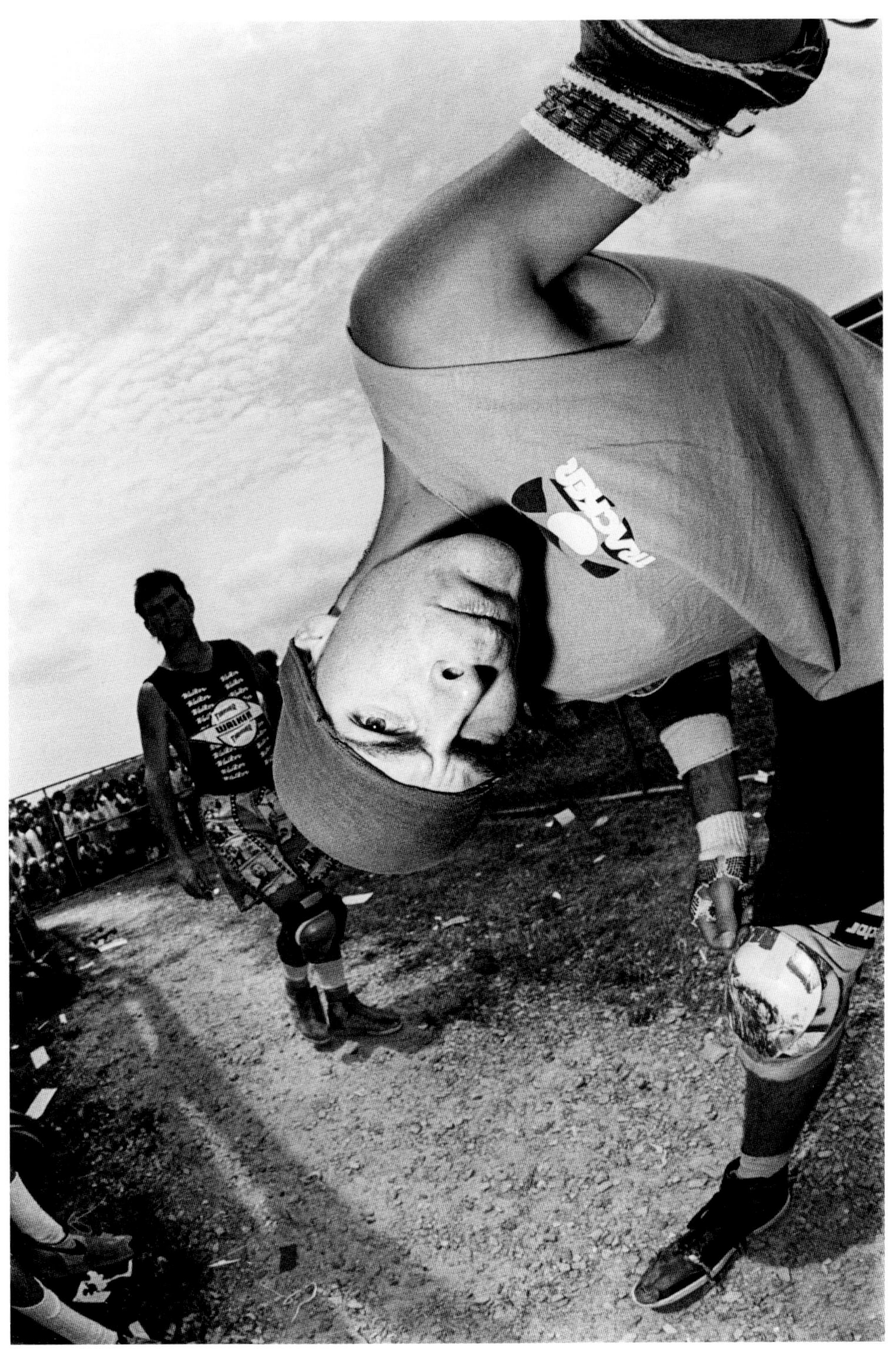

Neil Blender, Portrait, Mt. Trashmore, Virginia Beach, VA, 1986

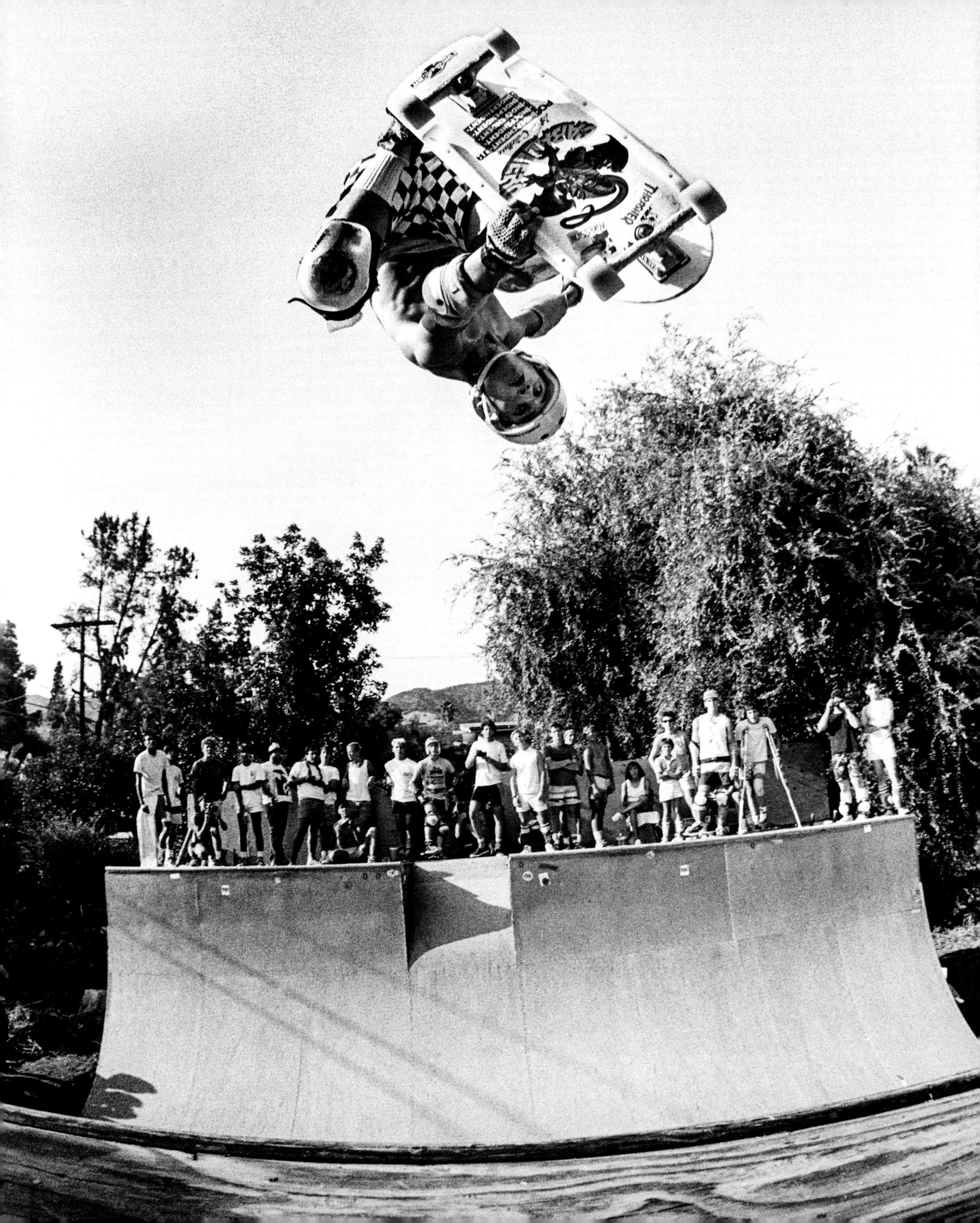

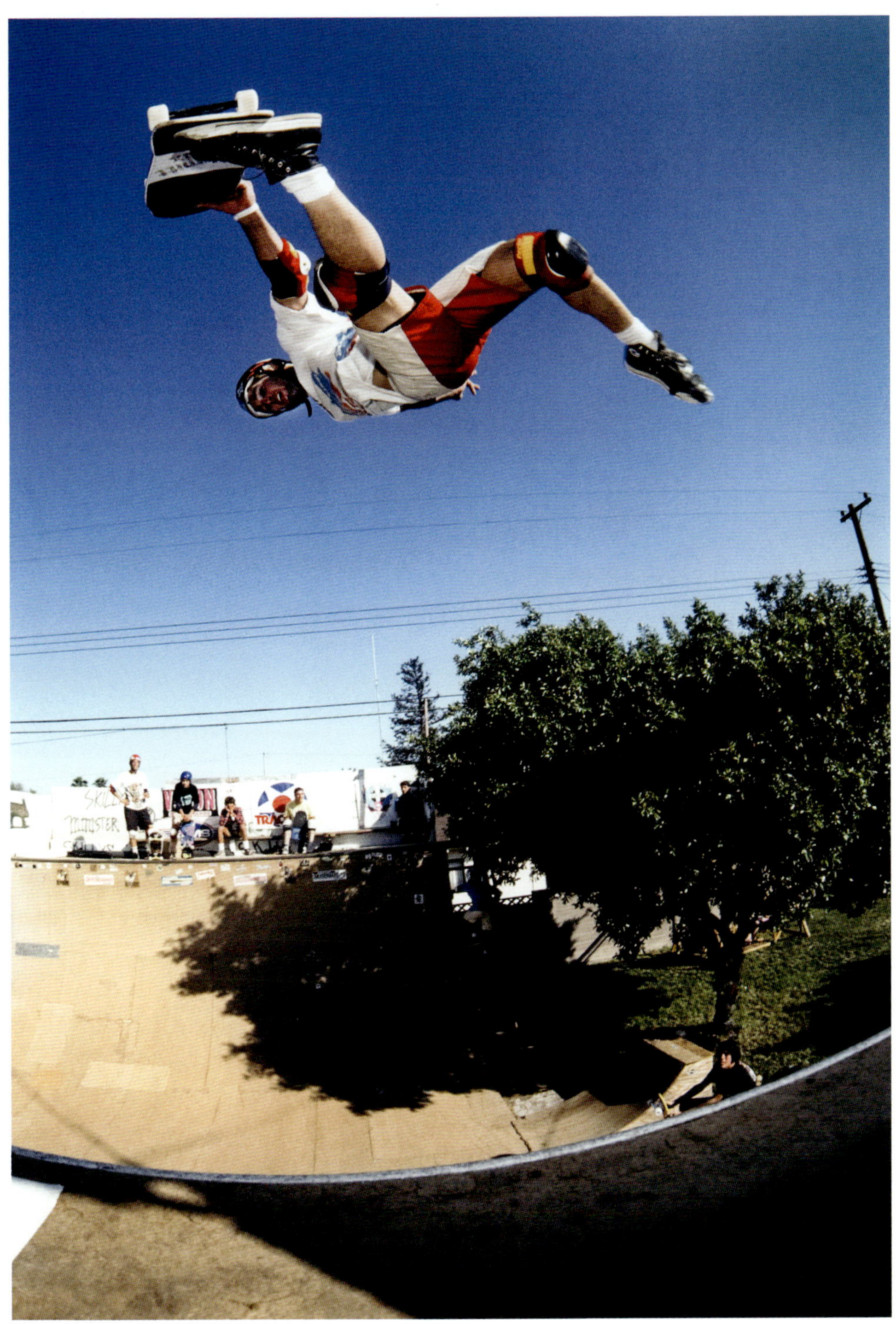

Monty Nolder, Frigid air, Skilly's Ramp, Westminster, CA, 1986

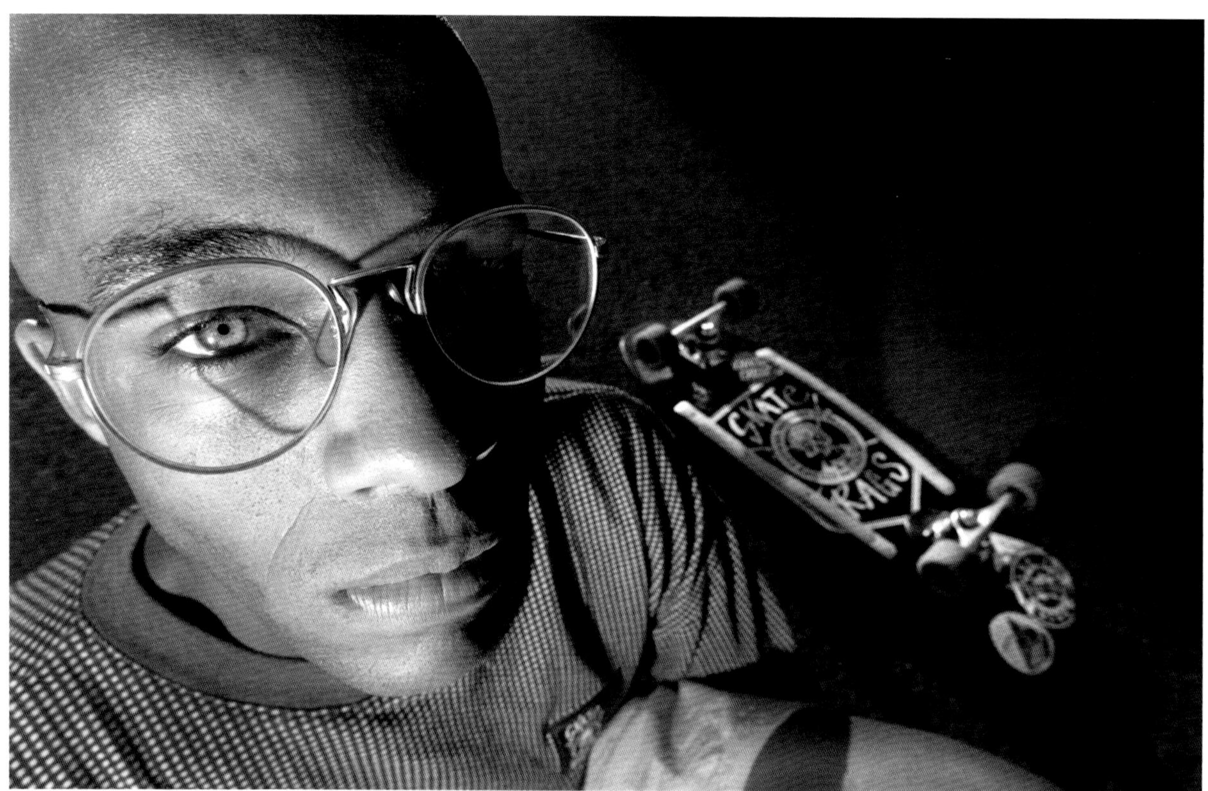

Chuck Treece, Portrait, Oceanside, CA, 1988

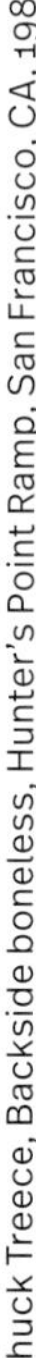

Chuck Treece, Backside boneless, Hunter's Point Ramp, San Francisco, CA, 1984

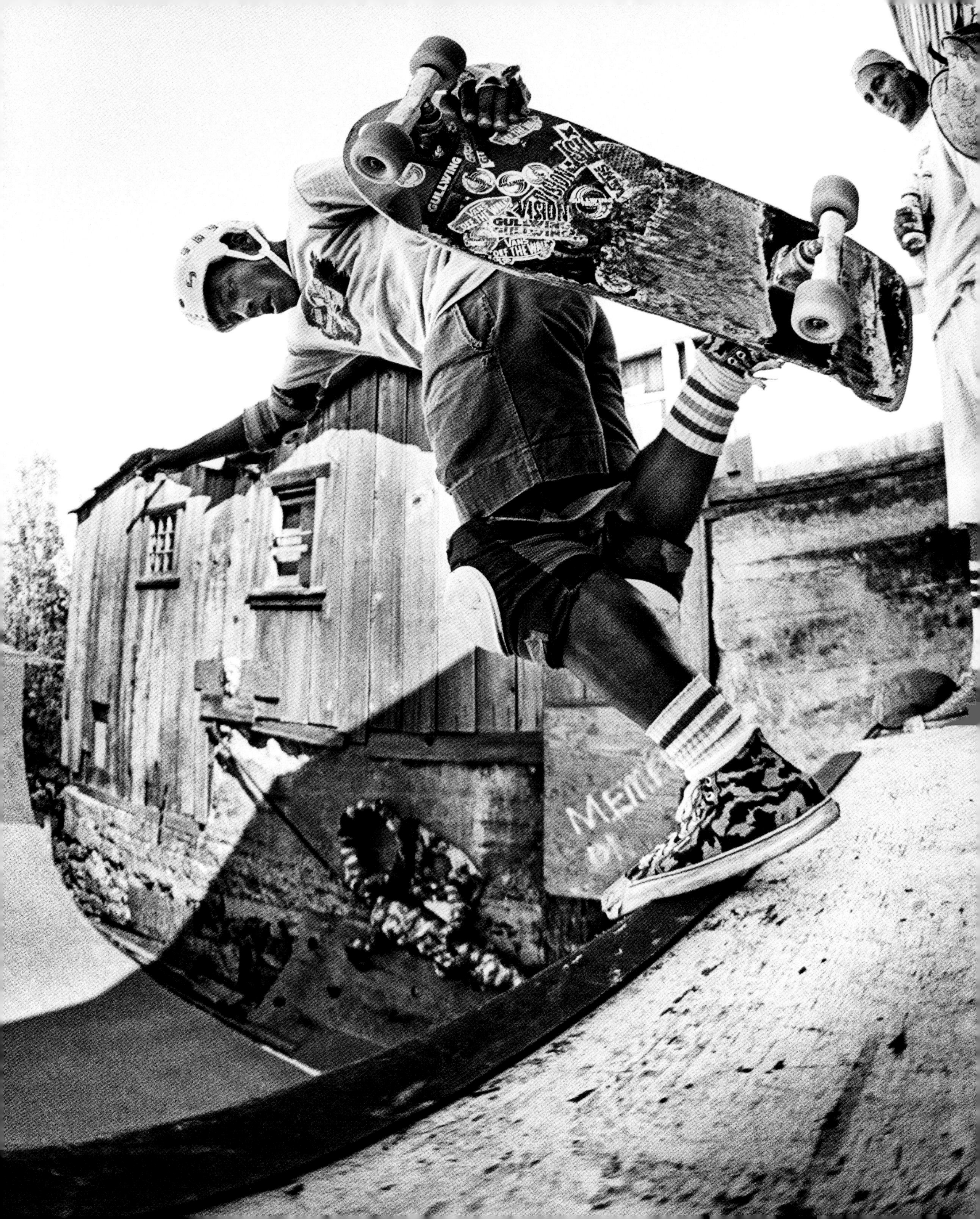
GULLWING
VISION
VANS OFF THE WALL

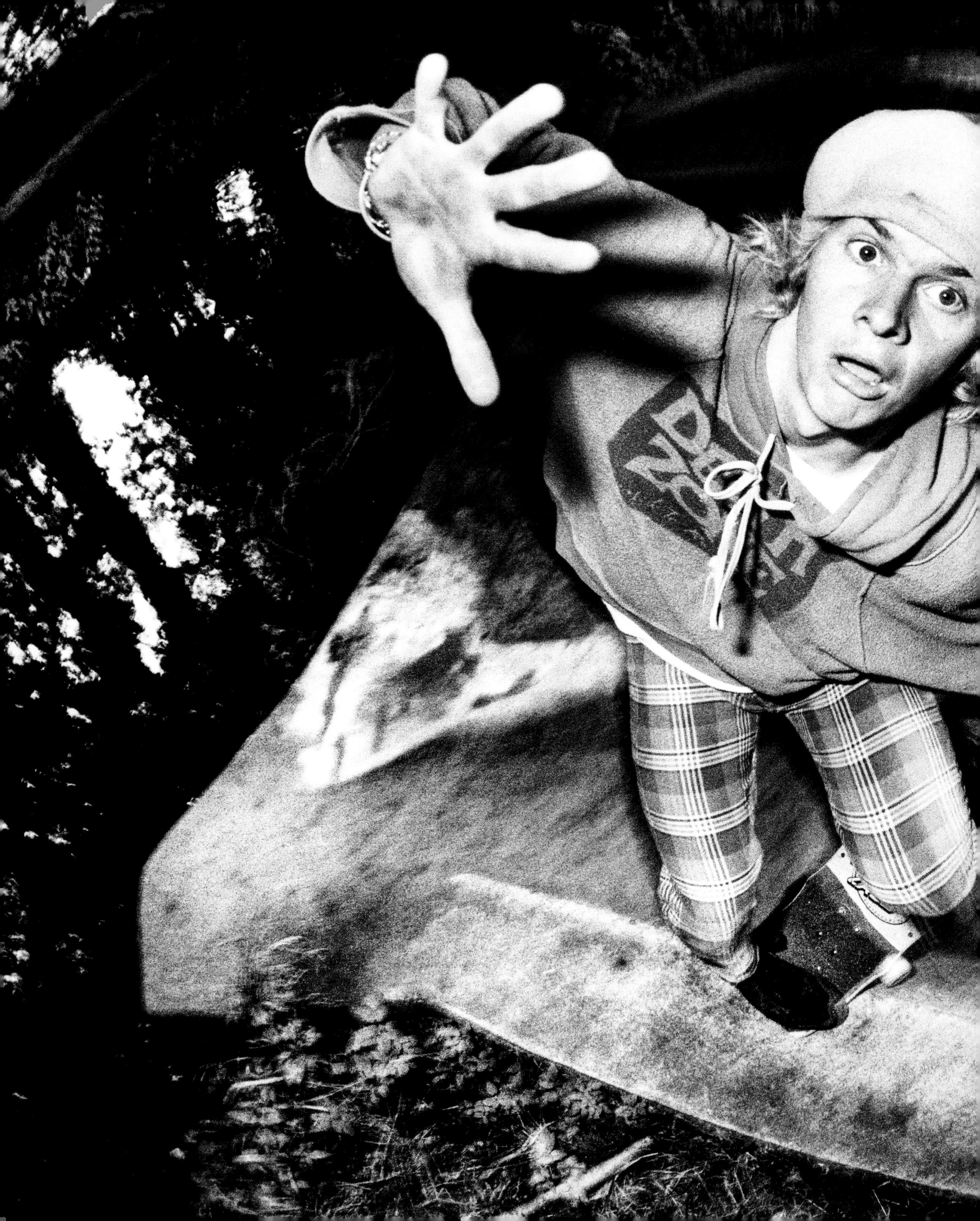

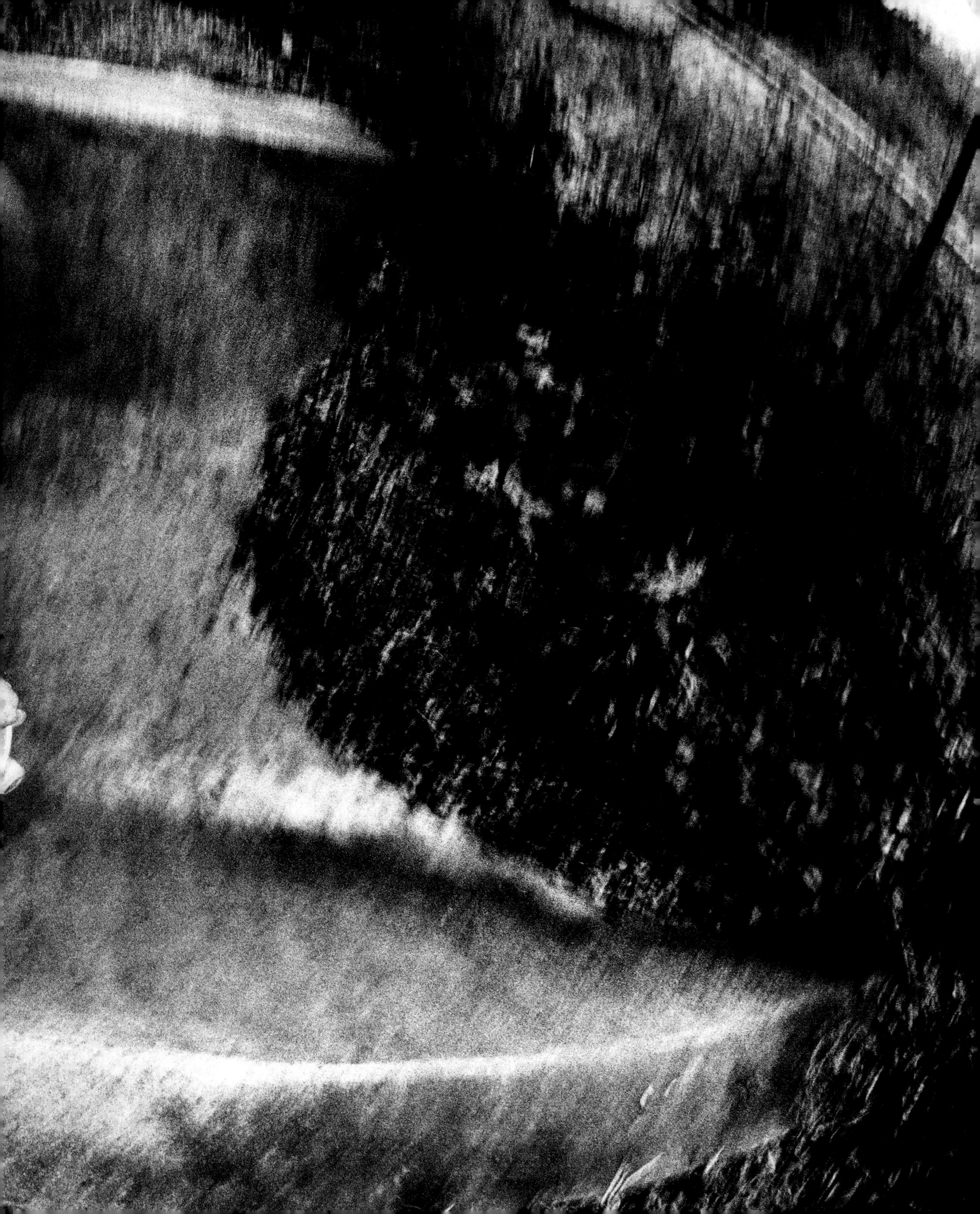

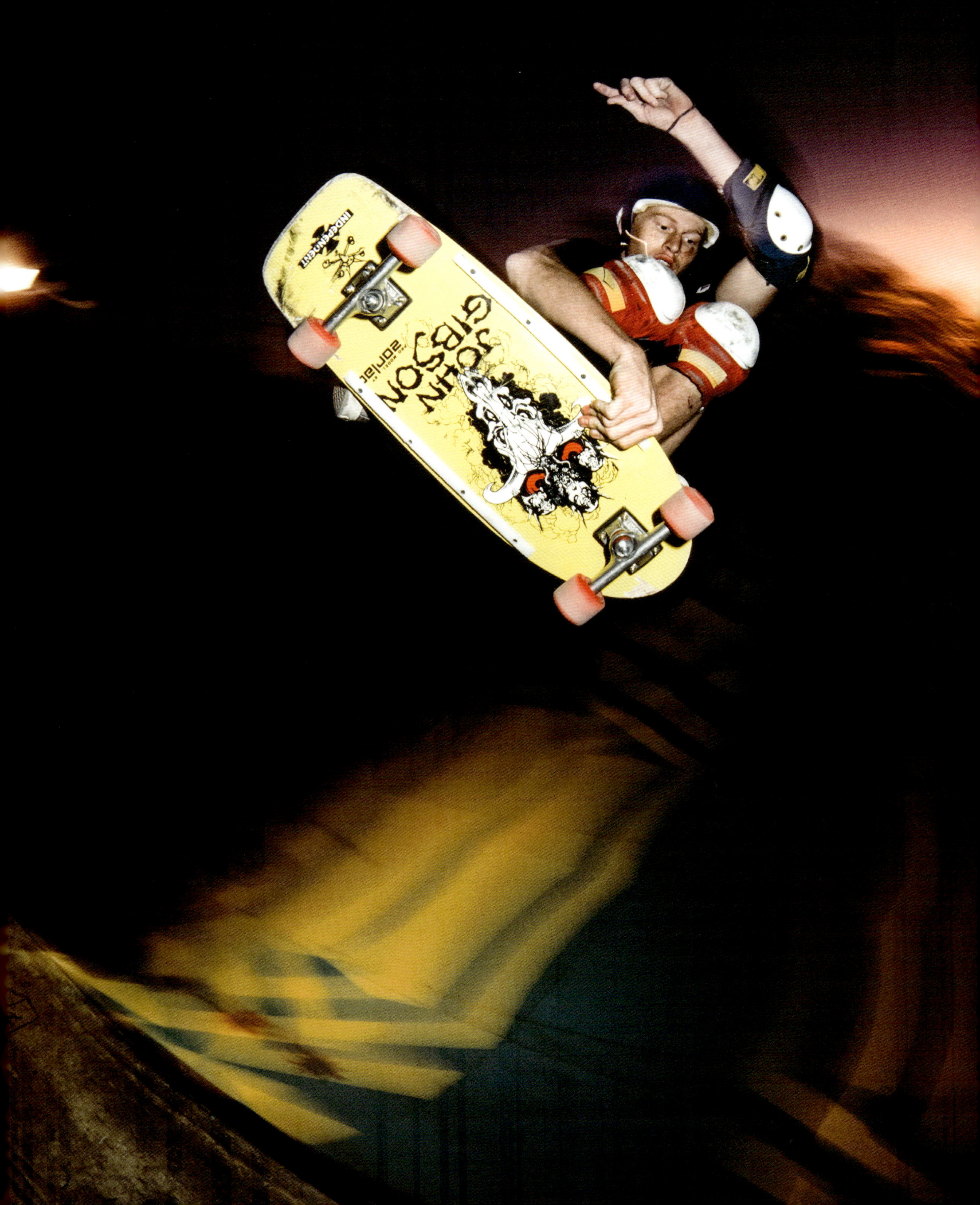
INDEPENDENT
JOHN GIBSON

Previous spread: Claus Grabke, Tailslide, Gütersloh Ditch, Gütersloh, Germany, 1987

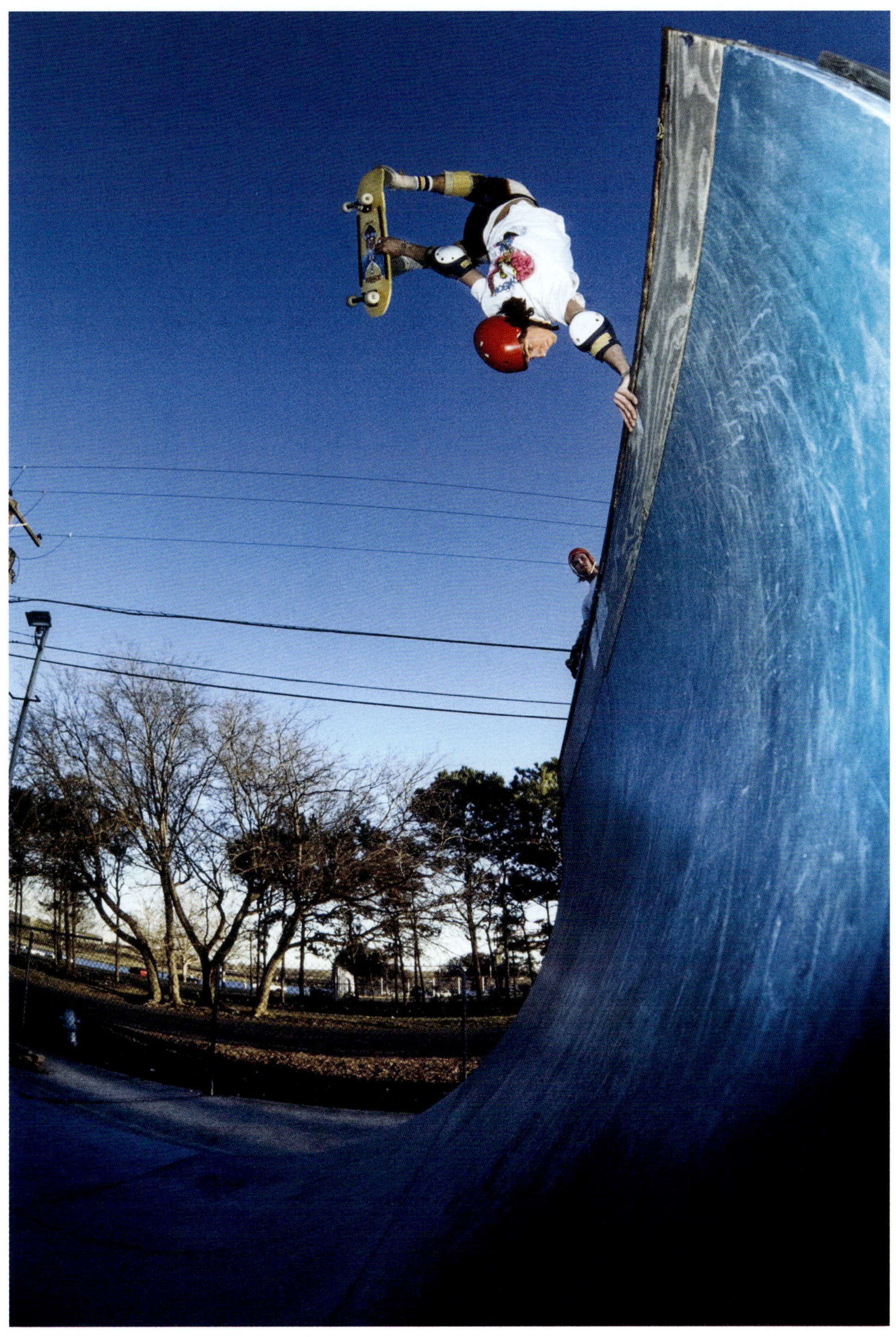

Craig Johnson, Andrecht plant, Blue Ramp, Dallas, TX, 1986

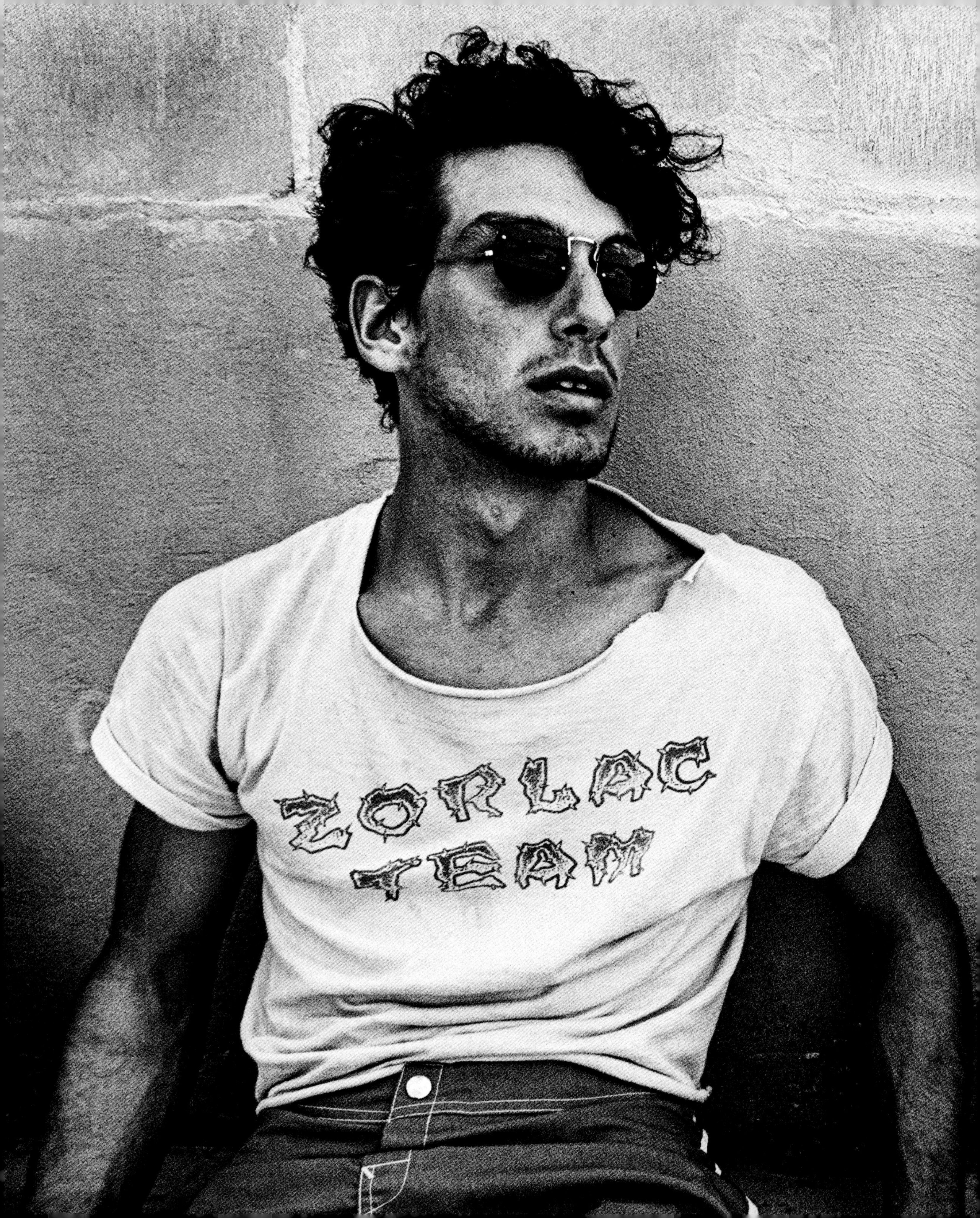
ZORLAC
TEAM

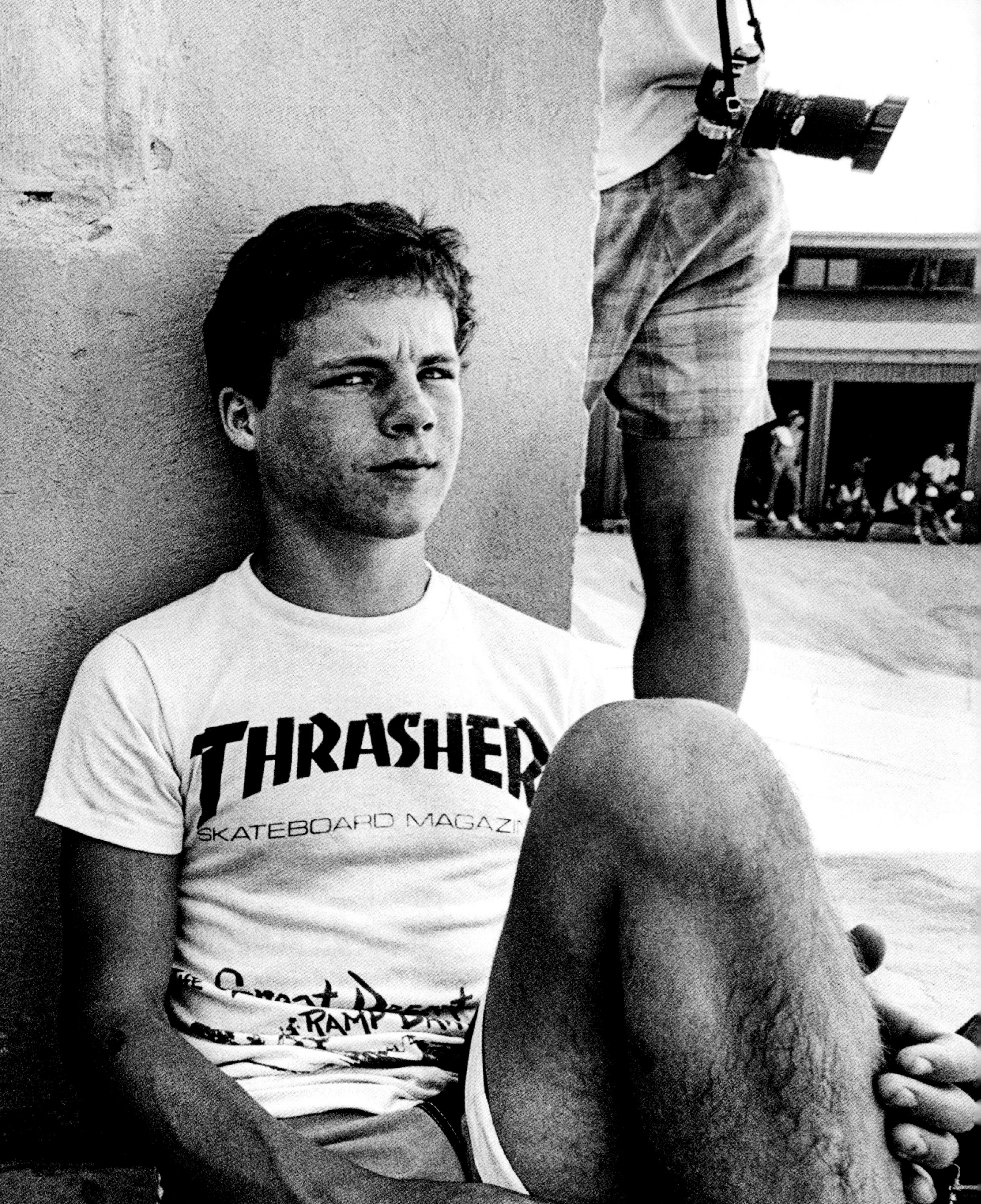
THRASHER
SKATEBOARD MAGAZIN

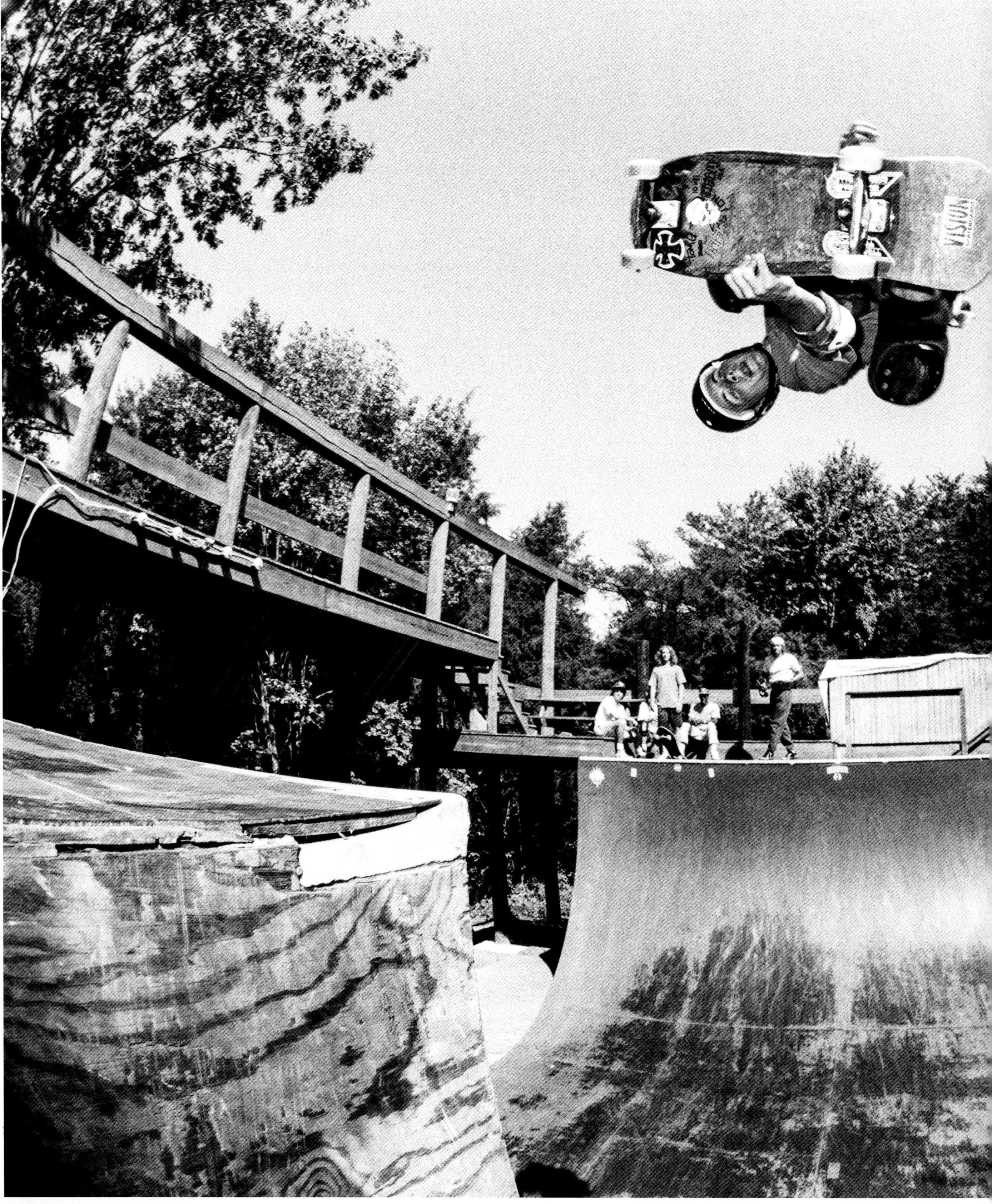
VISION

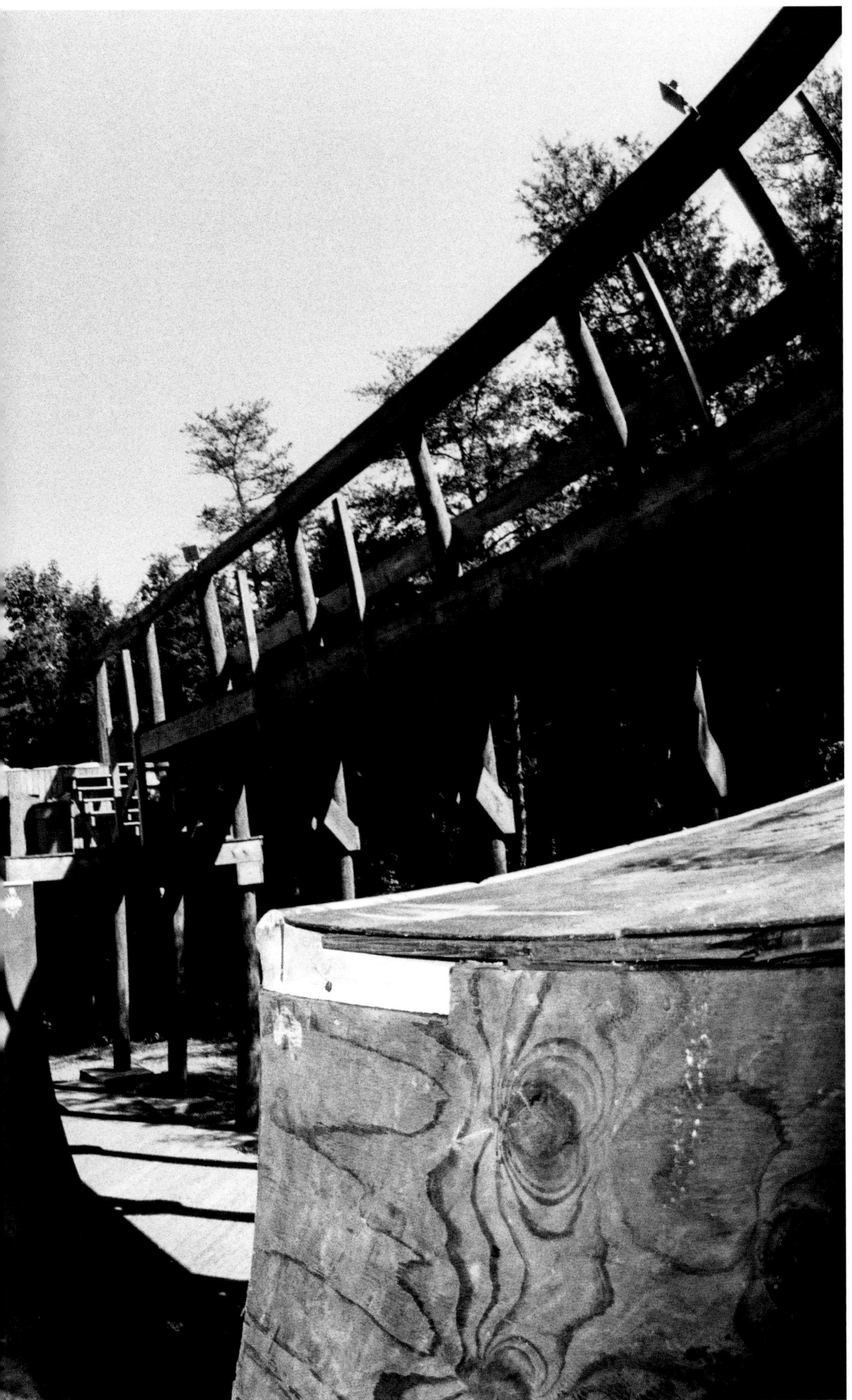

Tom Groholski, Indy over channel, Cedar Crest Country Club, Centreville, VA, 1988

Previous spread: Craig Johnson and Tom Groholski, Portrait, Kona Skatepark, Jacksonville, FL, 1984

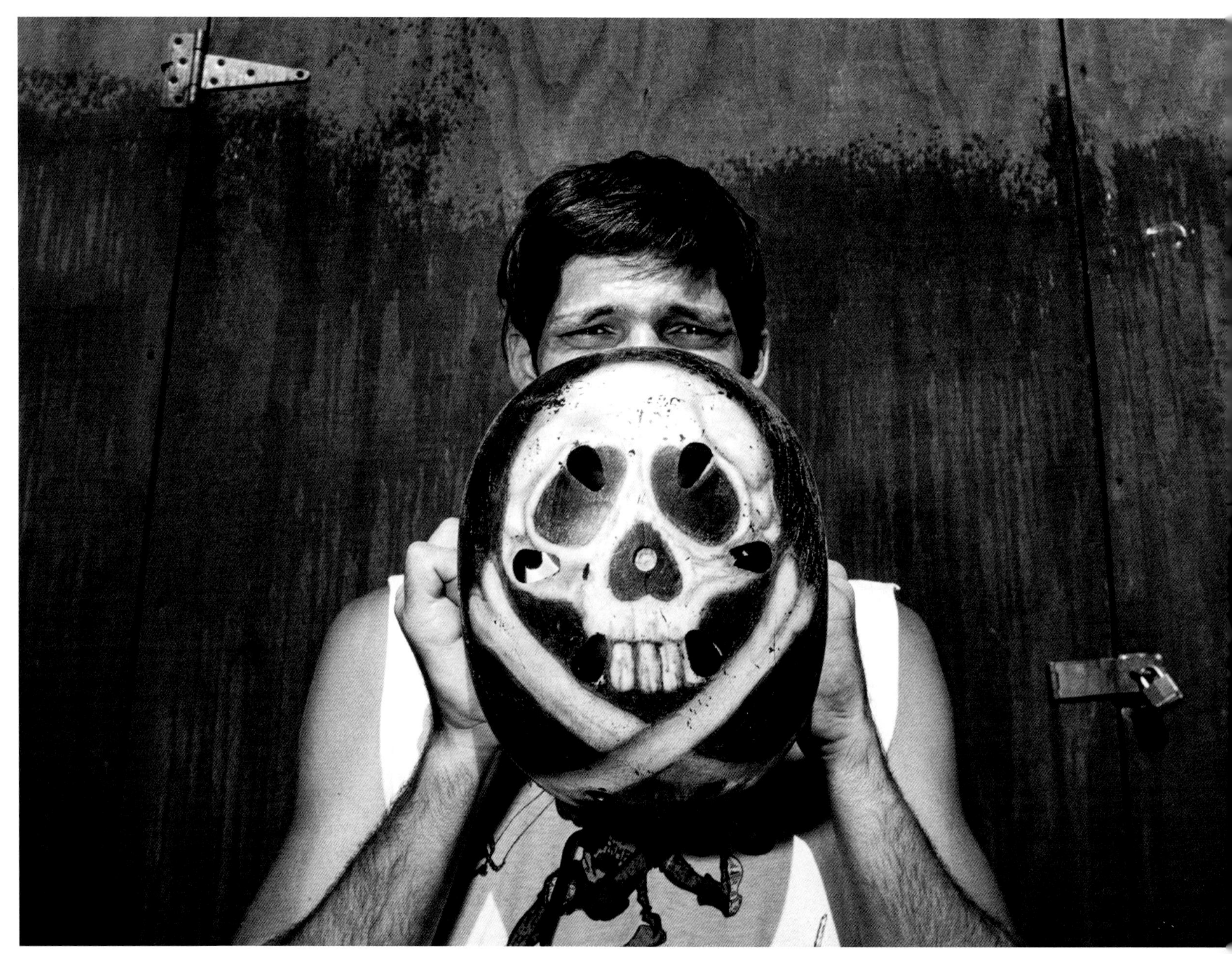

Jeff Phillips, Portrait, Skatepark of Houston, Houston, TX, 1988

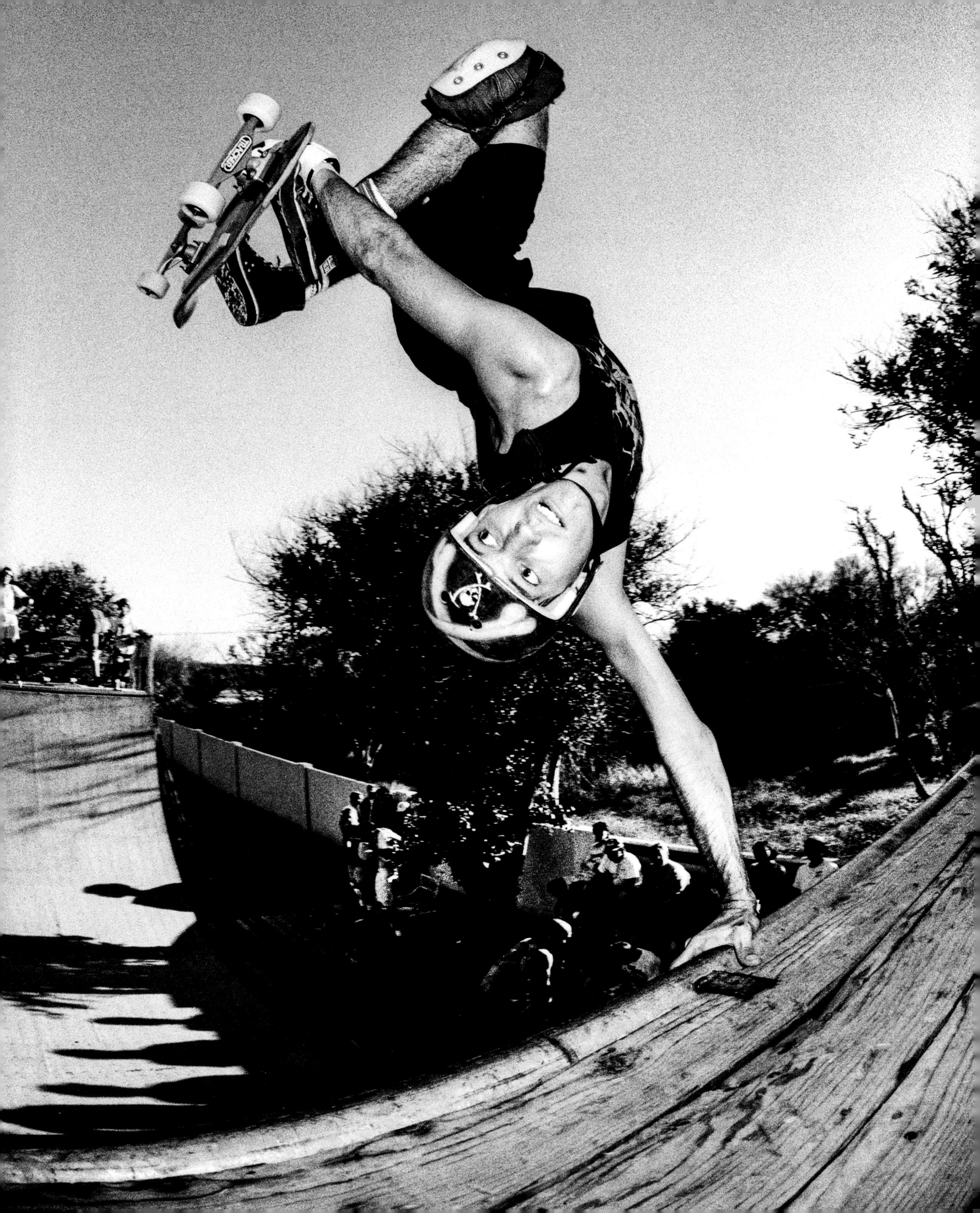

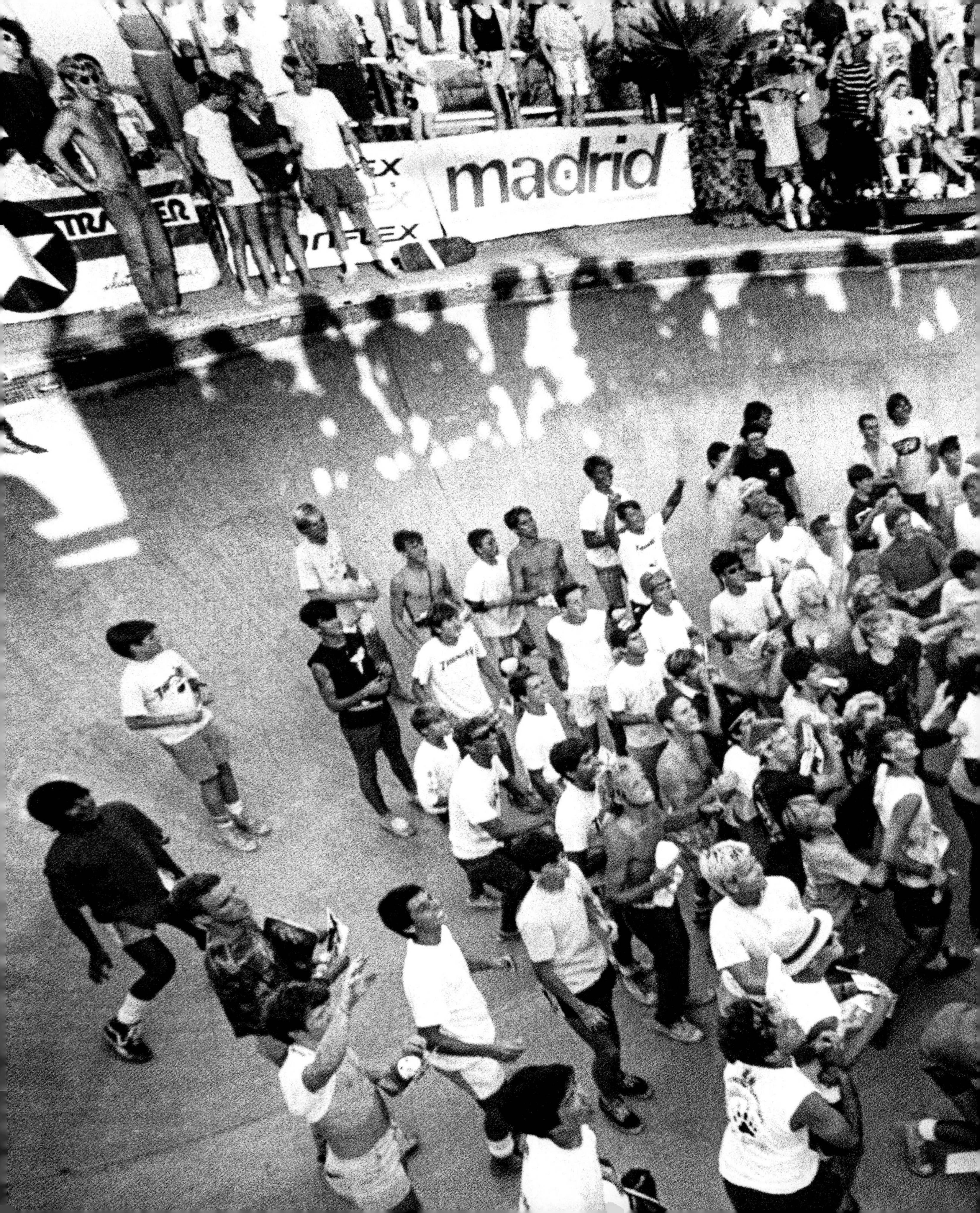
madrid

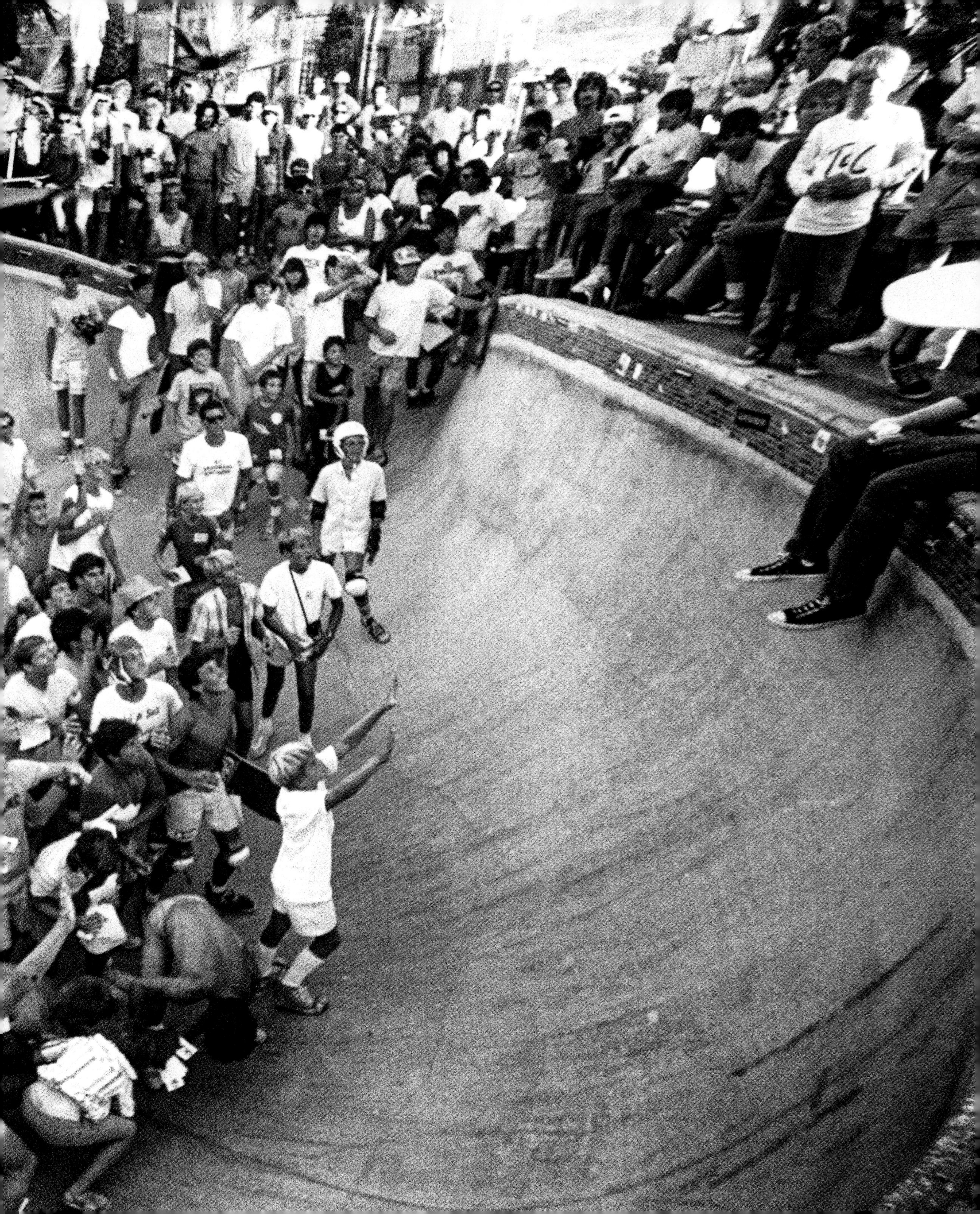

Previous spread: Sticker Toss at Del Mar contest, Del Mar Skate Ranch, Del Mar, CA, 1984

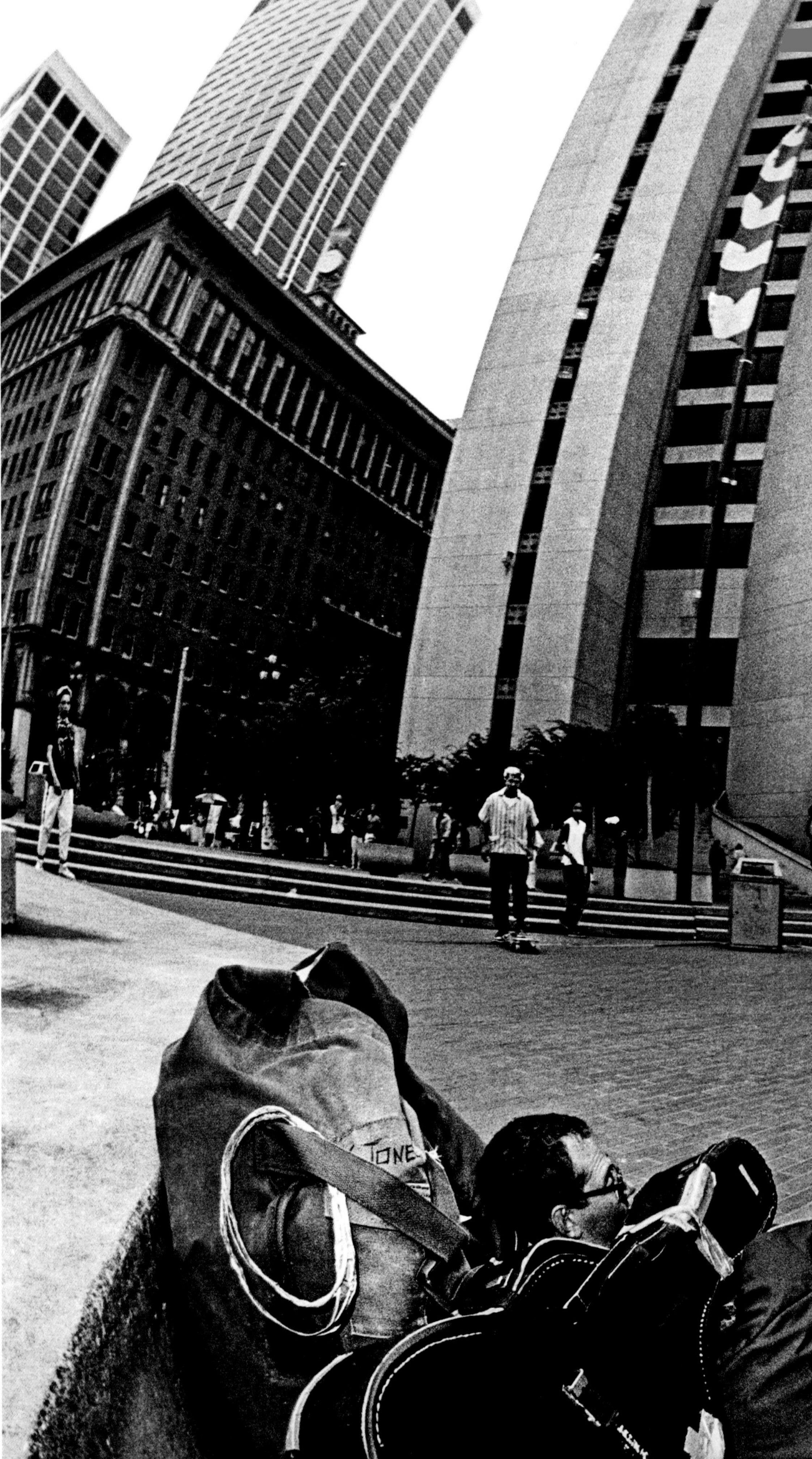

Orb, Ollie over sleeper, Embarcadero, San Francisco, CA, 1986

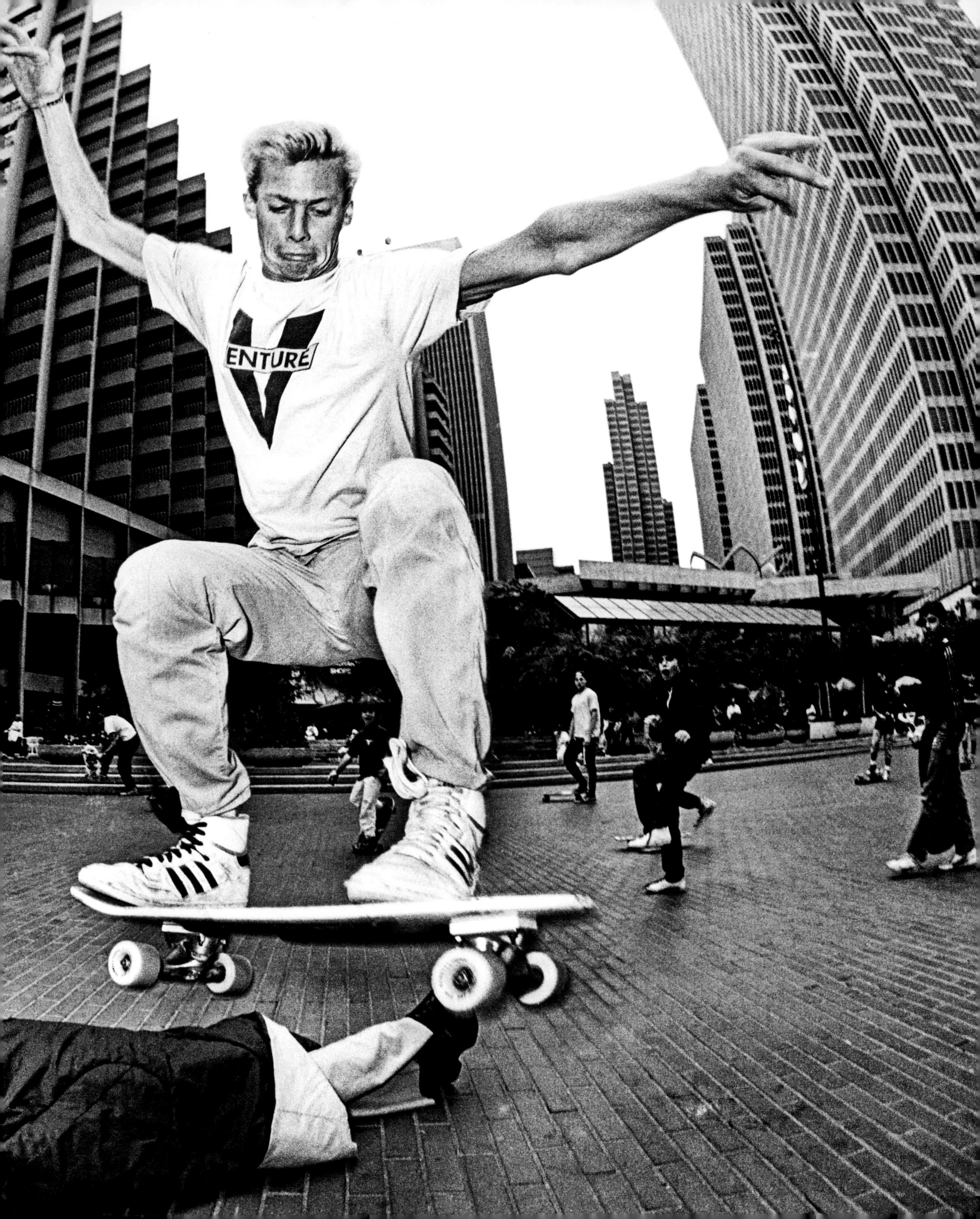
ENTURE

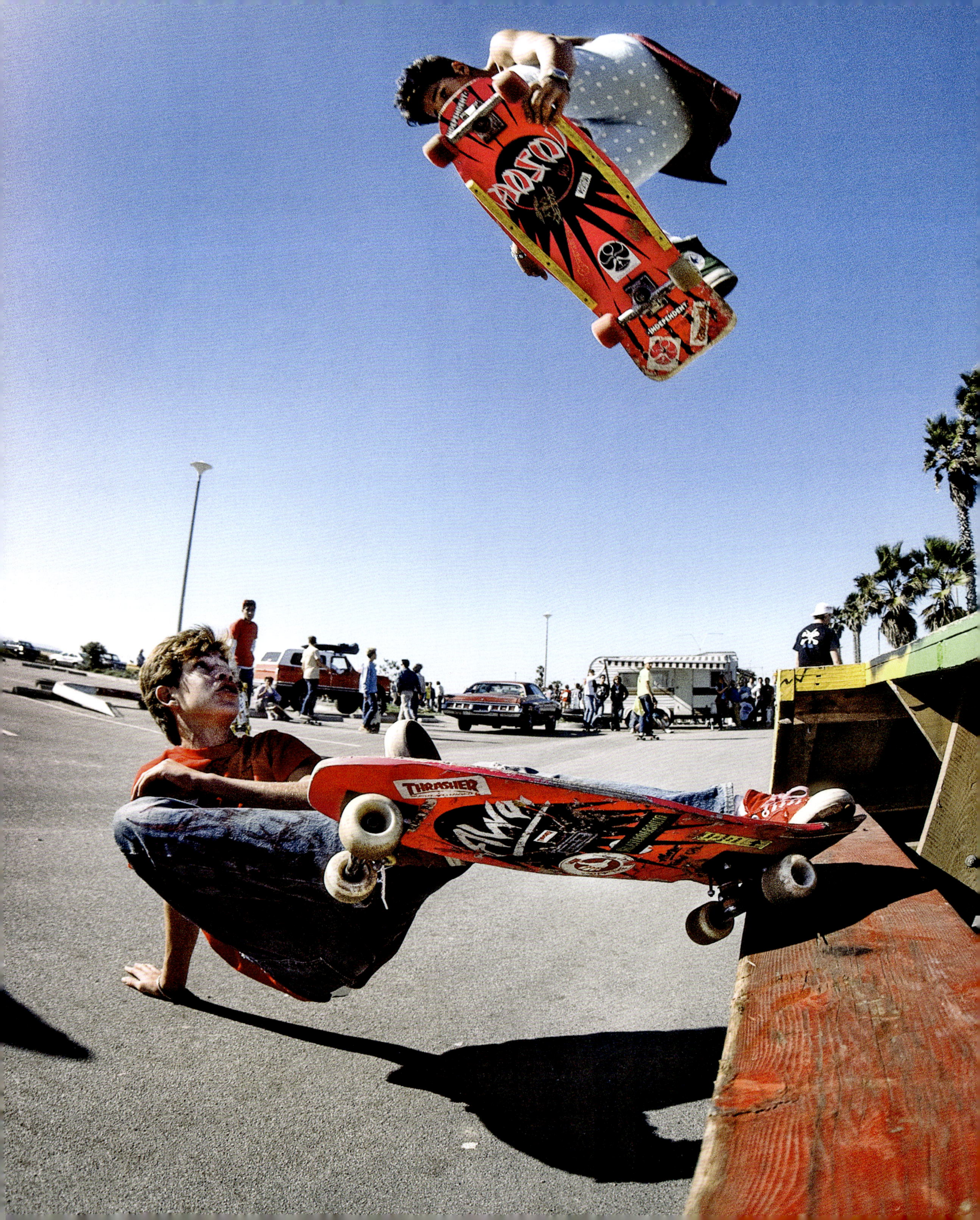
THRASHER

Mark Gonzales and Christian Hosoi, HB Contest, Huntington Beach, CA, 1984

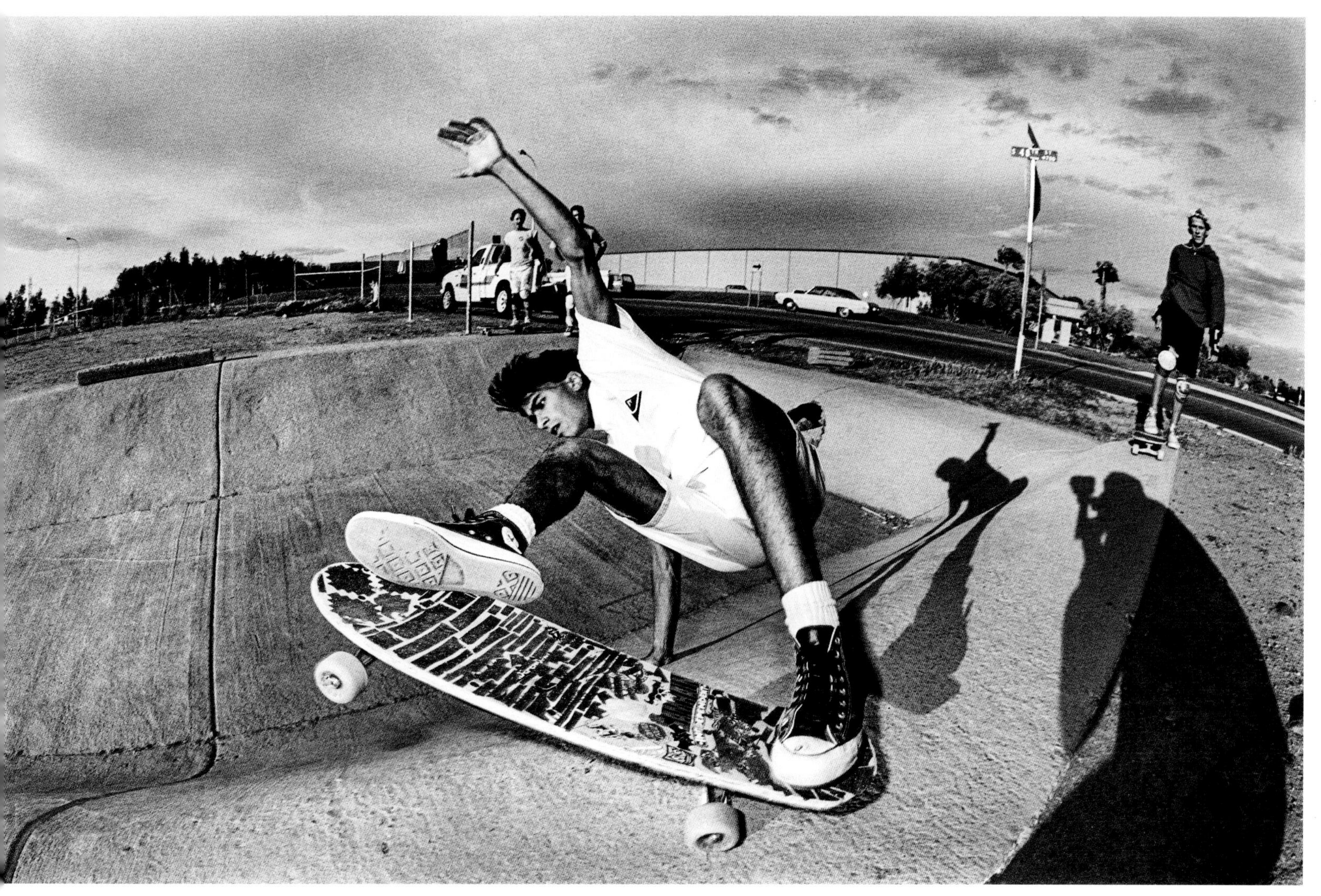

Rick "Spidey" De Montrond, Hohokam Ditch, Tempe, AZ, 1987

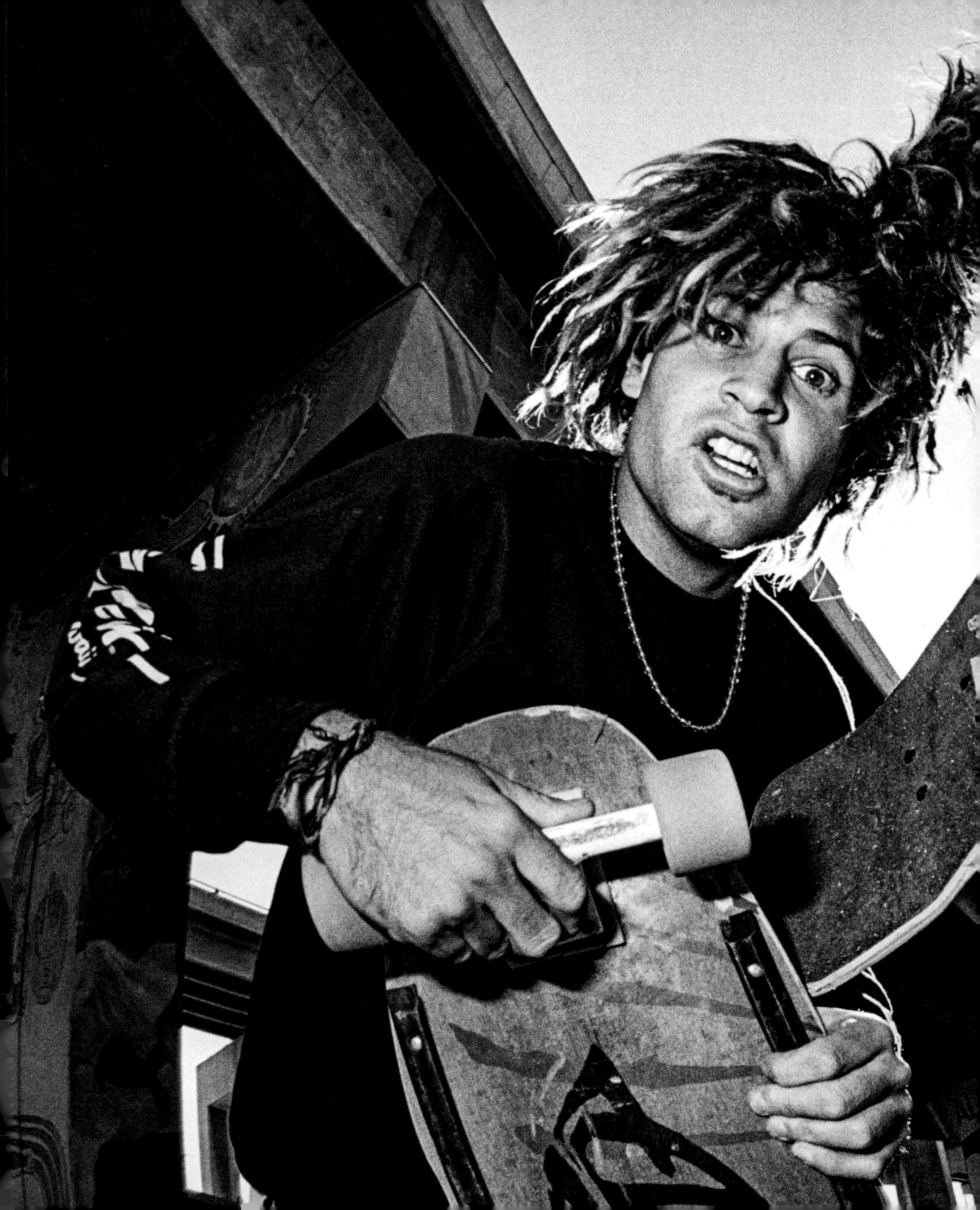

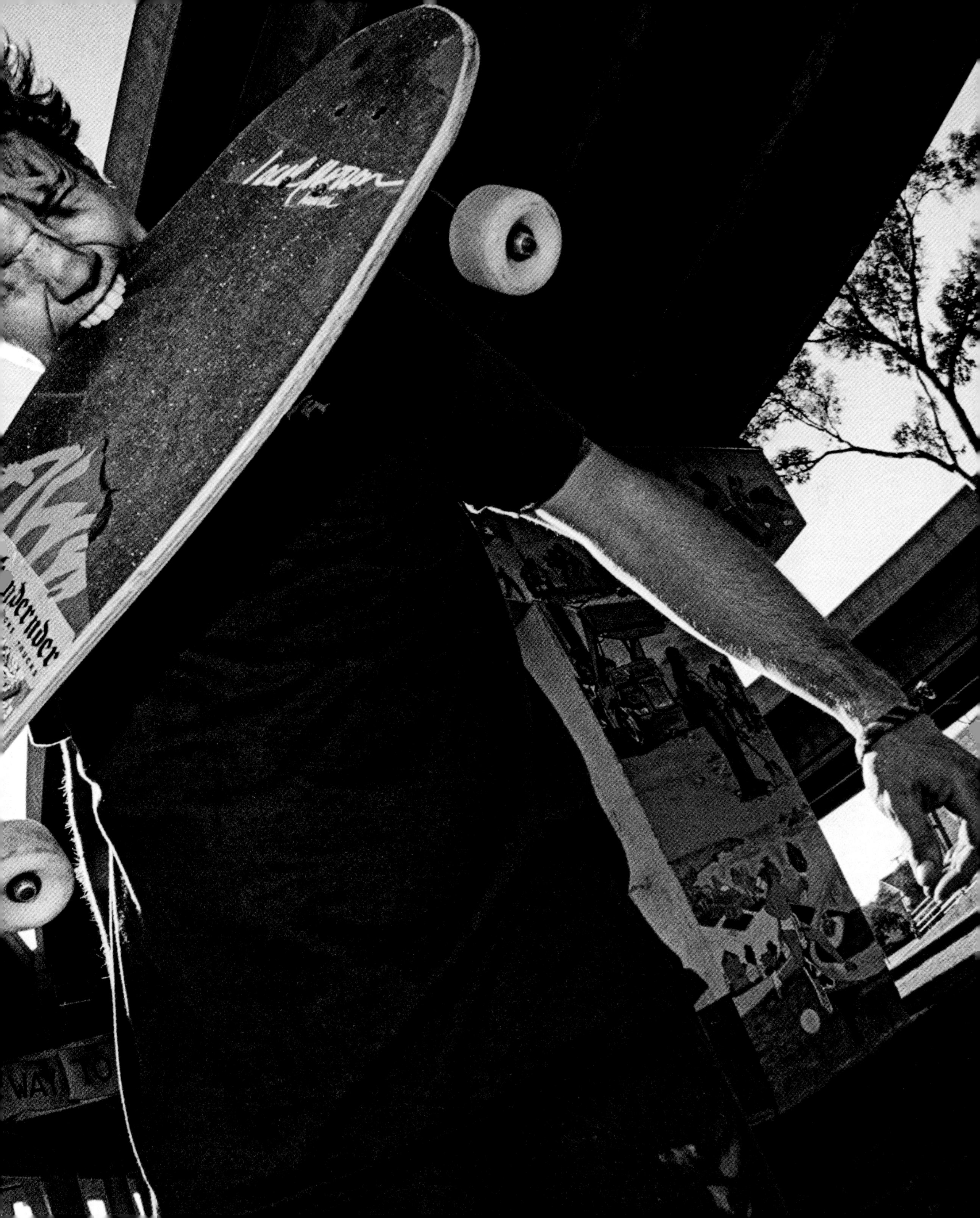
WAY

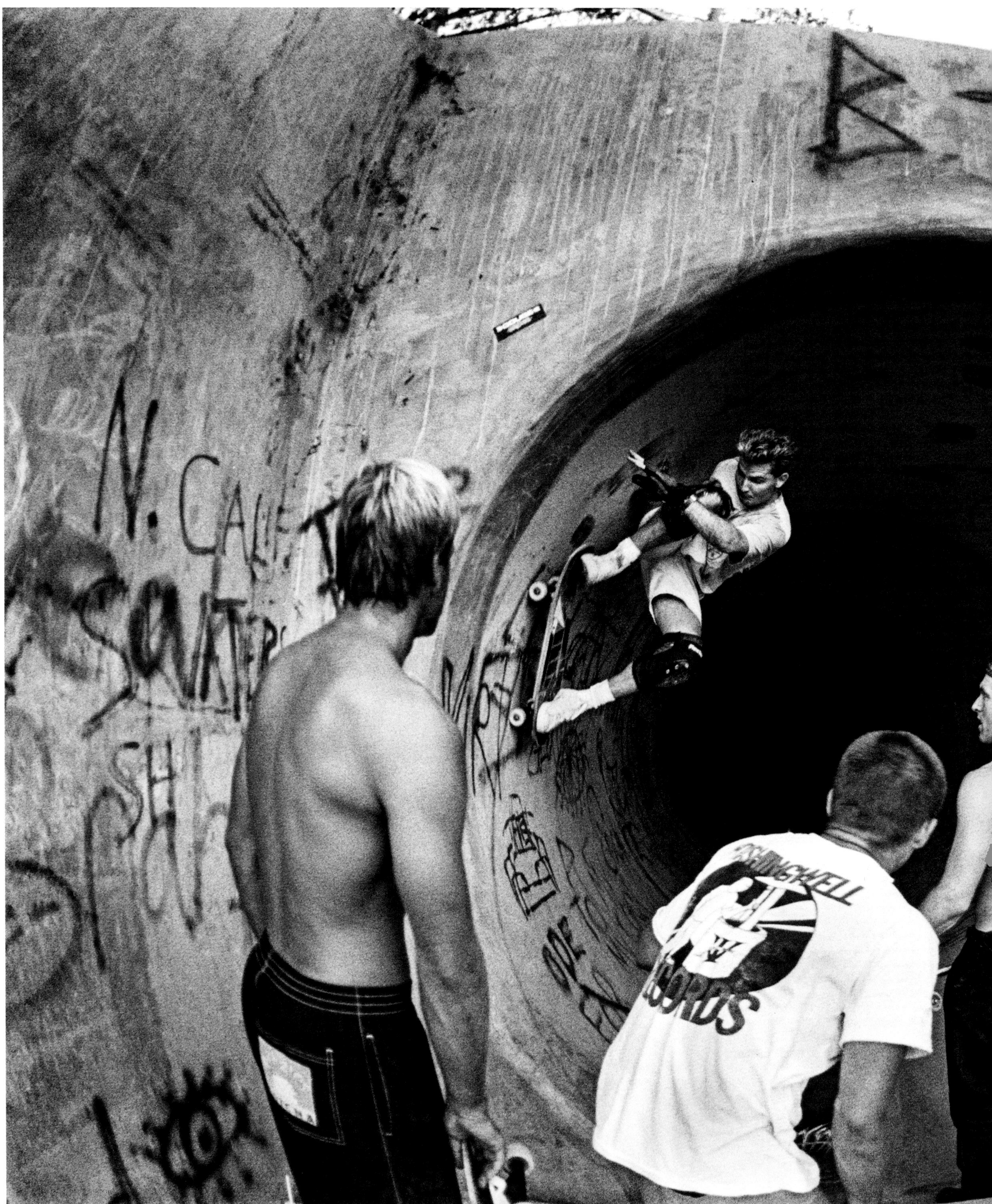

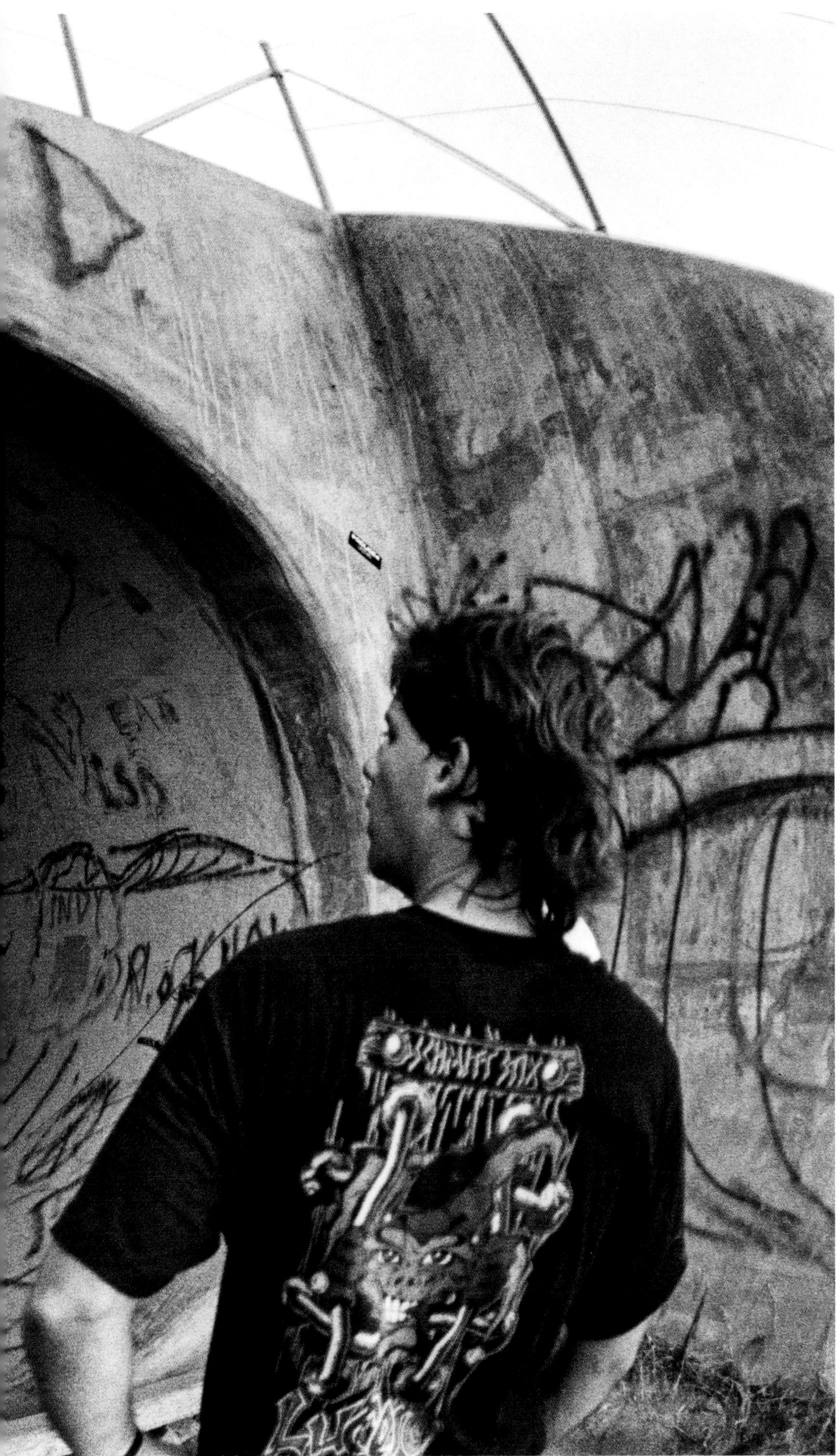

Jim Gray, Pico Pipe session, San Clemente, CA, 1987

Previous spread: Dave Duncan and John Thomas, Portrait, Chicano Park, San Diego, CA, 1987

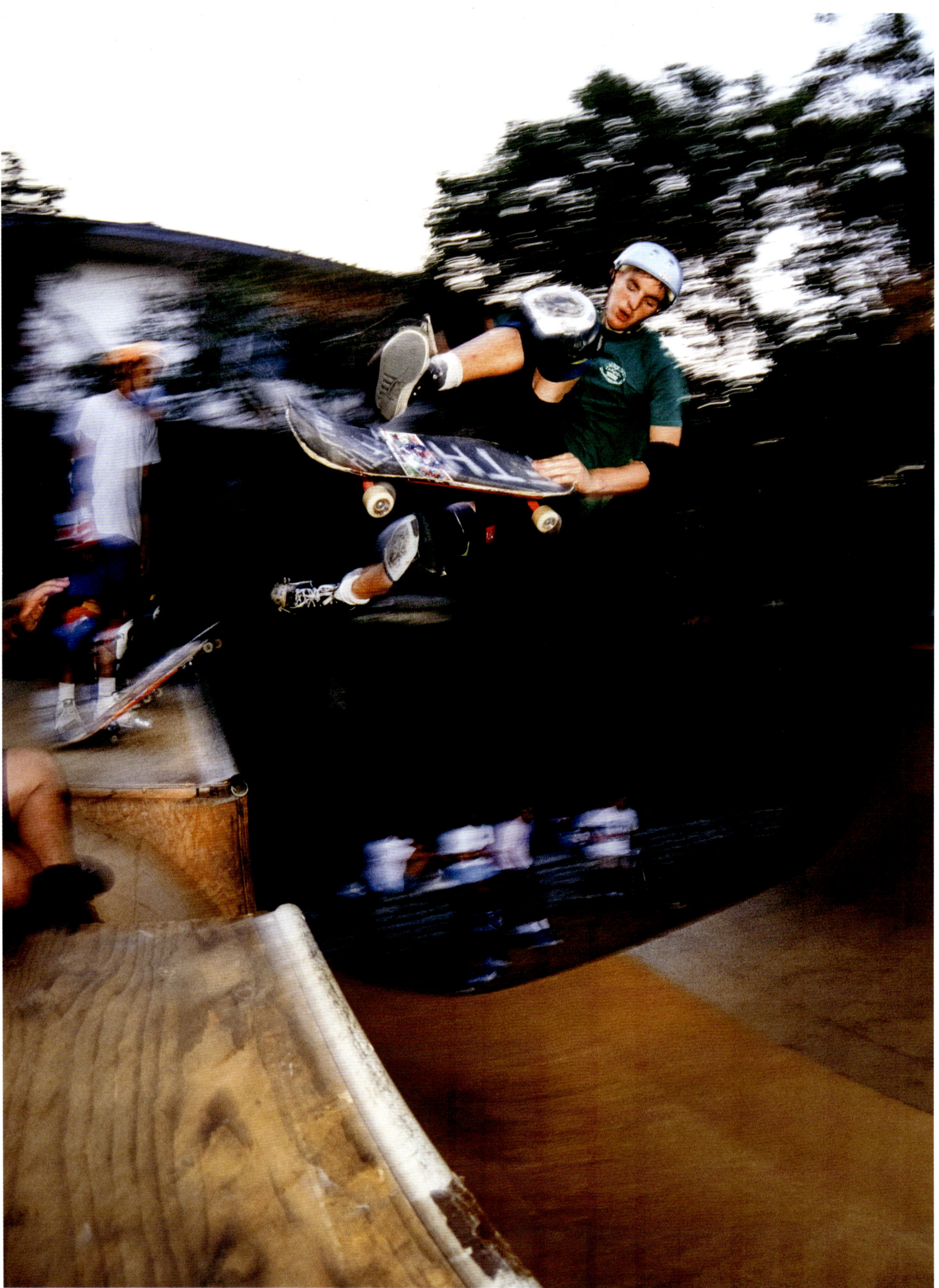

Ben Schroeder, Channel crossing, Mountain Manor, Alhambra, CA, 1987

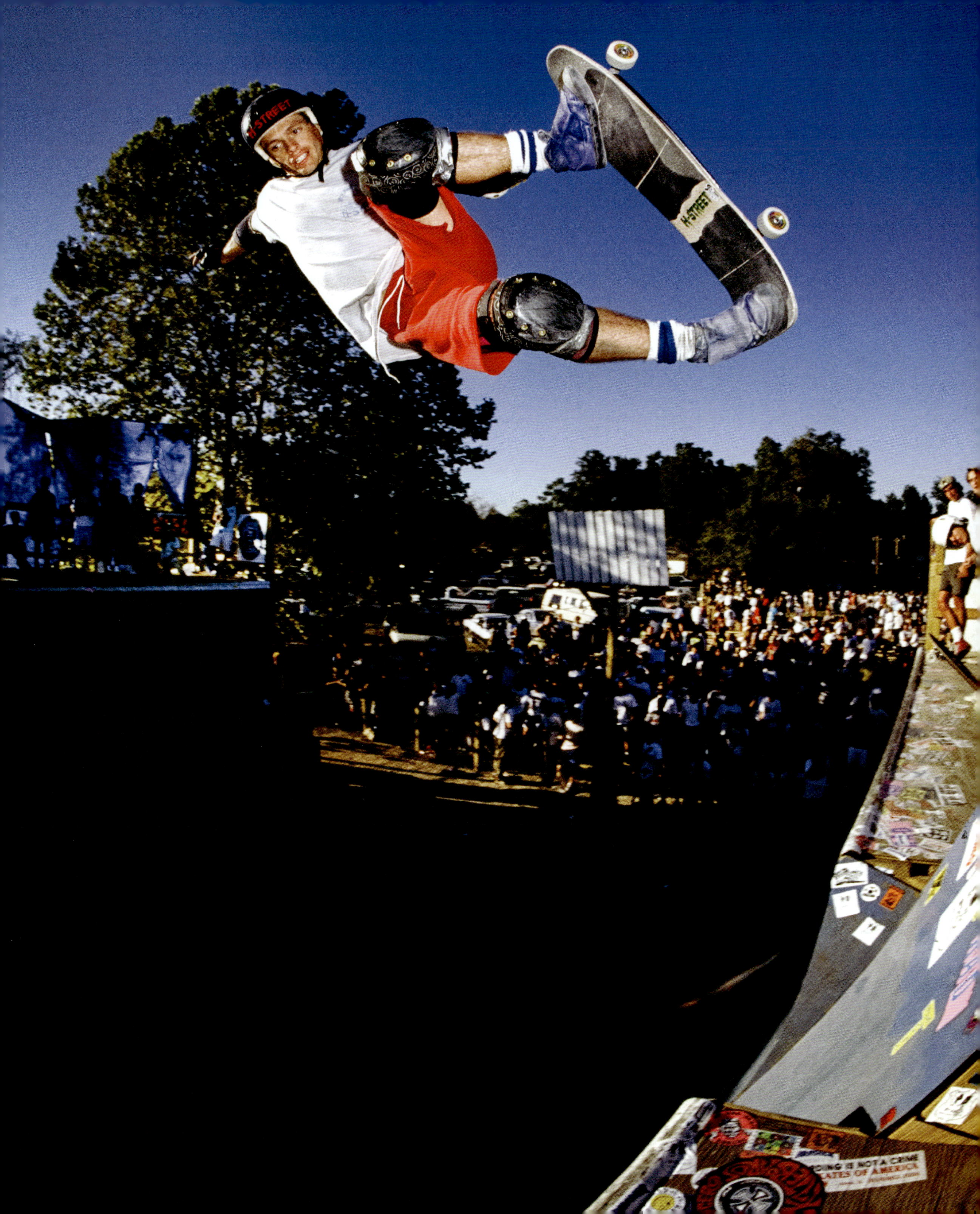
H-STREET
H-STREET

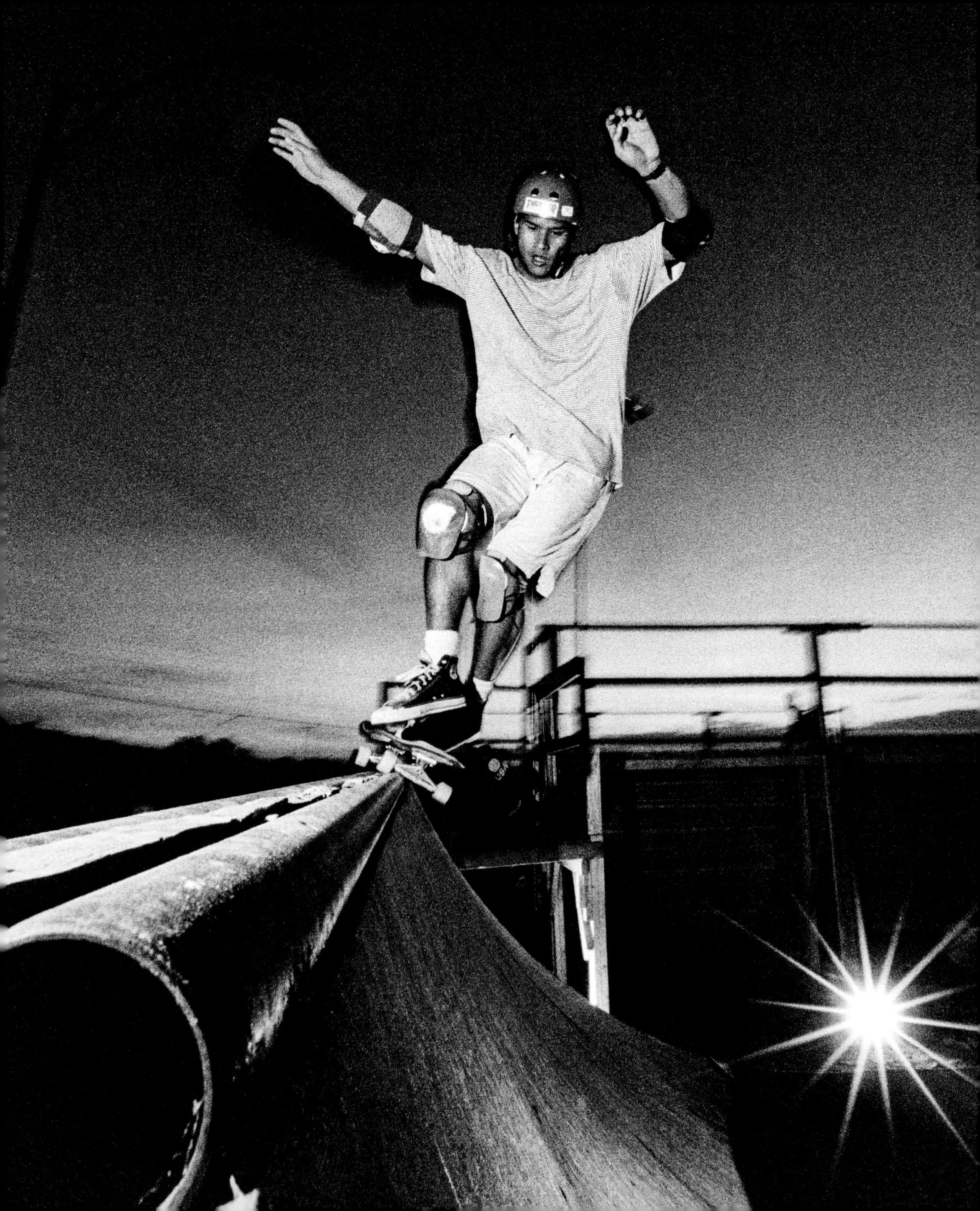

Pat Ngoho, Cross-step spine transfer, McGill's Skatepark, Carlsbad, CA, 1989

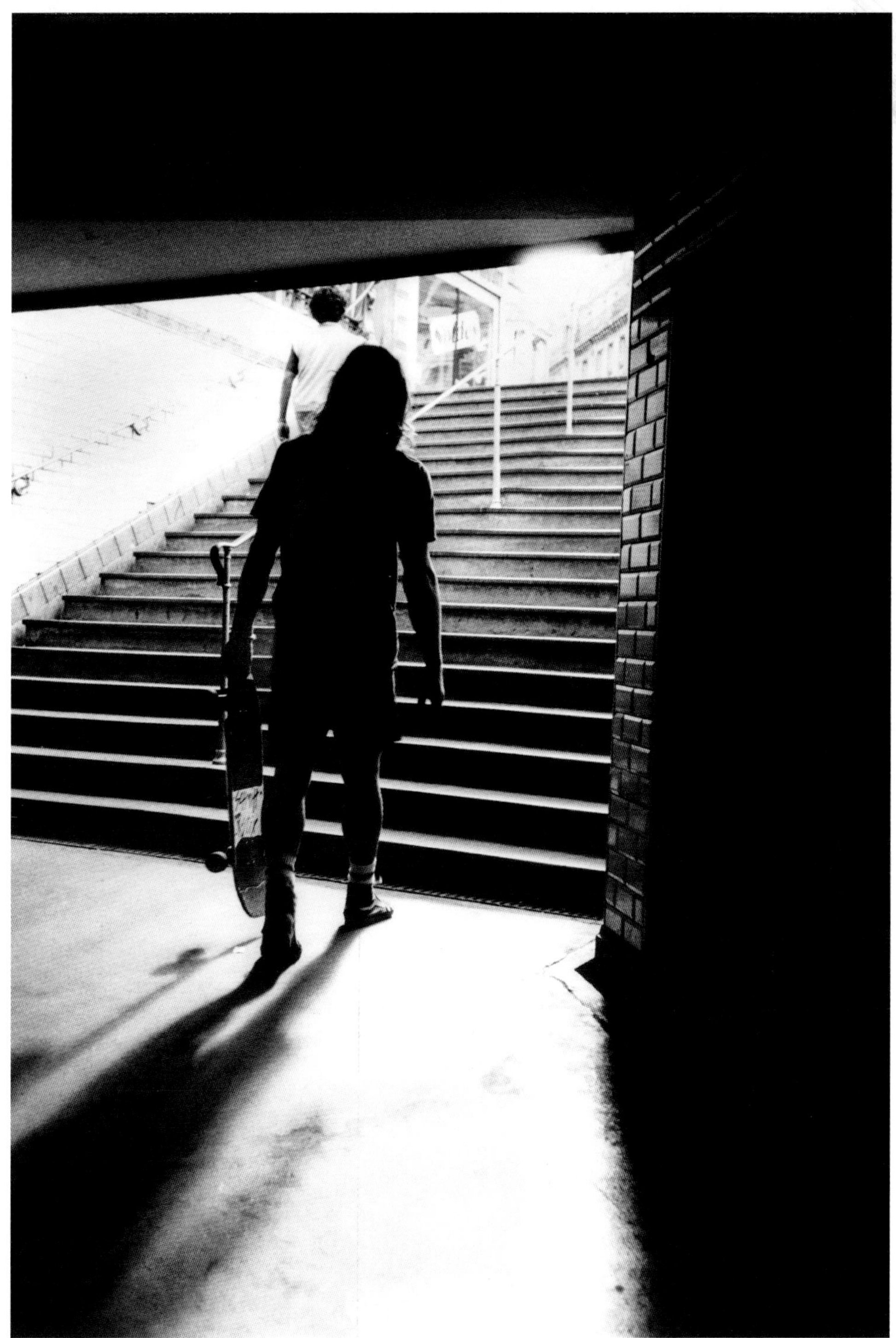

Bruno Peeters, Subway, Amsterdam, The Netherlands, 1987

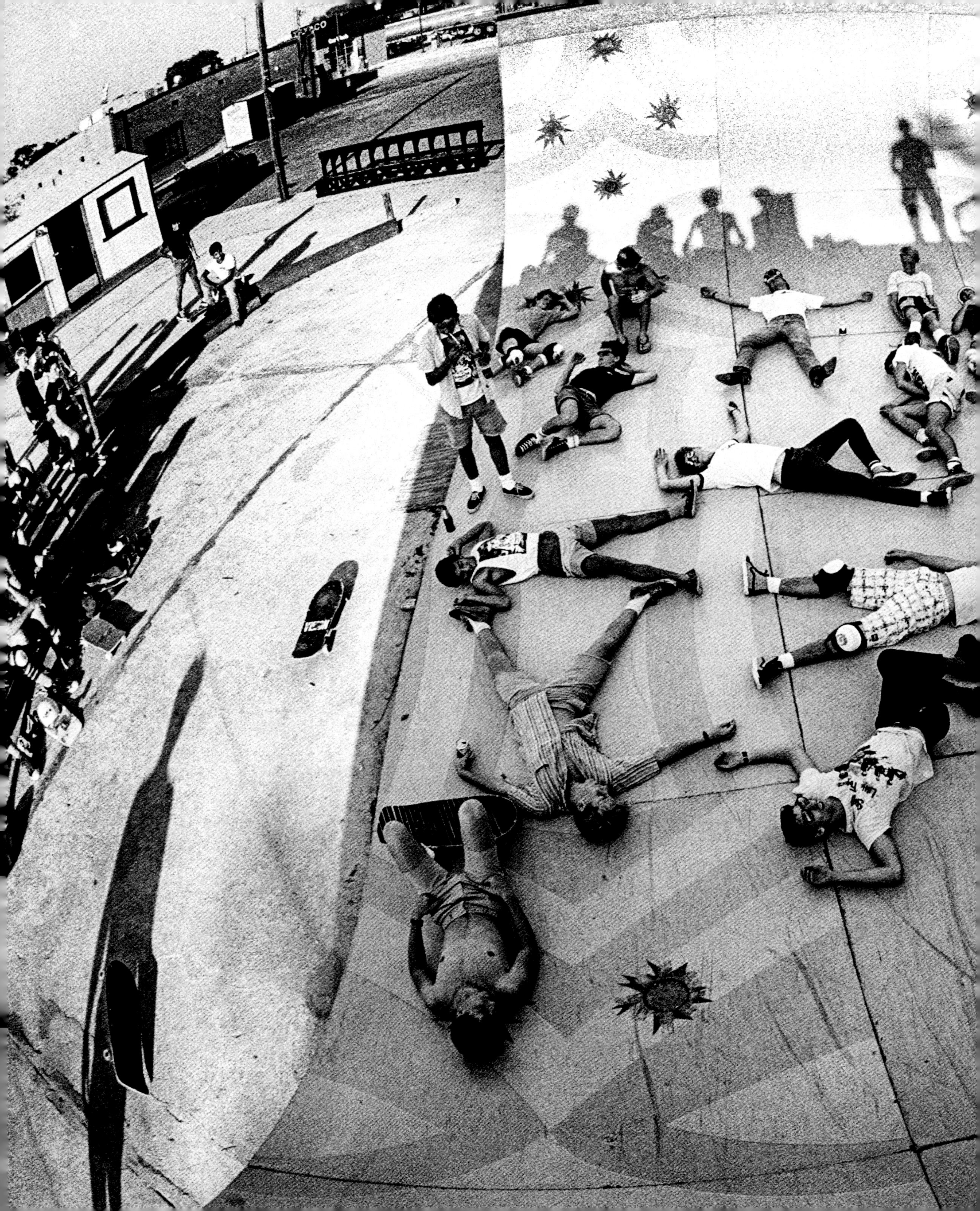

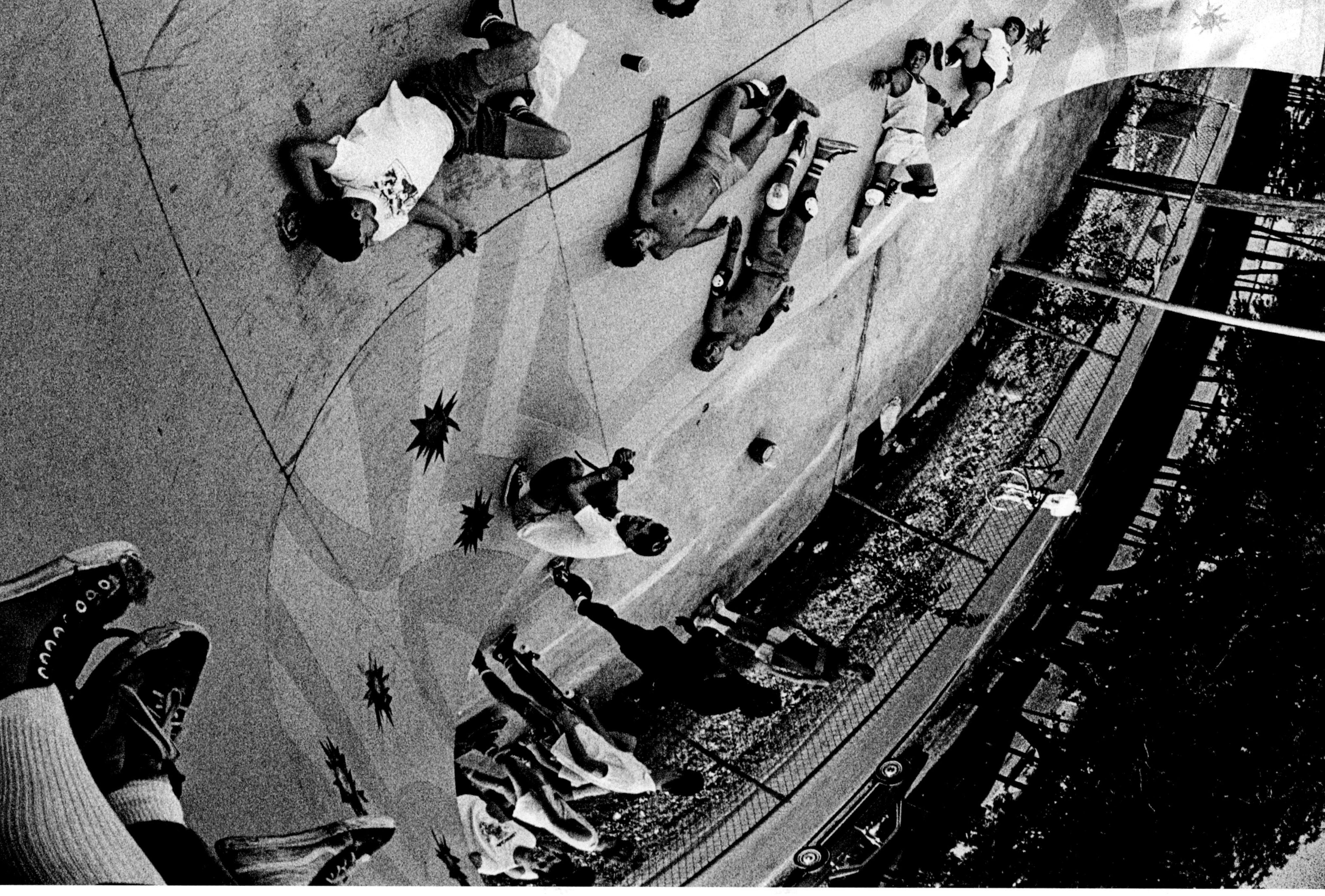

John Lucero and friends waiting for ambulance, Clown Ramp, Dallas, TX, 1984

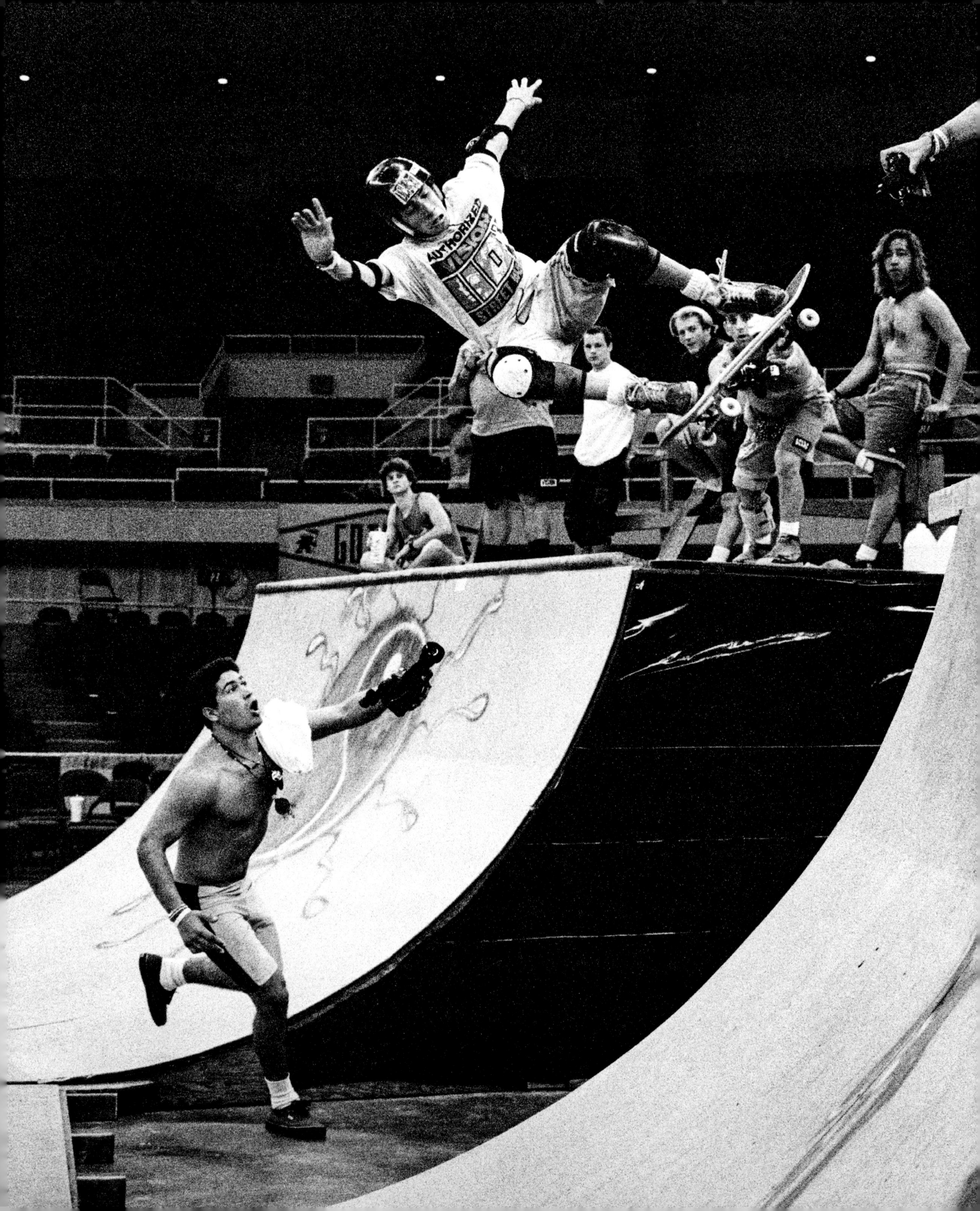
AUTHORIZED

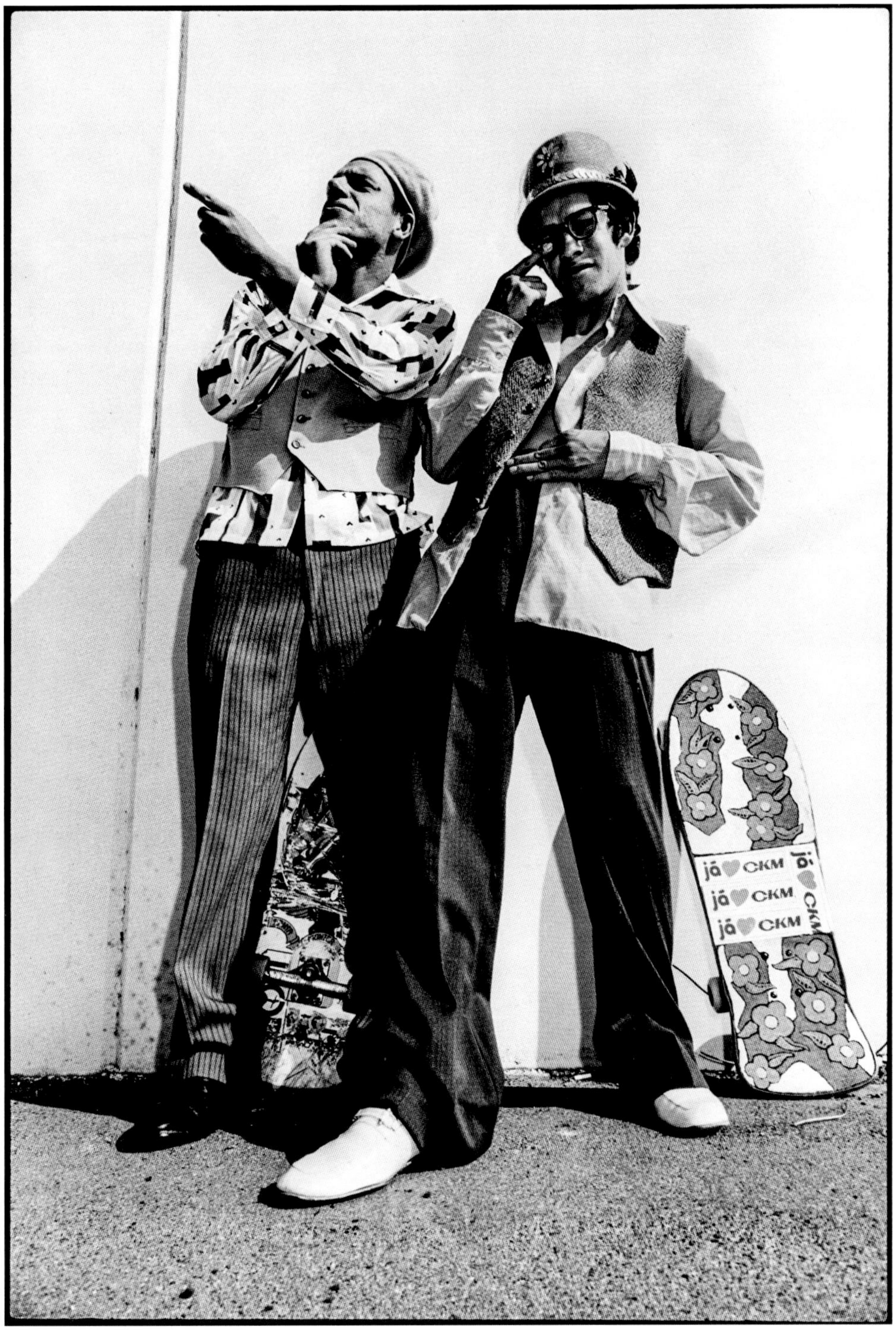

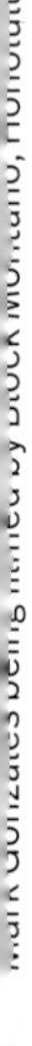

Natas Kaupas and Mark Gonzales, Street Sheet Thrifting, Oceanside, CA, 1987

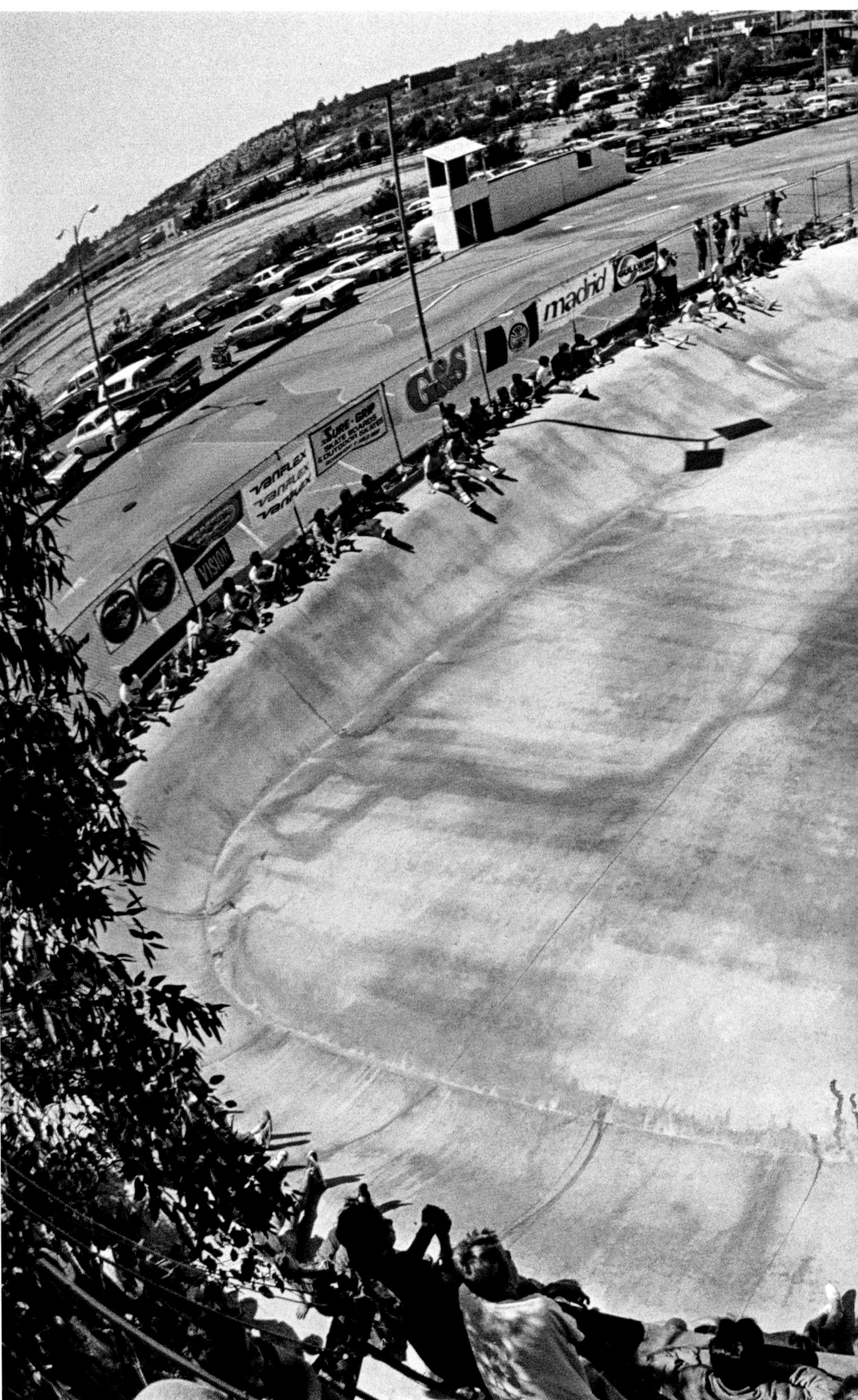

Per Welinder, Freestyle contest, Del Mar Skate Ranch, Del Mar, CA, 1985

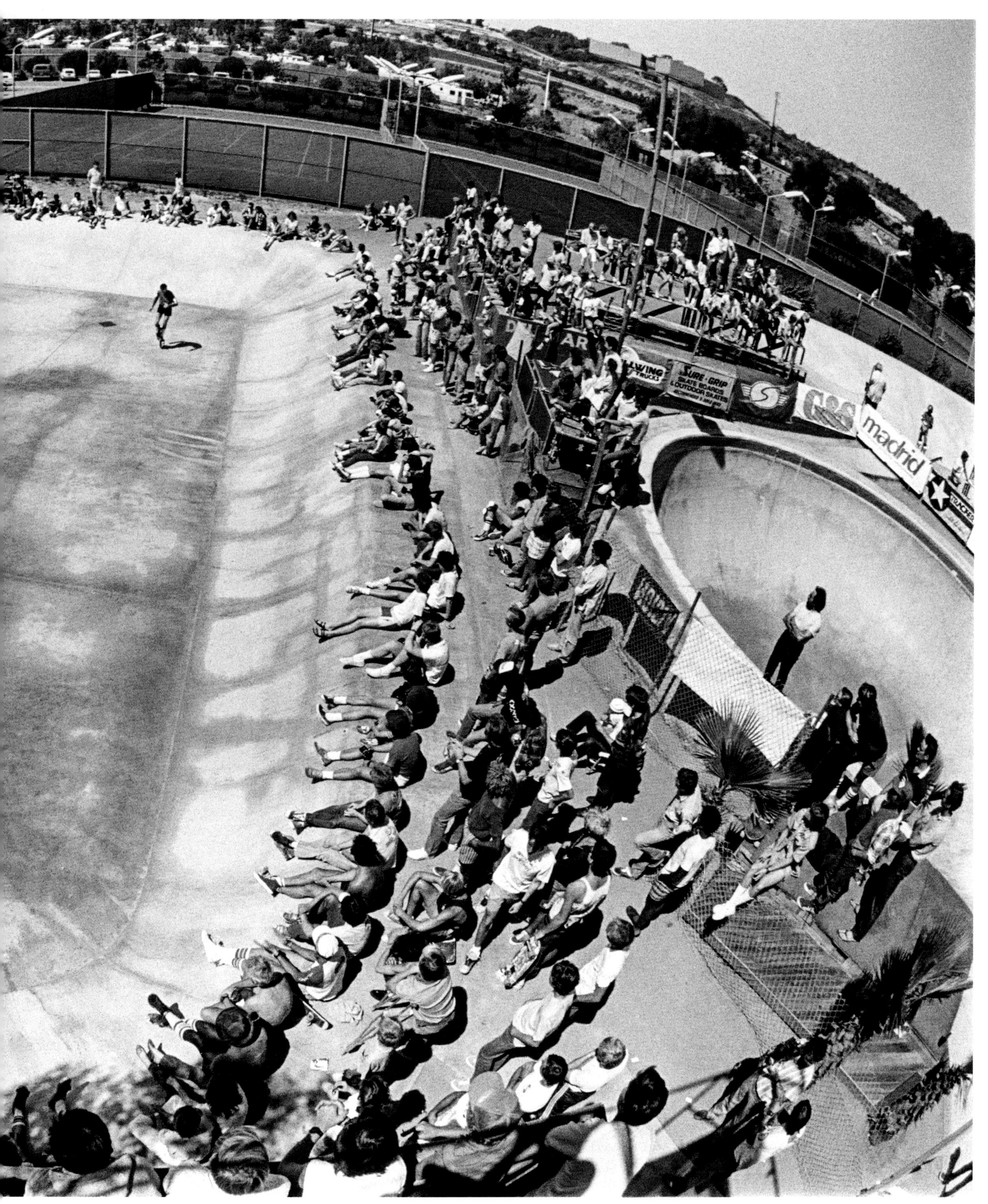
SURE · GRIP
SKATE BOARDS
& OUTDOOR SKATES
G&S
madrid

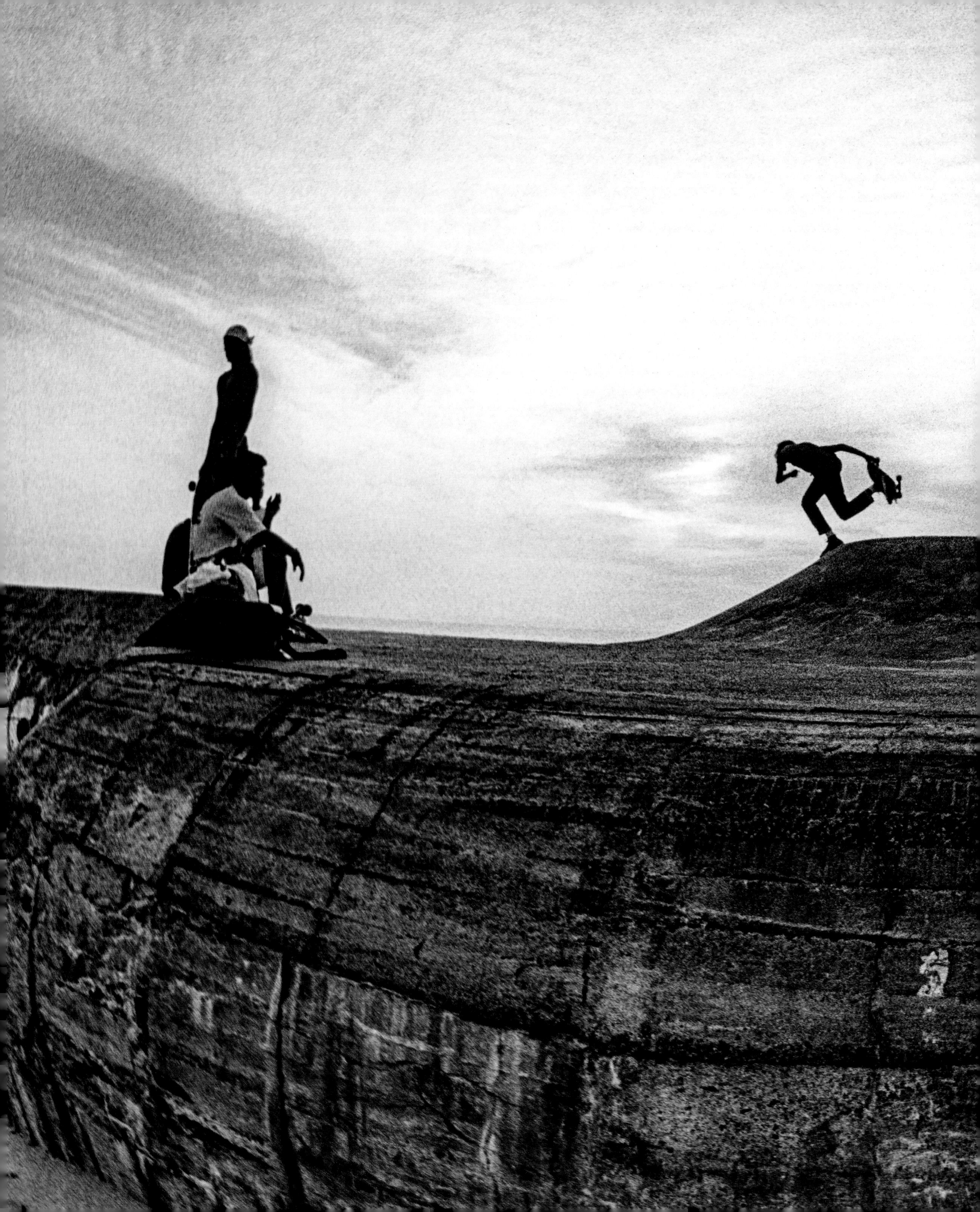

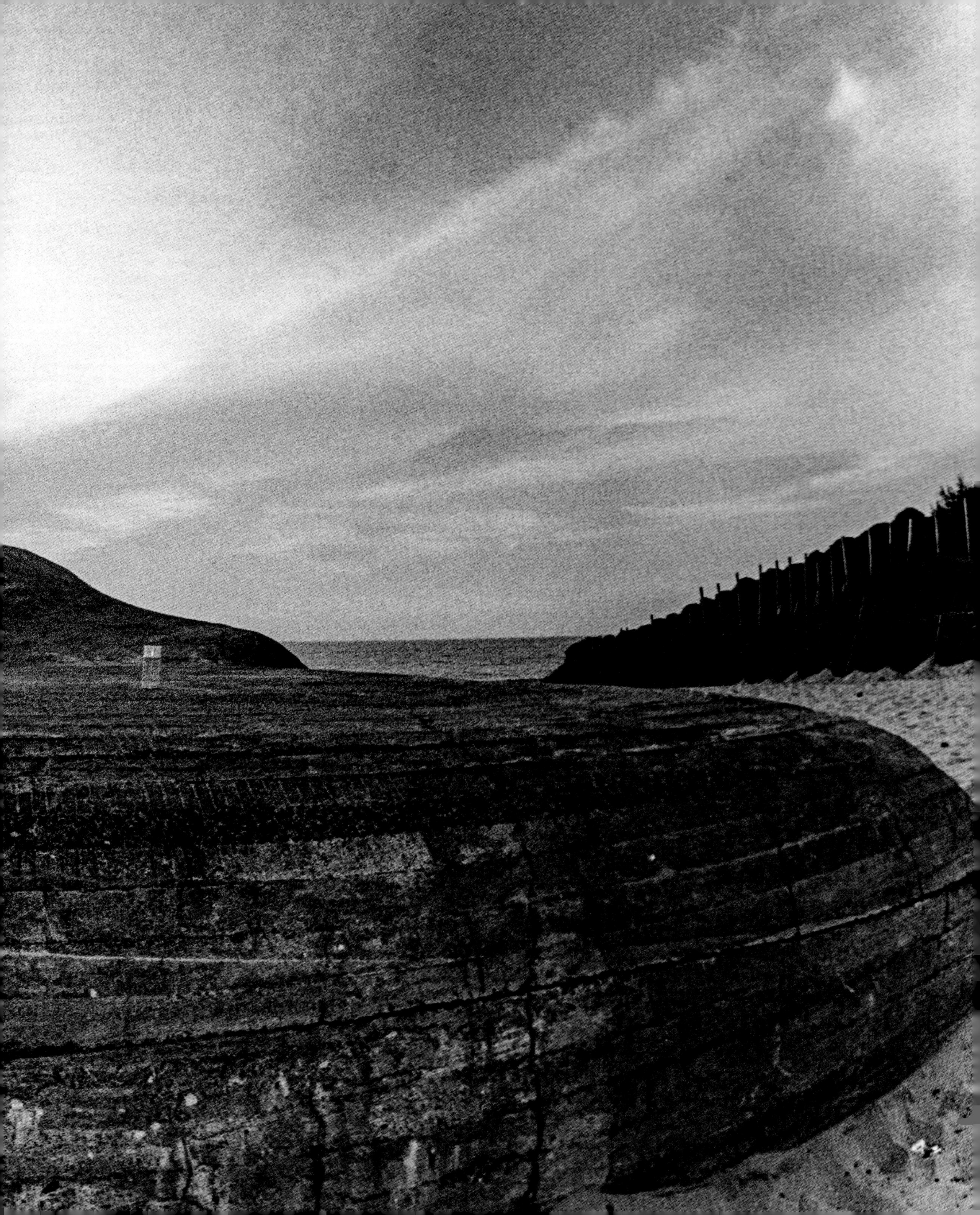

Previous spread: Christian Seewaldt, German bunker near Biarritz, France, 1985

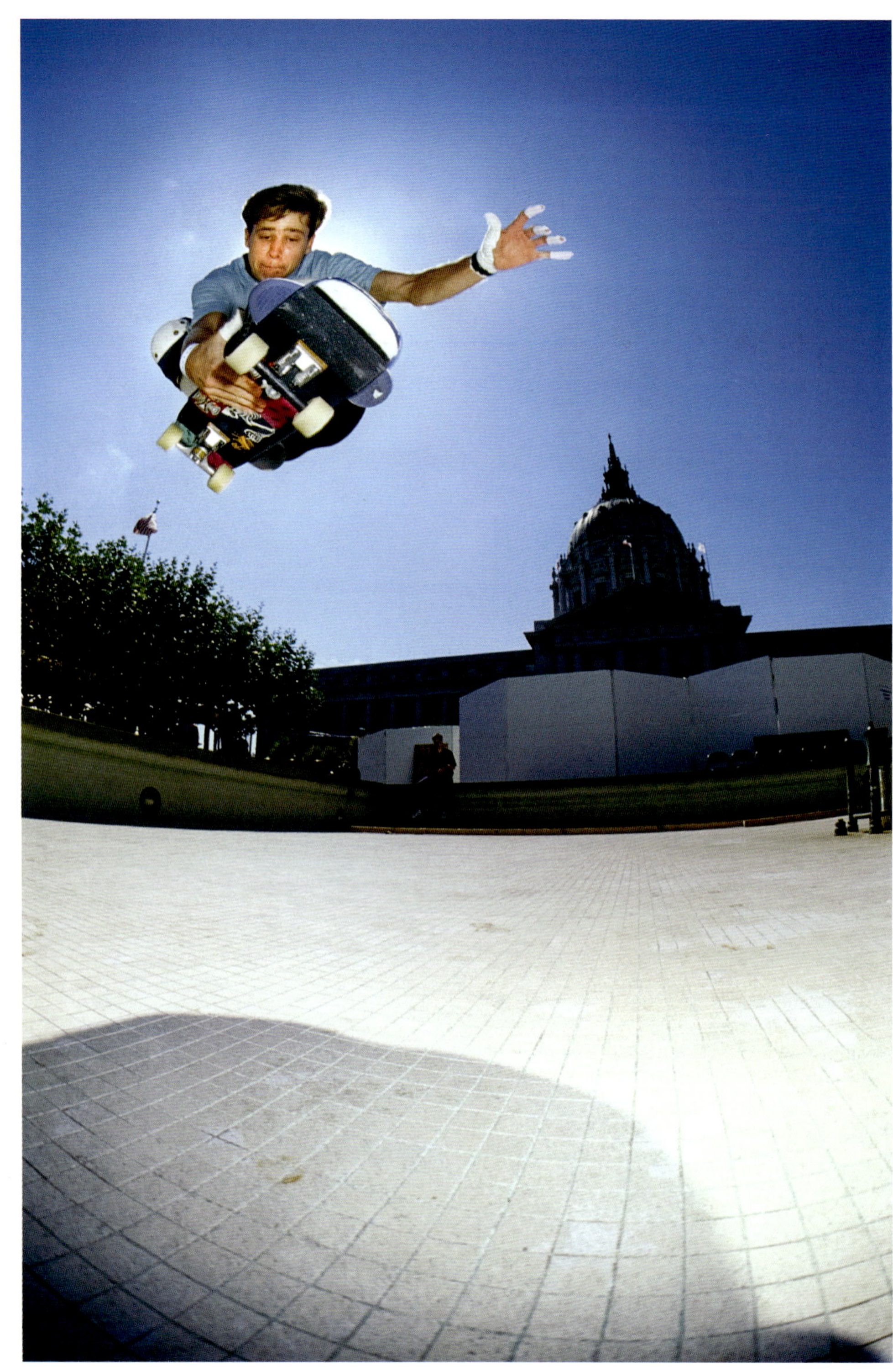

Rodney Mullen, Ollie grab, San Francisco, CA, 1988

Tony Hawk, Witt's Carlsbad Ringling Dome, Carlsbad, CA, 1985

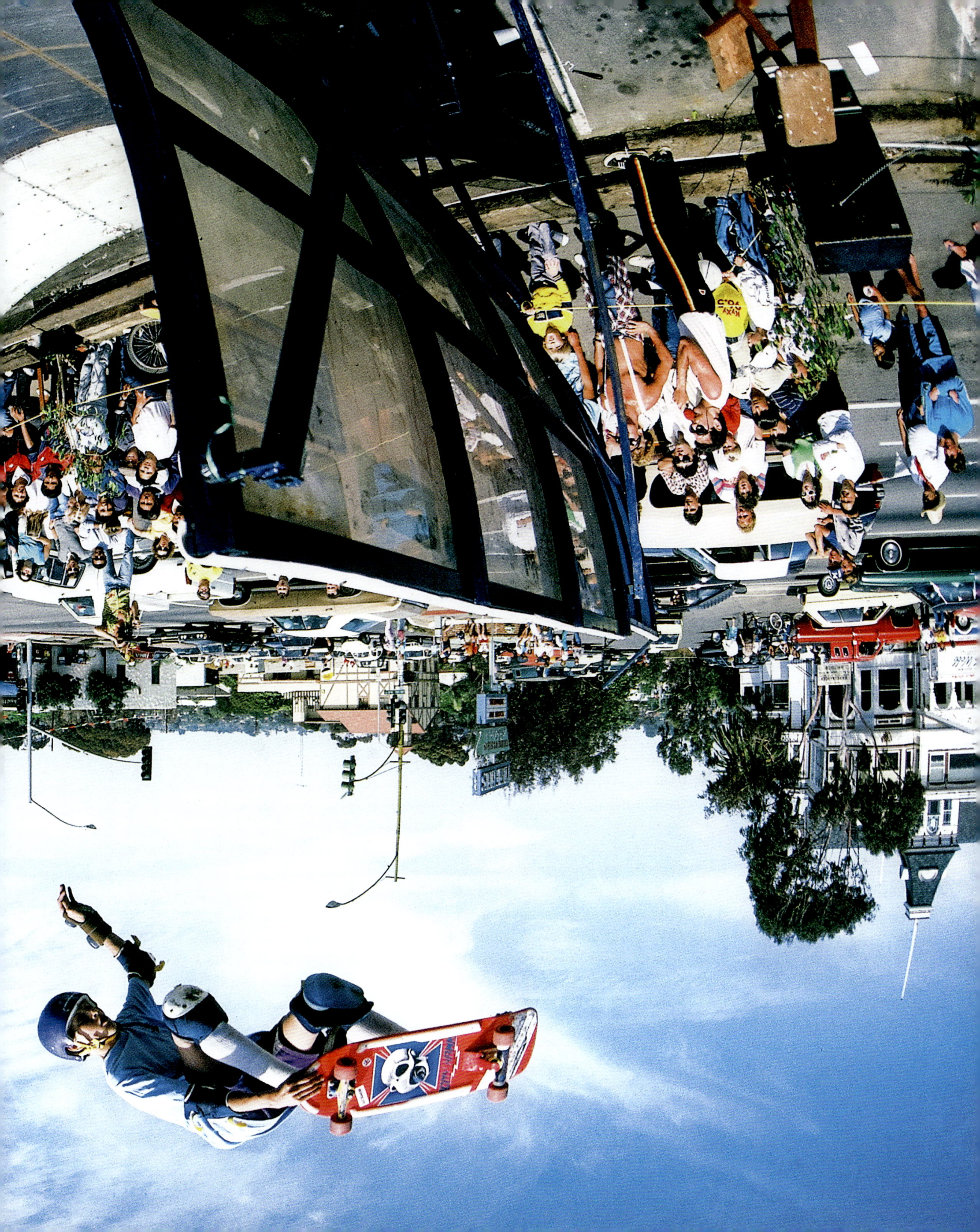

1975

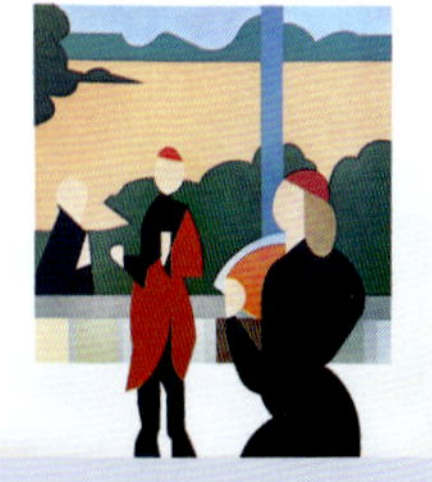

After the advent of urethane wheels in 1973 and *Skateboarder Magazine* in 1975, Grant gets more into skateboarding. On the music front, Grant's friends Rich Apple and Rob Morton introduce him to David Bowie, Pink Floyd, Iggy Pop, Genesis, Todd Rundgren, Yes, Kraftwerk's *Autobahn*, Roxy Music, and Brian Eno's *Another Green World*—the latter of which leads him to discover a lot of different kinds of non-mainstream music. "I was kind of stuck between generations. A lot of the people who were my age just kept listening to classic rock. Skateboarding got me into looking at other kinds of art and music."

1978

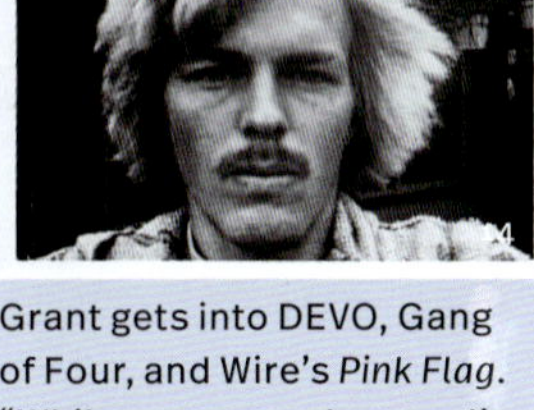

Grant gets into DEVO, Gang of Four, and Wire's *Pink Flag*. "While everyone else was listening to punk, I was getting into artier stuff."

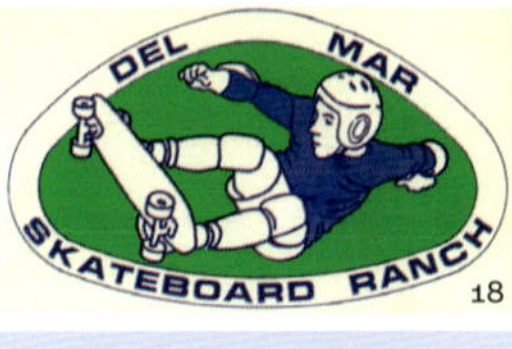

Tom "Wally" Inouye gives Grant one of his brand-new Caster pro model decks and in August helps him score a job sweeping out pools and renting out safety gear at the newly opened Del Mar Skate Ranch. "On my first day, I had just gotten back from a surf trip to Mexico. I was sunburned and my eyes were all red. So, the manager, Wayne Searle, sent me home because he thought I was stoned." Indeed, during this time period, Grant can be seen rocking long, frizzy hair and a big, bushy mustache, like your crazed-looking Uncle Meth Head.

1979

In February, inspired by the photography of Warren Bolster, James Cassimus, and Glen E. Friedman in *Skateboarder*, Grant borrows a 35mm camera from his roommate, Rich Apple, buys a roll of Kodak Kodachrome film, and shoots it at Del Mar. Only two photos out of a roll of 36 are in focus and composed well, including one of Kyle Jensen doing an invert. "I didn't know what I was doing. I was pretty much floundering. I shot a lot of film to get one good photo." To save money, Grant starts shooting in black and white and only has negatives developed—no proofsheets or prints. Grant cuts off his long hair and, eventually, his mustache—completely changing over to a more clean-cut appearance.

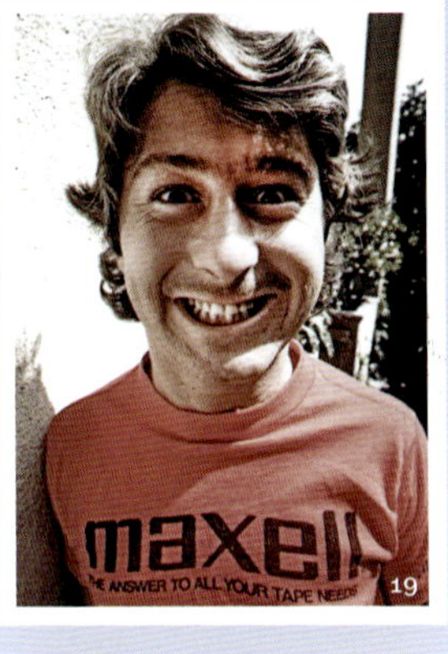
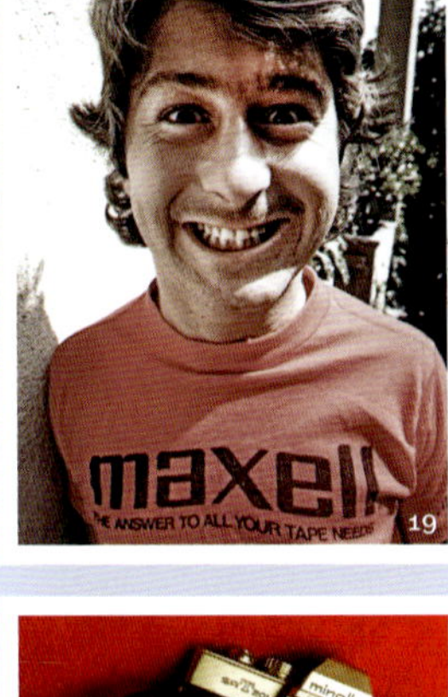

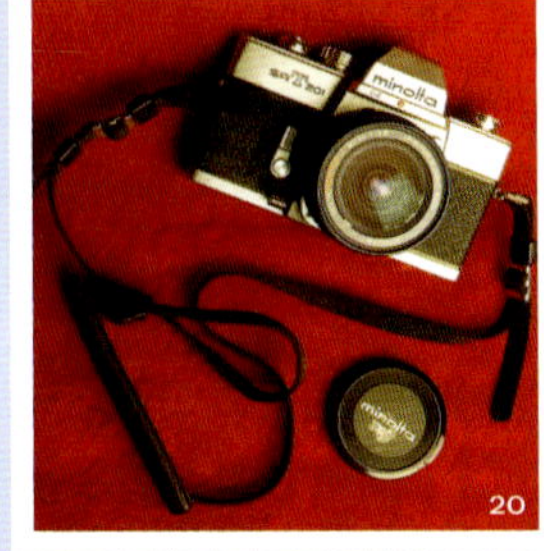

1981

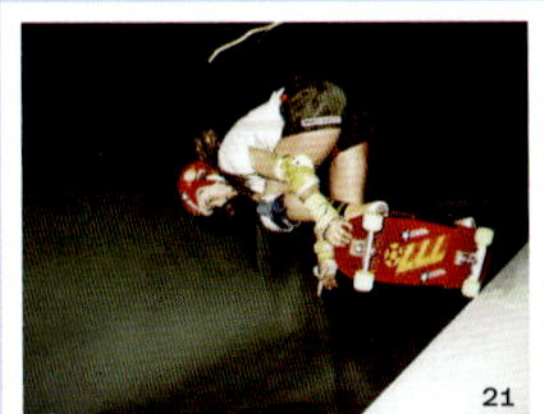

Surf and skate photographer Sonny Miller invites Grant to print one of his photos in the darkroom at Palomar College. Fully stoked on the whole developing process, Grant exclaims, "Oh, my God! I've got to get into this," then switches all of his classes from art and general education to photography. "My goal was to learn every kind of photography so I would never have to say, 'I don't know how to do that.' When *Transworld Skateboarding* Magazine (TWS) started up, I realized that I needed to know how to shoot landscapes, portraits, and product shots." A photography teacher at Palomar, Kean Wilcox, becomes Grant's mentor. Ditto art teacher Doug Durrant, who teaches Grant to look at everything differently.

13. New roommates from LA turn him onto Brian Eno and change his musical tastes, 1975

14. Still has long hair and mustache—takes selfie with camera, but still hasn't taken up photography, 1977
15. Becomes DEVO devotee, 1978

16. Neighbor Wally Inouye gets him job at DMSR, 1978
17. DMSR membership, 1978
18. DMSR sticker, 1978

19. Roommate Rich Apple lends his camera to Grant, 1979
20. Buys first camera—Minolta SRT201, 1979

21. Practices shooting DMSR locals like Leigh Parkin, 1980
22. Photographer friend Sonny Miller introduces Grant to Palomar photo darkroom, 1981

J. GRANT BRITTAIN TIMELINE

By Garry Scott Davis • All quotes–JGB

1955

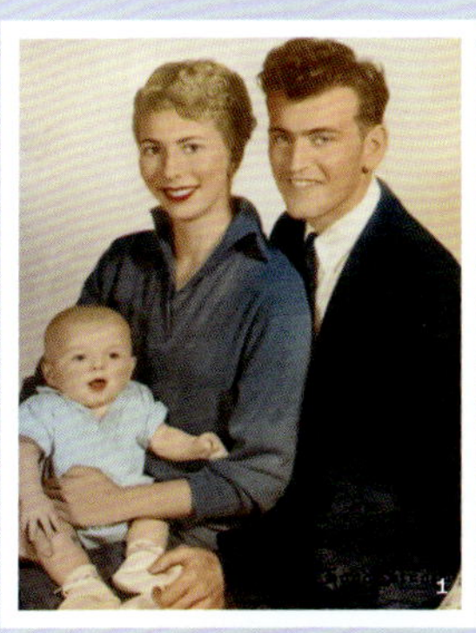

Jordan Grant Brittain is born on July 28, in Fallbrook, CA.

Late 1950s

As a young boy, Grant's mom dresses him up in a little cowboy outfit and a coonskin cap (not at the same time), which are all the rage in the 1950s.

1. Grant and parents, 1955
2. Cowboy, 1960

1965

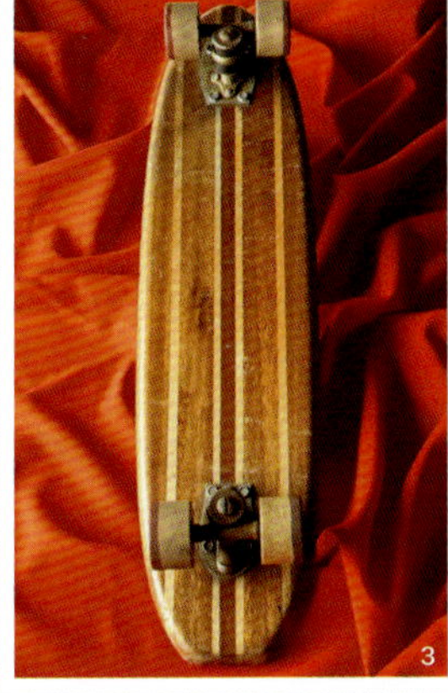

Grant starts skateboarding on Christmas Day, mostly buttboarding. After seeing the film *Skater Dater*, he starts standing up and, conversely, laying down (doing coffins).

3. Skateboard for Christmas, 1965
4. Boy Scout, 1966
5. Psychedelic shirt, 1967

1970

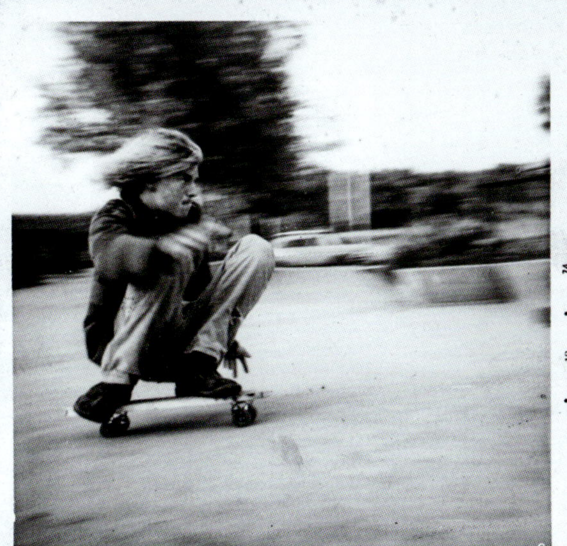

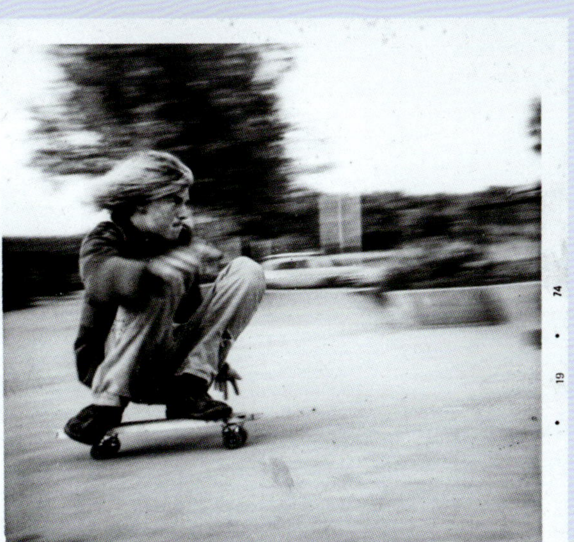

Grant starts surfing and continues riding skateboards with clay wheels–mainly surf skating (pretending to get tubed).

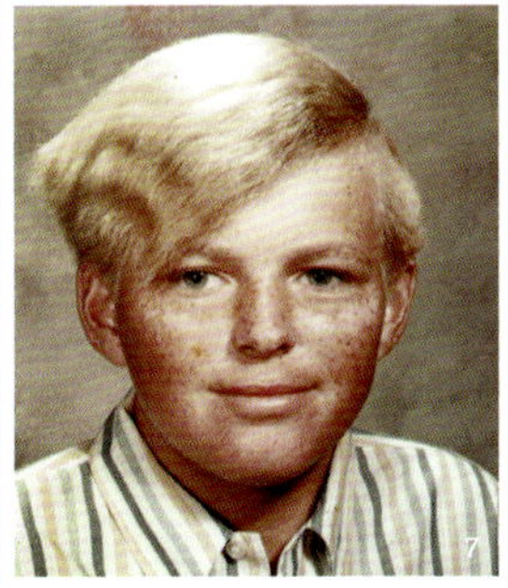

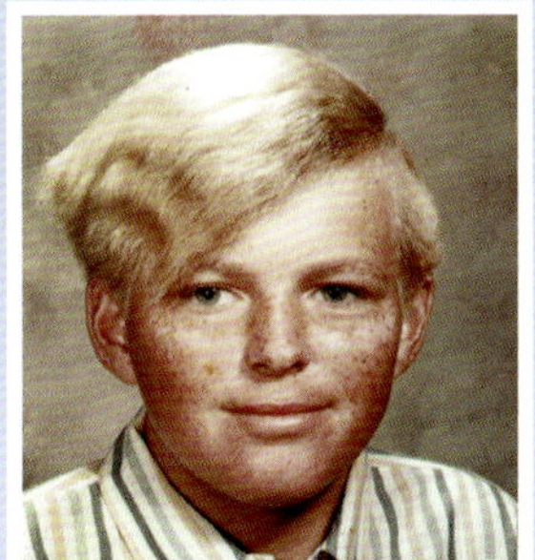

6. Skating when the waves are flat, 1974
7. Starts surfing and toasts skin, 1970

1973

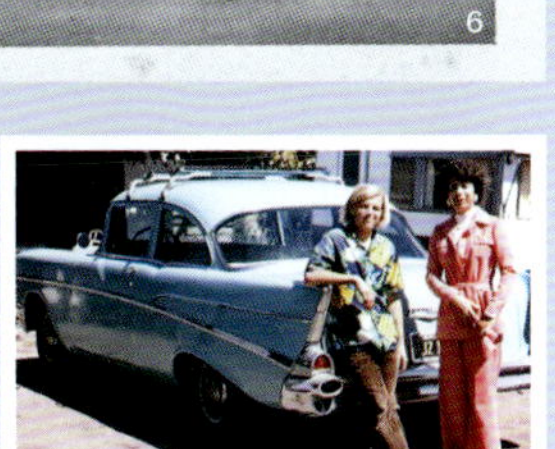

8. Grant buys his first car–'57 Chevy – for $300, 1973
9. Graduates high school in groovy threads, 1973

1974

A year out of high school, Grant moves from Fallbrook to Cardiff-by-the-Sea and starts surfing Cardiff Reef, where he enjoys kneeboarding because "it's easier to get barreled." Grant gets a job at the Del Mar Surf Shop.

Early 1970s

Grant does weird drawings influenced by the art of Rick Griffin.

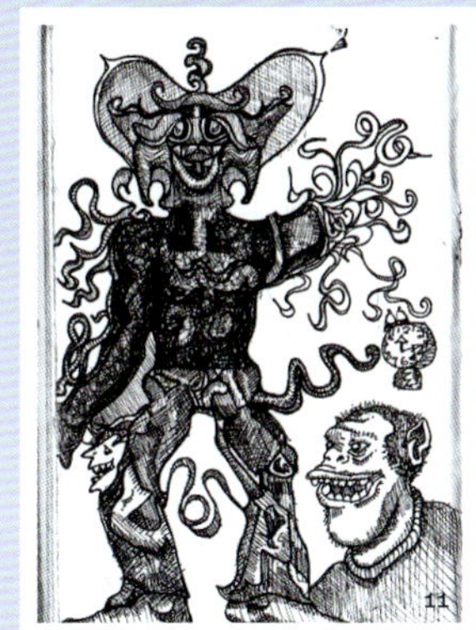

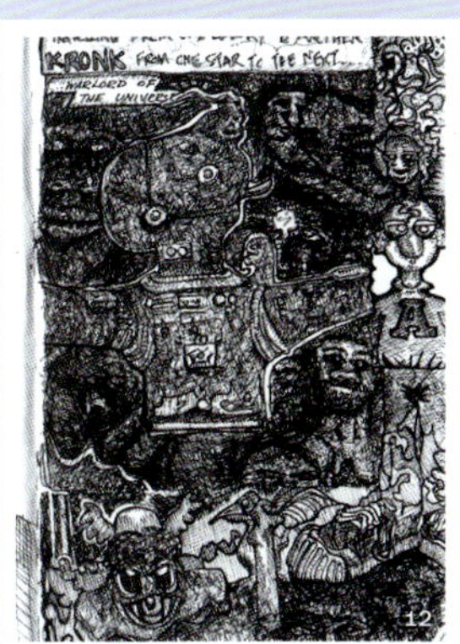

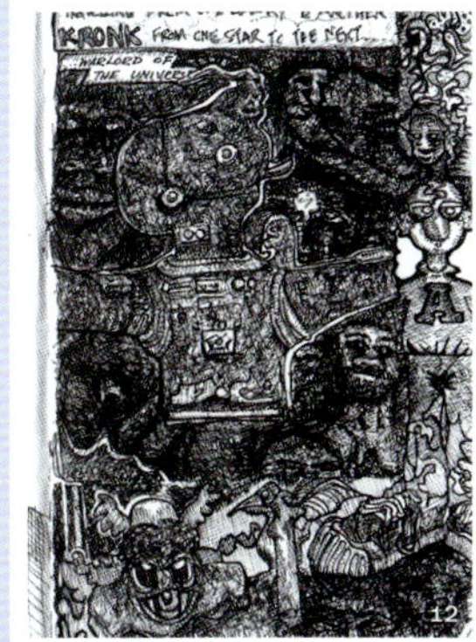

10. Leaves parents' home in Fallbrook to surf this wave, 1974
11–12. Makes wild Rick Griffin-inspired drawings, 1974

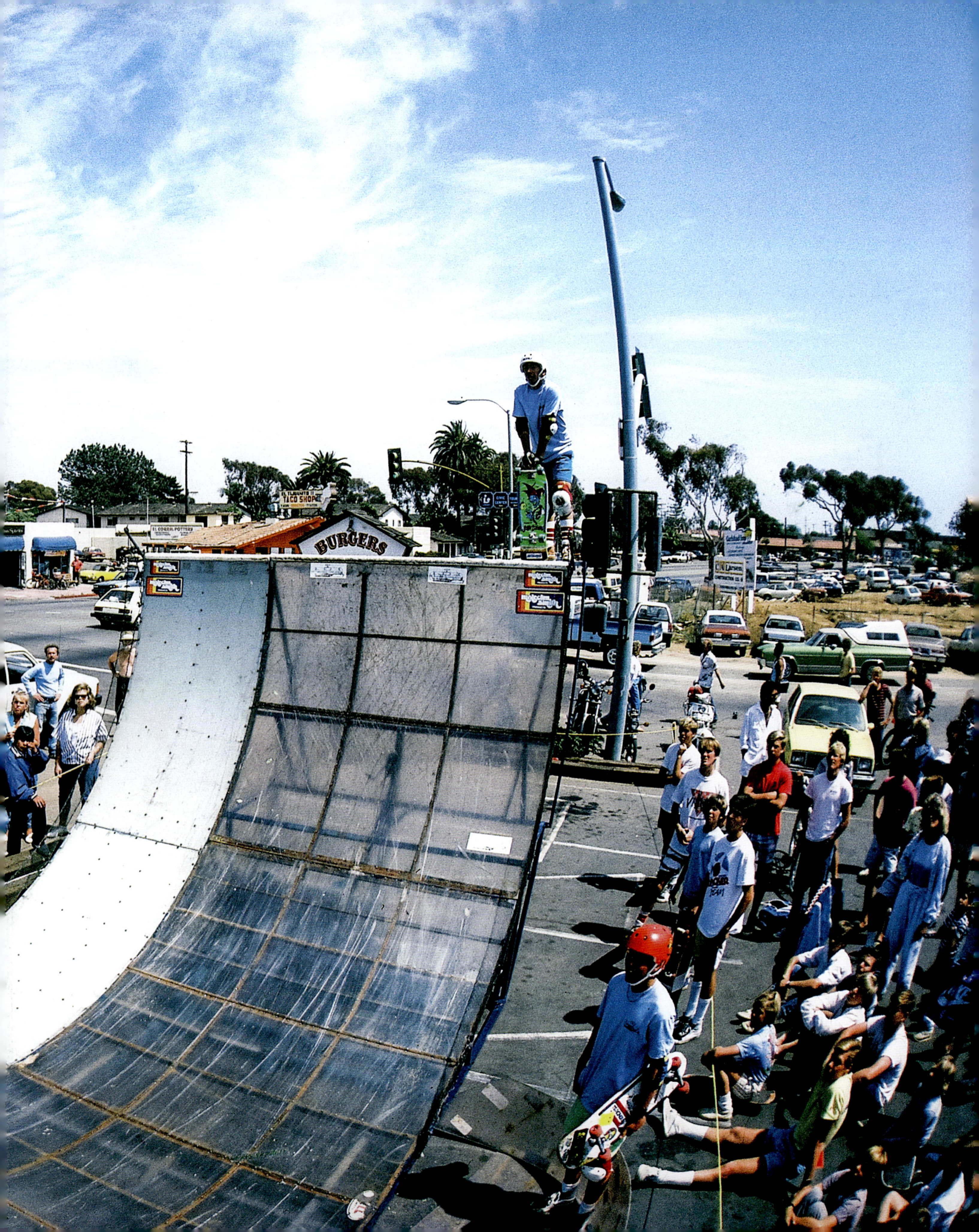
TACO SHOP
BURGERS

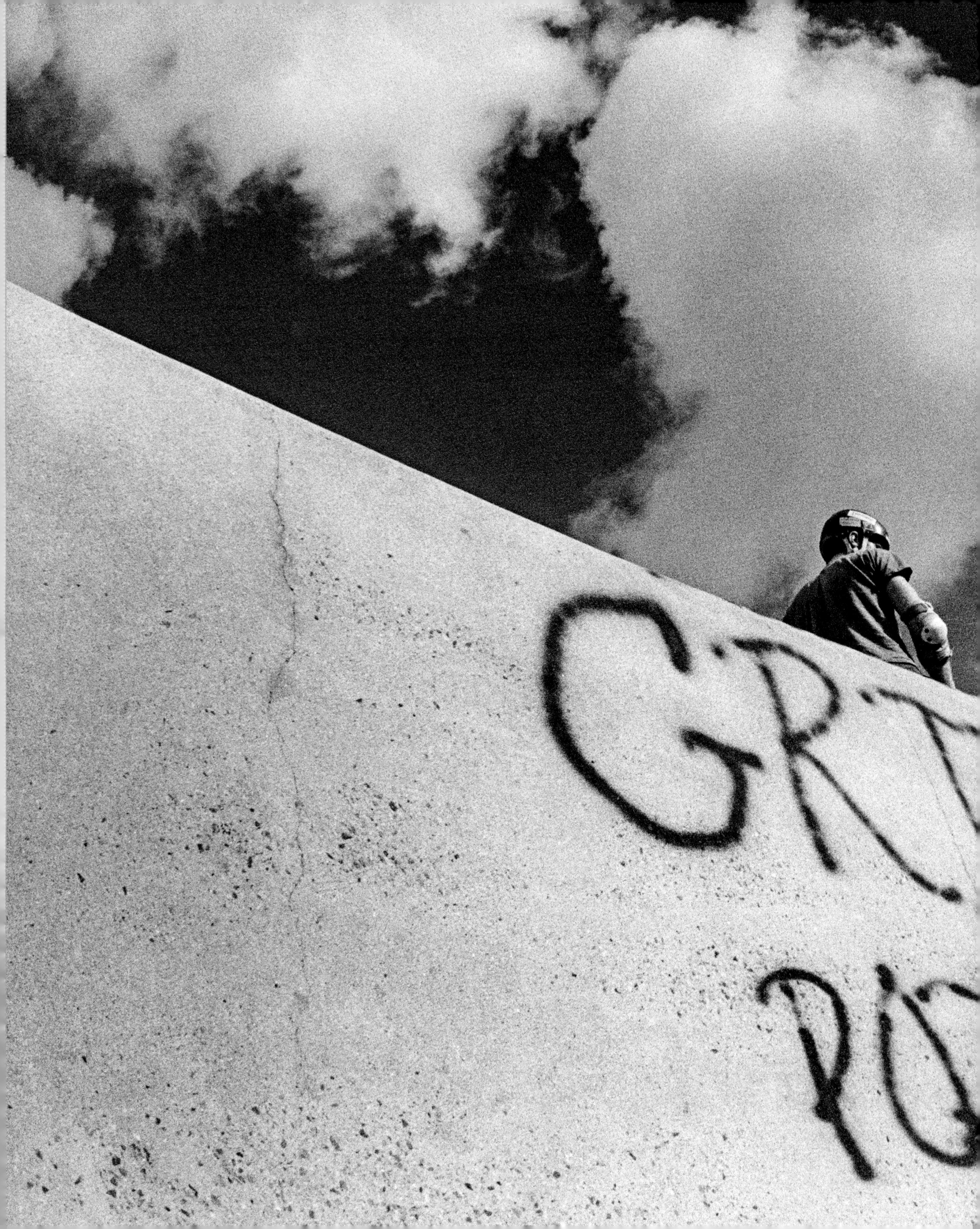

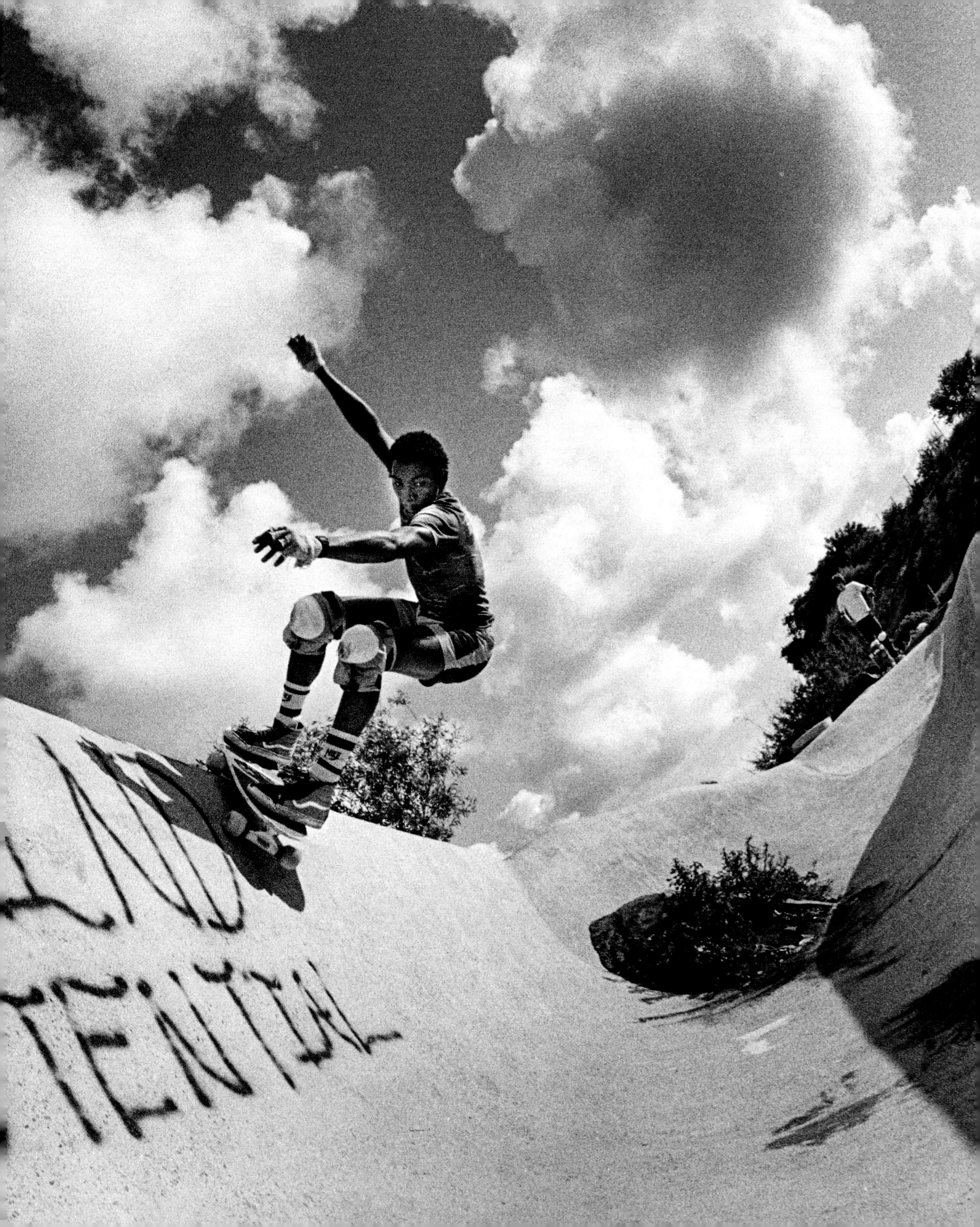

teve Steadham, Grind Potential, Surf de Earth, Vista CA, 1983

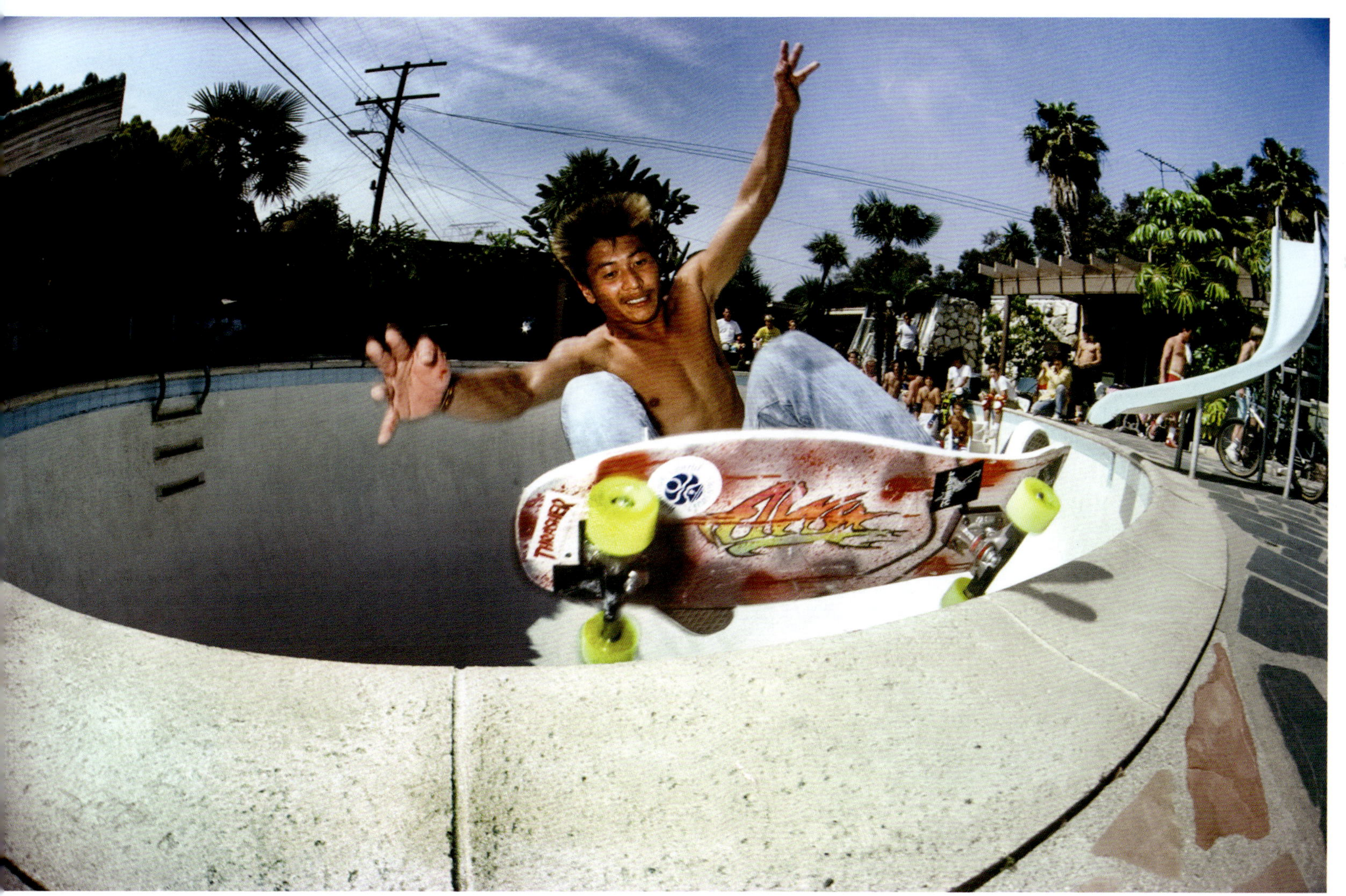

f Hartsel, Frontside grind, Gonzales Pool, Mar Vista, CA, 1986

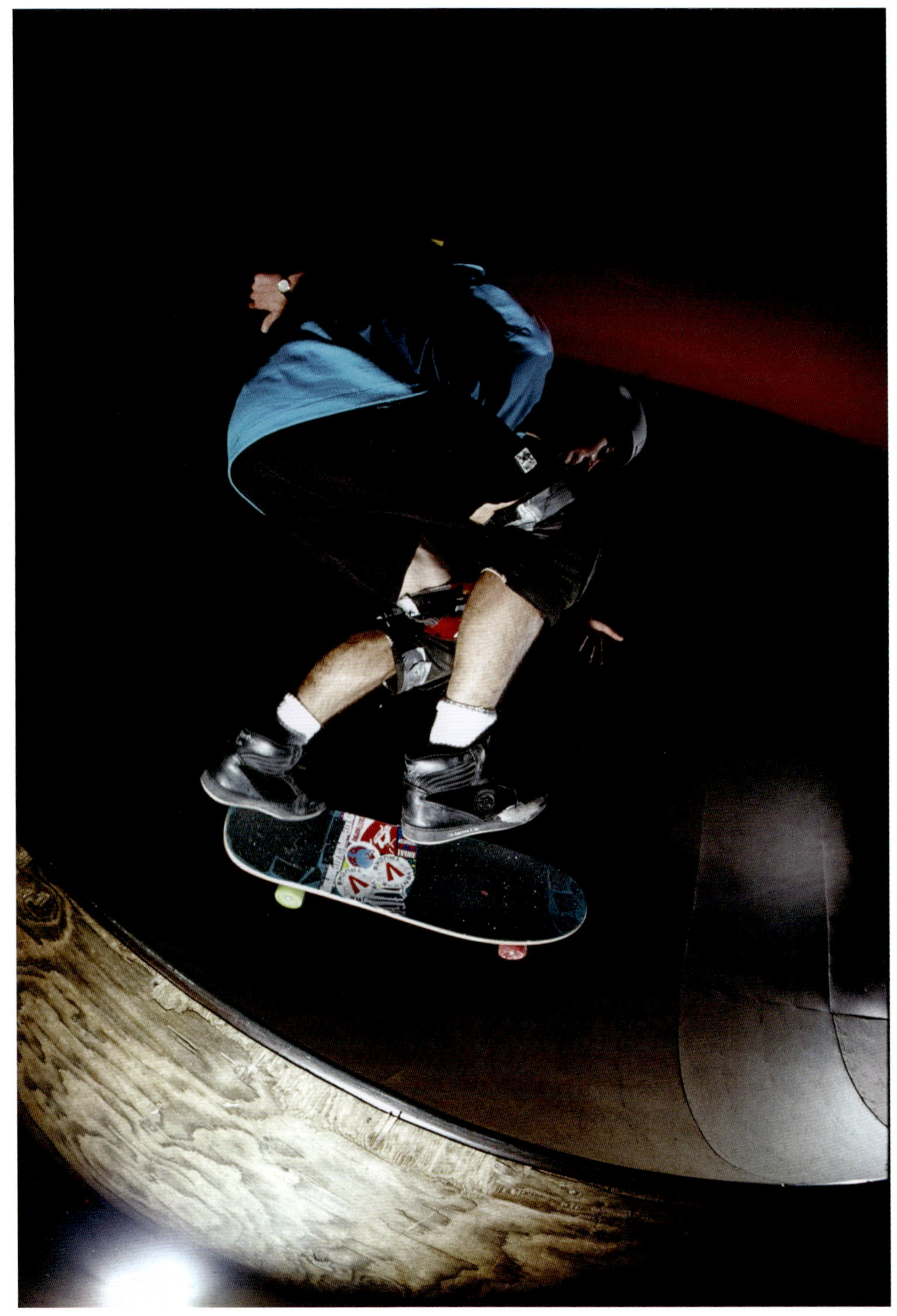

Jason Lee, Kickflip to tail, Mike McGill's Skatepark, Carlsbad, CA, 1989

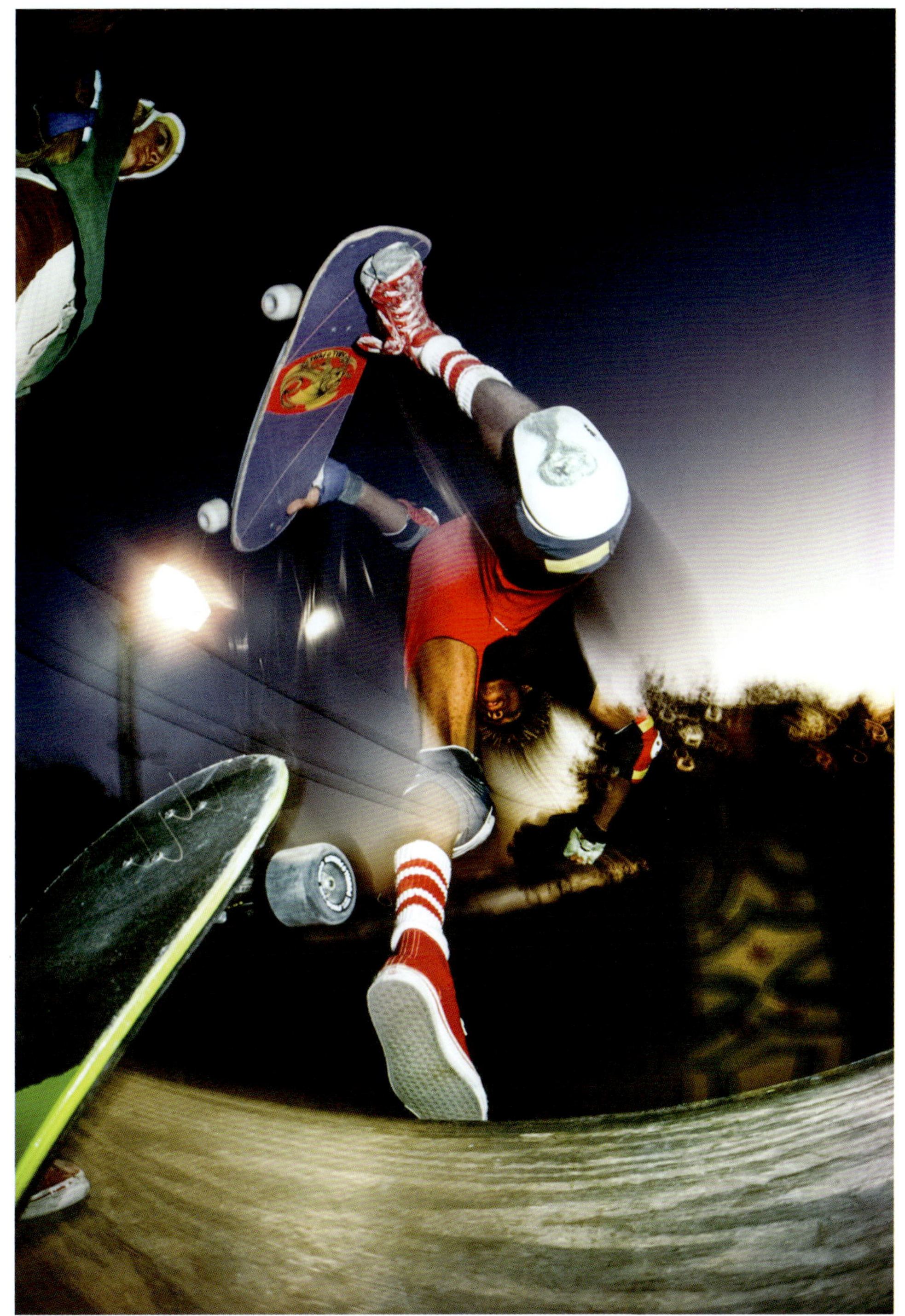

Steve Steadham, Backside boneless, Clown Ramp, Dallas, TX, 1984

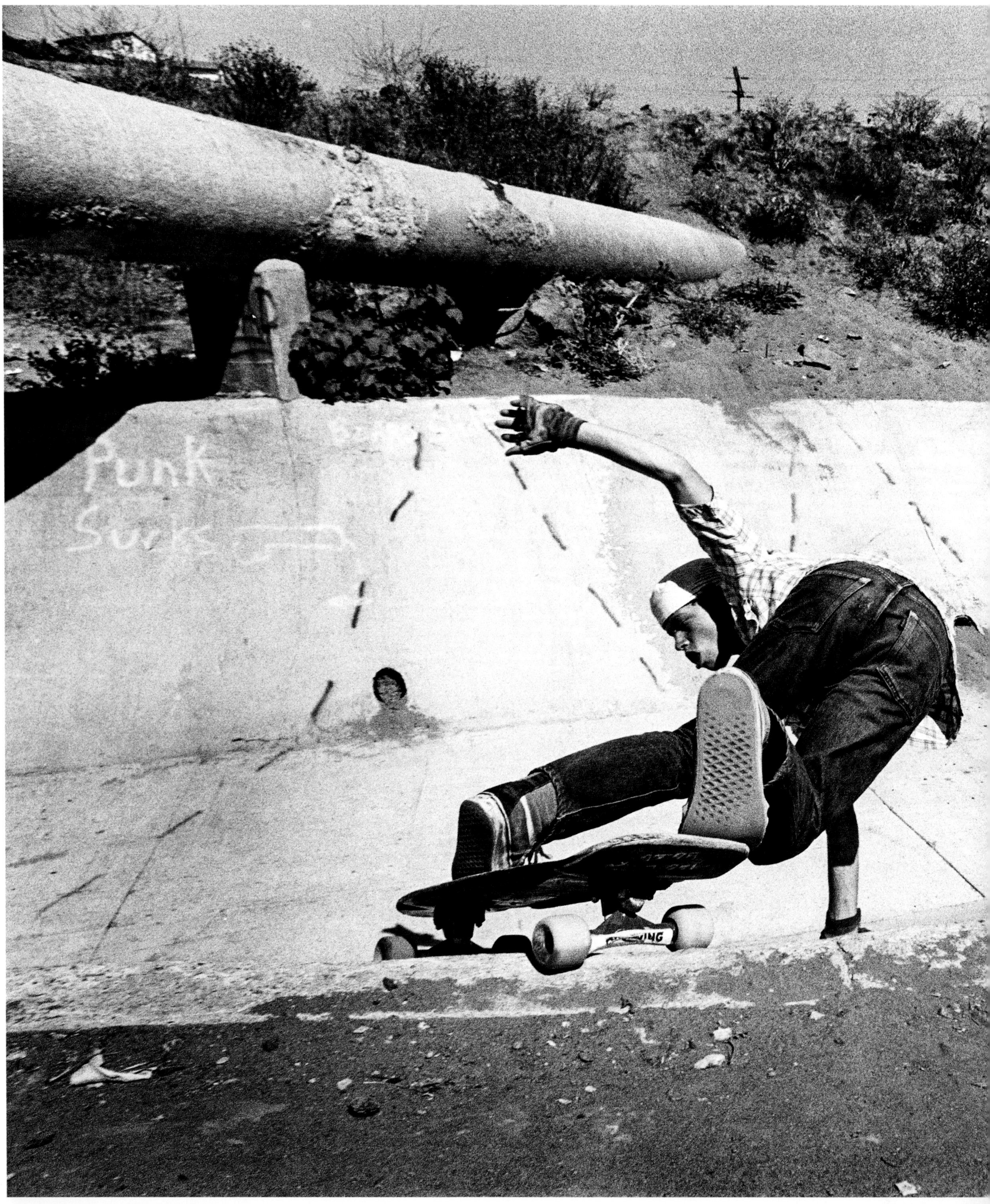
Punk
Sucks

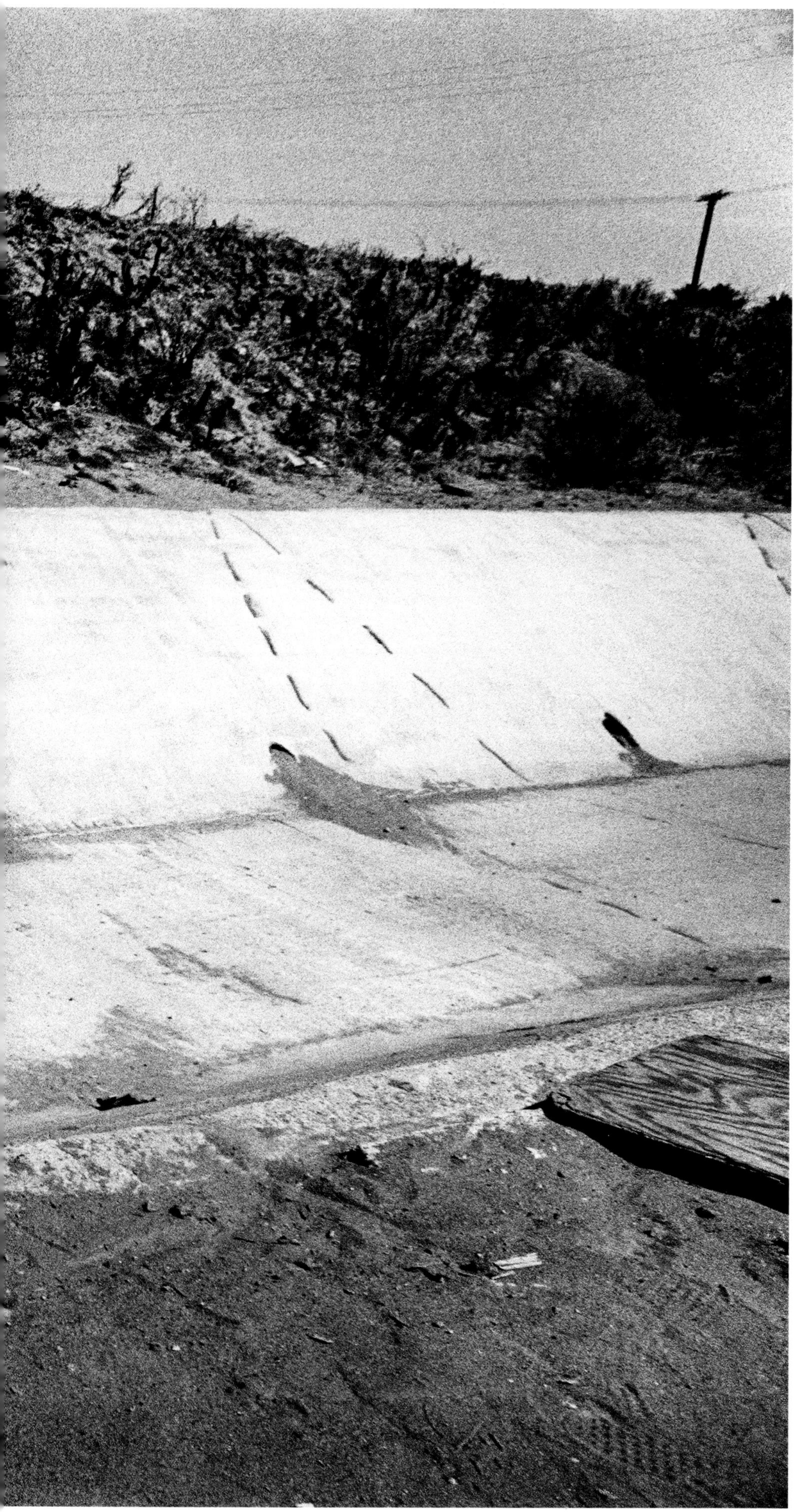

Owen Nieder, Sanoland, Cardiff-by-the-Sea, CA, 1984

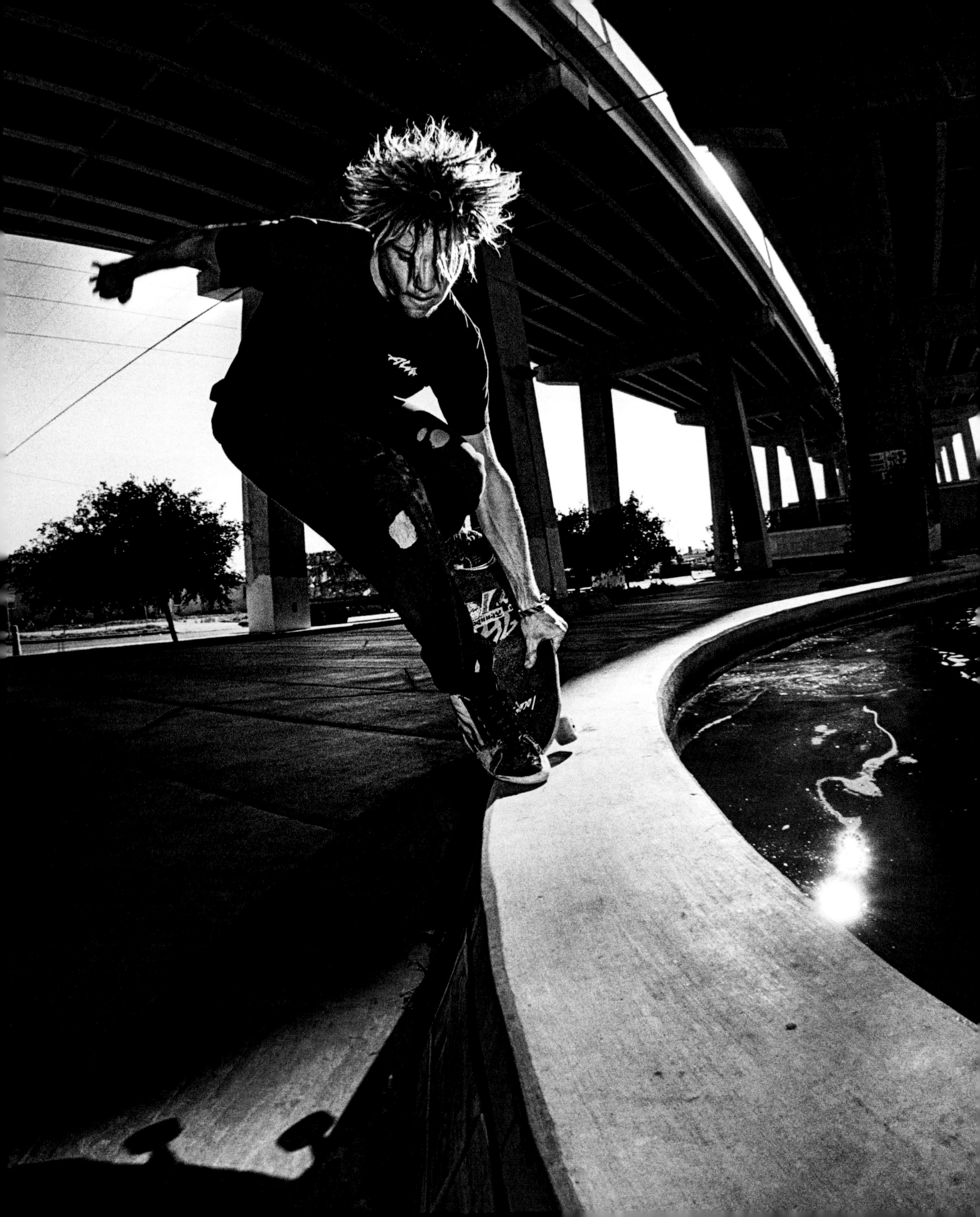

John Thomas, Frontside nosepick, Chicano Park, San Diego, CA, 1987

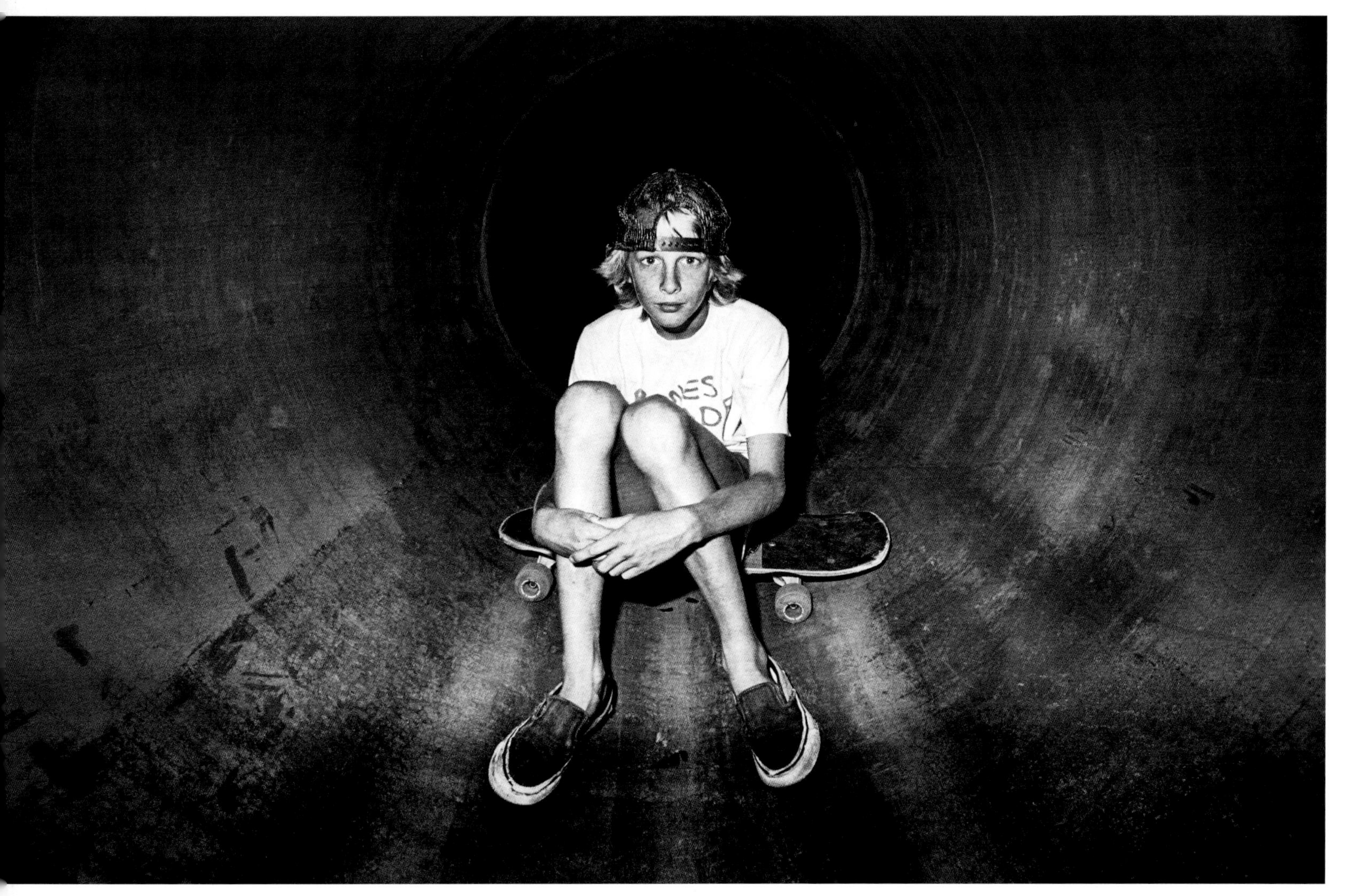

Tony Hawk, Portrait, Sanoland, Cardiff-by-the-Sea, CA, 1983

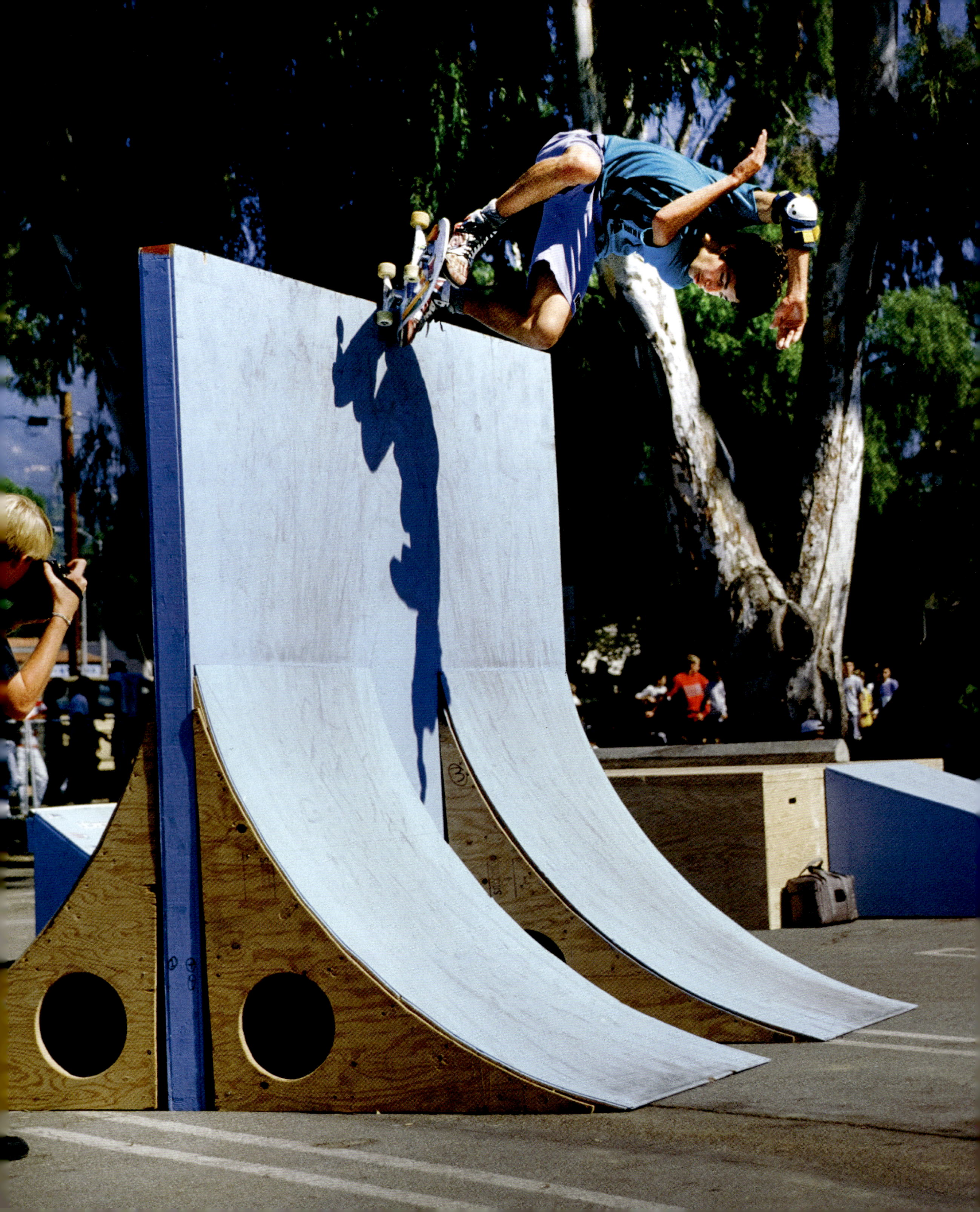

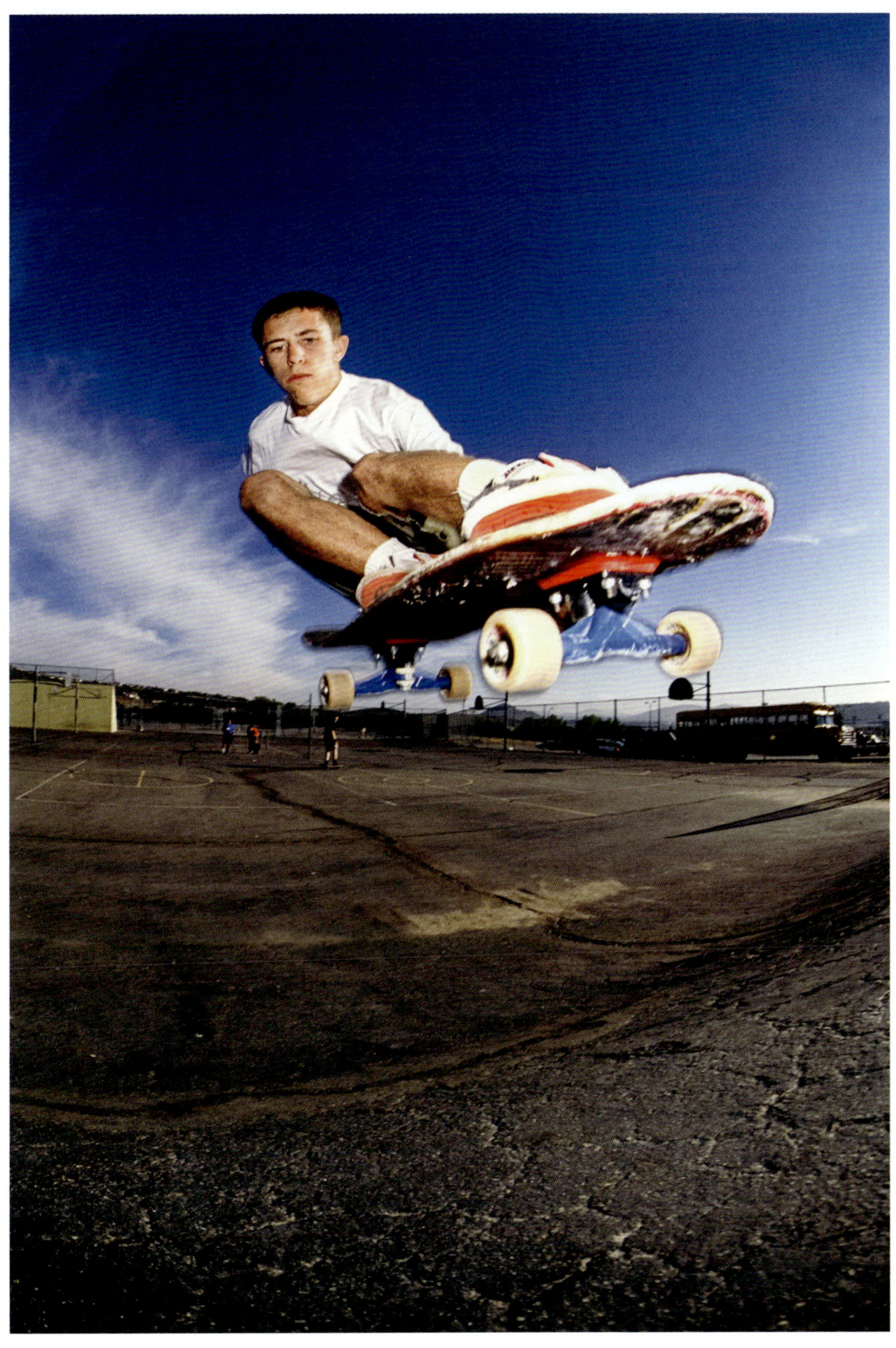

Matt Hensley, Ollie grab, San Pasqual High, San Pasqual, CA, 1989

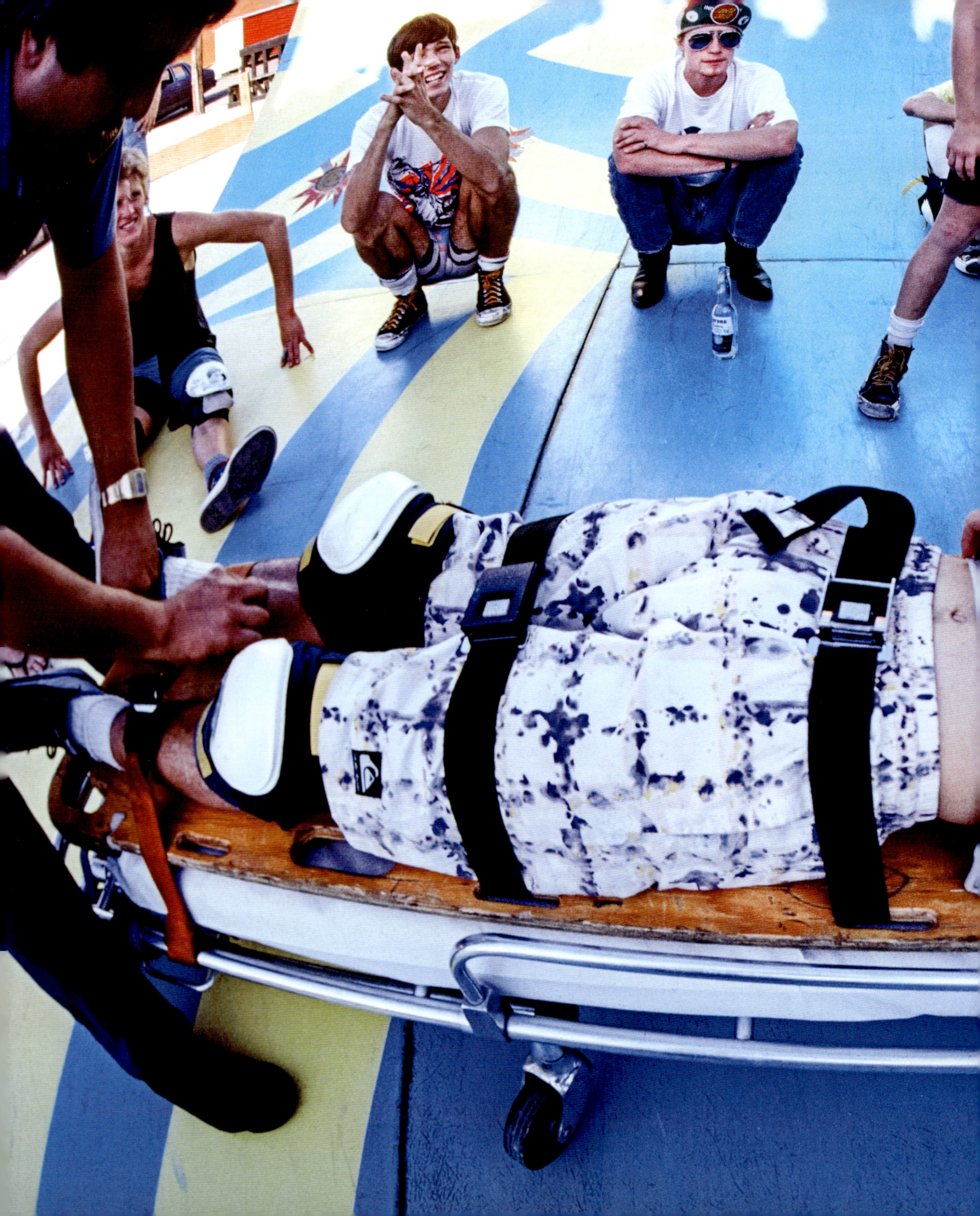

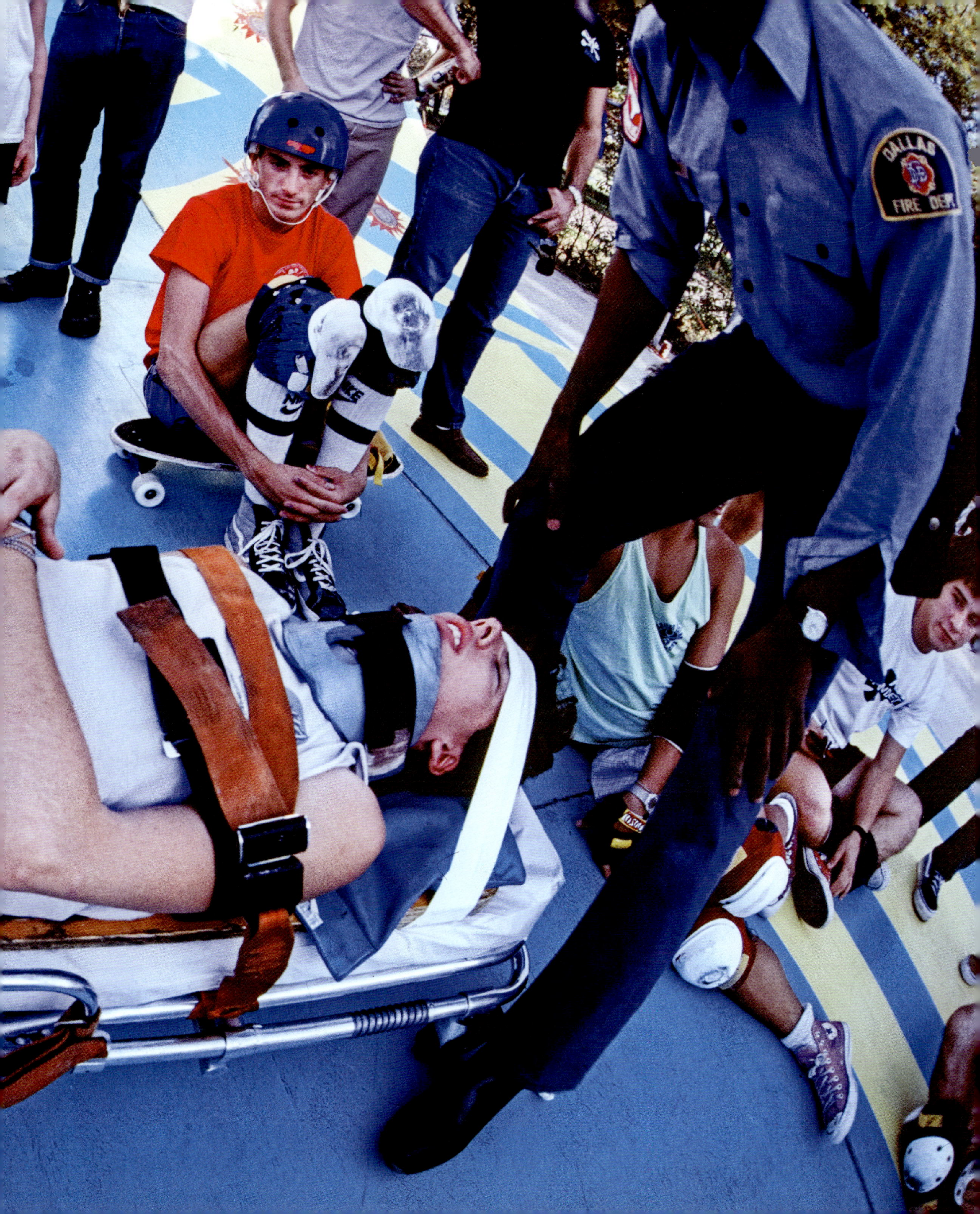
DALLAS
FIRE DEPT

THANK YOU FOR ALL OF THE INSPIRATION, IDEAS, AND SUPPORT THROUGH THE YEARS:

Larry Balma, Peggy Cozens, Josh Higgins, Tony Hawk, Miki Vuckovich, Garry S. Davis, the entire Brittain family, the Del Mar Skate Ranch locals, David Swift, Chris Miller, Mike Blabac, Tod Swank, the Bones Brigade, and Mörizen "Mofo" Föche.

Aaron Regan, Adrian Demain, Ako Jefferson, Alphonzo Rawls, Andy Jenkins, Anthony Acosta, Anthony Donez, APA San Diego, Atiba Jefferson, Barry Zaritsky, Bill Billing, Bob Denike, Bob Pribble, Brad Dorfman, Brendan Klein, Brett Stokes, Brian "Pushead" Schroeder, Brian Sellstrom, Britt Parrot, Bruno Peeters, Bryan Ridgeway, Bryce Kanights, Bucky Lasek, Chad DiNenna, Chip Morton, Chris Conway, Chris "Twinkie" Ray, Chris Fessenden, Chris Ortiz, Chris Strople, Christian Hosoi, Christopher Donez, Chuck Treece, Claus Grabke, Cowboy Steve Morris and Adrianne Smith, Craig Stecyk, Culture Brewing, Curtis Hesselgrave, Cynthia Cebula, Dale Smith, Daniel H. Sturt, Dave Bergthold, David and Barbarella Fokos, David Carson, David Mock, Dennis McGrath, Dennis Rieder, Desiree Astorga, Diane Launder, Don and Danielle Bostick, Don Brown, Donna Cosentino, Don Hoffman, Doug Durrant, Dwayne Carter, Ed Economy, Eddie Elguera, Ed Templeton, Eric Grisham, Eric Sentianin, Fabrice Le Mao, Fran Richards, Frank and Nancy Hawk, FTC San Francisco, Glen E. Friedman, George Powell, Greg Hunt, Grind for Life, Hagop Najarian, Heather Rose, Heather Yaryan, Jaimie Muehlhausen, Jaime Owens, Jack Smith, James Cassimus, Jamie Mosberg, Jamie Thomas, Jared Prindle, Jeff Grosso, Jeff Phillips, Jim Alesi, Jim Fitzpatrick, Jim Goodrich, Jim Gray, Jim Thiebaud, Joe Johnson, Joe Polevy, Joel Patterson, John Lucero, Jon Foster, Jon Holland, Jon Humphries, Jonny Donhowe, Kean Wilcox, Keith Carter, Keith Stephenson, Ken Park, Kevin Kinnear, Kevin Staab, Kevin Wilkins, Kyle Jensen, Lance Mountain, Lester Kasai, Look Back Library, Lou's Records, Louise Balma, Mac Premo, Mark Gonzales, Mark Oblow, Mark Waters, Marty Jimenez, Masanori "Nisi" Nishioka, Massimo van der Plas, Matt Hensley, Matt Price, Medium Photo, Michael Furukawa, Mike Farber, Mike McGill, Mike Mihaly, Mike Nelson, Mike Rogers, Mike Vallely, Natas Kaupas, Nayland Wilkins, Neil Blender, Nixon Watches, Otis Barthoulameu, Owen Nieder, Ozzie Ausband, Patrick Emerick and Holly LeFrois, Paul Schmitt, Paul Sunman, Per Welinder, Pete Thompson, Peter McBride, Pierre André Senizergues, Ray Barbee, Ray Underhill, Ray Zimmerman, Reggie Barnes, Rich Apple, Rodney Mullen, Ron Cameron, Sam Mullen, Chrome Digital, Sharon Harrison, Sean Mortimer, Sheri Farber, Sinisa Egelja, Skin Phillips, Sonja Catalano, Sonny Miller, Spike Jonze, Stacy Peralta, Stan and Jeanne Hoffman, Steve Caballero, Steve Douglas, Steve Rocco, Steve Sherman, Steve Steadham, Steve Van Doren, Ted Newsome, Ted Terrebonne, The Museum of Photographic Arts, The Newton family, The Palomar College Photo Department, The Photographer's Eye Collective, The Skatepark Foundation, Thomas Campbell, Tim Wrisley, Tobin Yelland, Tom Cozens, Tom "Wally" Inouye, Tommy Guerrero, Tony Alva, Tracy Storer, *Transworld Skateboarding* Magazine, Ty Evans, Warren Bolster, Wayne Searle, William Gullette, William Sharp, Gordon Eckler, and David Lopes and Gingko Press.

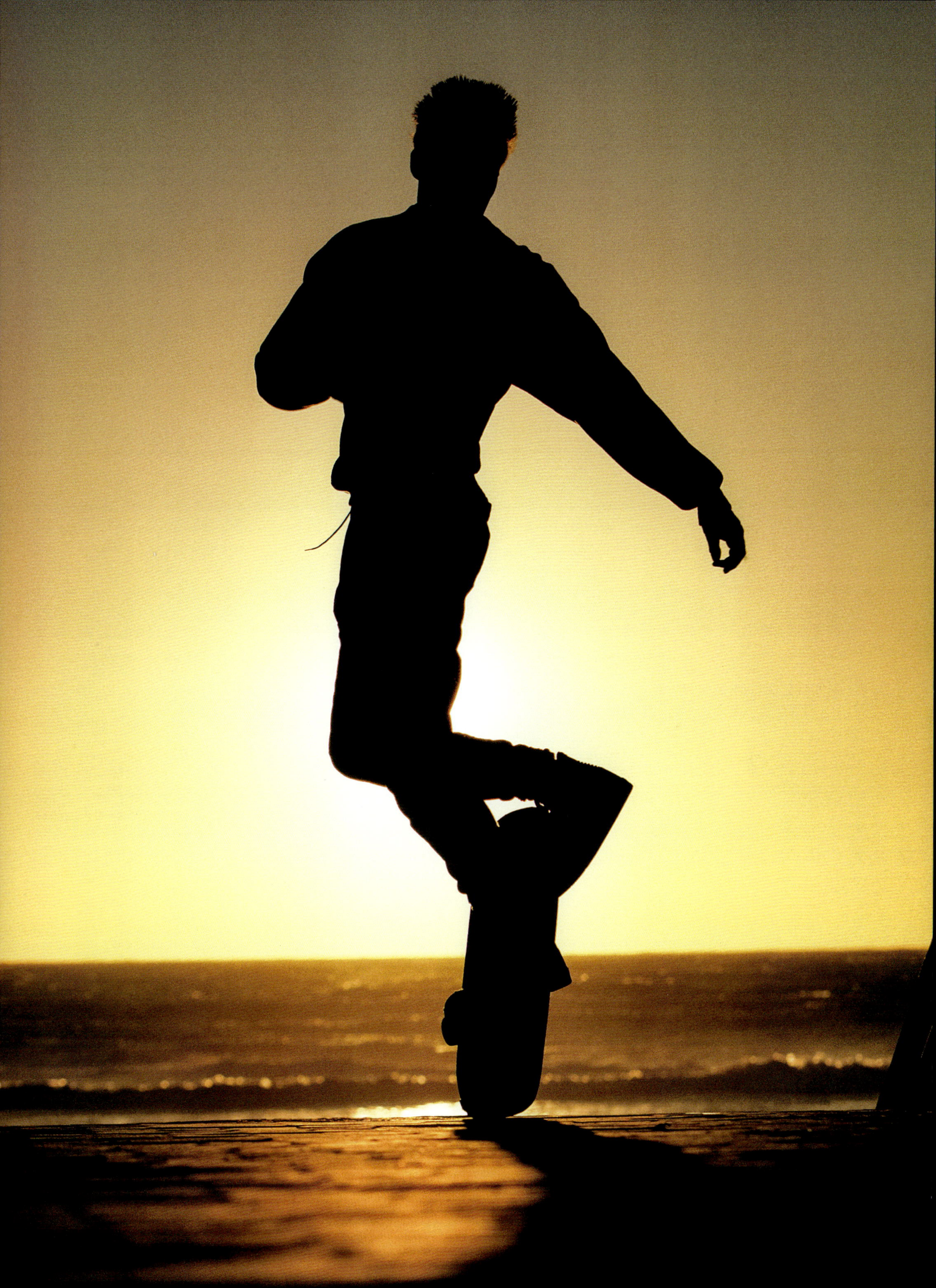

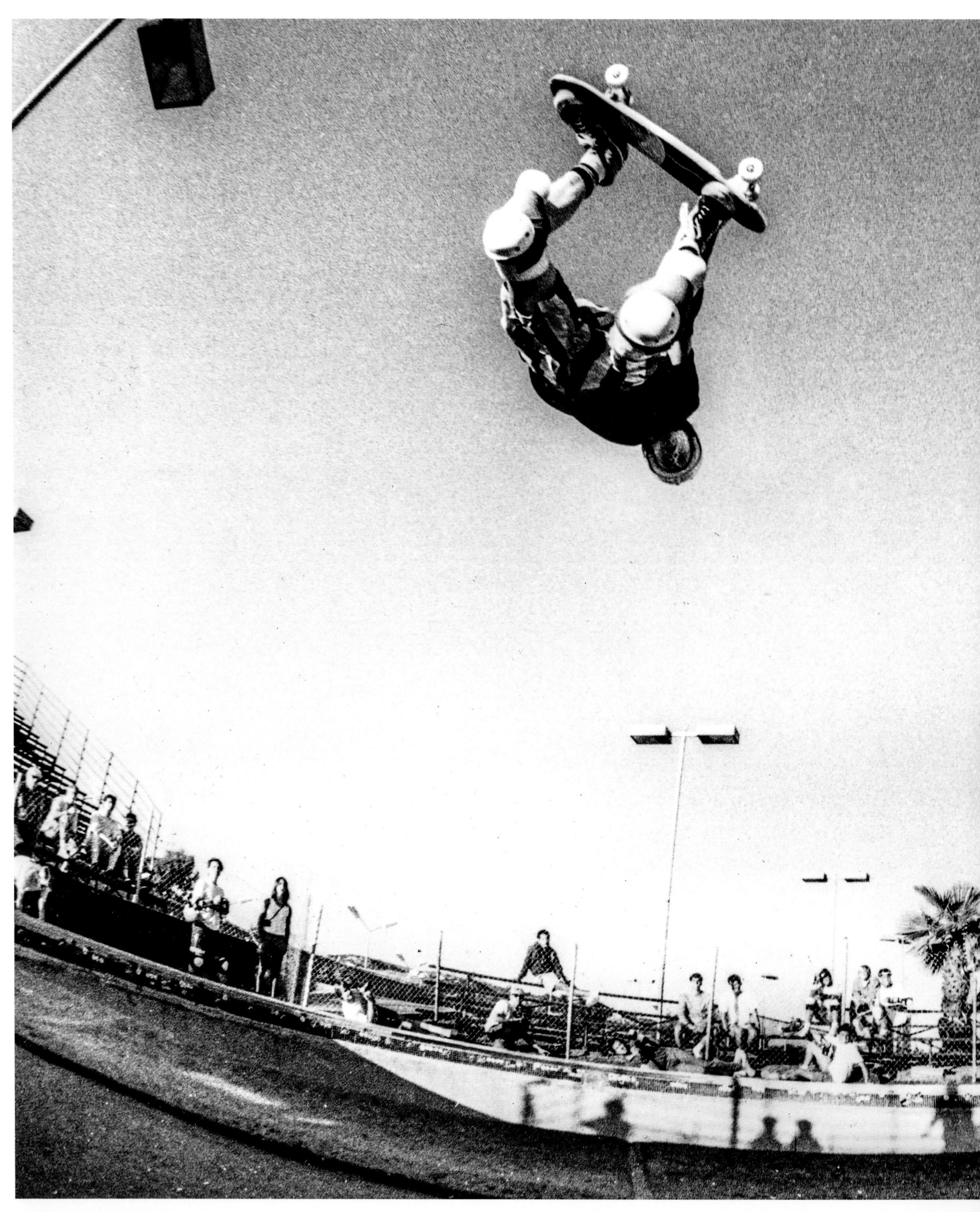

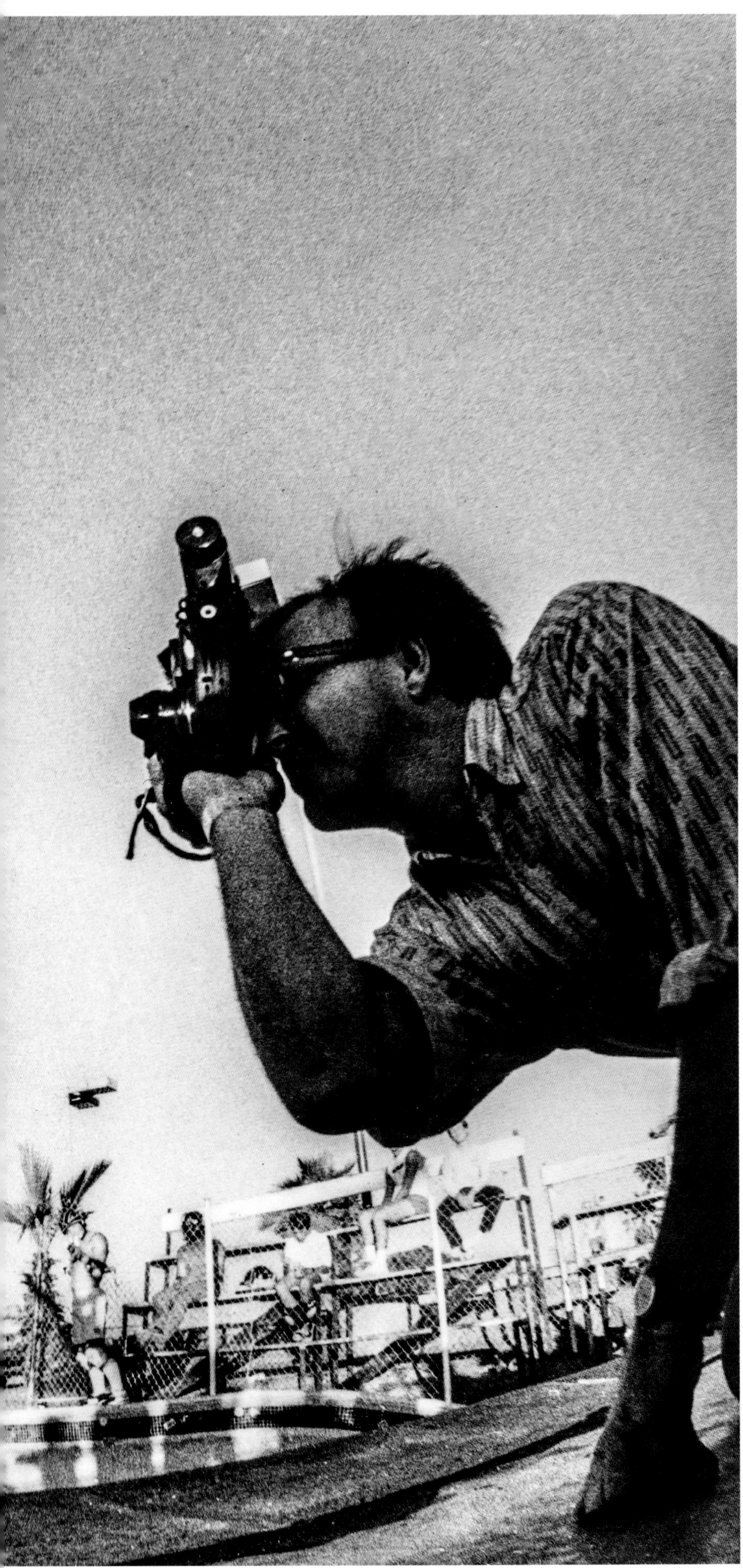

Grant Brittain shooting Tony Hawk, Del Mar Skate Ranch, Del Mar, CA, 1986 – Photo by Miki Vuckovich

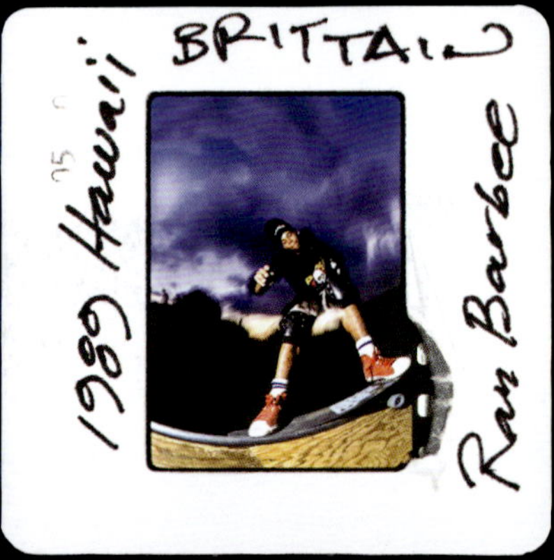

BRITTAIN
1989 Hawaii
Ron Barbee

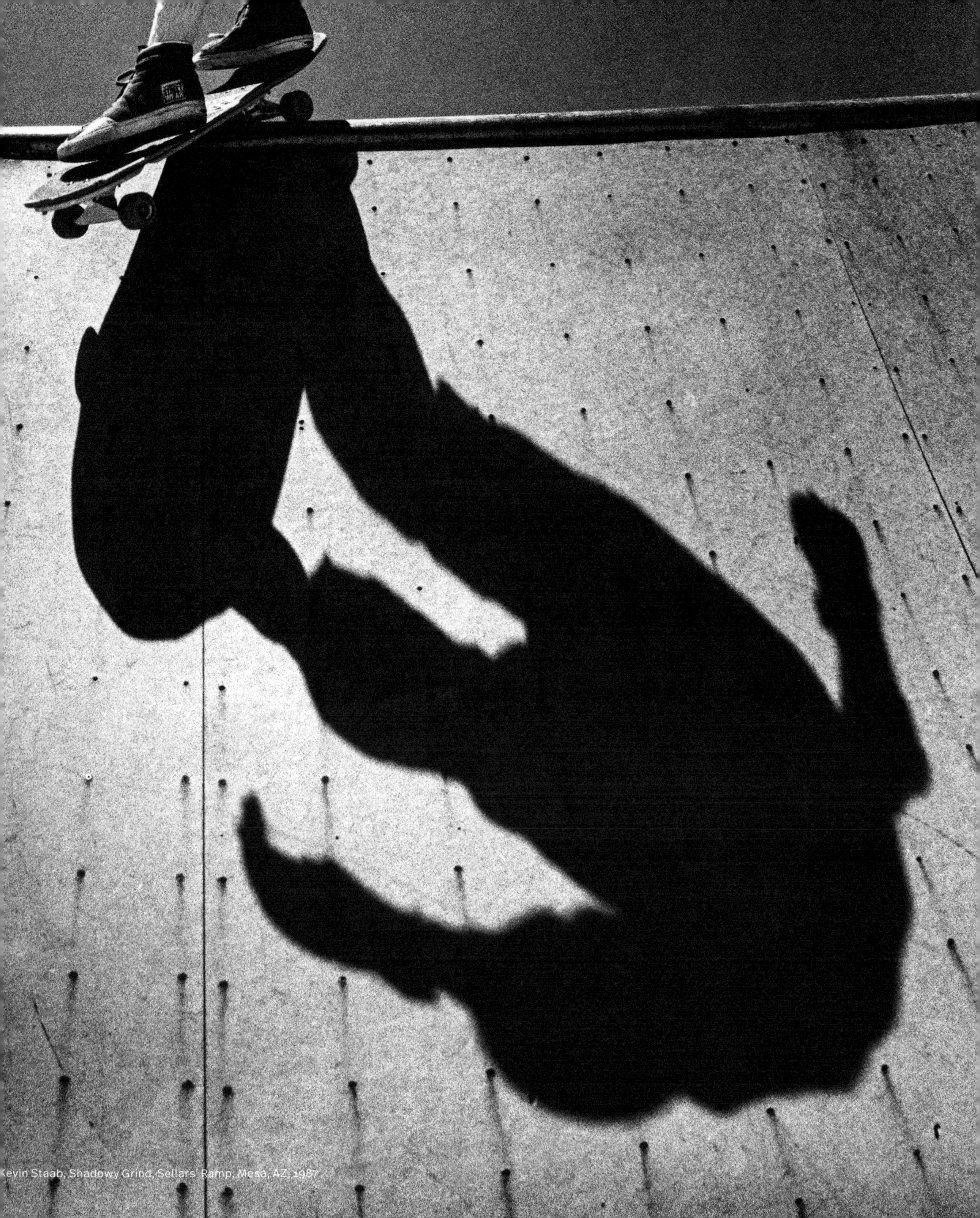

Kevin Staab, Shadowy Grind, Sellars' Ramp, Mesa, AZ, 1987

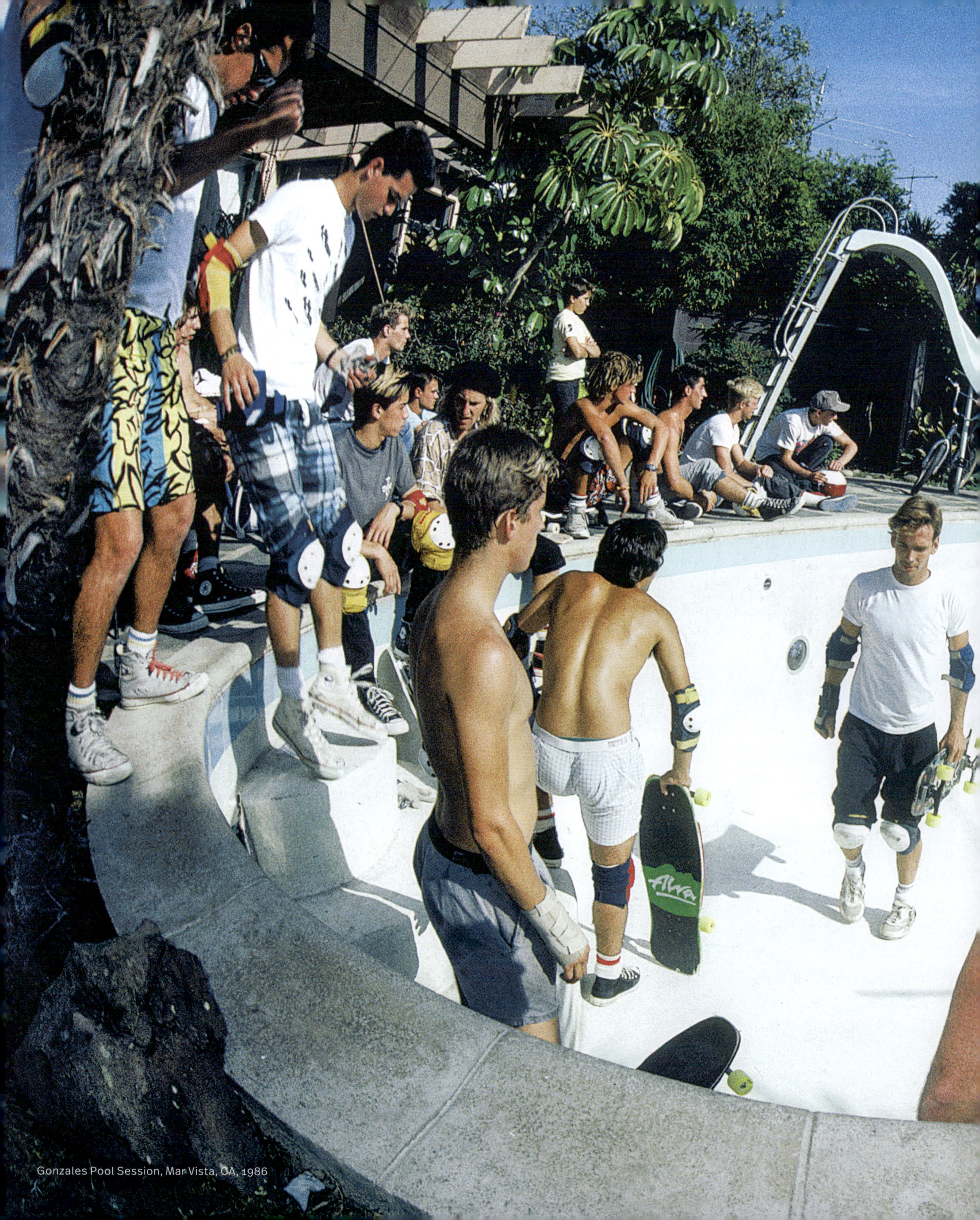

Gonzales Pool Session, Mar Vista, CA, 1986